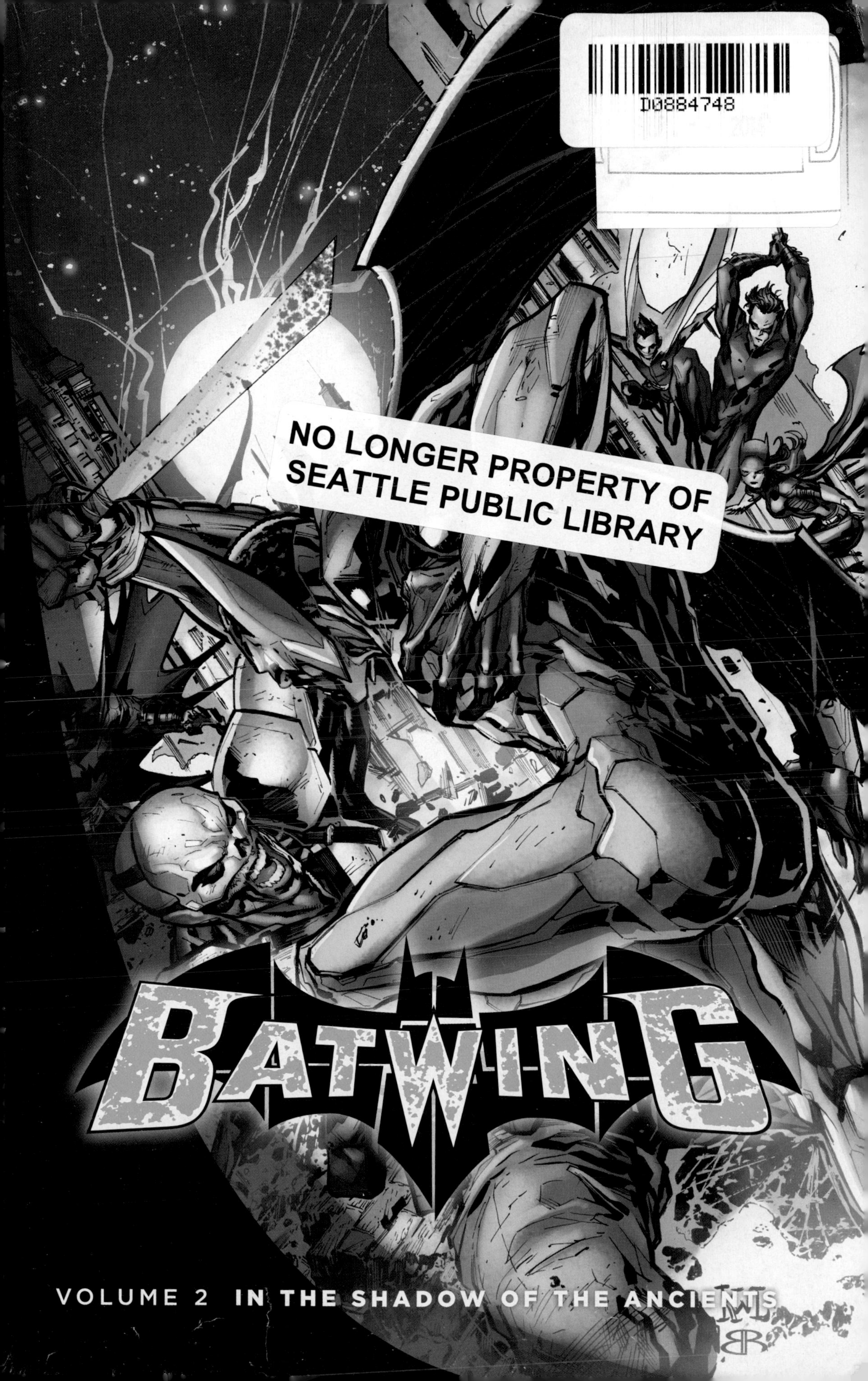
BATWING
VOLUME 2 IN THE SHADOW OF THE ANCIENTS

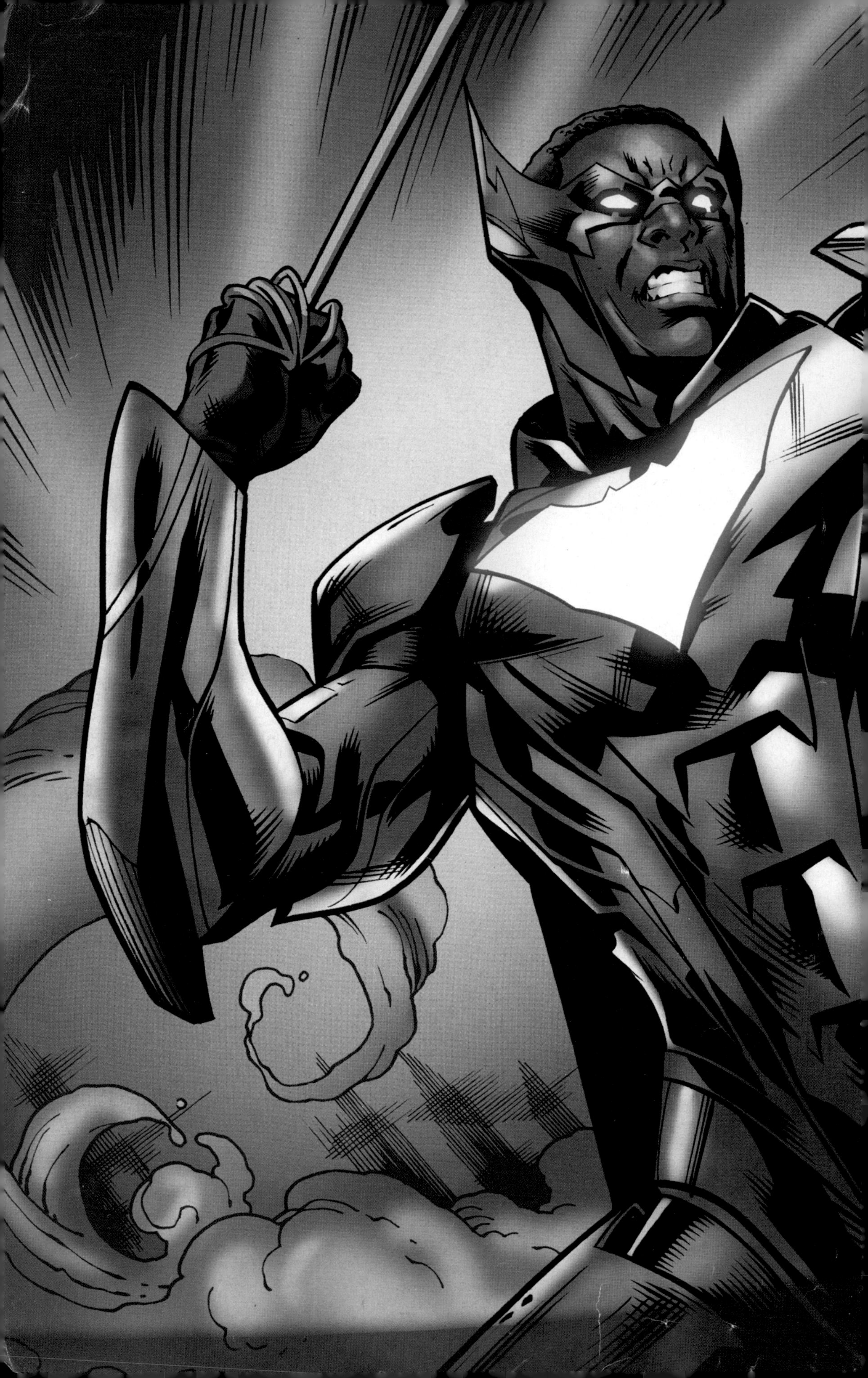

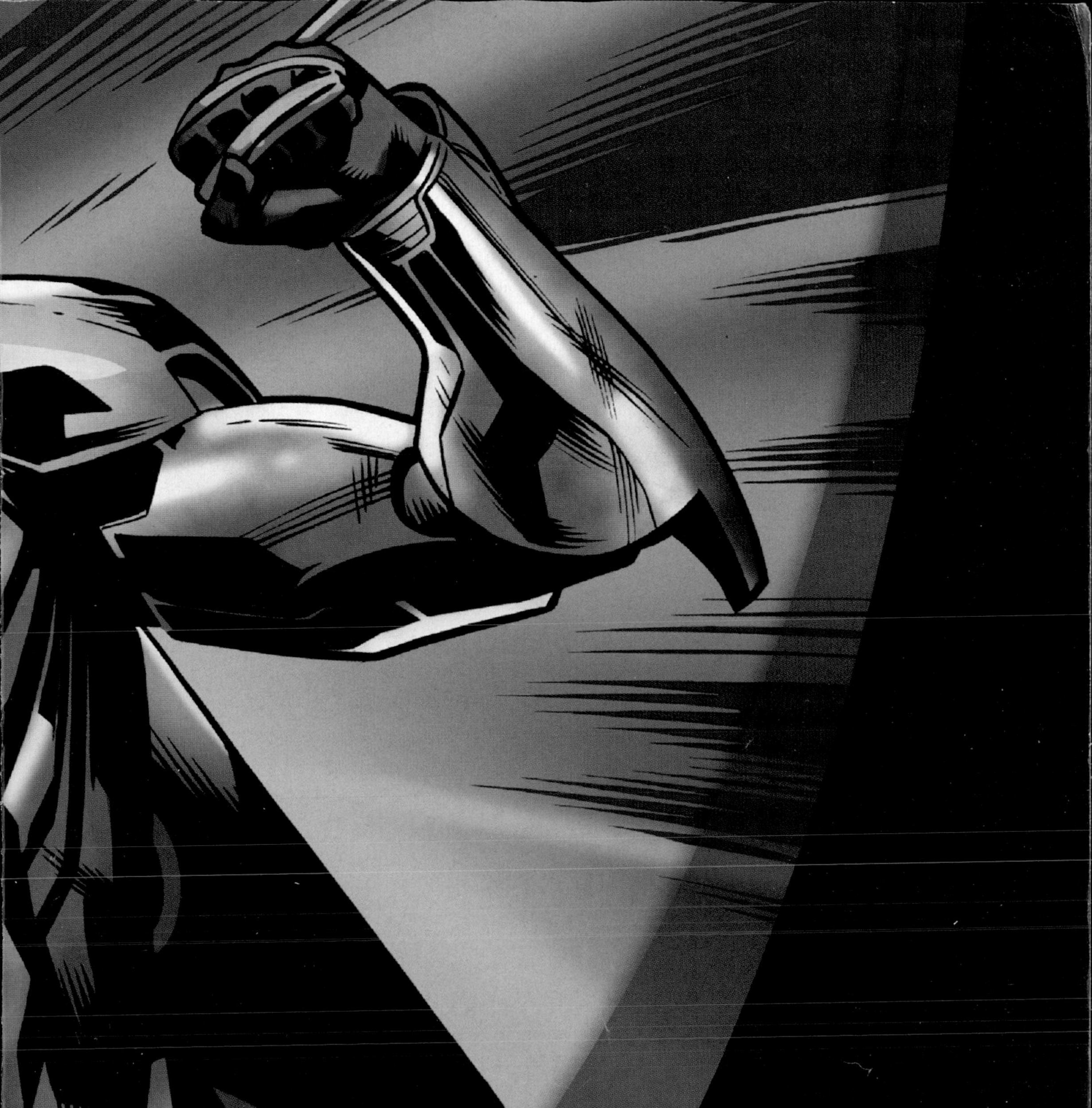

BATWING

VOLUME 2

IN THE SHADOW OF THE ANCIENTS

JUDD **WINICK** writer

MARCUS **TO** RYAN **WINN** Dustin **Nguyen** Derek **Fridolfs** Le Beau **Underwood** Richard **Zajac** artists

BRIAN **REBER** JASON **WRIGHT** colorists

CARLOS M. **MANGUAL** DEZI **SIENTY** PAT **BROSSEAU** DAVE **SHARPE** letterers

MARCUS **TO** & BRIAN **REBER** collection cover artists

BATMAN created by BOB **KANE**

MIKE MARTS HARVEY RICHARDS Editors – Original Series RICKEY PURDIN Assistant Editor – Original Series
ROWENA YOW Editor ROBBIN BROSTERMAN Design Director – Books
ROBBIE BIEDERMAN Publication Design

BOB HARRAS VP – Editor-in-Chief

DIANE NELSON President DAN DIDIO and JIM LEE Co-Publishers
GEOFF JOHNS Chief Creative Officer
JOHN ROOD Executive VP – Sales, Marketing and Business Development
AMY GENKINS Senior VP – Business and Legal Affairs NAIRI GARDINER Senior VP – Finance
JEFF BOISON VP – Publishing Operations MARK CHIARELLO VP – Art Direction and Design
JOHN CUNNINGHAM VP – Marketing TERRI CUNNINGHAM VP – Talent Relations and Services
ALISON GILL Senior VP – Manufacturing and Operations HANK KANALZ Senior VP - Digital
JAY KOGAN VP – Business and Legal Affairs, Publishing JACK MAHAN VP – Business Affairs, Talent
NICK NAPOLITANO VP – Manufacturing Administration SUE POHJA VP – Book Sales
COURTNEY SIMMONS Senior VP – Publicity BOB WAYNE Senior VP - Sales

BATWING VOLUME 2: IN THE SHADOW OF THE ANCIENTS

DC Comics, 1700 Broadway, New York, NY 10019
A Warner Bros. Entertainment Company.
Printed by RR Donnelley, Salem, VA, USA. 2/22/13. First Printing.

ISBN: 978-1-4012-3791-2

SUSTAINABLE
FORESTRY
INITIATIVE

Certified Chain of Custody
At Least 20% Certified Forest Content
www.sfiprogram.org
SFI-01042
APPLIES TO TEXT STOCK ONLY

Library of Congress Cataloging-in-Publication Data

Winick, Judd.
Batwing. Volume 2, In the Shadow of the Ancients / Judd Winick, Marcus To, Dustin Nguyen.
pages cm
"Originally published in single magazine form in Batwing 0, 7-12."
ISBN 978-1-4012-3791-2
1. Graphic novels. I. To, Marcus, illustrator. II. Nguyen, Dustin, illustrator. III. Title. IV. Title: In the Shadow of the Ancients.
PN6728.B3647W57 2013
741.5'973—dc23
                                                        2012048553

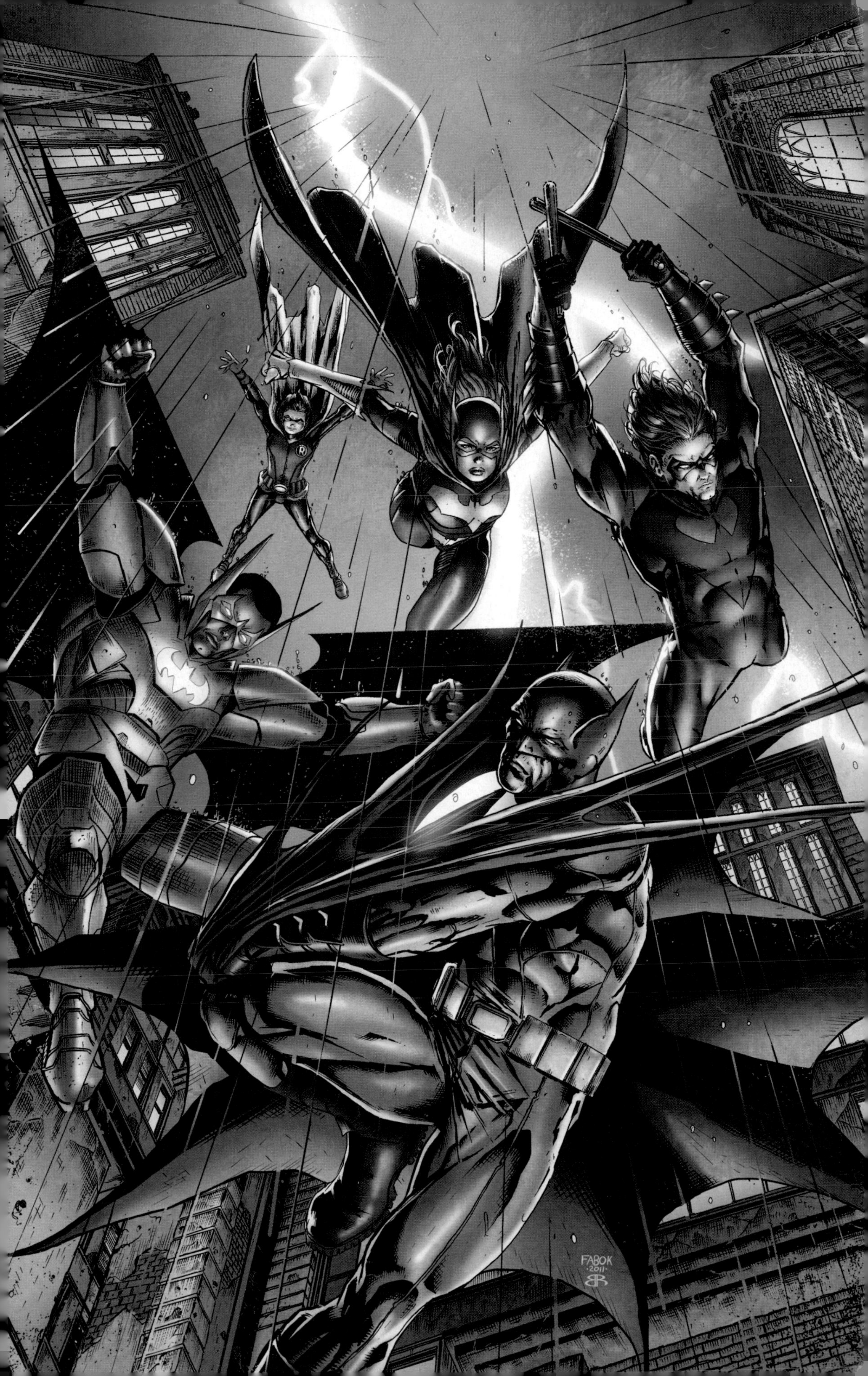
FABOK
2011

“BUT THERE WERE CONSEQUENCES FOR US.”

JUDD WINICK writer DUSTIN NGUYEN penciller DEREK FRIDOLFS inker cover art by JASON FABOK & BRIAN REBER

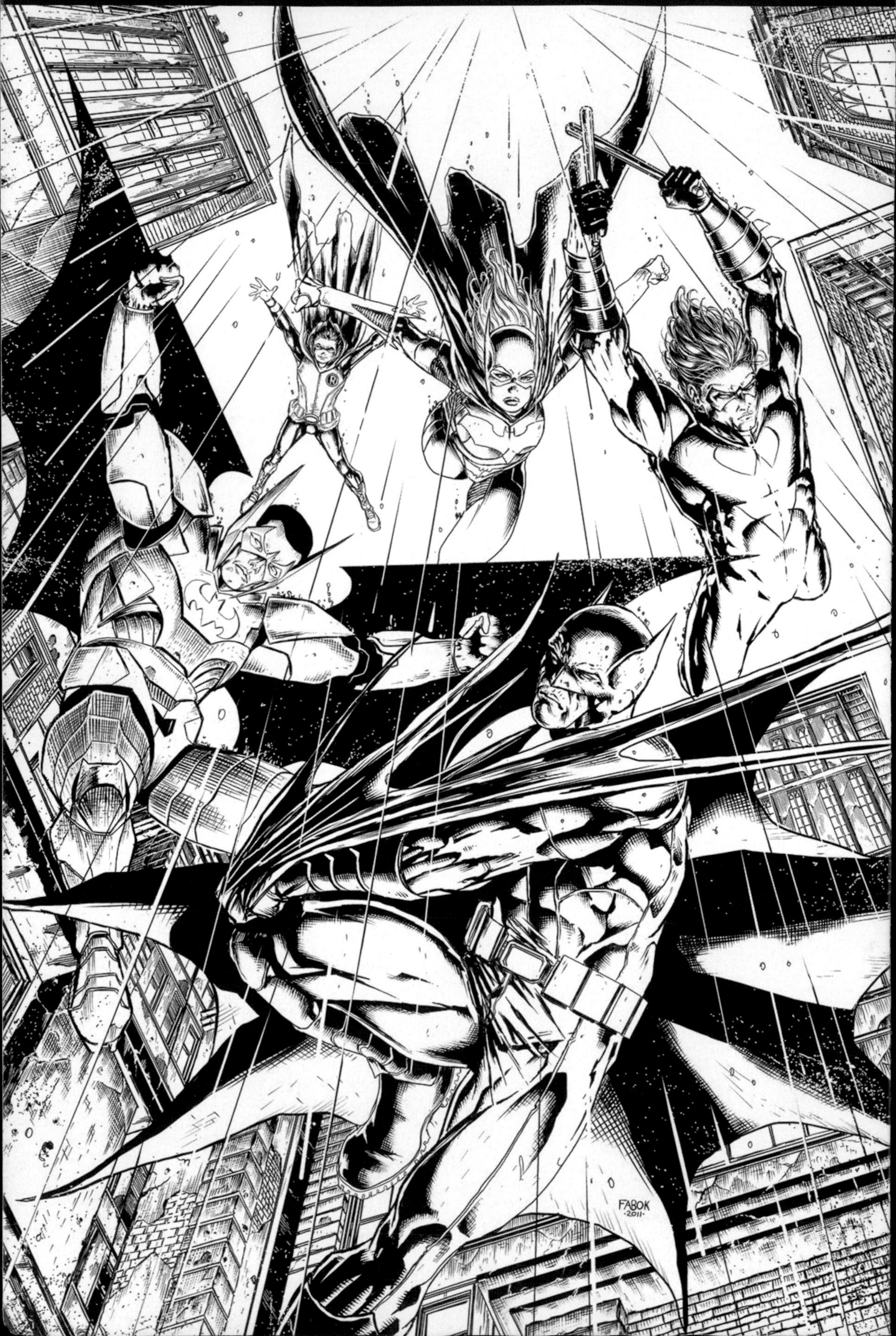

FABOK
2011

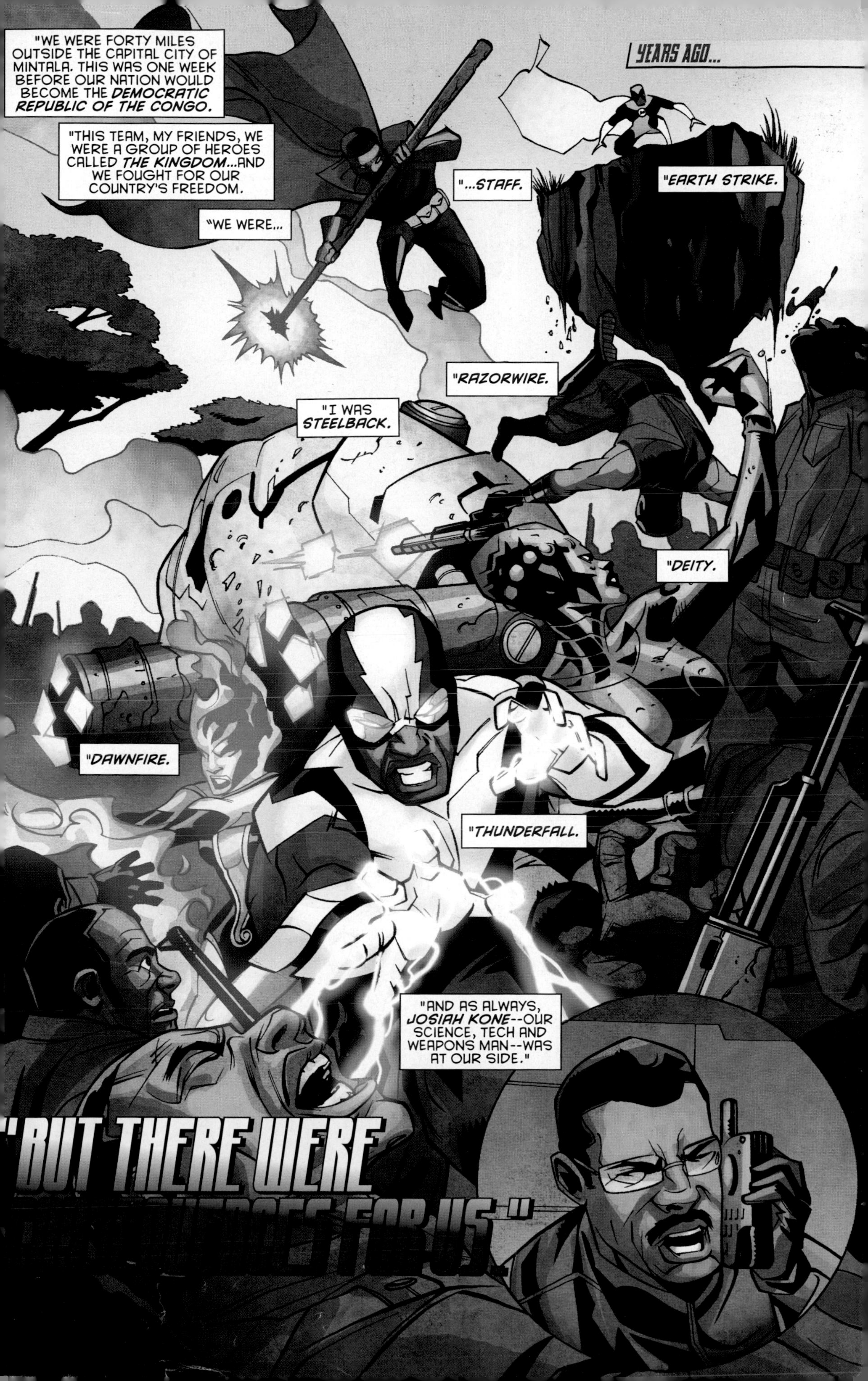
"WE WERE FORTY MILES OUTSIDE THE CAPITAL CITY OF MINTALA. THIS WAS ONE WEEK BEFORE OUR NATION WOULD BECOME THE DEMOCRATIC REPUBLIC OF THE CONGO.
YEARS AGO...
"THIS TEAM, MY FRIENDS, WE WERE A GROUP OF HEROES CALLED THE KINGDOM...AND WE FOUGHT FOR OUR COUNTRY'S FREEDOM.
"WE WERE...
"...STAFF.
"EARTH STRIKE.
"RAZORWIRE.
"I WAS STEELBACK.
"DEITY.
"DAWNFIRE.
"THUNDERFALL.
"AND AS ALWAYS, JOSIAH KONE--OUR SCIENCE, TECH AND WEAPONS MAN--WAS AT OUR SIDE."
"BUT THERE WERE
FOR US."

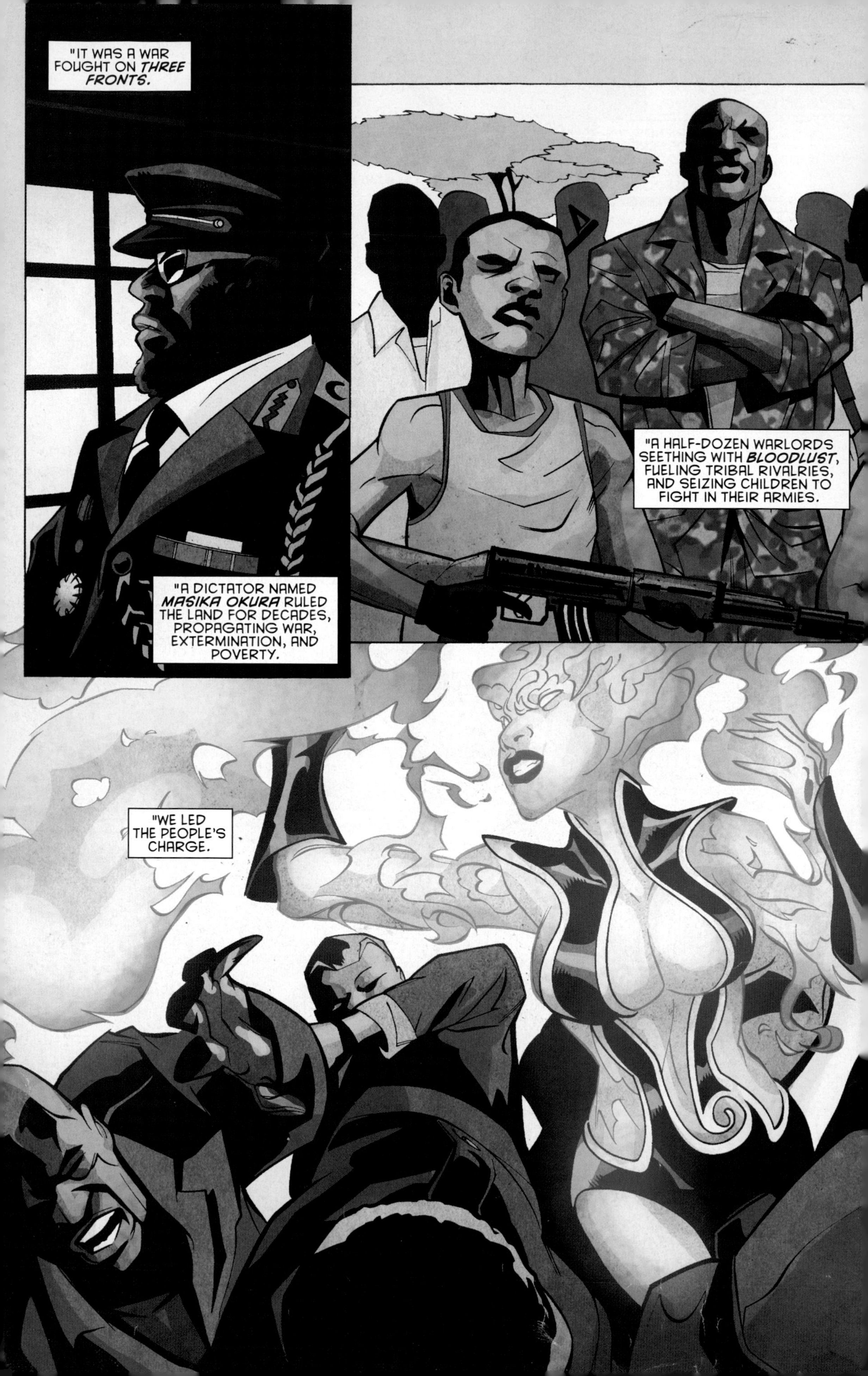
"IT WAS A WAR FOUGHT ON THREE FRONTS.
"A DICTATOR NAMED MASIKA OKURA RULED THE LAND FOR DECADES, PROPAGATING WAR, EXTERMINATION, AND POVERTY.
"A HALF-DOZEN WARLORDS SEETHING WITH BLOODLUST, FUELING TRIBAL RIVALRIES, AND SEIZING CHILDREN TO FIGHT IN THEIR ARMIES.
"WE LED THE PEOPLE'S CHARGE.

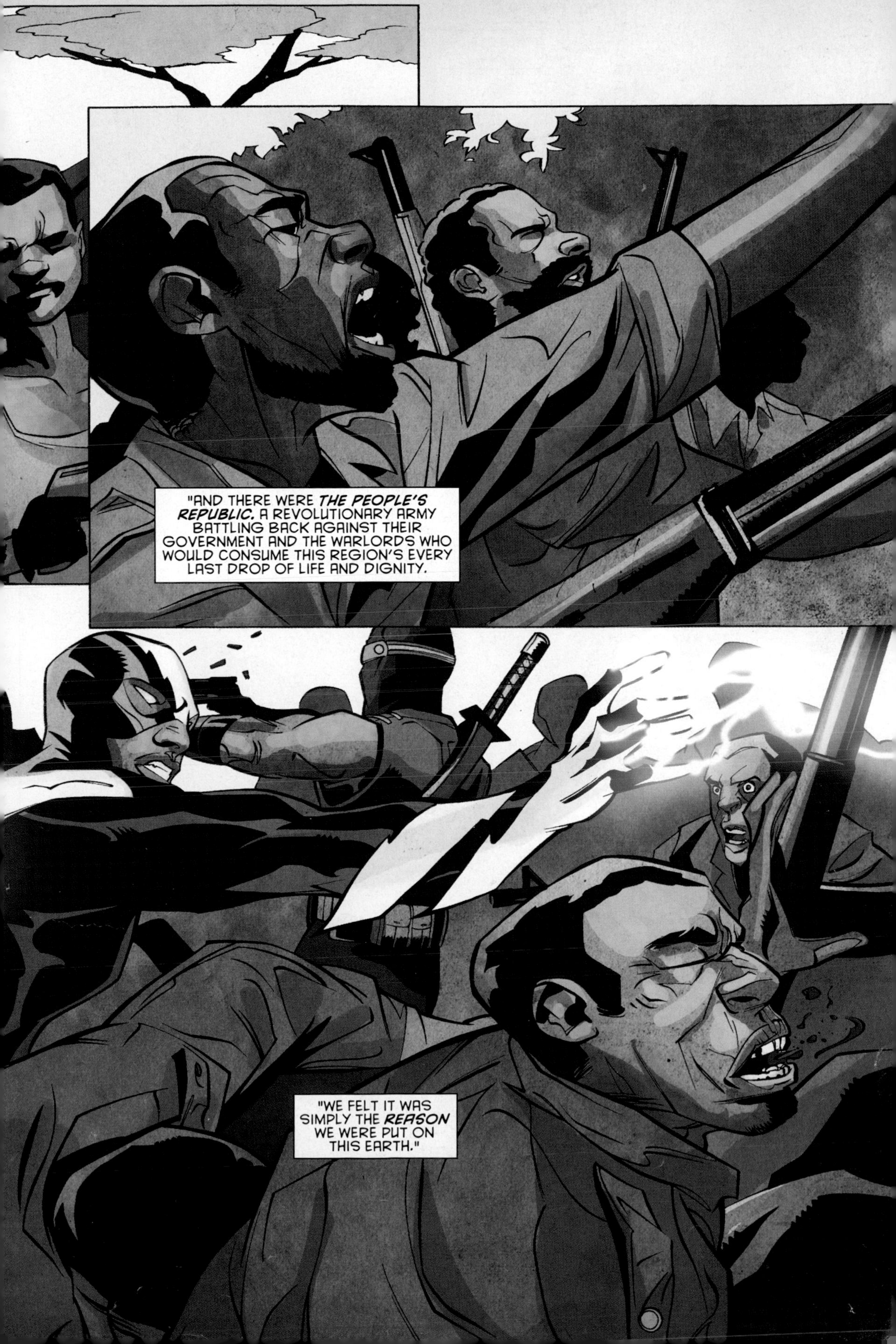
"AND THERE WERE *THE PEOPLE'S REPUBLIC.* A REVOLUTIONARY ARMY BATTLING BACK AGAINST THEIR GOVERNMENT AND THE WARLORDS WHO WOULD CONSUME THIS REGION'S EVERY LAST DROP OF LIFE AND DIGNITY.
"WE FELT IT WAS SIMPLY THE *REASON* WE WERE PUT ON THIS EARTH."

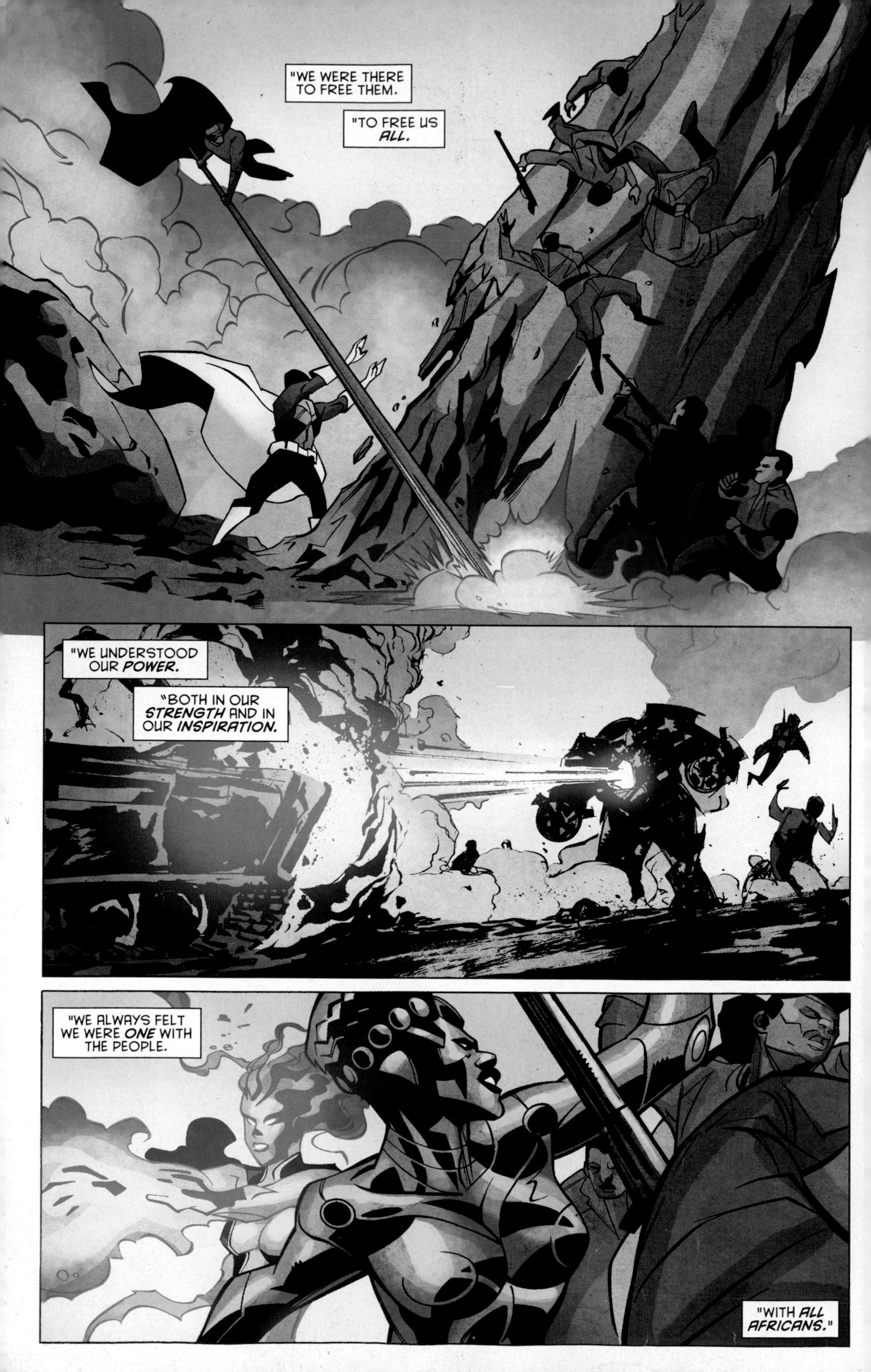
"WE WERE THERE TO FREE THEM.
"TO FREE US ALL.
"WE UNDERSTOOD OUR POWER.
"BOTH IN OUR STRENGTH AND IN OUR INSPIRATION.
"WE ALWAYS FELT WE WERE ONE WITH THE PEOPLE.
"WITH ALL AFRICANS."

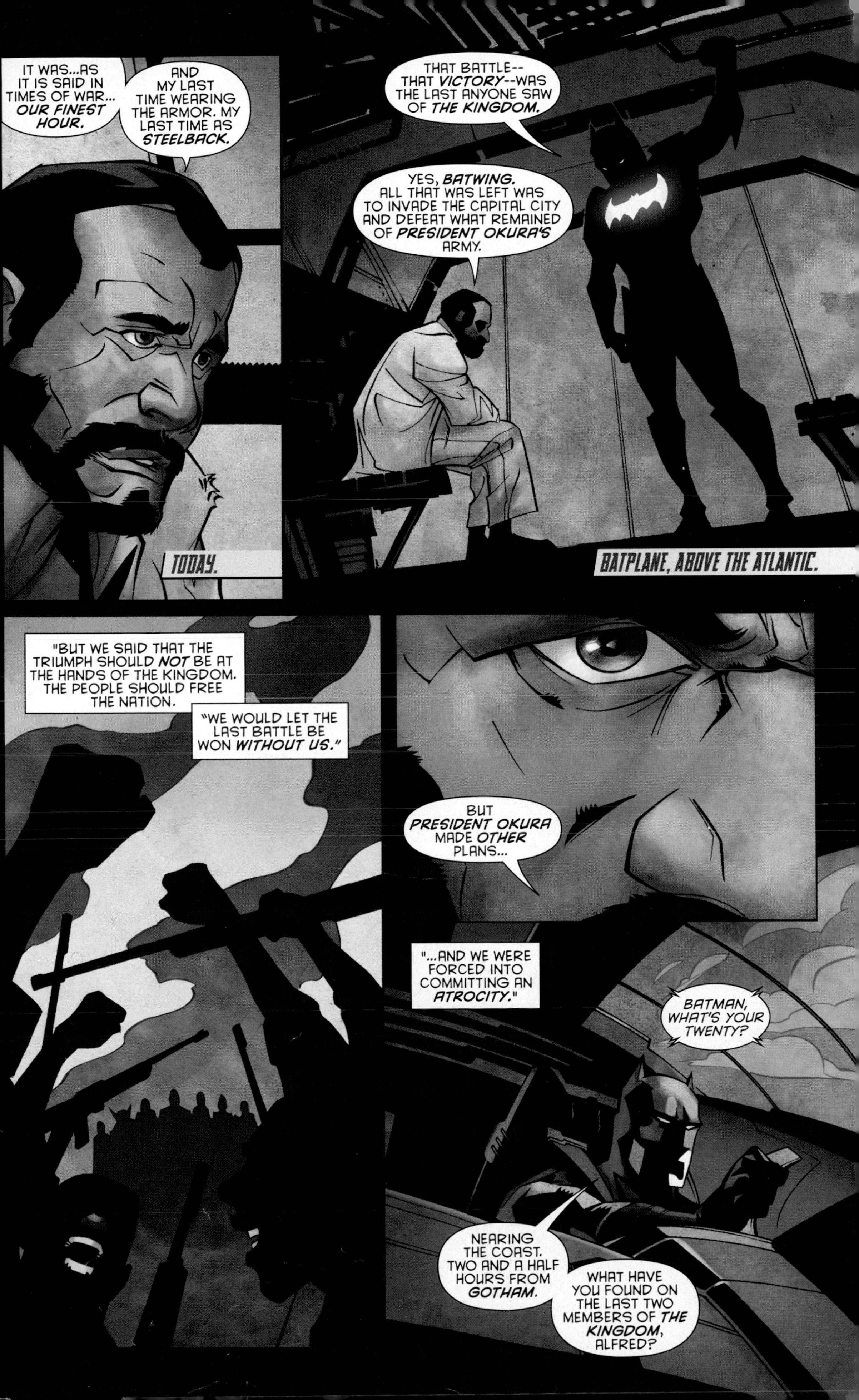
IT WAS...AS IT IS SAID IN TIMES OF WAR... OUR FINEST HOUR.
AND MY LAST TIME WEARING THE ARMOR. MY LAST TIME AS STEELBACK.
TODAY.
THAT BATTLE-- THAT VICTORY--WAS THE LAST ANYONE SAW OF THE KINGDOM.
YES, BATWING. ALL THAT WAS LEFT WAS TO INVADE THE CAPITAL CITY AND DEFEAT WHAT REMAINED OF PRESIDENT OKURA'S ARMY.
BATPLANE, ABOVE THE ATLANTIC.
"BUT WE SAID THAT THE TRIUMPH SHOULD NOT BE AT THE HANDS OF THE KINGDOM. THE PEOPLE SHOULD FREE THE NATION.
"WE WOULD LET THE LAST BATTLE BE WON WITHOUT US."
BUT PRESIDENT OKURA MADE OTHER PLANS...
"...AND WE WERE FORCED INTO COMMITTING AN ATROCITY."
BATMAN, WHAT'S YOUR TWENTY?
NEARING THE COAST. TWO AND A HALF HOURS FROM GOTHAM.
WHAT HAVE YOU FOUND ON THE LAST TWO MEMBERS OF THE KINGDOM, ALFRED?

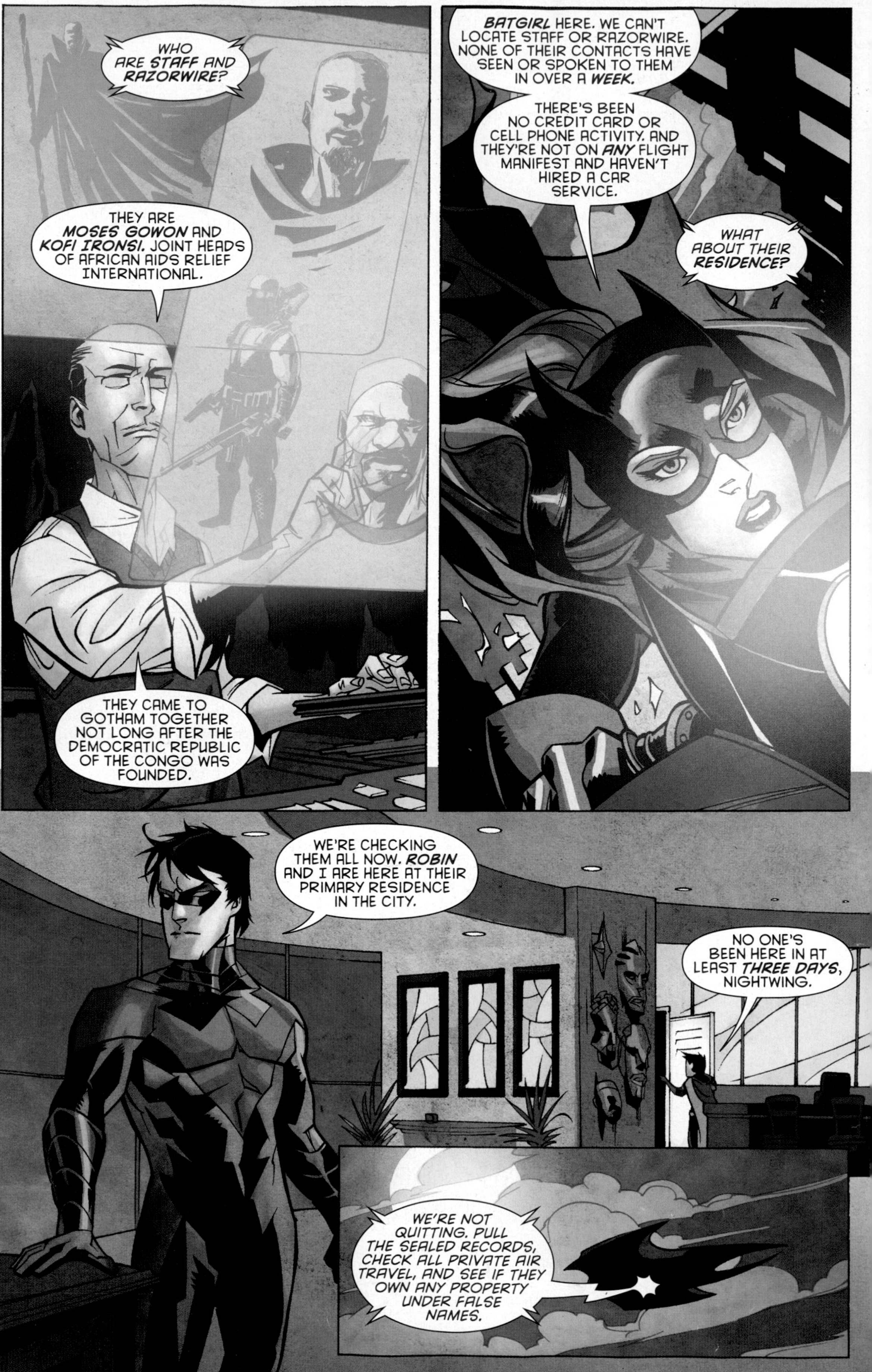
WHO ARE STAFF AND RAZORWIRE?
THEY ARE MOSES GOWON AND KOFI IRONSI. JOINT HEADS OF AFRICAN AIDS RELIEF INTERNATIONAL.
THEY CAME TO GOTHAM TOGETHER NOT LONG AFTER THE DEMOCRATIC REPUBLIC OF THE CONGO WAS FOUNDED.
BATGIRL HERE. WE CAN'T LOCATE STAFF OR RAZORWIRE. NONE OF THEIR CONTACTS HAVE SEEN OR SPOKEN TO THEM IN OVER A WEEK.
THERE'S BEEN NO CREDIT CARD OR CELL PHONE ACTIVITY. AND THEY'RE NOT ON ANY FLIGHT MANIFEST AND HAVEN'T HIRED A CAR SERVICE.
WHAT ABOUT THEIR RESIDENCE?
WE'RE CHECKING THEM ALL NOW. ROBIN AND I ARE HERE AT THEIR PRIMARY RESIDENCE IN THE CITY.
NO ONE'S BEEN HERE IN AT LEAST THREE DAYS, NIGHTWING.
WE'RE NOT QUITTING. PULL THE SEALED RECORDS, CHECK ALL PRIVATE AIR TRAVEL, AND SEE IF THEY OWN ANY PROPERTY UNDER FALSE NAMES.

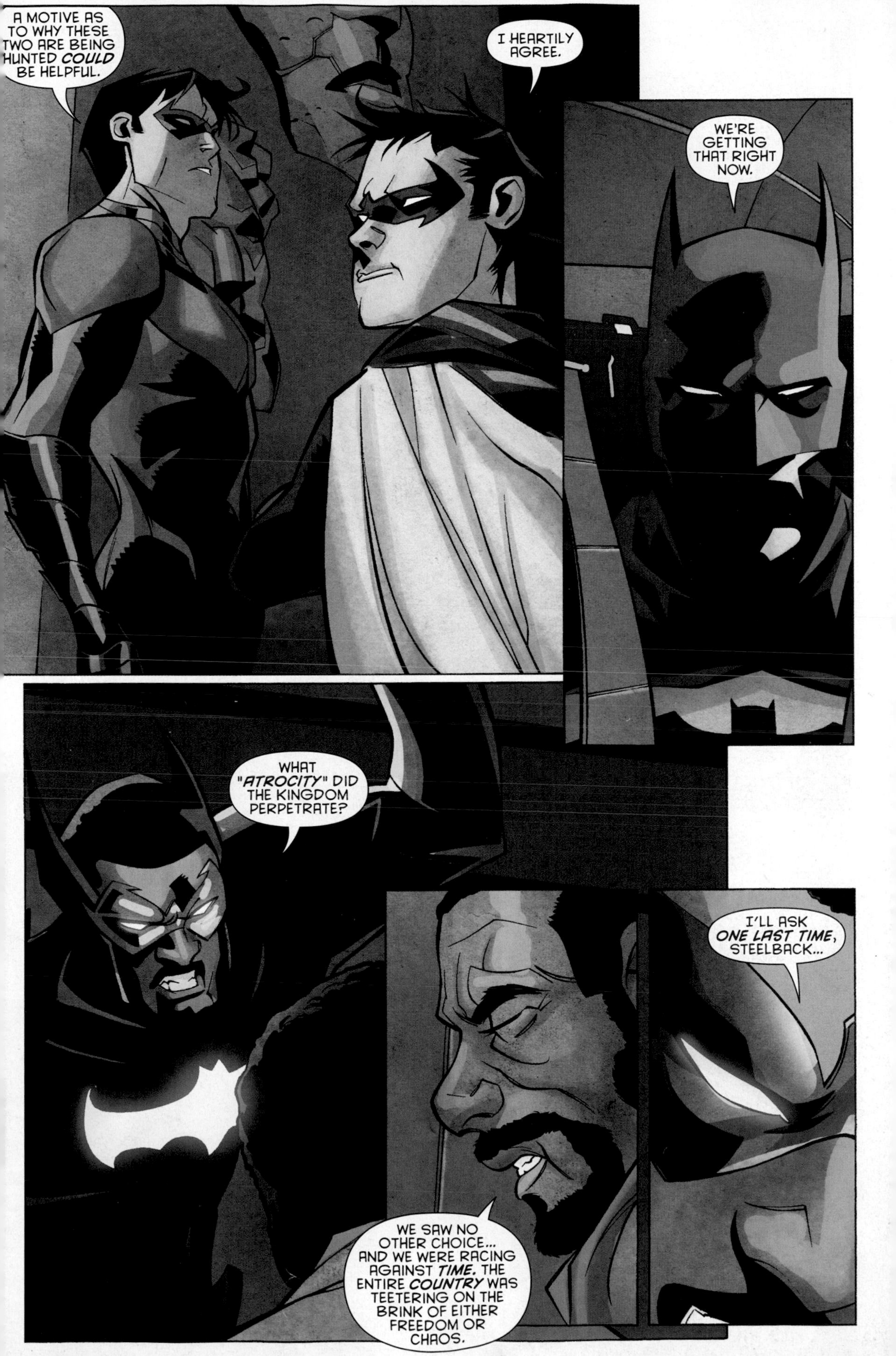
A MOTIVE AS TO WHY THESE TWO ARE BEING HUNTED *COULD* BE HELPFUL.
I HEARTILY AGREE.
WE'RE GETTING THAT RIGHT NOW.
WHAT "*ATROCITY*" DID THE KINGDOM PERPETRATE?
I'LL ASK *ONE LAST TIME*, STEELBACK...
WE SAW NO OTHER CHOICE... AND WE WERE RACING AGAINST *TIME*. THE ENTIRE *COUNTRY* WAS TEETERING ON THE BRINK OF EITHER FREEDOM OR CHAOS.

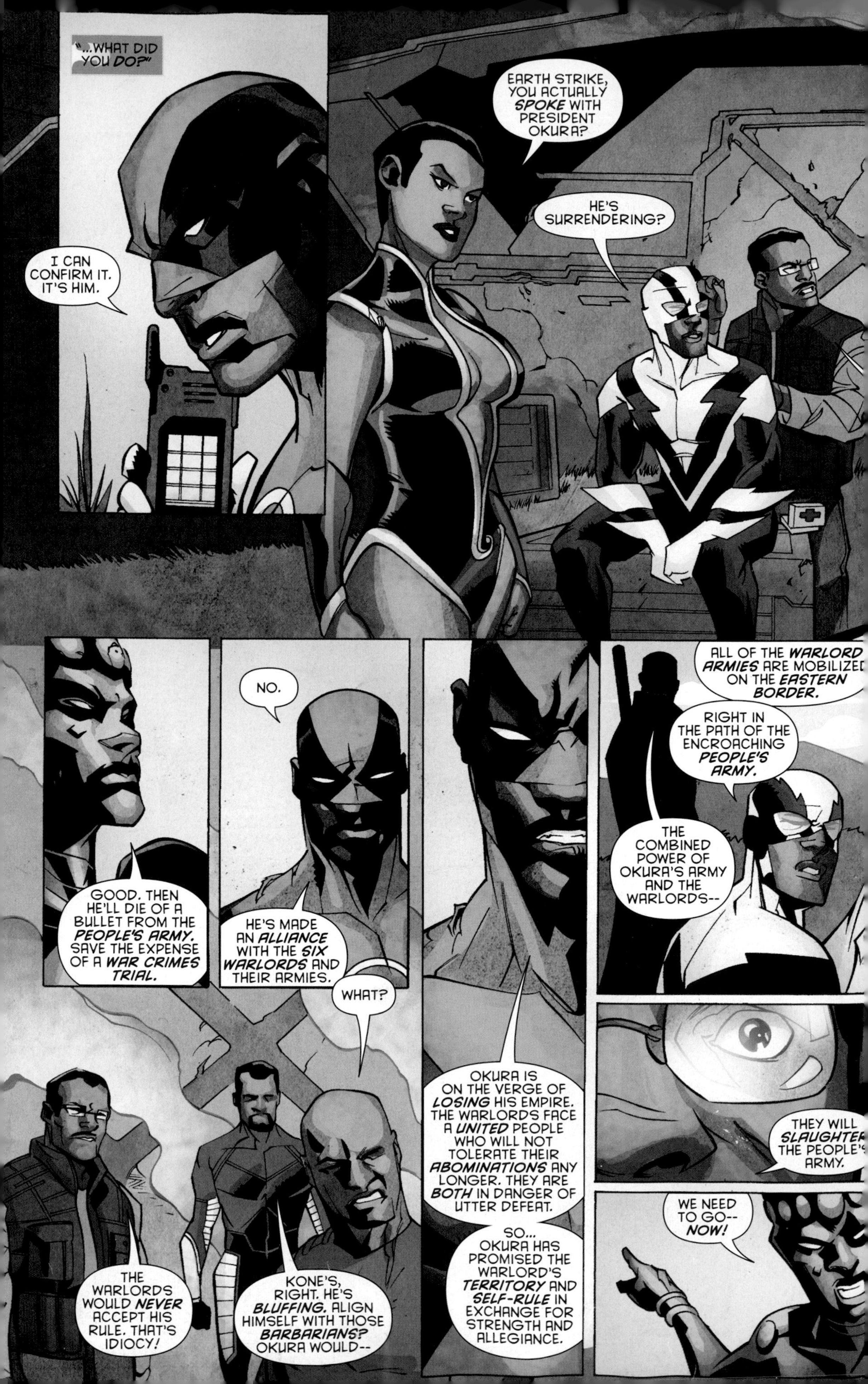
"...WHAT DID YOU DO?"
I CAN CONFIRM IT. IT'S HIM.
EARTH STRIKE, YOU ACTUALLY SPOKE WITH PRESIDENT OKURA?
HE'S SURRENDERING?
GOOD. THEN HE'LL DIE OF A BULLET FROM THE PEOPLE'S ARMY. SAVE THE EXPENSE OF A WAR CRIMES TRIAL.
NO.
HE'S MADE AN ALLIANCE WITH THE SIX WARLORDS AND THEIR ARMIES.
WHAT?
ALL OF THE WARLORD ARMIES ARE MOBILIZED ON THE EASTERN BORDER.
RIGHT IN THE PATH OF THE ENCROACHING PEOPLE'S ARMY.
THE COMBINED POWER OF OKURA'S ARMY AND THE WARLORDS--
THEY WILL SLAUGHTER THE PEOPLE'S ARMY.
THE WARLORDS WOULD NEVER ACCEPT HIS RULE. THAT'S IDIOCY!
KONE'S, RIGHT. HE'S BLUFFING. ALIGN HIMSELF WITH THOSE BARBARIANS? OKURA WOULD--
OKURA IS ON THE VERGE OF LOSING HIS EMPIRE. THE WARLORDS FACE A UNITED PEOPLE WHO WILL NOT TOLERATE THEIR ABOMINATIONS ANY LONGER. THEY ARE BOTH IN DANGER OF UTTER DEFEAT.
SO... OKURA HAS PROMISED THE WARLORD'S TERRITORY AND SELF-RULE IN EXCHANGE FOR STRENGTH AND ALLEGIANCE.
WE NEED TO GO-- NOW!

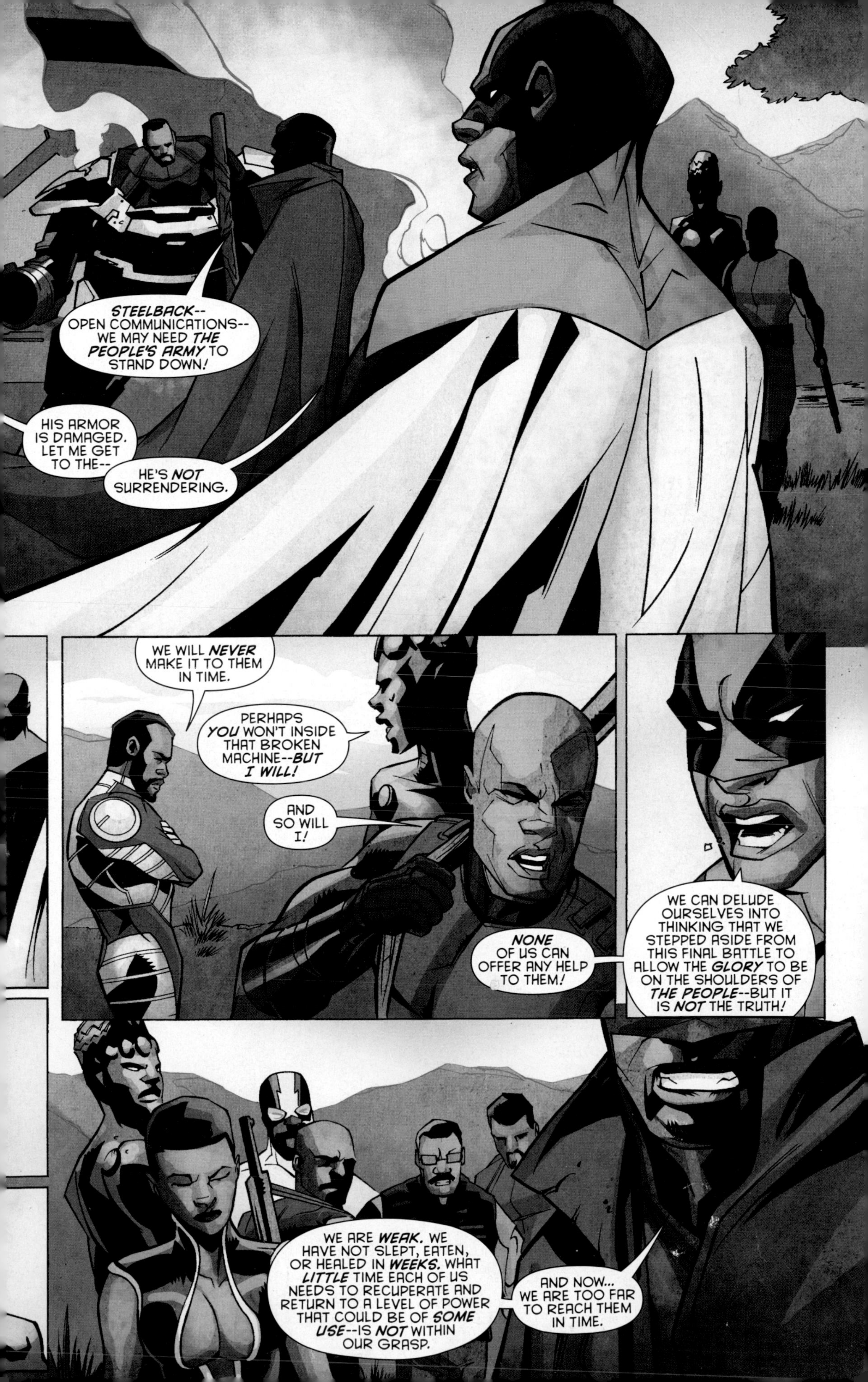
STEELBACK--
OPEN COMMUNICATIONS--
WE MAY NEED THE PEOPLE'S ARMY TO STAND DOWN!
HIS ARMOR IS DAMAGED. LET ME GET TO THE--
HE'S NOT SURRENDERING.
WE WILL NEVER MAKE IT TO THEM IN TIME.
PERHAPS YOU WON'T INSIDE THAT BROKEN MACHINE--BUT I WILL!
AND SO WILL I!
NONE OF US CAN OFFER ANY HELP TO THEM!
WE CAN DELUDE OURSELVES INTO THINKING THAT WE STEPPED ASIDE FROM THIS FINAL BATTLE TO ALLOW THE GLORY TO BE ON THE SHOULDERS OF THE PEOPLE--BUT IT IS NOT THE TRUTH!
WE ARE WEAK. WE HAVE NOT SLEPT, EATEN, OR HEALED IN WEEKS. WHAT LITTLE TIME EACH OF US NEEDS TO RECUPERATE AND RETURN TO A LEVEL OF POWER THAT COULD BE OF SOME USE--IS NOT WITHIN OUR GRASP.
AND NOW... WE ARE TOO FAR TO REACH THEM IN TIME.

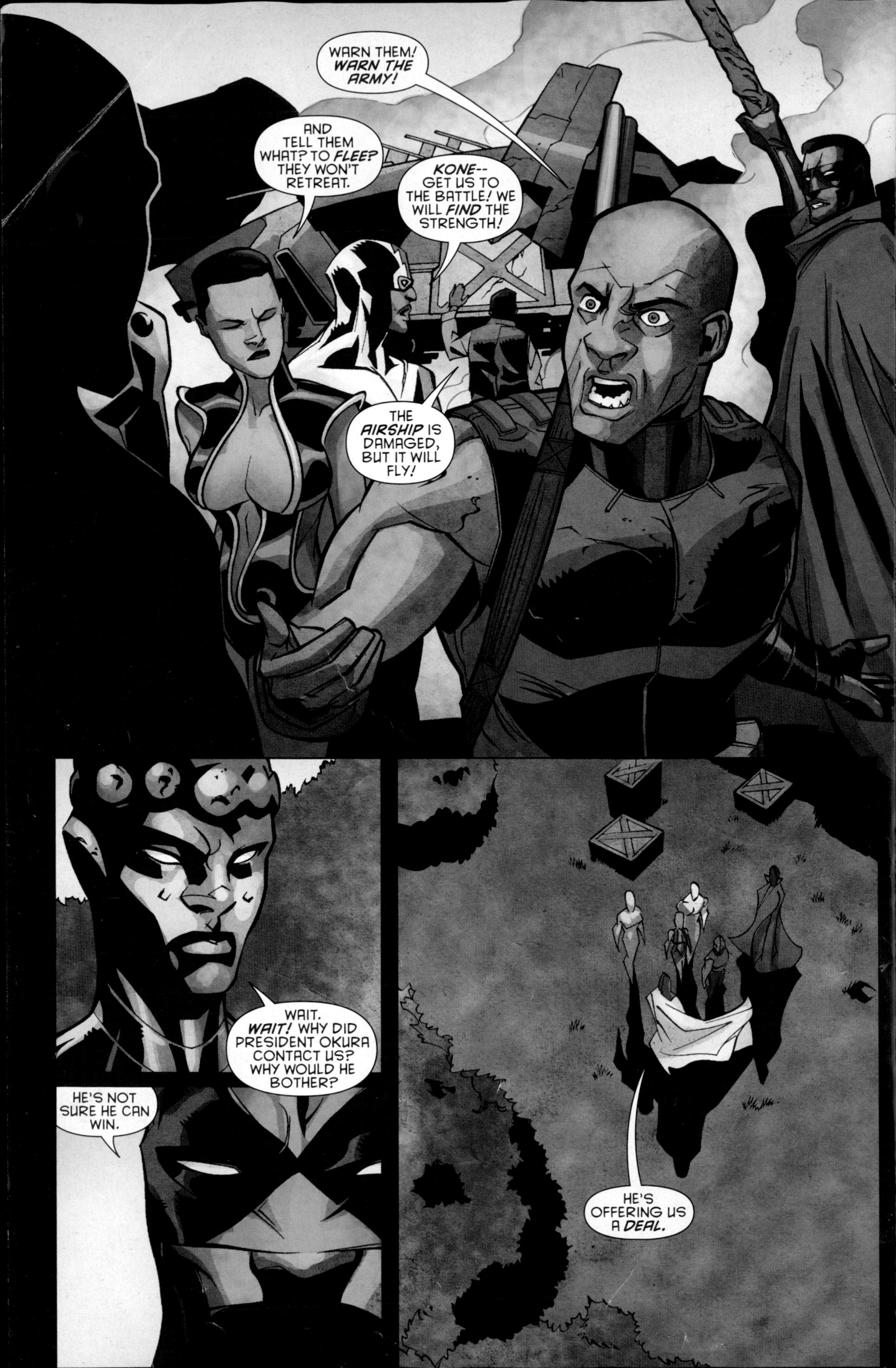
WARN THEM! WARN THE ARMY!
AND TELL THEM WHAT? TO FLEE? THEY WON'T RETREAT.
KONE-- GET US TO THE BATTLE! WE WILL FIND THE STRENGTH!
THE AIRSHIP IS DAMAGED, BUT IT WILL FLY!
WAIT. WAIT! WHY DID PRESIDENT OKURA CONTACT US? WHY WOULD HE BOTHER?
HE'S NOT SURE HE CAN WIN.
HE'S OFFERING US A DEAL.

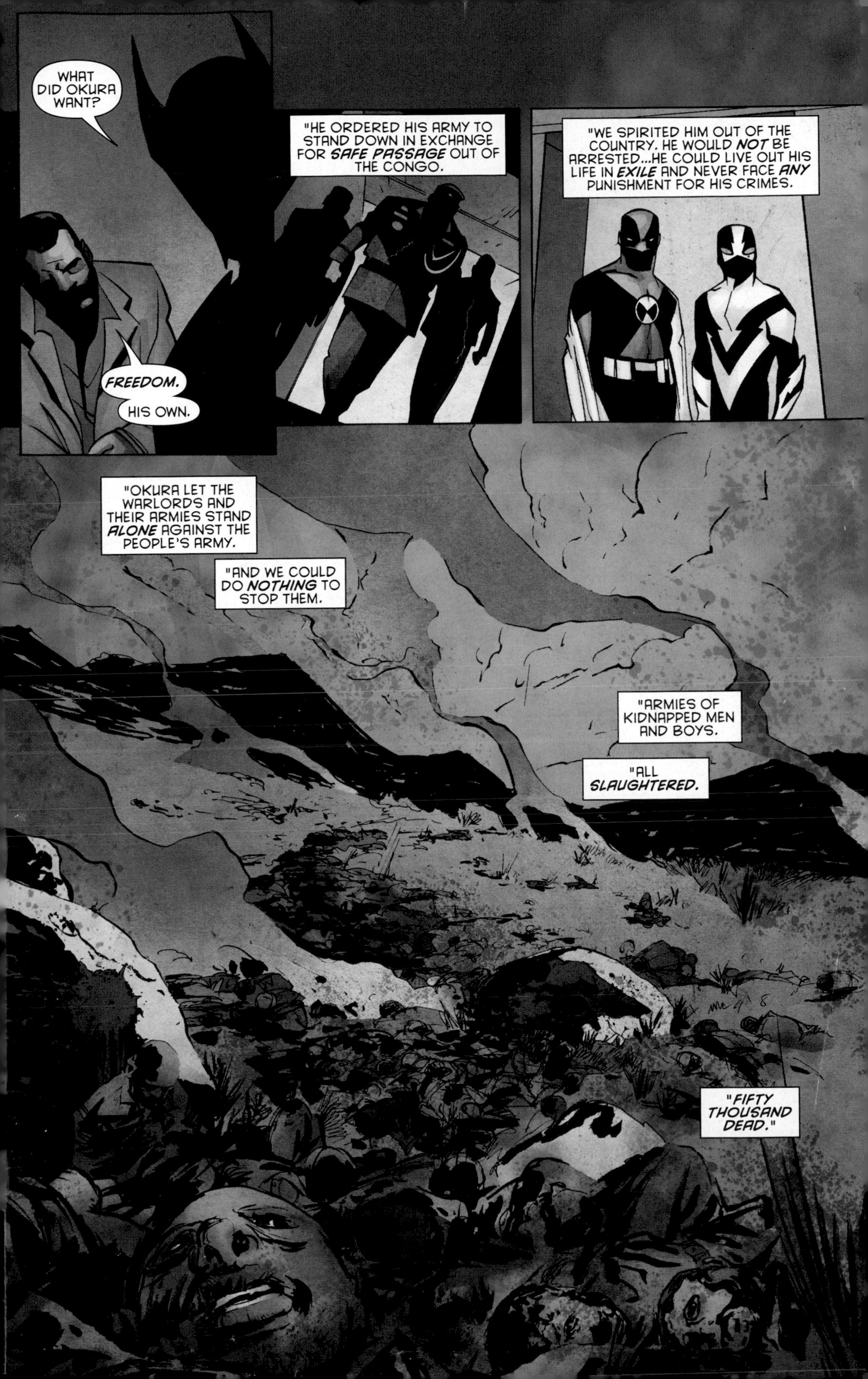
WHAT DID OKURA WANT?
"HE ORDERED HIS ARMY TO STAND DOWN IN EXCHANGE FOR SAFE PASSAGE OUT OF THE CONGO.
"WE SPIRITED HIM OUT OF THE COUNTRY. HE WOULD NOT BE ARRESTED...HE COULD LIVE OUT HIS LIFE IN EXILE AND NEVER FACE ANY PUNISHMENT FOR HIS CRIMES.
FREEDOM.
HIS OWN.
"OKURA LET THE WARLORDS AND THEIR ARMIES STAND ALONE AGAINST THE PEOPLE'S ARMY.
"AND WE COULD DO NOTHING TO STOP THEM.
"ARMIES OF KIDNAPPED MEN AND BOYS.
"ALL SLAUGHTERED.
"FIFTY THOUSAND DEAD."

"OKURA OFFERED HIS SURRENDER FROM A VERY SAFE DISTANCE.

"BUT THERE WERE *CONSEQUENCES* FOR US."

HOW COULD YOU LET HIM *GO?!* AFTER ALL THAT'S HE'S *DONE!* YOU LET THAT MONSTER *WALK AWAY?!* WHY?!

WE GAVE OUR *WORD!* WHAT ARE WE IF WE ACT WITHOUT HONOR?!

HONOR?!

HOW COULD YOU SPEAK OF *HONOR?!* THAT SCUM, WHO'S *RAPED, TORTURED* AND *MURDERED* OUR PEOPLE FOR TWENTY YEARS--

HE'S COMMITTED *GENOCIDE!* AND *YOU* LET HIM *LIVE!*

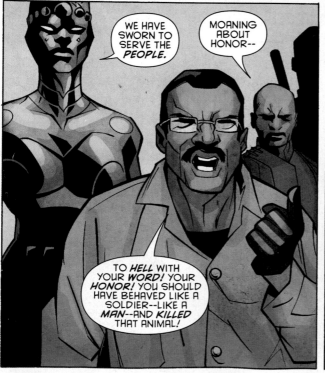

WE HAVE SWORN TO SERVE THE *PEOPLE.*

MOANING ABOUT HONOR--

TO *HELL* WITH YOUR *WORD!* YOUR *HONOR!* YOU SHOULD HAVE BEHAVED LIKE A SOLDIER--LIKE A *MAN*--AND *KILLED* THAT ANIMAL!

KONE, THIS IS *NOT* YOUR PLACE.

OH, BECAUSE I AM SIMPLY THE *MORTAL* IN THE RANKS! *TRUE!* IF I *DID* POSSESS YOUR *GOD-GIVEN POWER,* I *WOULD HAVE BROKEN HIM IN HALF!*

I WOULDN'T HAVE TURNED AWAY FROM MY DUTY LIKE A WEAK, FRIGHTENED BOY--*LIKE A DAMNED* **COWARD!**

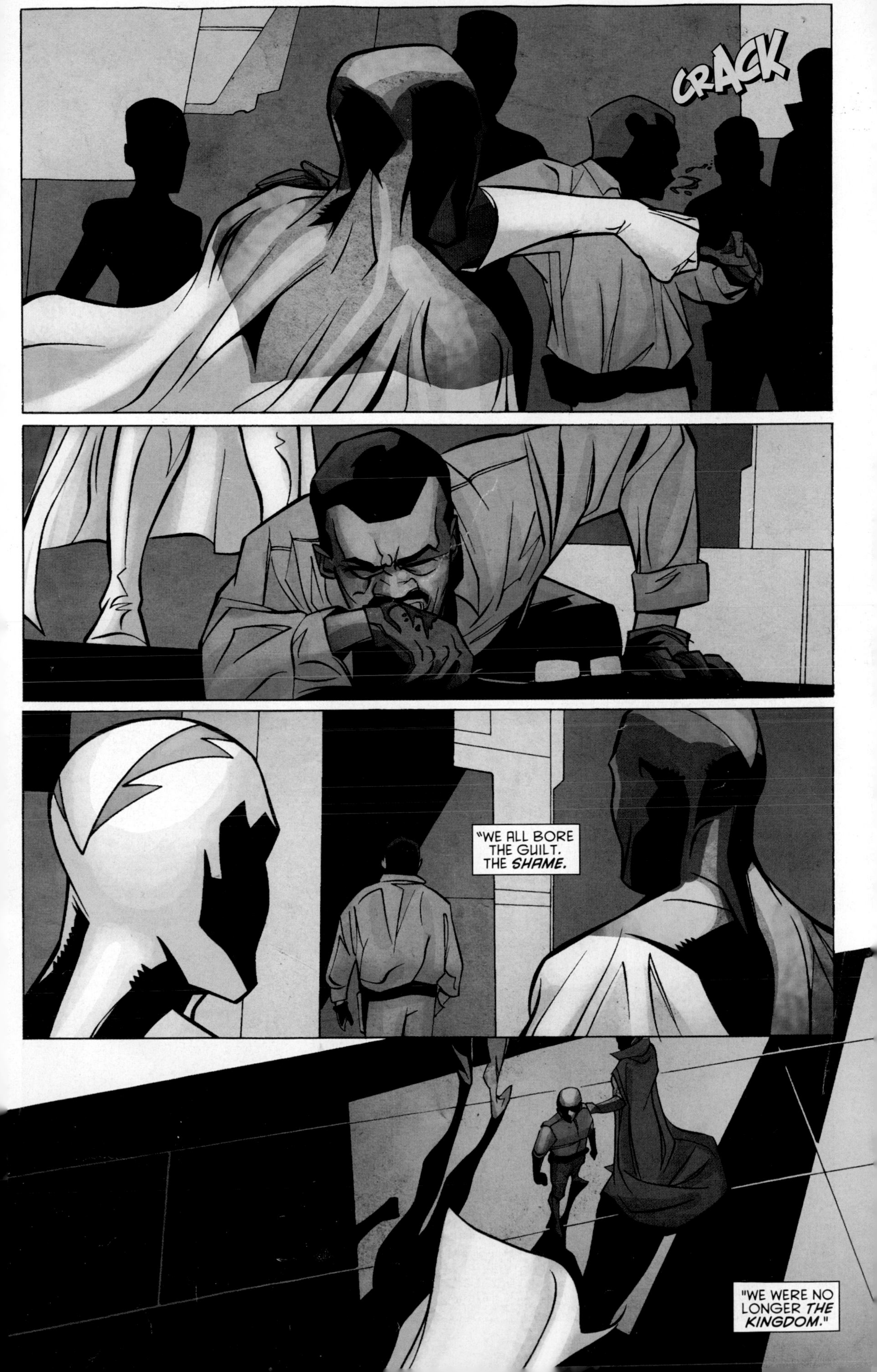
CRACK
"WE ALL BORE THE GUILT. THE *SHAME*.
"WE WERE NO LONGER *THE KINGDOM*."

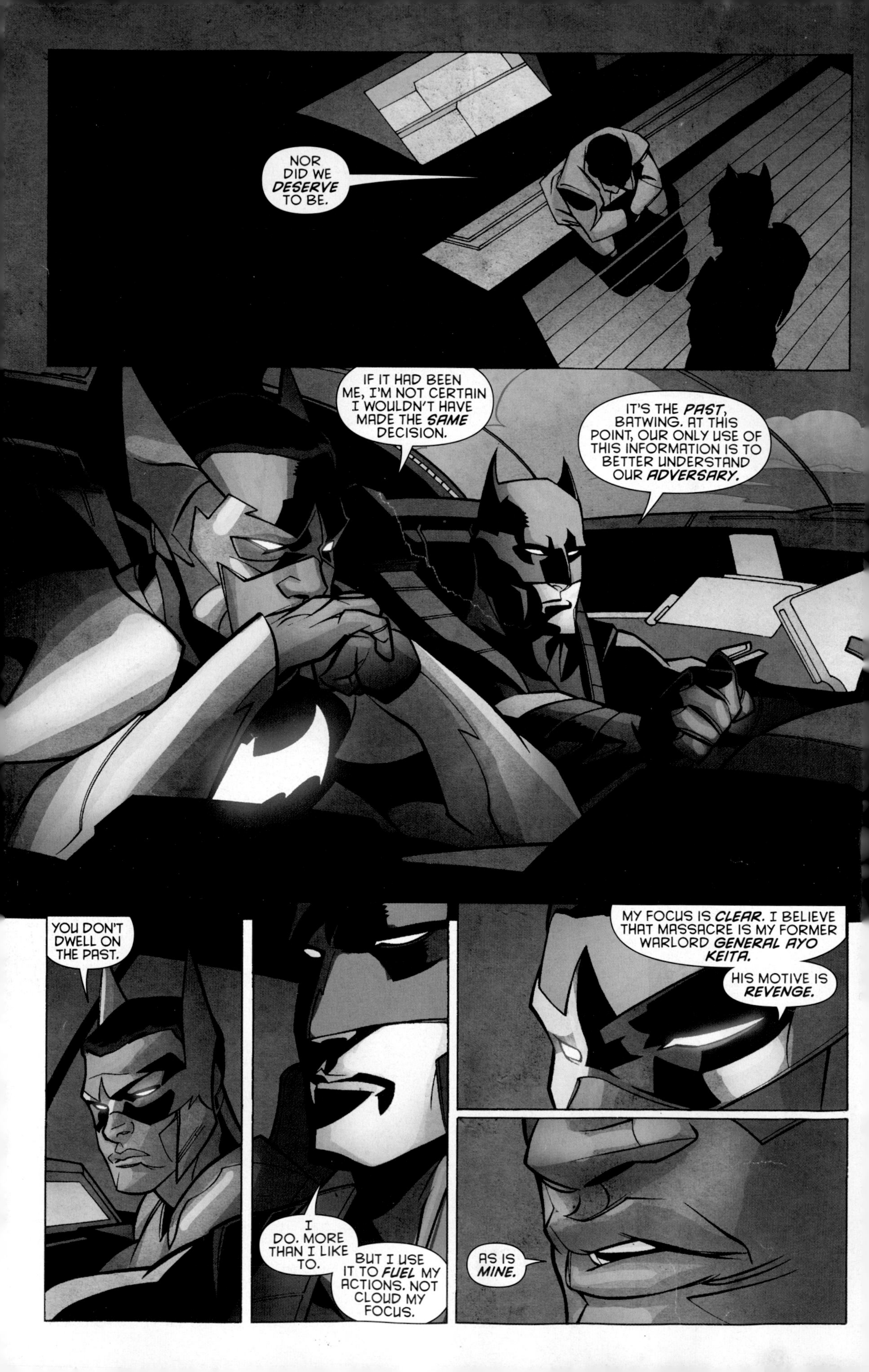
NOR DID WE DESERVE TO BE.
IF IT HAD BEEN ME, I'M NOT CERTAIN I WOULDN'T HAVE MADE THE SAME DECISION.
IT'S THE PAST, BATWING. AT THIS POINT, OUR ONLY USE OF THIS INFORMATION IS TO BETTER UNDERSTAND OUR ADVERSARY.
YOU DON'T DWELL ON THE PAST.
I DO. MORE THAN I LIKE TO.
BUT I USE IT TO FUEL MY ACTIONS. NOT CLOUD MY FOCUS.
MY FOCUS IS CLEAR. I BELIEVE THAT MASSACRE IS MY FORMER WARLORD GENERAL AYO KEITA.
HIS MOTIVE IS REVENGE.
AS IS MINE.

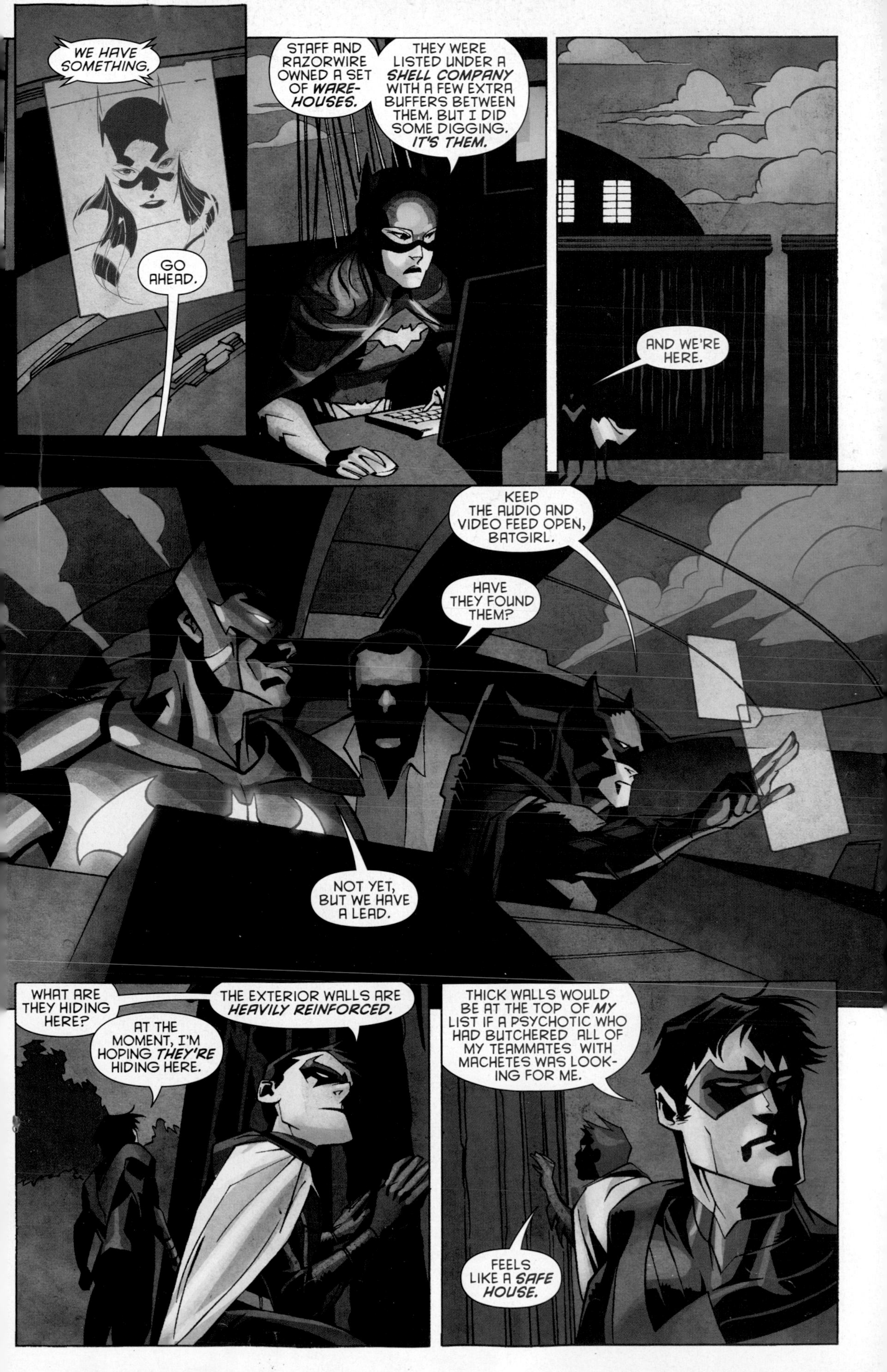
WE HAVE SOMETHING.
GO AHEAD.
STAFF AND RAZORWIRE OWNED A SET OF WARE-HOUSES.
THEY WERE LISTED UNDER A SHELL COMPANY WITH A FEW EXTRA BUFFERS BETWEEN THEM. BUT I DID SOME DIGGING. IT'S THEM.
AND WE'RE HERE.
KEEP THE AUDIO AND VIDEO FEED OPEN, BATGIRL.
HAVE THEY FOUND THEM?
NOT YET, BUT WE HAVE A LEAD.
WHAT ARE THEY HIDING HERE?
THE EXTERIOR WALLS ARE HEAVILY REINFORCED.
AT THE MOMENT, I'M HOPING THEY'RE HIDING HERE.
THICK WALLS WOULD BE AT THE TOP OF MY LIST IF A PSYCHOTIC WHO HAD BUTCHERED ALL OF MY TEAMMATES WITH MACHETES WAS LOOK-ING FOR ME.
FEELS LIKE A SAFE HOUSE.

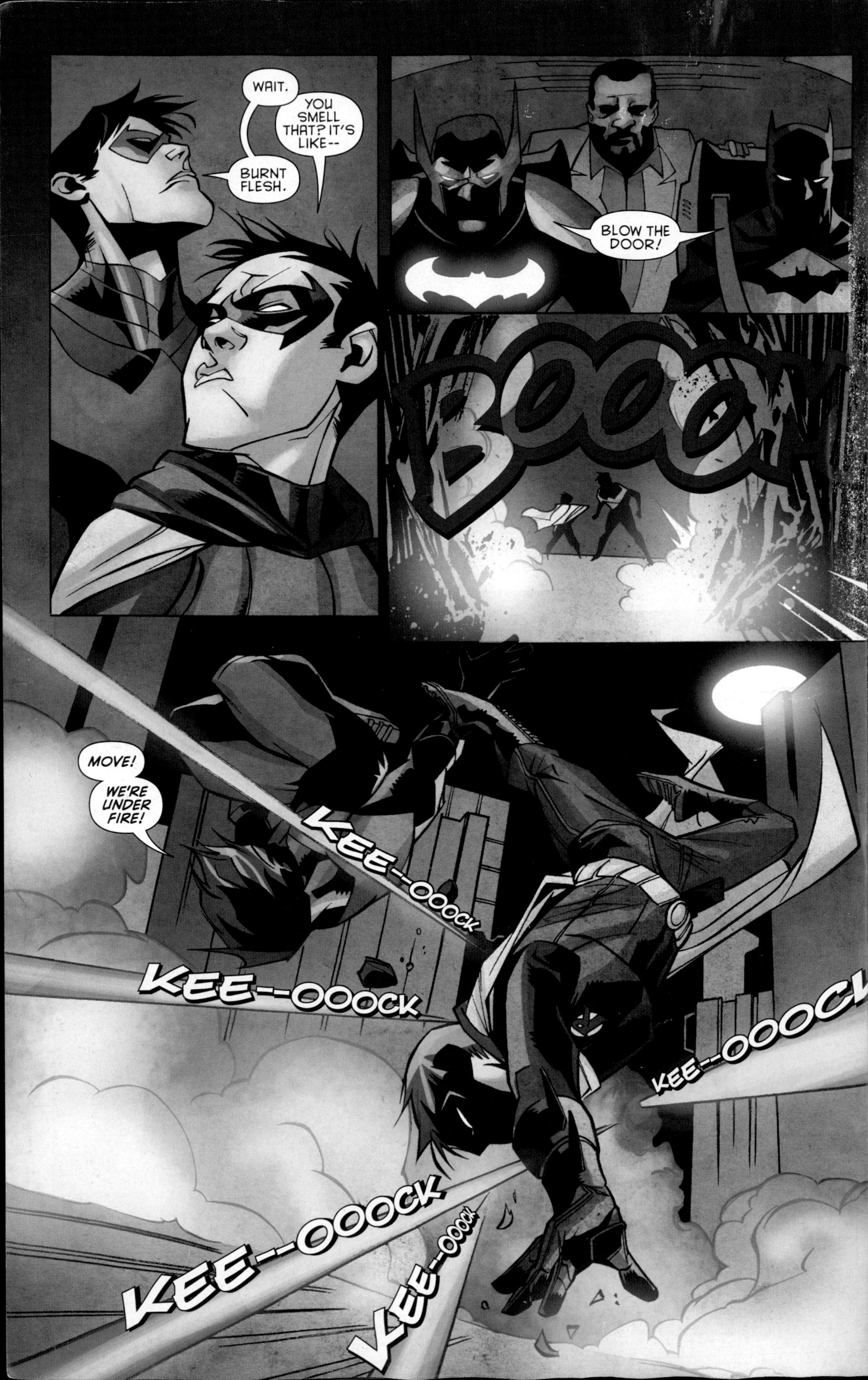

WAIT.
YOU SMELL THAT? IT'S LIKE--
BURNT FLESH.
BLOW THE DOOR!
BOOOOM
MOVE! WE'RE UNDER FIRE!
KEE--OOOCK
KEE--OOOCK
KEE--OOOCK
KEE--OOOCK
KEE--OOOCK

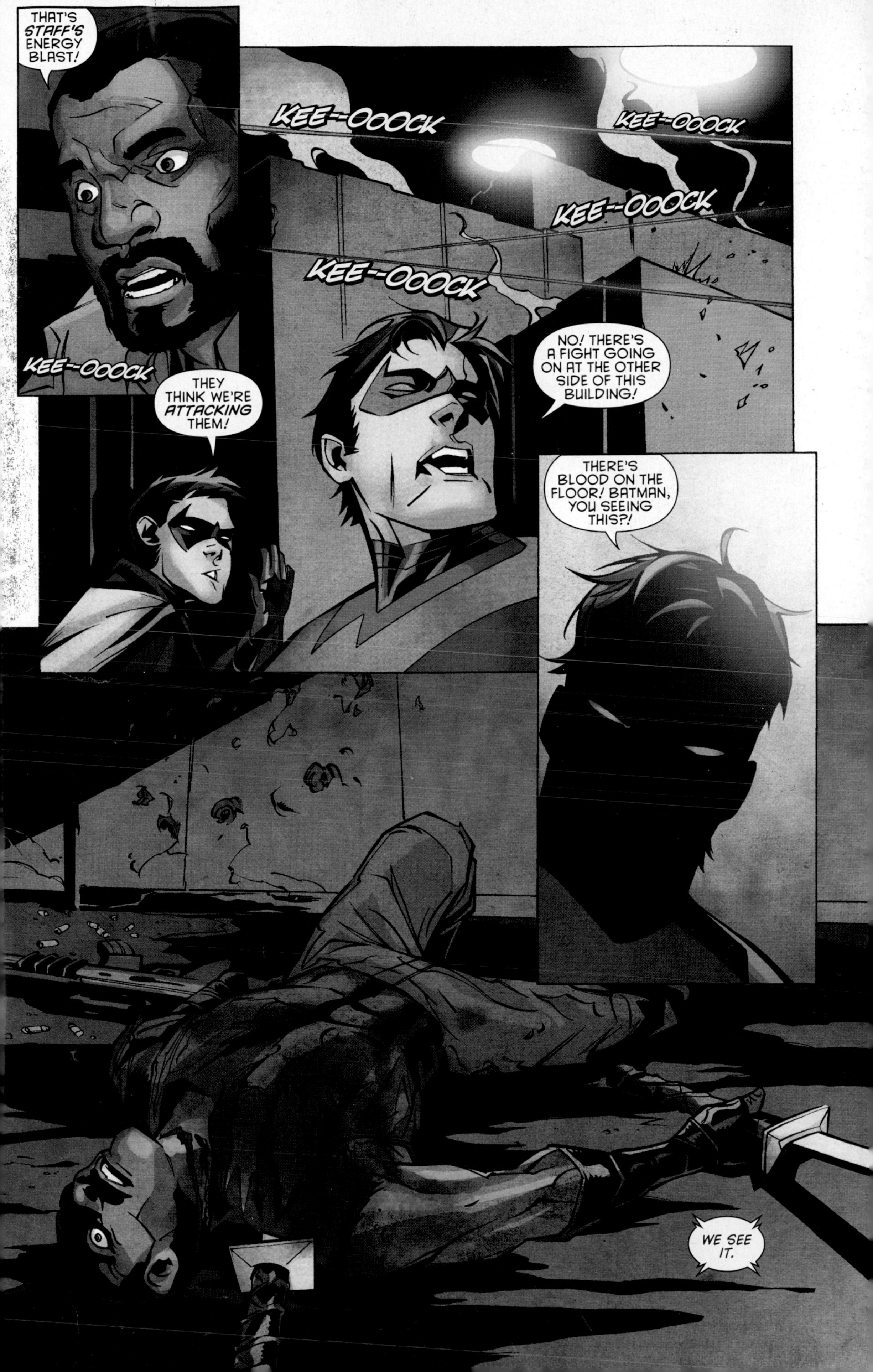
THAT'S STAFF'S ENERGY BLAST!
KEE--OOOCK
KEE--OOOCK
KEE--OOOCK
KEE--OOOCK
KEE--OOOCK
THEY THINK WE'RE ATTACKING THEM!
NO! THERE'S A FIGHT GOING ON AT THE OTHER SIDE OF THIS BUILDING!
THERE'S BLOOD ON THE FLOOR! BATMAN, YOU SEEING THIS?!
WE SEE IT.

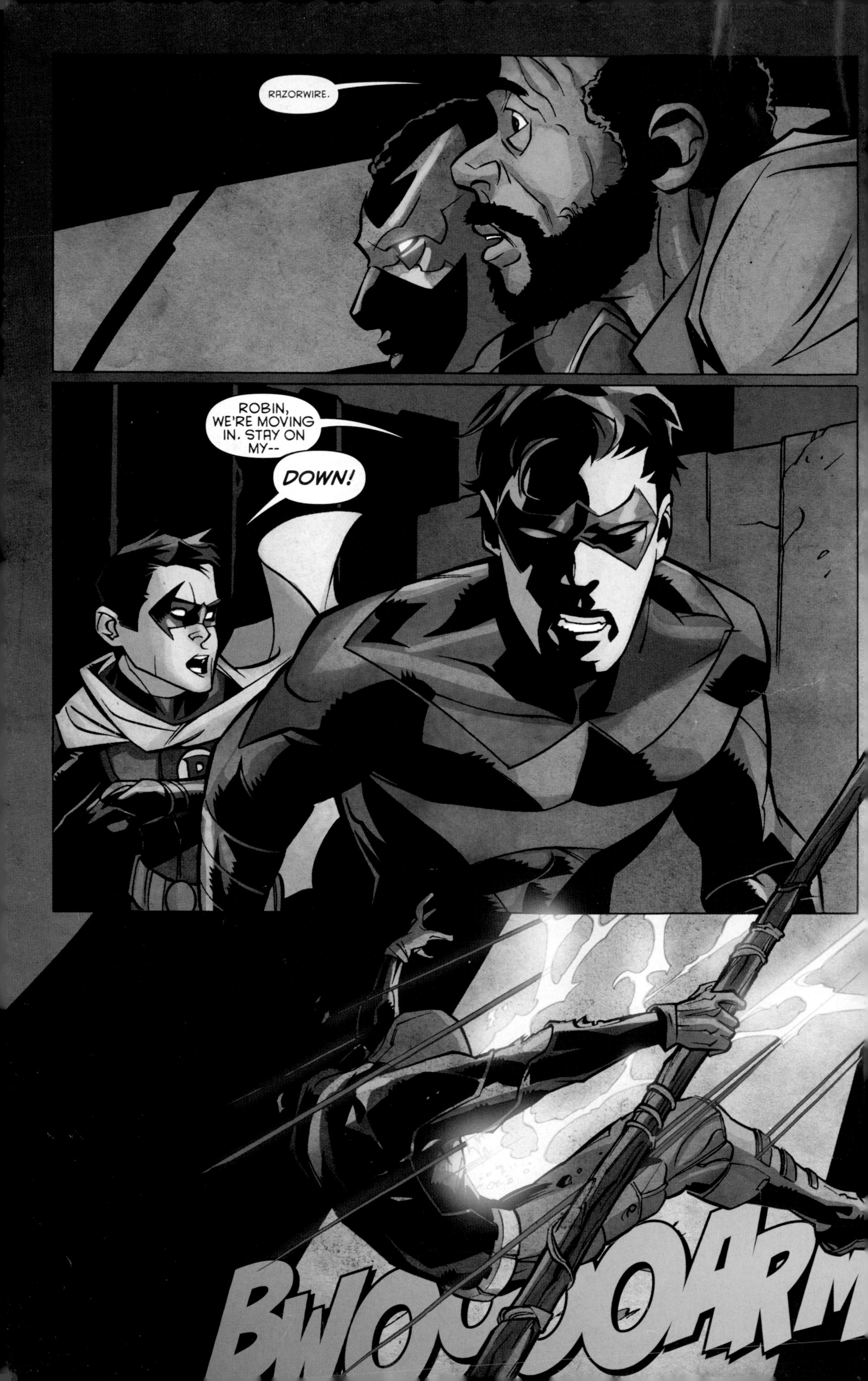
RAZORWIRE.
ROBIN, WE'RE MOVING IN. STAY ON MY--
DOWN!

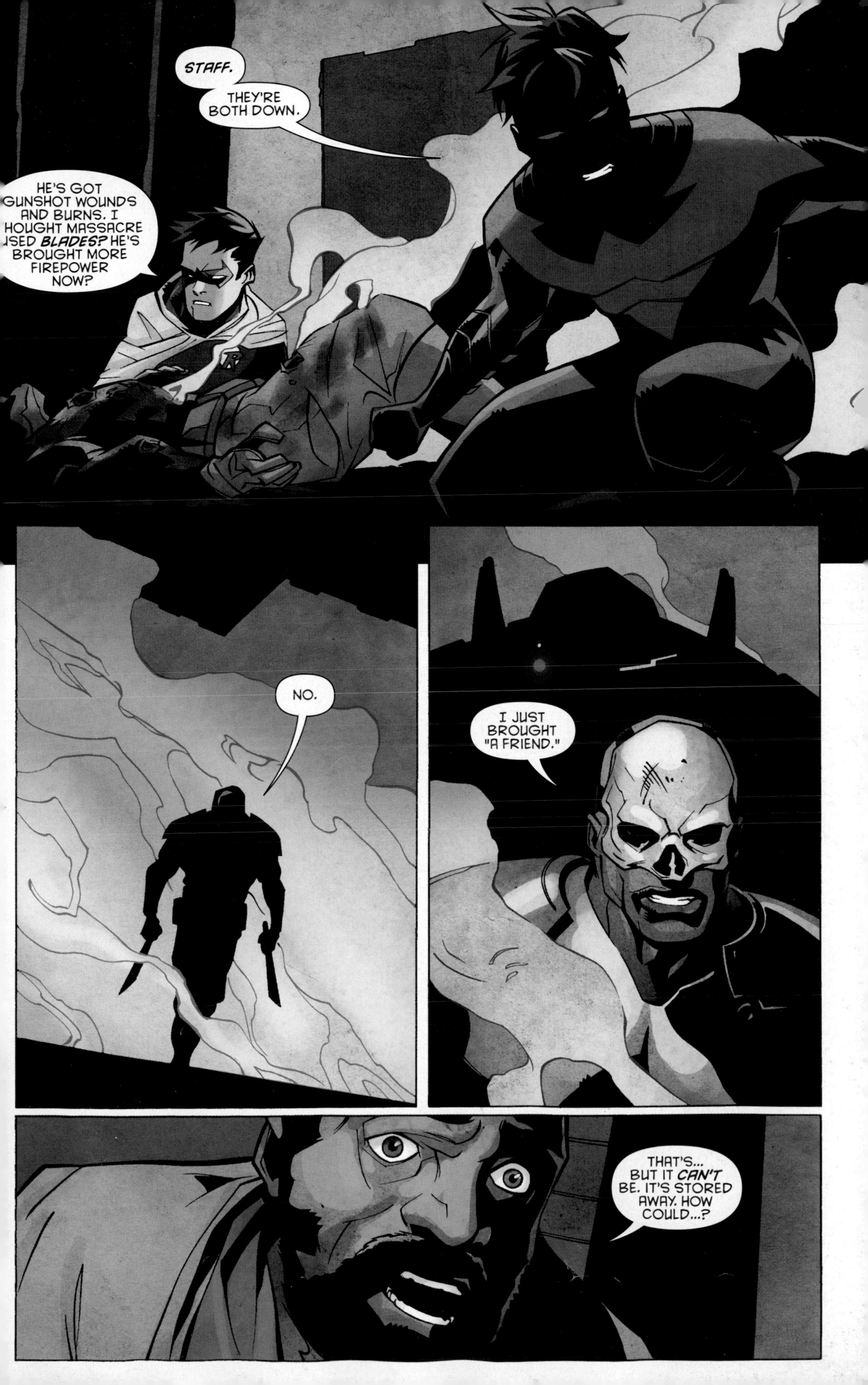
STAFF.
THEY'RE BOTH DOWN.
HE'S GOT GUNSHOT WOUNDS AND BURNS. I HOUGHT MASSACRE USED BLADES? HE'S BROUGHT MORE FIREPOWER NOW?
NO.
I JUST BROUGHT "A FRIEND."
THAT'S... BUT IT CAN'T BE. IT'S STORED AWAY. HOW COULD...?

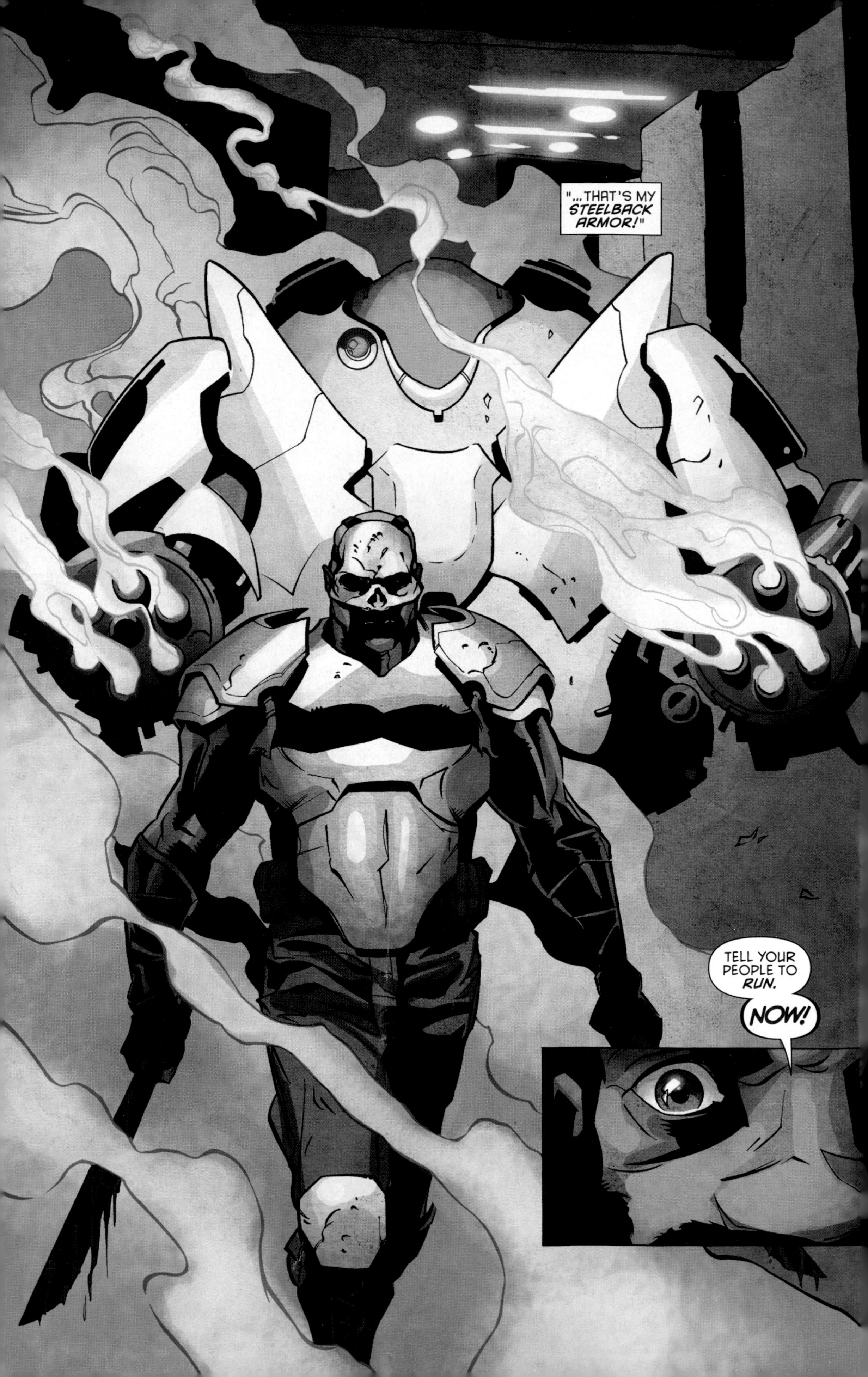
"...THAT'S MY STEELBACK ARMOR!"
TELL YOUR PEOPLE TO RUN.
NOW!

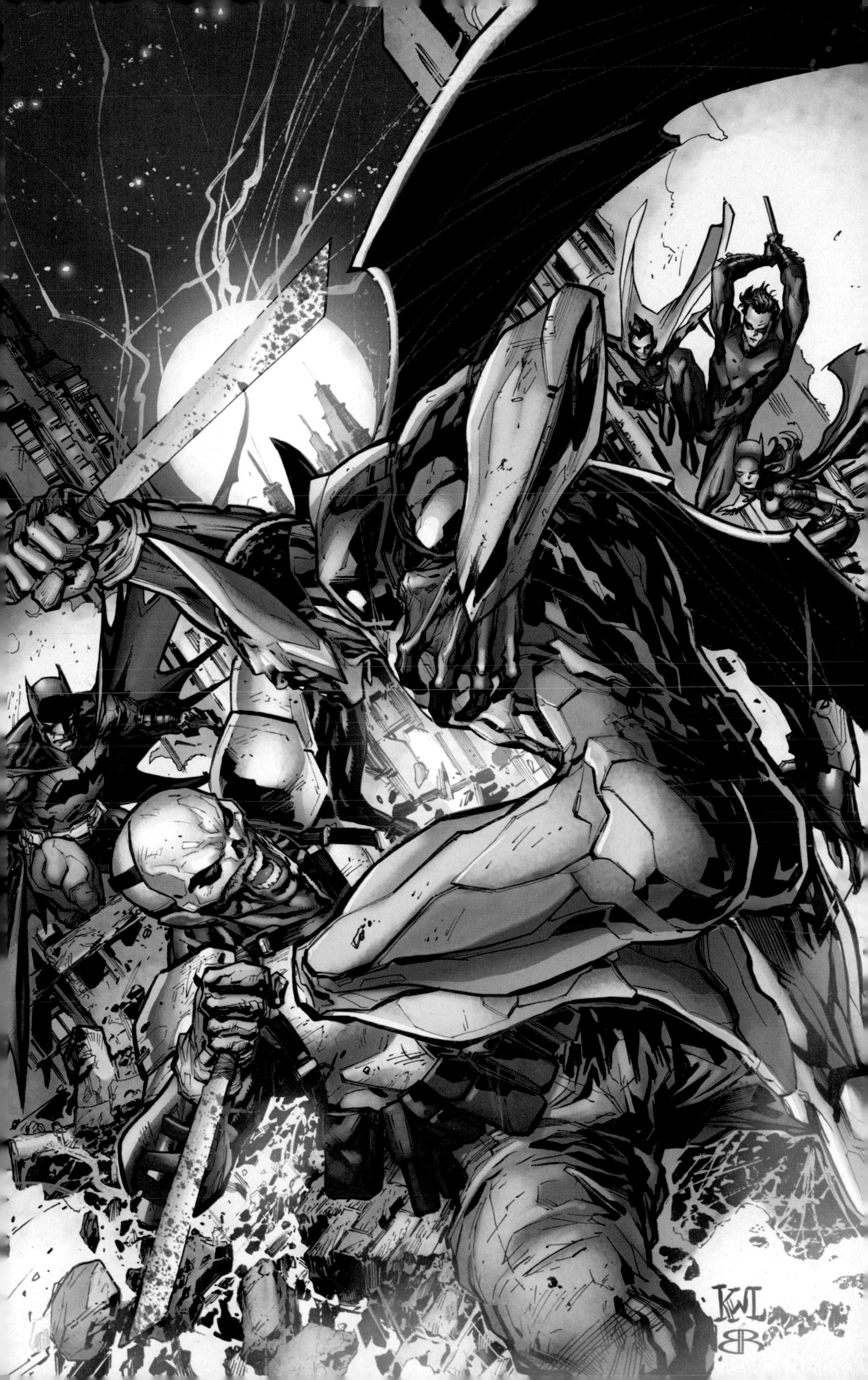

WHAT I AM... WAS BORN FROM DEATH

JUDD WINICK writer **DUSTIN NGUYEN** penciller **DEREK FRIDOLFS** inker cover art by **KEN LASHLEY & BRIAN REBER**

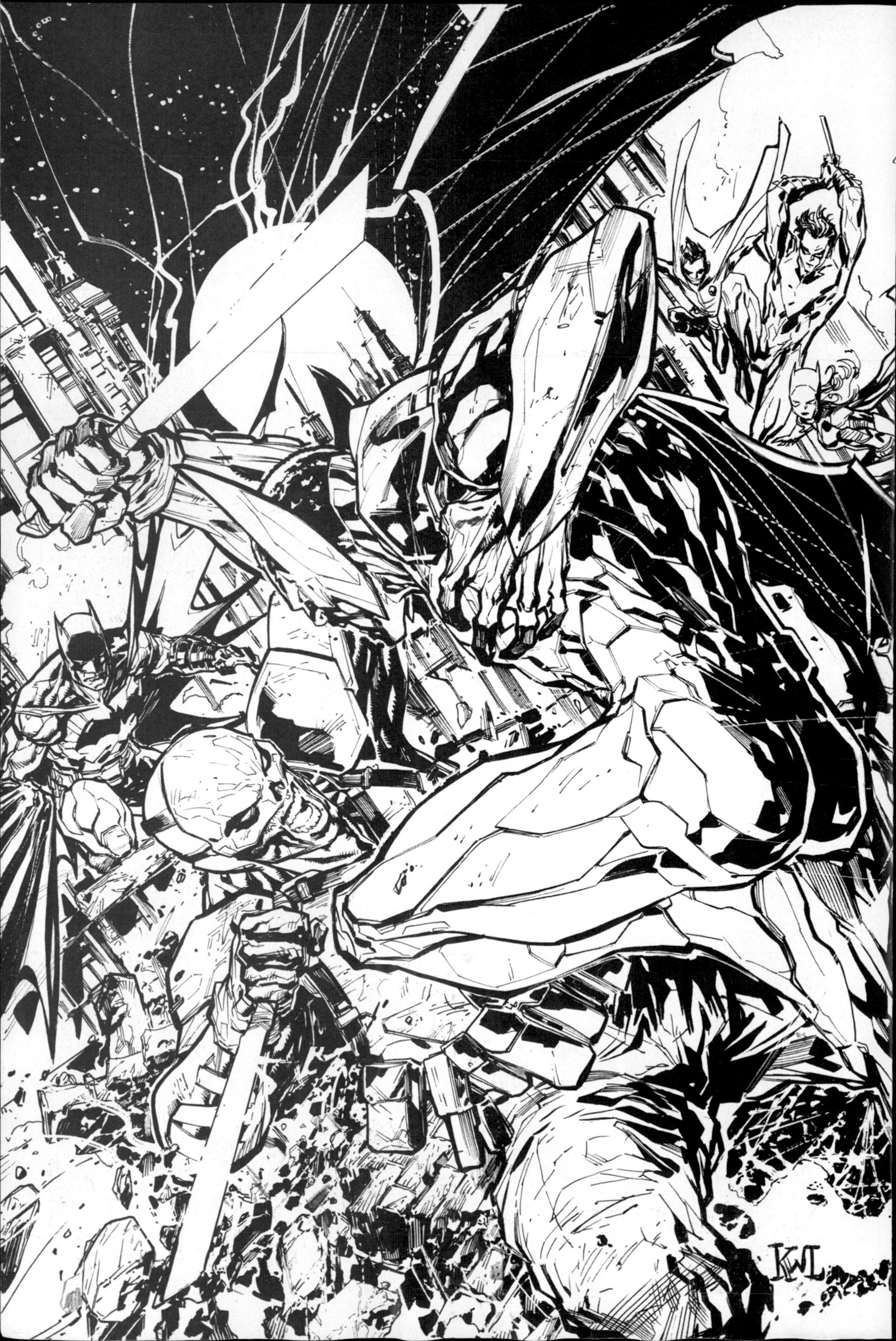

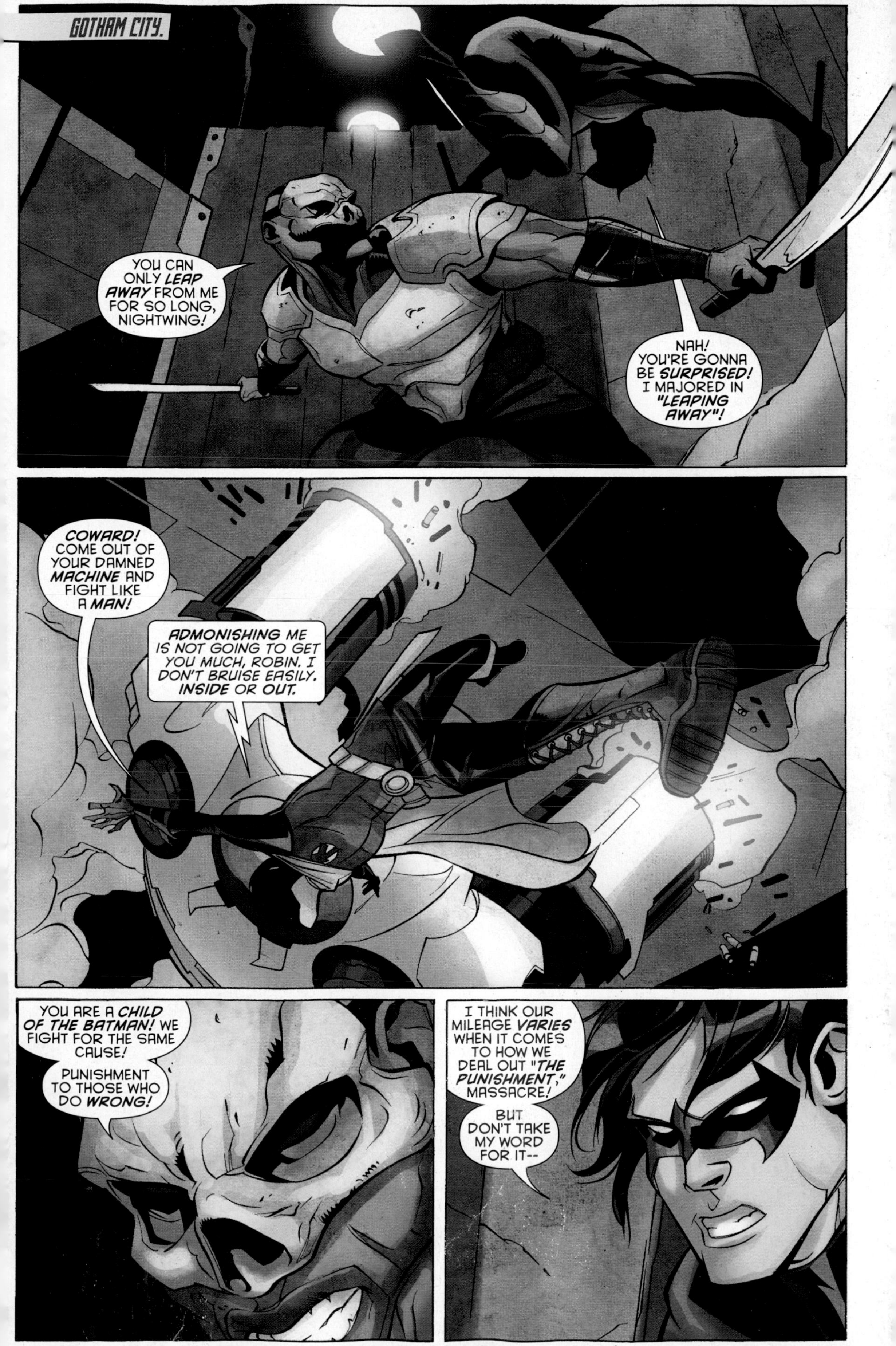
GOTHAM CITY.
YOU CAN ONLY LEAP AWAY FROM ME FOR SO LONG, NIGHTWING!
NAH! YOU'RE GONNA BE SURPRISED! I MAJORED IN "LEAPING AWAY"!
COWARD! COME OUT OF YOUR DAMNED MACHINE AND FIGHT LIKE A MAN!
ADMONISHING ME IS NOT GOING TO GET YOU MUCH, ROBIN. I DON'T BRUISE EASILY. INSIDE OR OUT.
YOU ARE A CHILD OF THE BATMAN! WE FIGHT FOR THE SAME CAUSE!
PUNISHMENT TO THOSE WHO DO WRONG!
I THINK OUR MILEAGE VARIES WHEN IT COMES TO HOW WE DEAL OUT "THE PUNISHMENT," MASSACRE!
BUT DON'T TAKE MY WORD FOR IT--

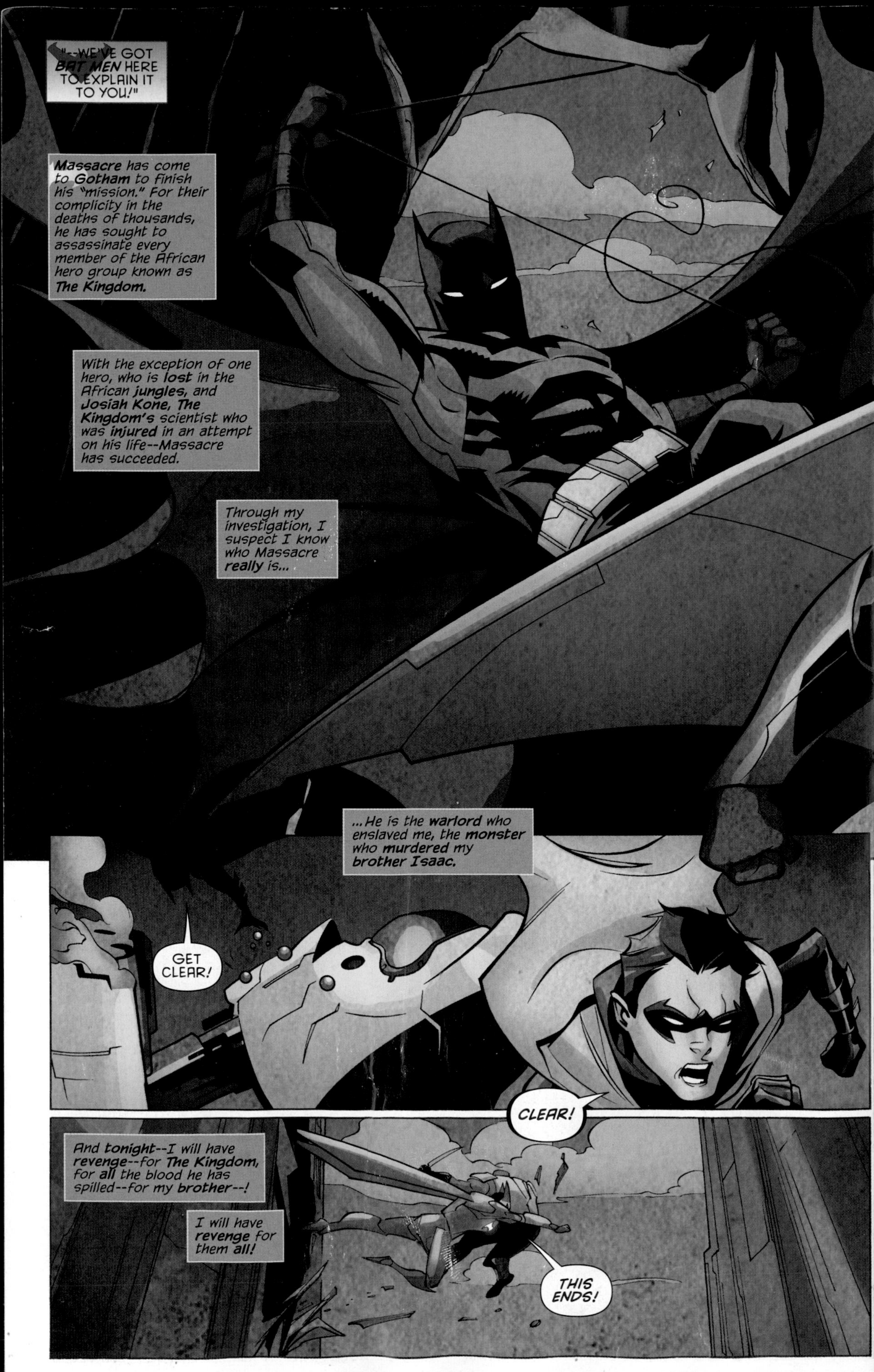
"--WE'VE GOT BAT MEN HERE TO EXPLAIN IT TO YOU!"
Massacre has come to Gotham to finish his "mission." For their complicity in the deaths of thousands, he has sought to assassinate every member of the African hero group known as The Kingdom.
With the exception of one hero, who is lost in the African jungles, and Josiah Kone, The Kingdom's scientist who was injured in an attempt on his life--Massacre has succeeded.
Through my investigation, I suspect I know who Massacre really is...
...He is the warlord who enslaved me, the monster who murdered my brother Isaac.
GET CLEAR!
CLEAR!
And tonight--I will have revenge--for The Kingdom, for all the blood he has spilled--for my brother--!
I will have revenge for them all!
THIS ENDS!

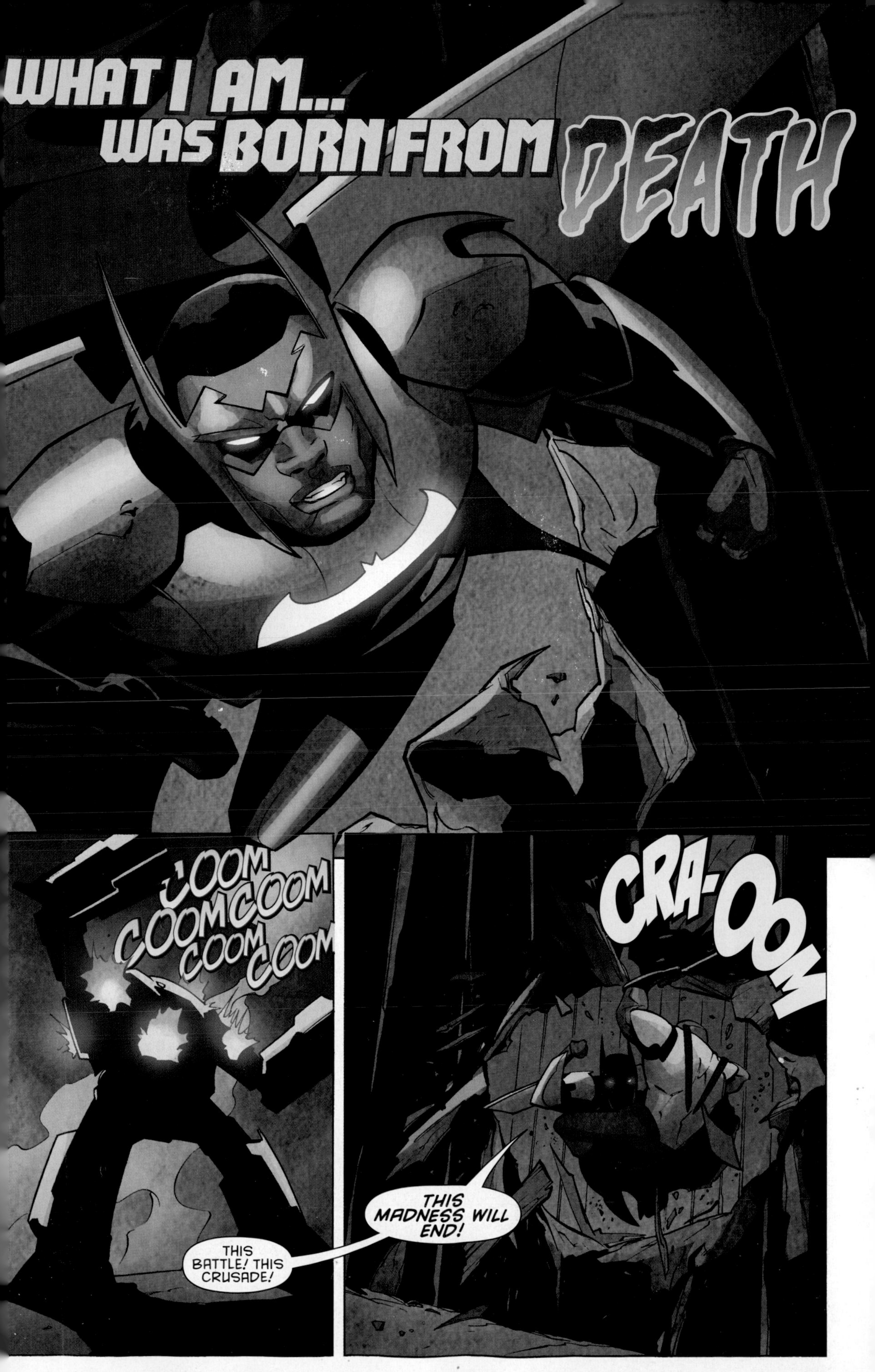
WHAT I AM...
WAS BORN FROM DEATH
COOM
COOM COOM
COOM COOM
CRA-OOM
THIS BATTLE! THIS CRUSADE!
THIS MADNESS WILL END!

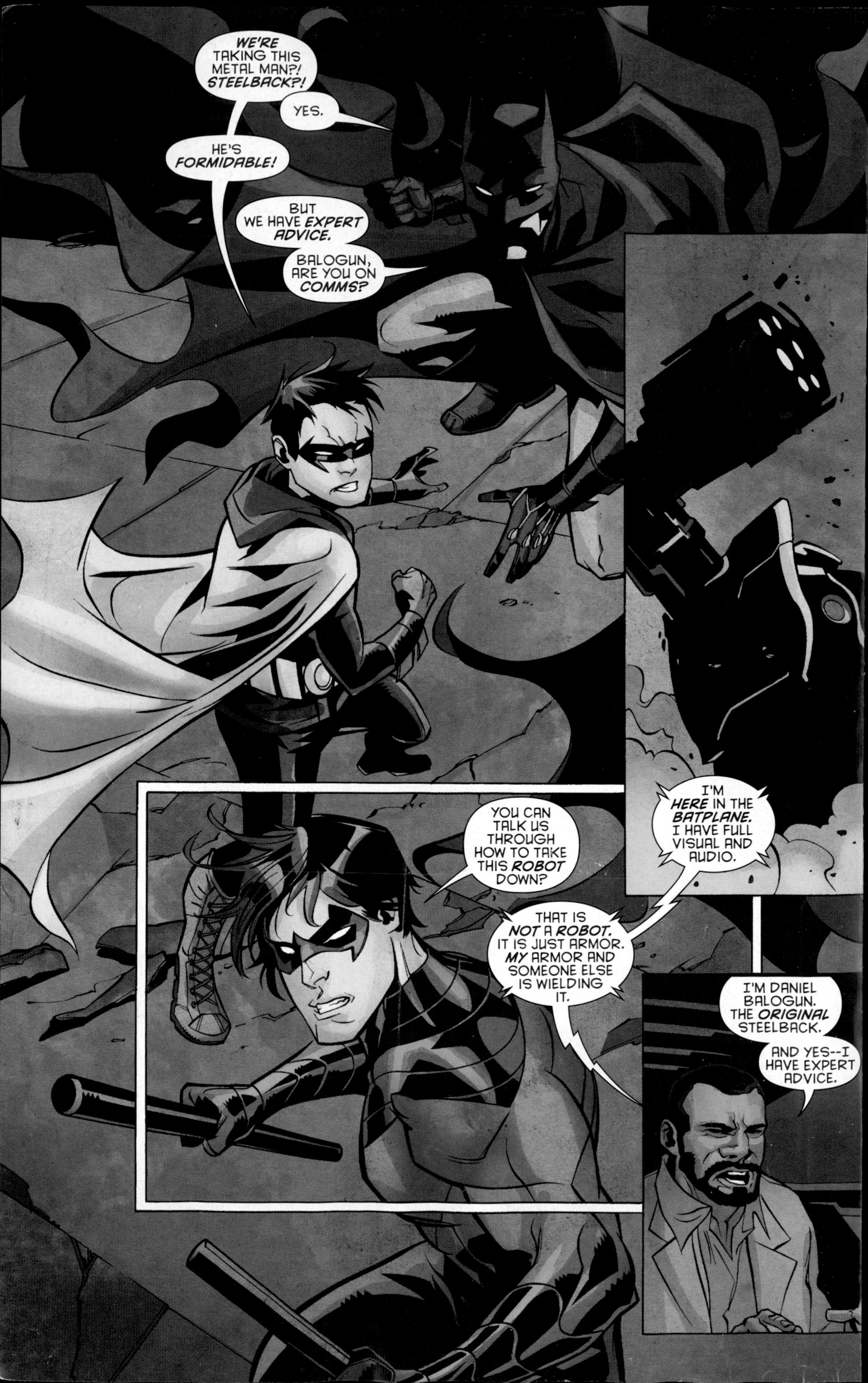
WE'RE TAKING THIS METAL MAN?! STEELBACK?!
YES.
HE'S FORMIDABLE!
BUT WE HAVE EXPERT ADVICE.
BALOGUN, ARE YOU ON COMMS?
I'M HERE IN THE BATPLANE. I HAVE FULL VISUAL AND AUDIO.
YOU CAN TALK US THROUGH HOW TO TAKE THIS ROBOT DOWN?
THAT IS NOT A ROBOT. IT IS JUST ARMOR. MY ARMOR AND SOMEONE ELSE IS WIELDING IT.
I'M DANIEL BALOGUN. THE ORIGINAL STEELBACK.
AND YES--I HAVE EXPERT ADVICE.

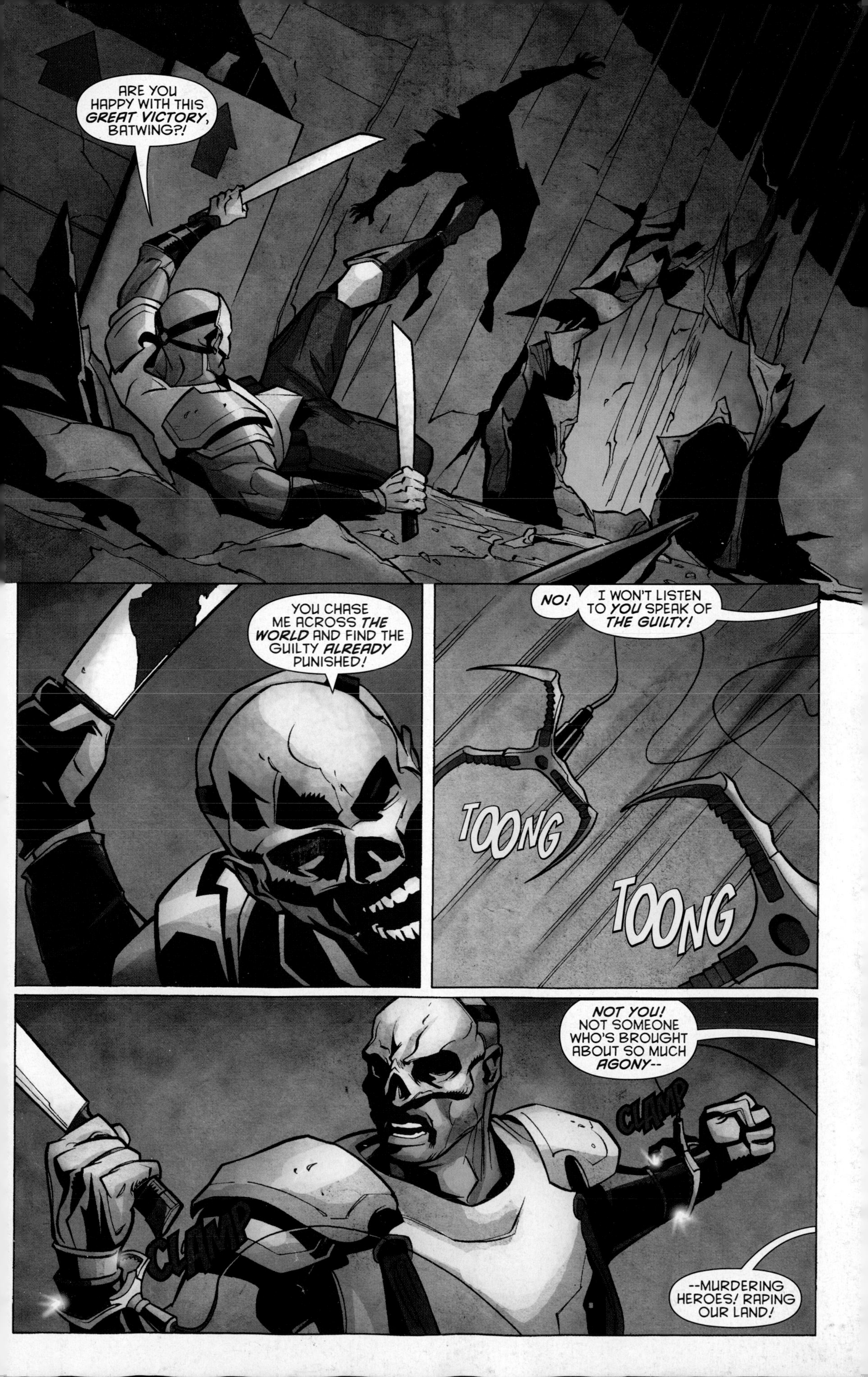
ARE YOU HAPPY WITH THIS GREAT VICTORY, BATWING?!
YOU CHASE ME ACROSS THE WORLD AND FIND THE GUILTY ALREADY PUNISHED!
NO!
I WON'T LISTEN TO YOU SPEAK OF THE GUILTY!
TOONG
TOONG
NOT YOU! NOT SOMEONE WHO'S BROUGHT ABOUT SO MUCH AGONY--
CLAMP
CLAMP
--MURDERING HEROES! RAPING OUR LAND!

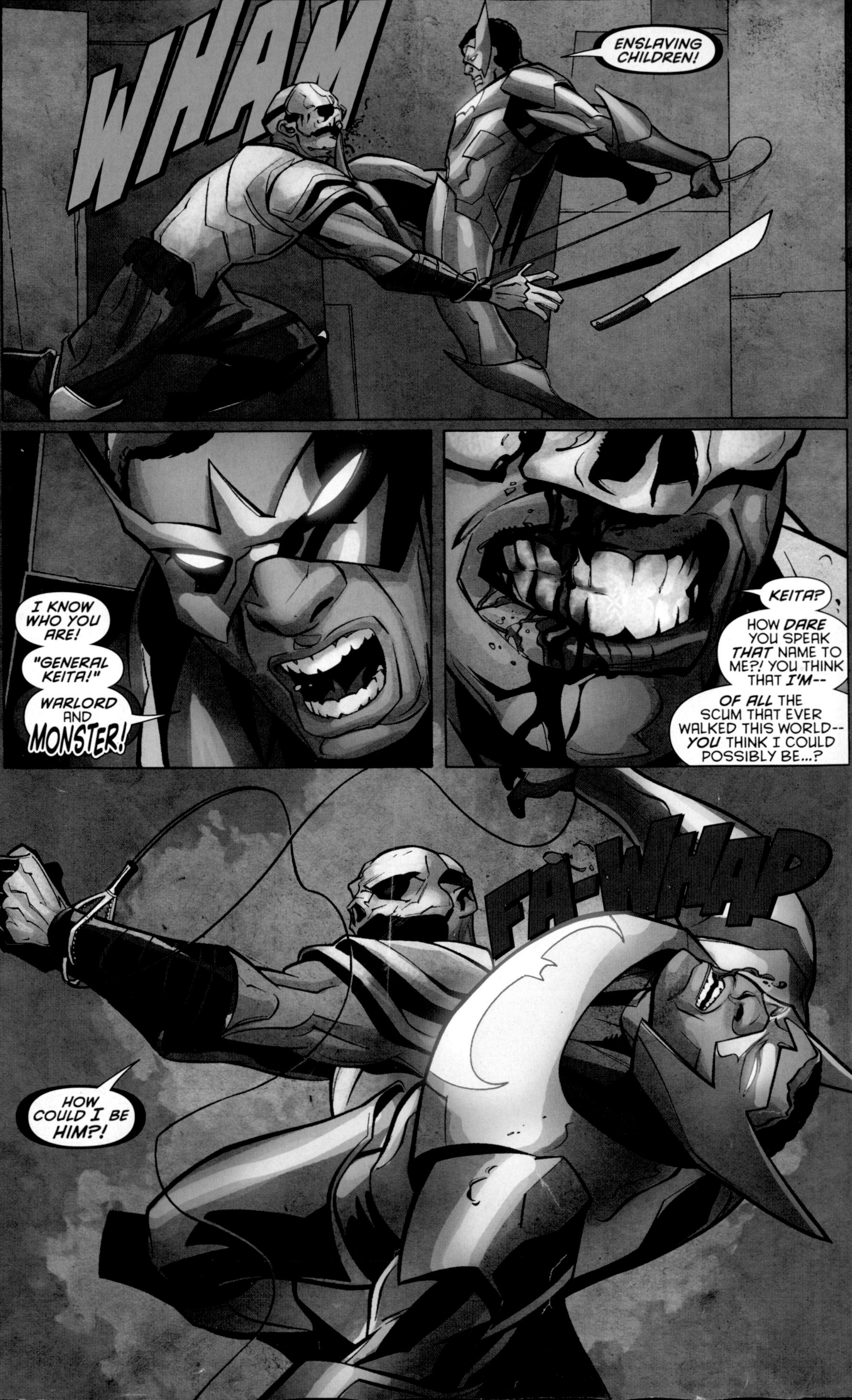
WHAM
ENSLAVING CHILDREN!
I KNOW WHO YOU ARE!
"GENERAL KEITA!"
WARLORD AND MONSTER!
KEITA?
HOW DARE YOU SPEAK THAT NAME TO ME?! YOU THINK THAT I'M--
OF ALL THE SCUM THAT EVER WALKED THIS WORLD-- YOU THINK I COULD POSSIBLY BE...?
FA-WHAP
HOW COULD I BE HIM?!

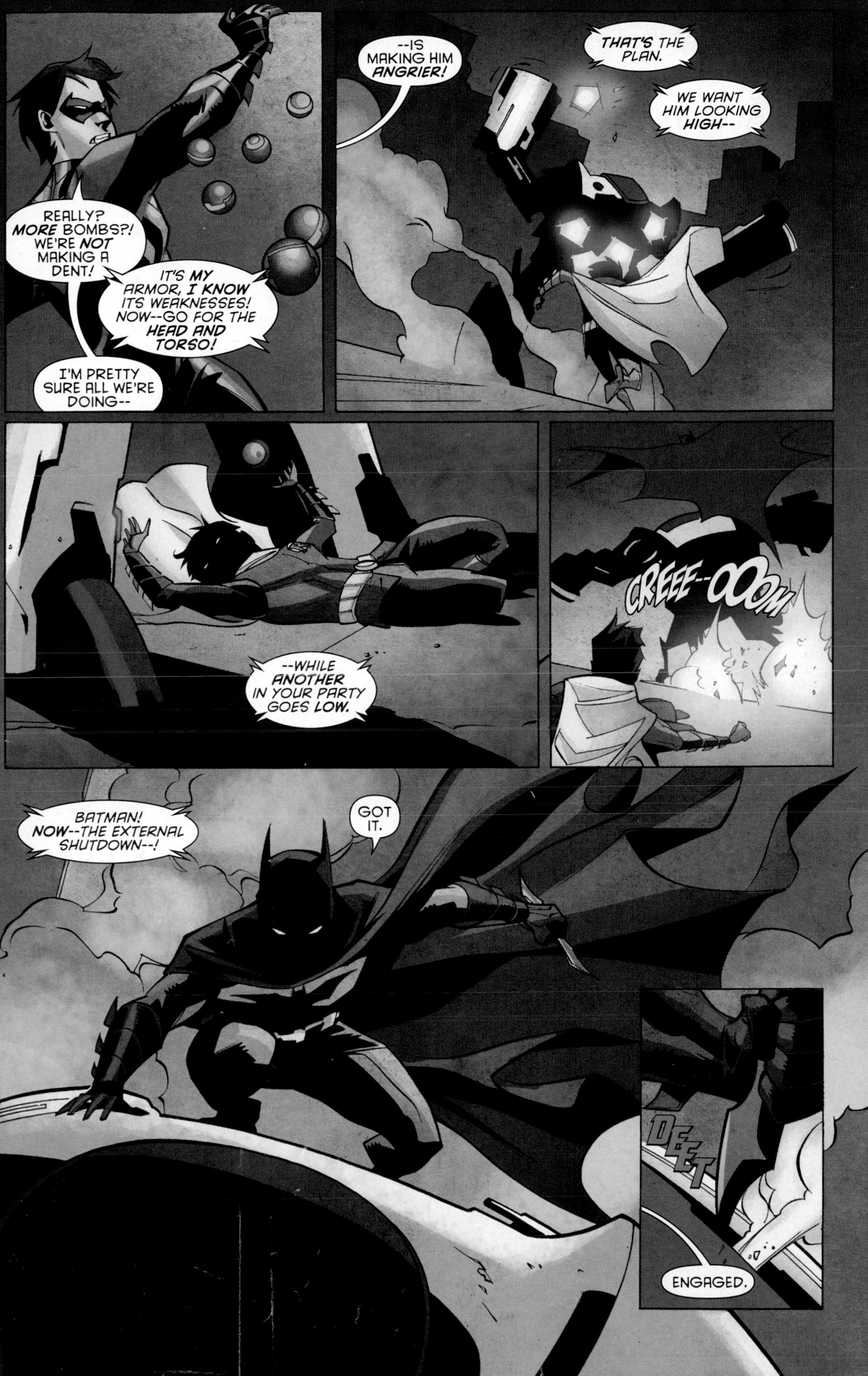
REALLY? MORE BOMBS?! WE'RE NOT MAKING A DENT!
IT'S MY ARMOR, I KNOW ITS WEAKNESSES! NOW--GO FOR THE HEAD AND TORSO!
I'M PRETTY SURE ALL WE'RE DOING--
--IS MAKING HIM ANGRIER!
THAT'S THE PLAN.
WE WANT HIM LOOKING HIGH--
--WHILE ANOTHER IN YOUR PARTY GOES LOW.
CREEE--OOOM
BATMAN! NOW--THE EXTERNAL SHUTDOWN--!
GOT IT.
DEET
ENGAGED.

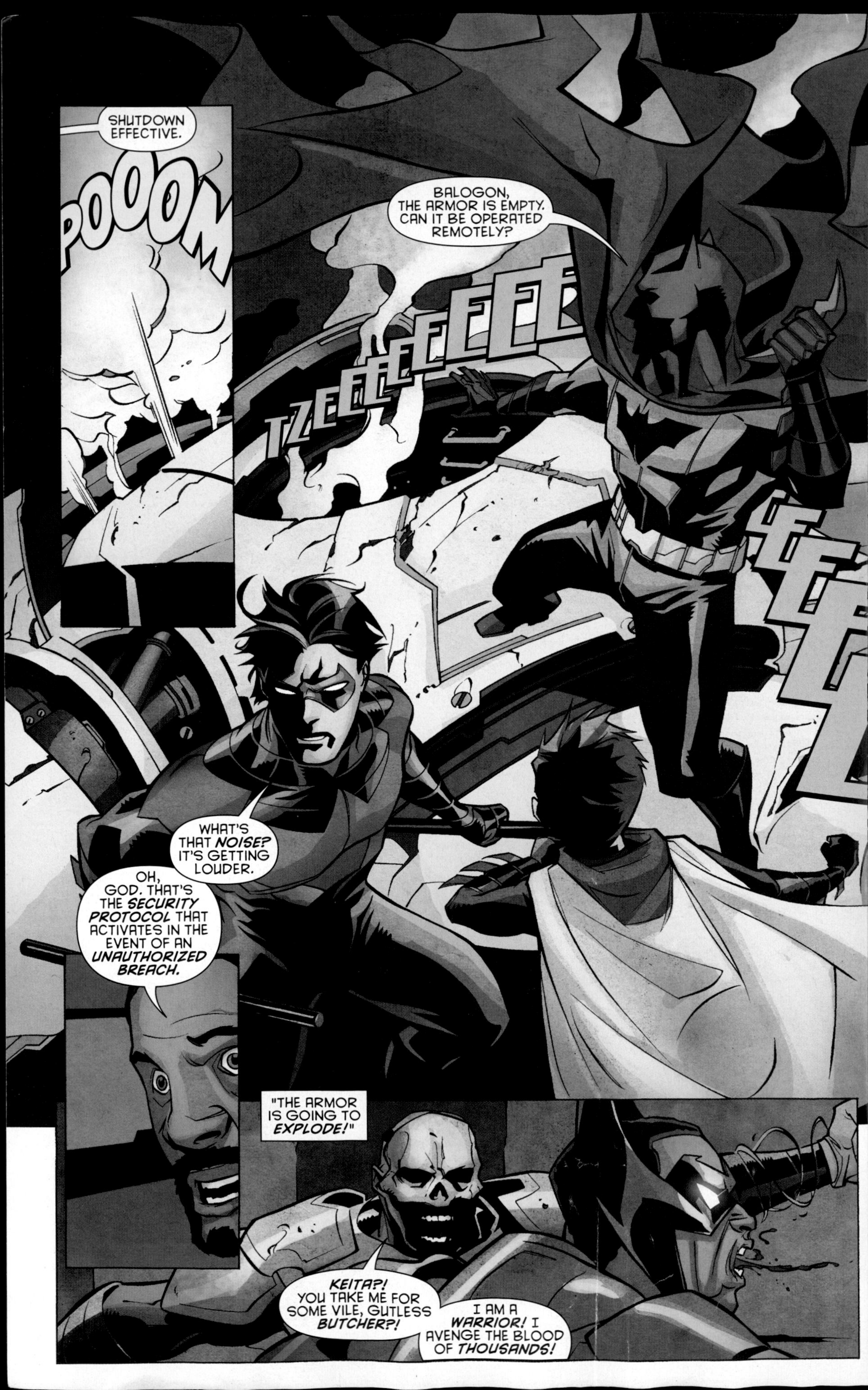
SHUTDOWN EFFECTIVE.
POOOOM
BALOGON, THE ARMOR IS EMPTY. CAN IT BE OPERATED REMOTELY?
TZEEEEEEEE
WHAT'S THAT NOISE? IT'S GETTING LOUDER.
OH, GOD. THAT'S THE SECURITY PROTOCOL THAT ACTIVATES IN THE EVENT OF AN UNAUTHORIZED BREACH.
"THE ARMOR IS GOING TO EXPLODE!"
KEITA?! YOU TAKE ME FOR SOME VILE, GUTLESS BUTCHER?!
I AM A WARRIOR! I AVENGE THE BLOOD OF THOUSANDS!

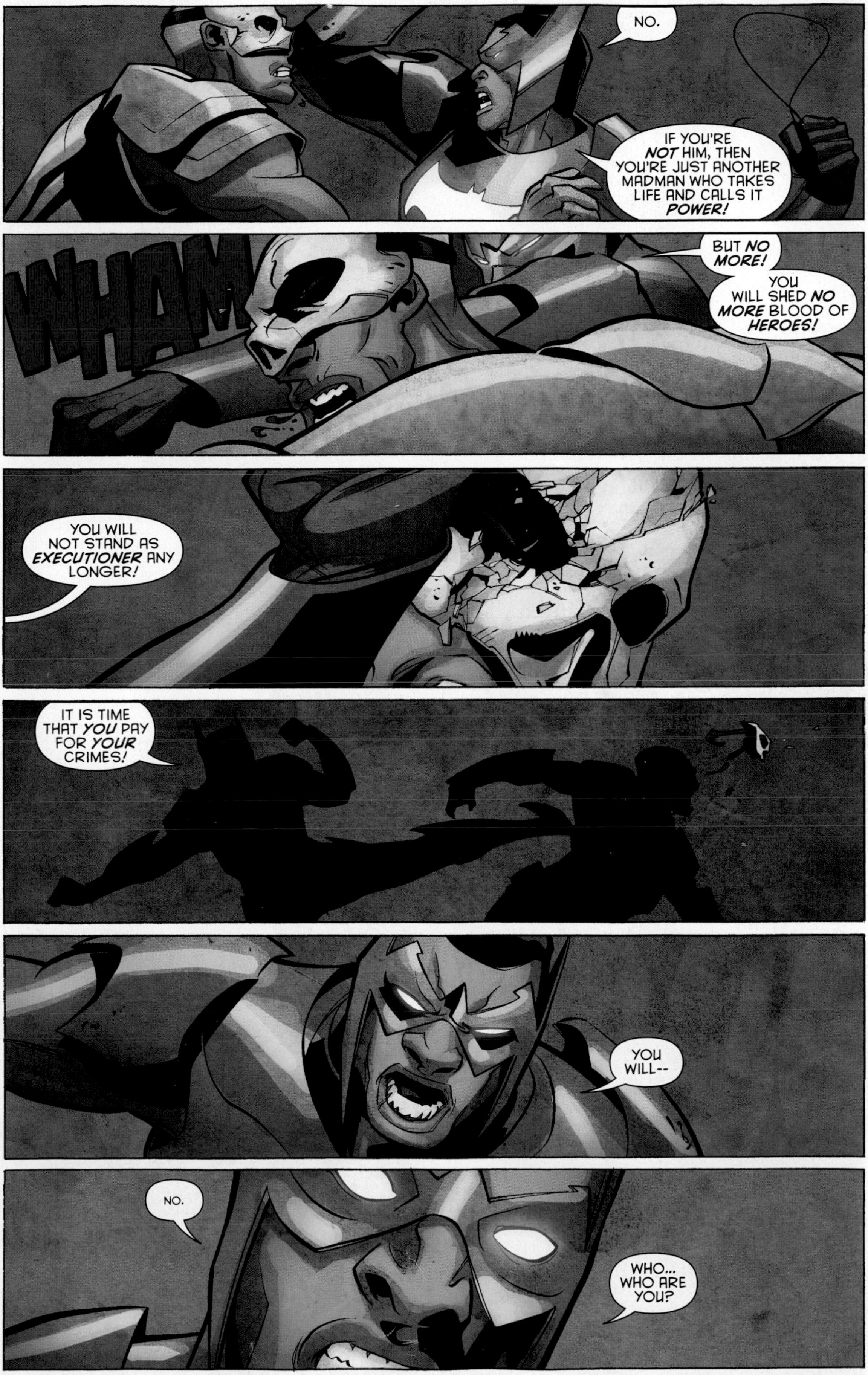
NO.
IF YOU'RE NOT HIM, THEN YOU'RE JUST ANOTHER MADMAN WHO TAKES LIFE AND CALLS IT POWER!
WHAM
BUT NO MORE!
YOU WILL SHED NO MORE BLOOD OF HEROES!
YOU WILL NOT STAND AS EXECUTIONER ANY LONGER!
IT IS TIME THAT YOU PAY FOR YOUR CRIMES!
YOU WILL--
NO.
WHO... WHO ARE YOU?

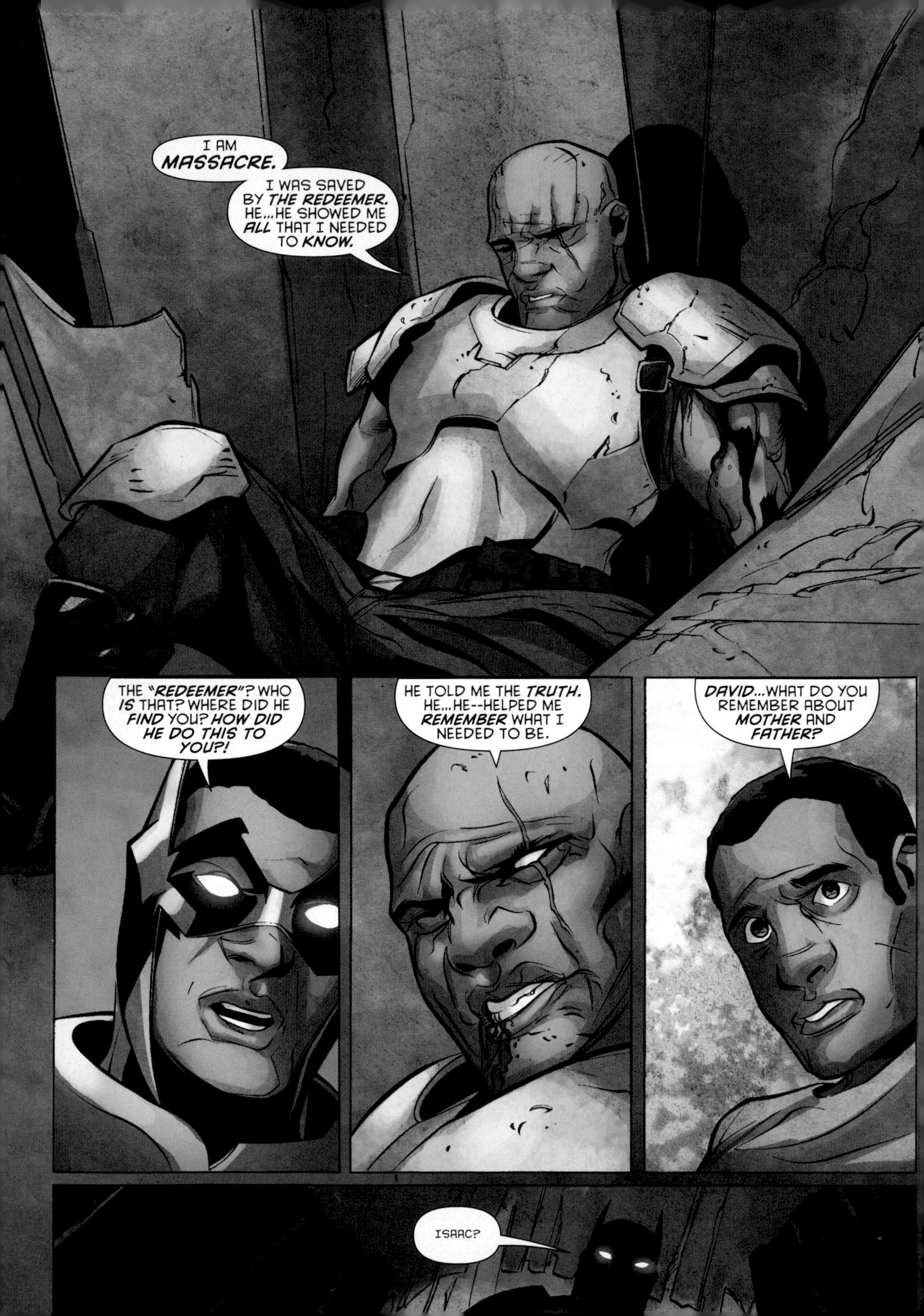
I AM MASSACRE.
I WAS SAVED BY THE REDEEMER. HE...HE SHOWED ME ALL THAT I NEEDED TO KNOW.
THE "REDEEMER"? WHO IS THAT? WHERE DID HE FIND YOU? HOW DID HE DO THIS TO YOU?!
HE TOLD ME THE TRUTH. HE...HE--HELPED ME REMEMBER WHAT I NEEDED TO BE.
DAVID...WHAT DO YOU REMEMBER ABOUT MOTHER AND FATHER?
ISAAC?

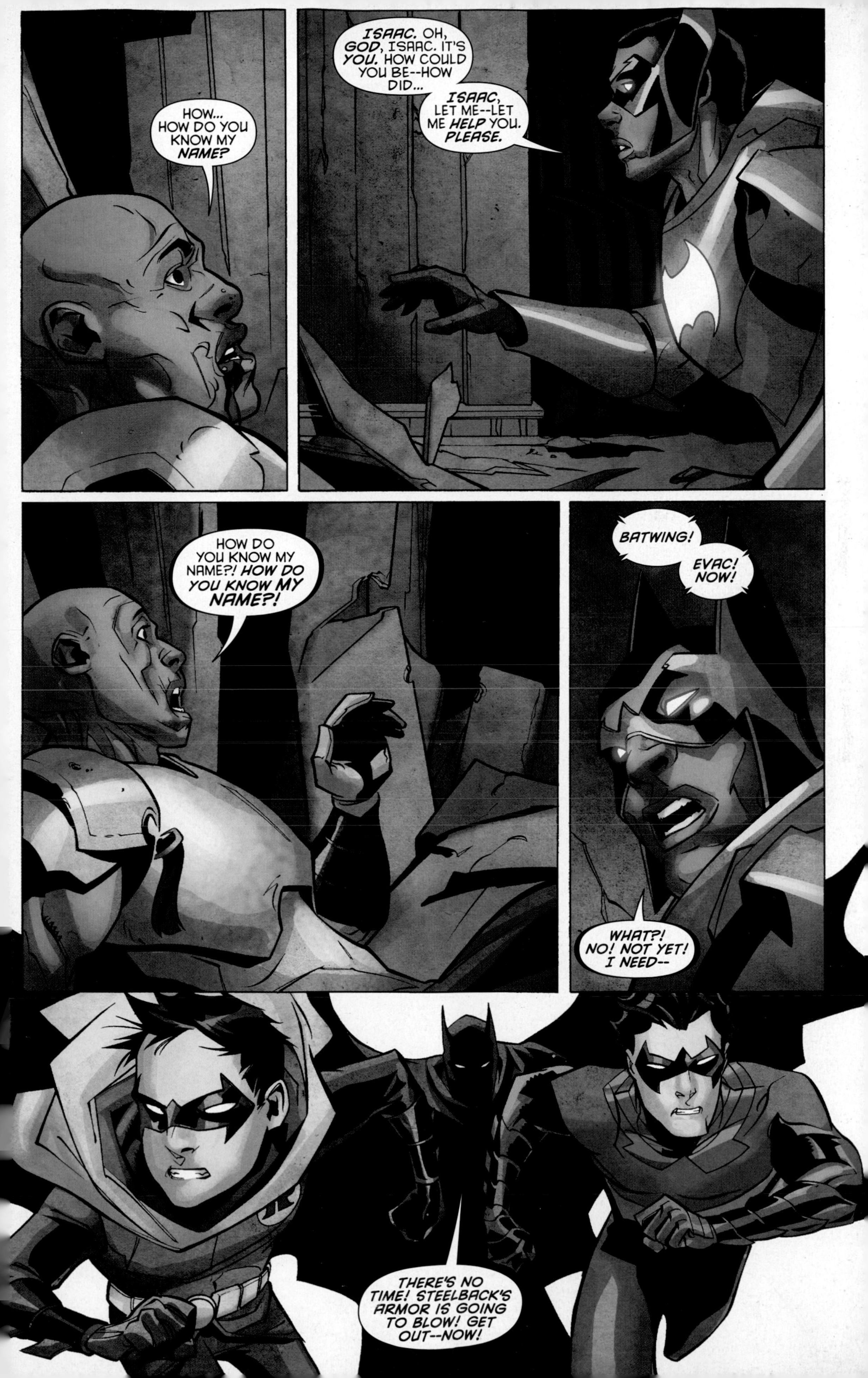
HOW... HOW DO YOU KNOW MY NAME?
ISAAC. OH, GOD, ISAAC. IT'S YOU. HOW COULD YOU BE--HOW DID...
ISAAC, LET ME--LET ME HELP YOU. PLEASE.
HOW DO YOU KNOW MY NAME?! HOW DO YOU KNOW MY NAME?!
BATWING!
EVAC! NOW!
WHAT?! NO! NOT YET! I NEED--
THERE'S NO TIME! STEELBACK'S ARMOR IS GOING TO BLOW! GET OUT--NOW!

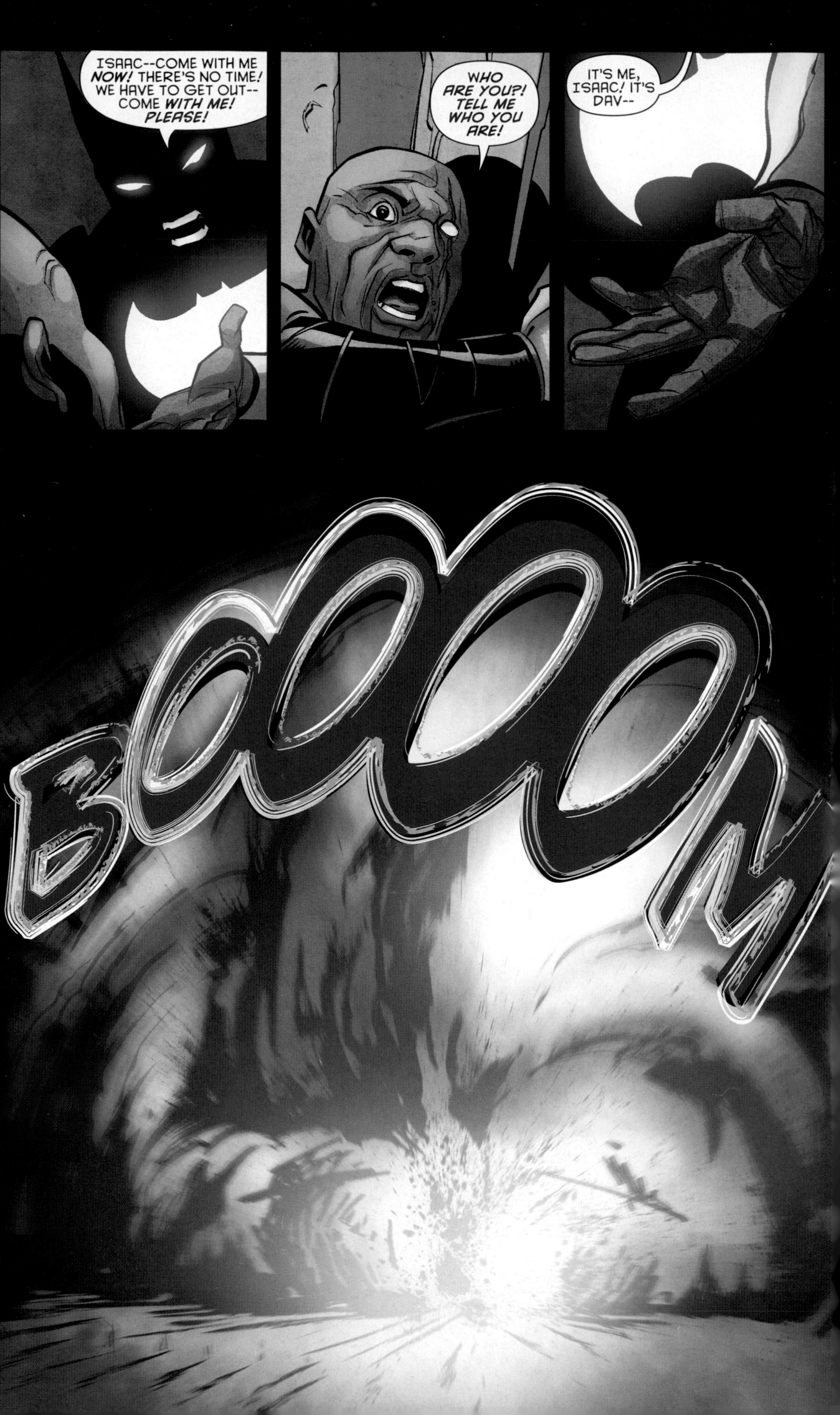
ISAAC--COME WITH ME NOW! THERE'S NO TIME! WE HAVE TO GET OUT-- COME WITH ME! PLEASE!
WHO ARE YOU?! TELL ME WHO YOU ARE!
IT'S ME, ISAAC! IT'S DAV--
BOOOOM

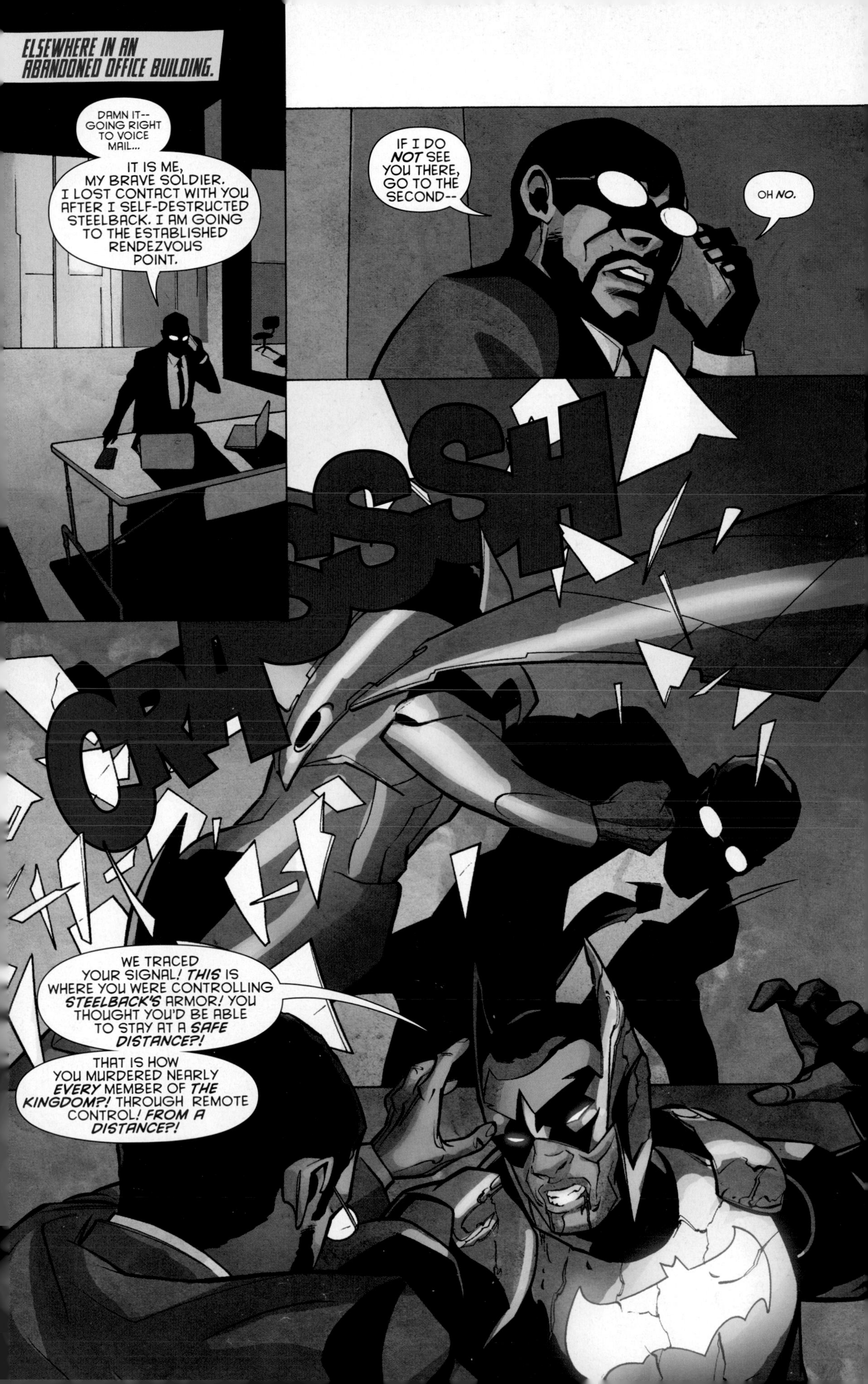

ELSEWHERE IN AN ABANDONED OFFICE BUILDING.
DAMN IT-- GOING RIGHT TO VOICE MAIL...
IT IS ME, MY BRAVE SOLDIER. I LOST CONTACT WITH YOU AFTER I SELF-DESTRUCTED STEELBACK. I AM GOING TO THE ESTABLISHED RENDEZVOUS POINT.
IF I DO NOT SEE YOU THERE, GO TO THE SECOND--
OH NO.
CRASSSH
WE TRACED YOUR SIGNAL! THIS IS WHERE YOU WERE CONTROLLING STEELBACK'S ARMOR! YOU THOUGHT YOU'D BE ABLE TO STAY AT A SAFE DISTANCE?!
THAT IS HOW YOU MURDERED NEARLY EVERY MEMBER OF THE KINGDOM?! THROUGH REMOTE CONTROL! FROM A DISTANCE?!

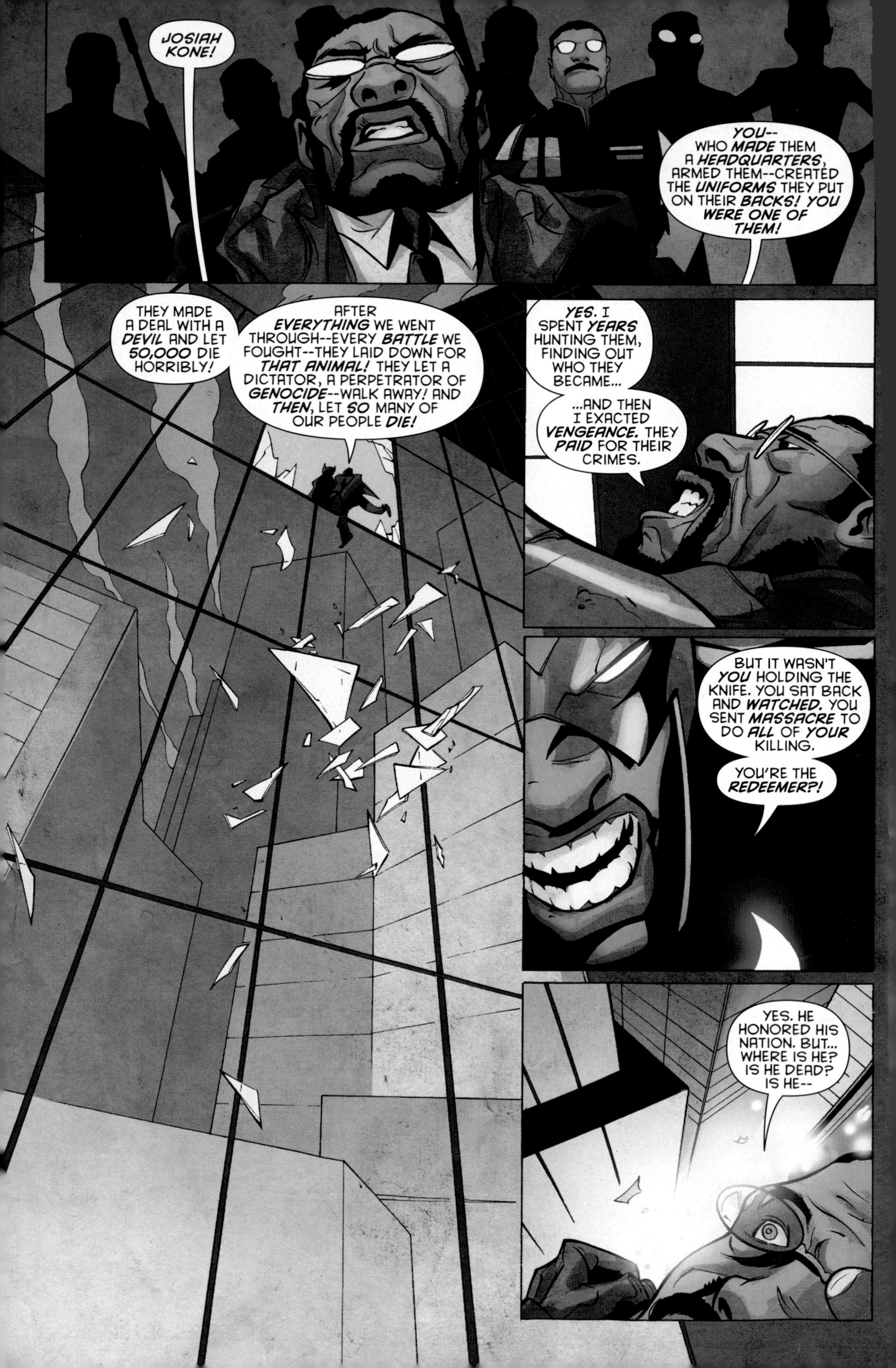
JOSIAH KONE!
YOU-- WHO MADE THEM A HEADQUARTERS, ARMED THEM--CREATED THE UNIFORMS THEY PUT ON THEIR BACKS! YOU WERE ONE OF THEM!
THEY MADE A DEAL WITH A DEVIL AND LET 50,000 DIE HORRIBLY!
AFTER EVERYTHING WE WENT THROUGH--EVERY BATTLE WE FOUGHT--THEY LAID DOWN FOR THAT ANIMAL! THEY LET A DICTATOR, A PERPETRATOR OF GENOCIDE--WALK AWAY! AND THEN, LET SO MANY OF OUR PEOPLE DIE!
YES. I SPENT YEARS HUNTING THEM, FINDING OUT WHO THEY BECAME...
...AND THEN I EXACTED VENGEANCE. THEY PAID FOR THEIR CRIMES.
BUT IT WASN'T YOU HOLDING THE KNIFE. YOU SAT BACK AND WATCHED. YOU SENT MASSACRE TO DO ALL OF YOUR KILLING.
YOU'RE THE REDEEMER?!
YES. HE HONORED HIS NATION. BUT... WHERE IS HE? IS HE DEAD? IS HE--

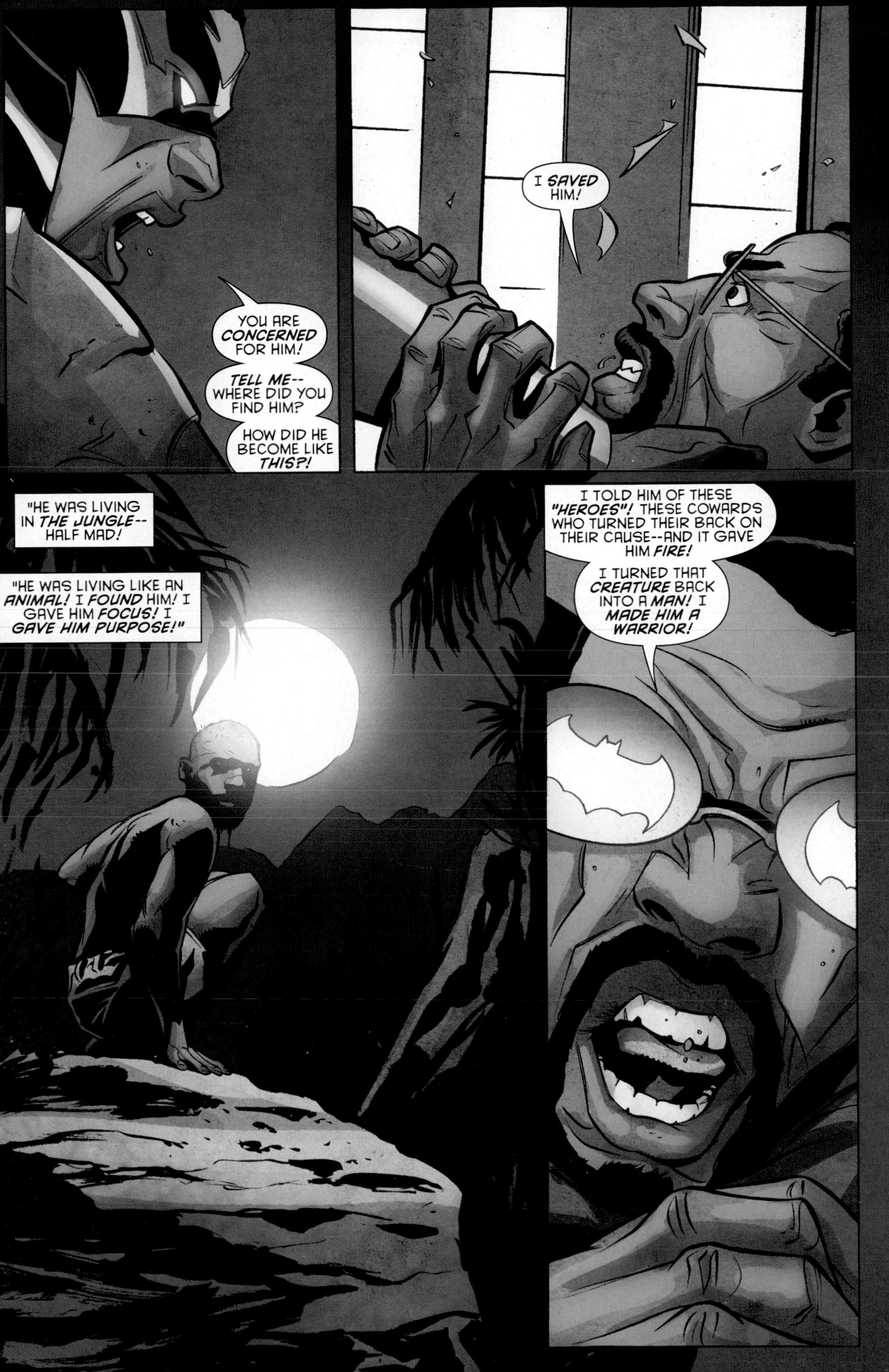
YOU ARE CONCERNED FOR HIM!
TELL ME-- WHERE DID YOU FIND HIM?
HOW DID HE BECOME LIKE THIS?!
I SAVED HIM!
"HE WAS LIVING IN THE JUNGLE-- HALF MAD!
"HE WAS LIVING LIKE AN ANIMAL! I FOUND HIM! I GAVE HIM FOCUS! I GAVE HIM PURPOSE!"
I TOLD HIM OF THESE "HEROES"! THESE COWARDS WHO TURNED THEIR BACK ON THEIR CAUSE--AND IT GAVE HIM FIRE!
I TURNED THAT CREATURE BACK INTO A MAN! I MADE HIM A WARRIOR!

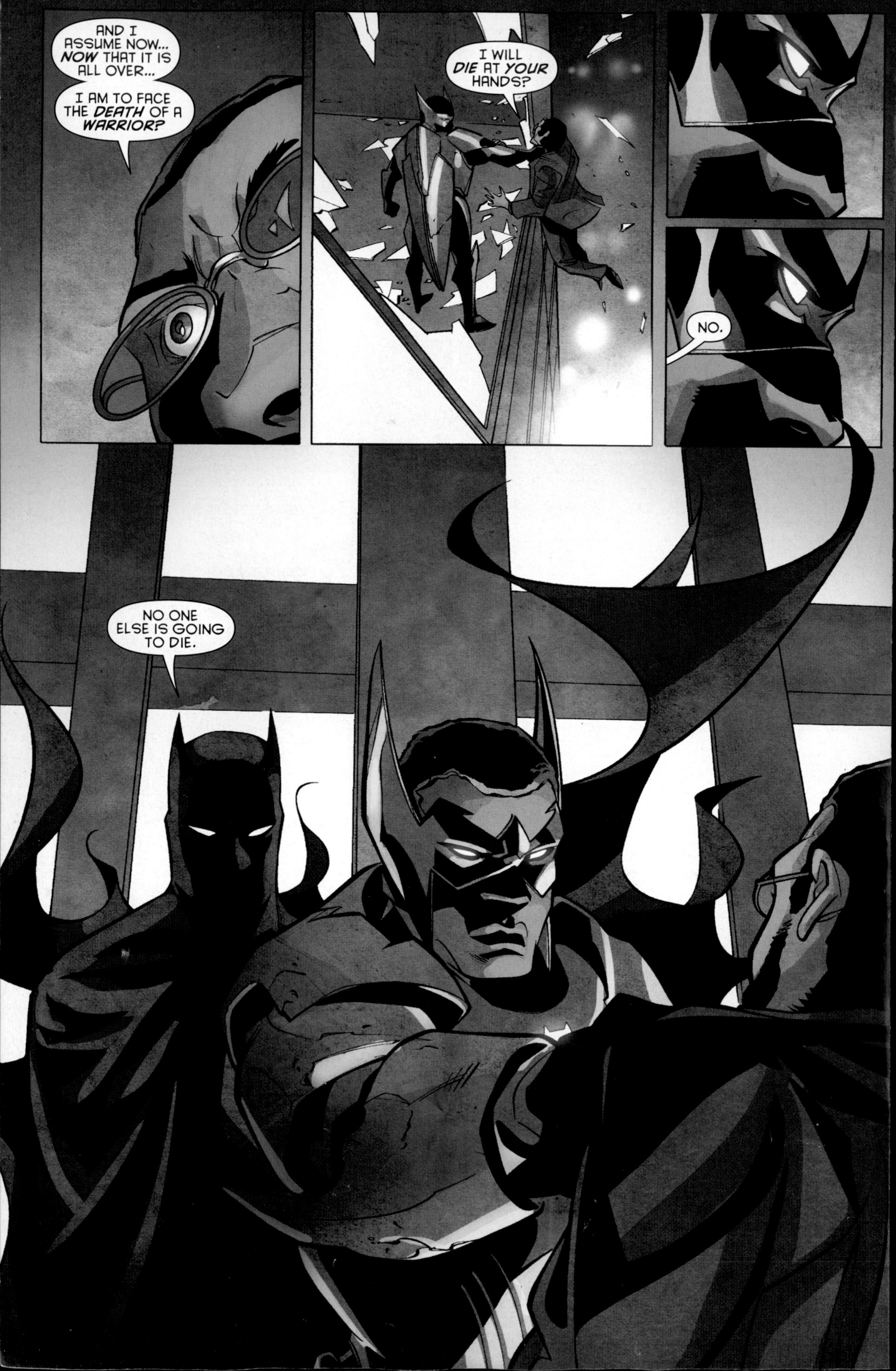
AND I ASSUME NOW... *NOW* THAT IT IS ALL OVER...
I AM TO FACE THE *DEATH* OF A *WARRIOR?*
I WILL *DIE* AT *YOUR* HANDS?
NO.
NO ONE ELSE IS GOING TO DIE.

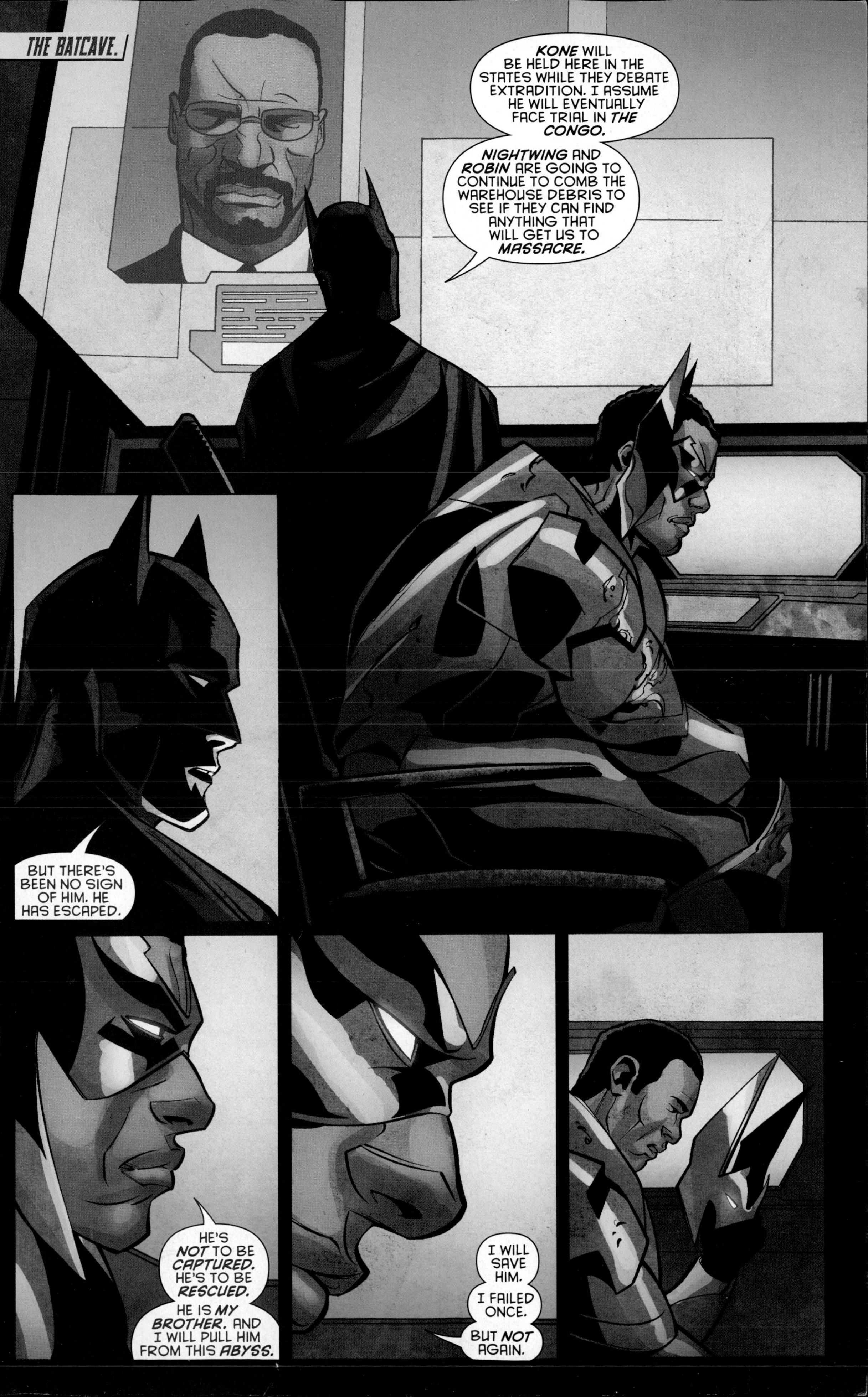
THE BATCAVE.
KONE WILL BE HELD HERE IN THE STATES WHILE THEY DEBATE EXTRADITION. I ASSUME HE WILL EVENTUALLY FACE TRIAL IN THE CONGO.
NIGHTWING AND ROBIN ARE GOING TO CONTINUE TO COMB THE WAREHOUSE DEBRIS TO SEE IF THEY CAN FIND ANYTHING THAT WILL GET US TO MASSACRE.
BUT THERE'S BEEN NO SIGN OF HIM. HE HAS ESCAPED.
HE'S NOT TO BE CAPTURED. HE'S TO BE RESCUED.
HE IS MY BROTHER. AND I WILL PULL HIM FROM THIS ABYSS.
I WILL SAVE HIM.
I FAILED ONCE.
BUT NOT AGAIN.

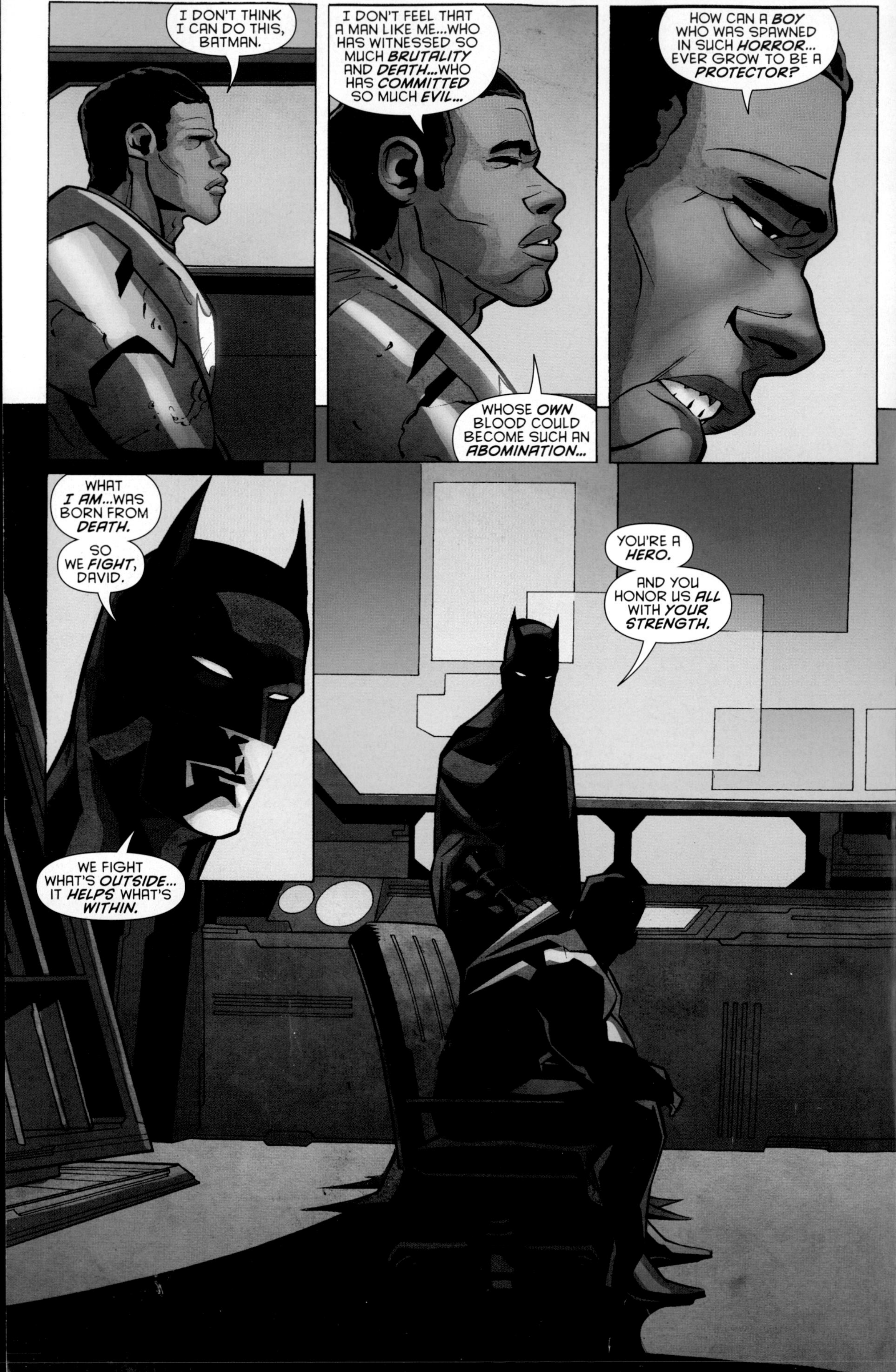
I DON'T THINK I CAN DO THIS, BATMAN.
I DON'T FEEL THAT A MAN LIKE ME...WHO HAS WITNESSED SO MUCH BRUTALITY AND DEATH...WHO HAS COMMITTED SO MUCH EVIL...
WHOSE OWN BLOOD COULD BECOME SUCH AN ABOMINATION...
HOW CAN A BOY WHO WAS SPAWNED IN SUCH HORROR... EVER GROW TO BE A PROTECTOR?
WHAT I AM...WAS BORN FROM DEATH.
SO WE FIGHT, DAVID.
WE FIGHT WHAT'S OUTSIDE... IT HELPS WHAT'S WITHIN.
YOU'RE A HERO.
AND YOU HONOR US ALL WITH YOUR STRENGTH.

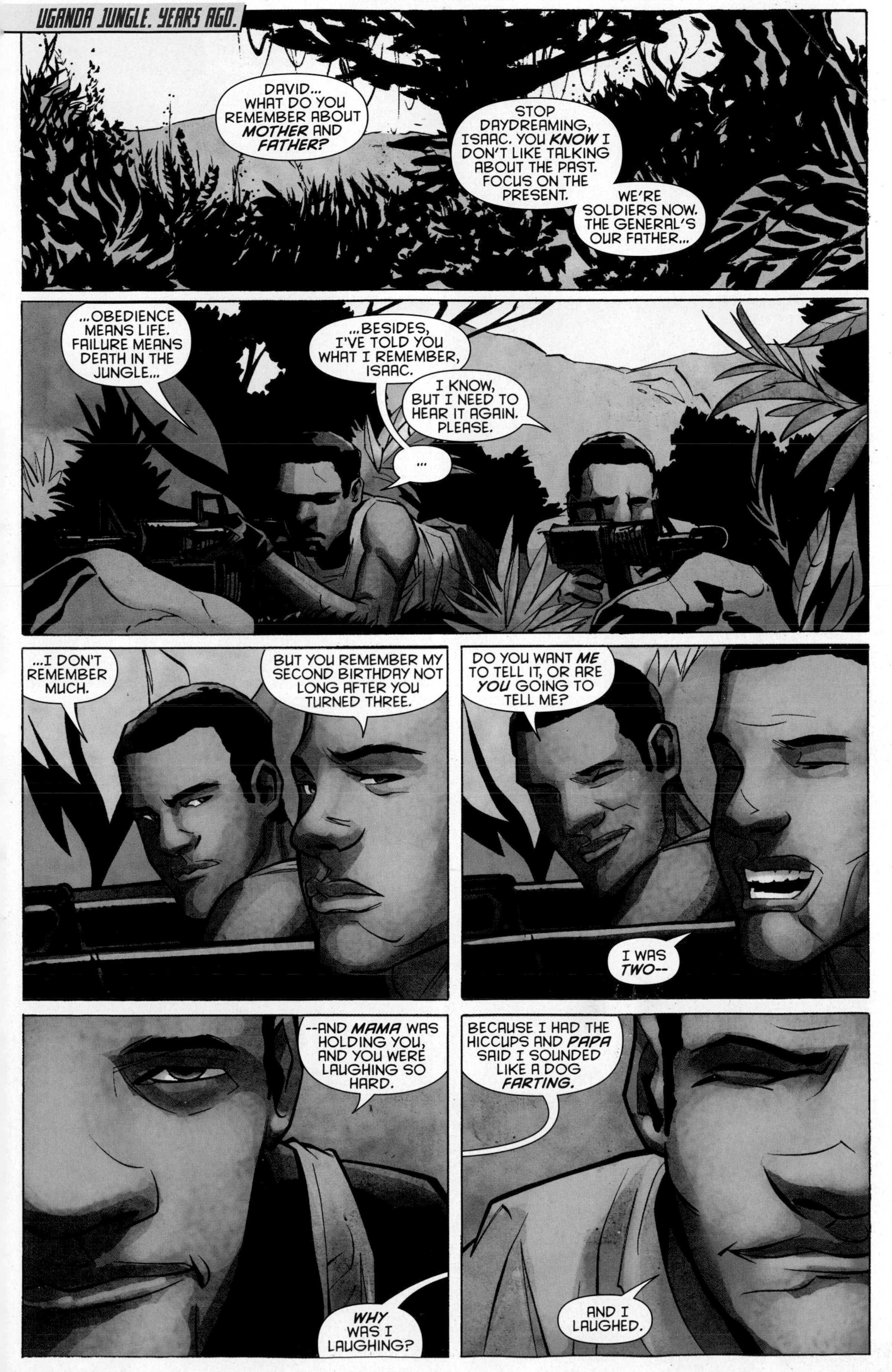
UGANDA JUNGLE. YEARS AGO.
DAVID... WHAT DO YOU REMEMBER ABOUT MOTHER AND FATHER?
STOP DAYDREAMING, ISAAC. YOU KNOW I DON'T LIKE TALKING ABOUT THE PAST. FOCUS ON THE PRESENT.
WE'RE SOLDIERS NOW. THE GENERAL'S OUR FATHER...
...OBEDIENCE MEANS LIFE. FAILURE MEANS DEATH IN THE JUNGLE...
...BESIDES, I'VE TOLD YOU WHAT I REMEMBER, ISAAC.
I KNOW, BUT I NEED TO HEAR IT AGAIN. PLEASE.
...
...I DON'T REMEMBER MUCH.
BUT YOU REMEMBER MY SECOND BIRTHDAY NOT LONG AFTER YOU TURNED THREE.
DO YOU WANT ME TO TELL IT, OR ARE YOU GOING TO TELL ME?
I WAS TWO--
--AND MAMA WAS HOLDING YOU, AND YOU WERE LAUGHING SO HARD.
WHY WAS I LAUGHING?
BECAUSE I HAD THE HICCUPS AND PAPA SAID I SOUNDED LIKE A DOG FARTING.
AND I LAUGHED.

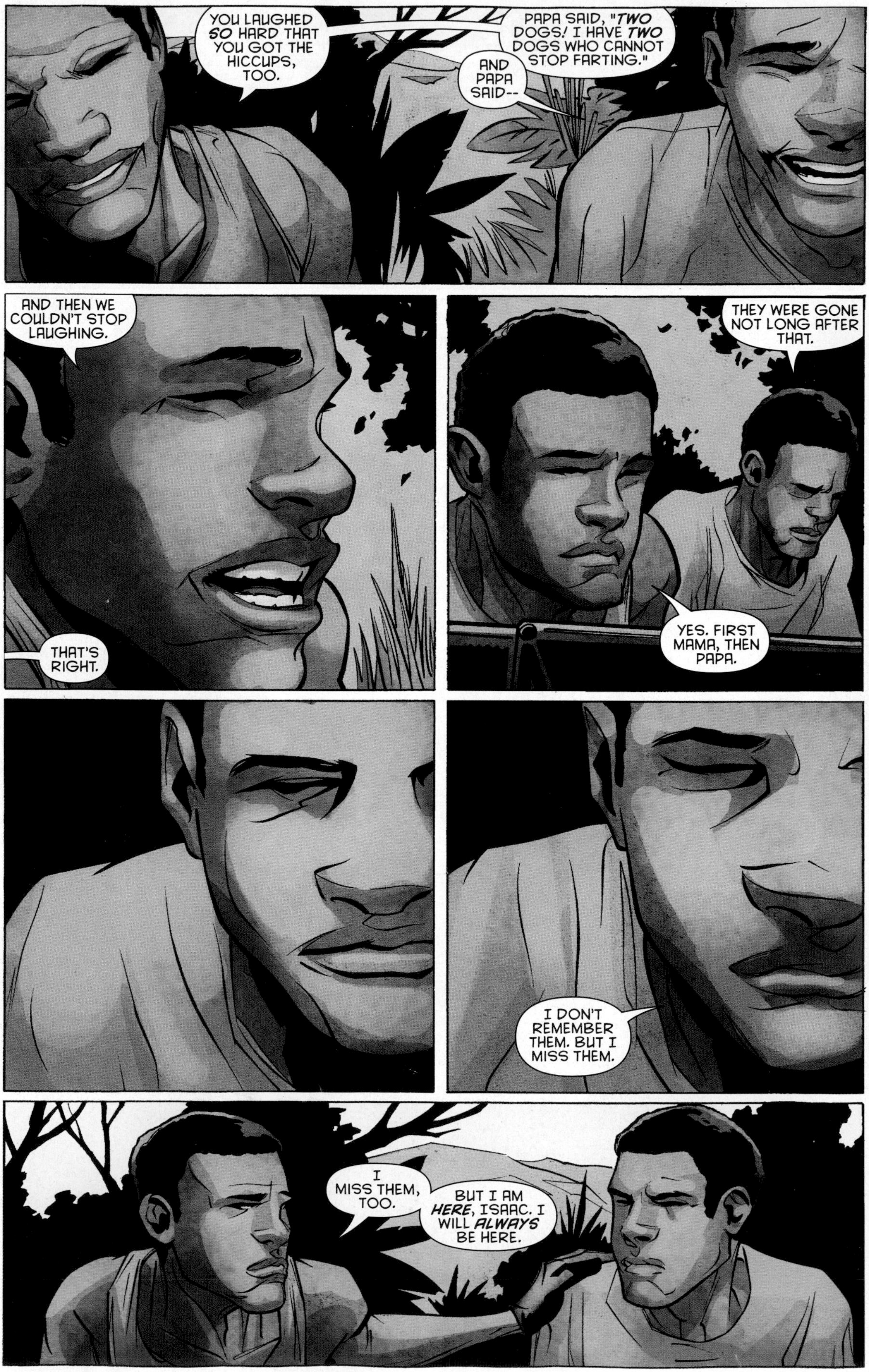
YOU LAUGHED SO HARD THAT YOU GOT THE HICCUPS, TOO.
AND PAPA SAID--
PAPA SAID, "TWO DOGS! I HAVE TWO DOGS WHO CANNOT STOP FARTING."
AND THEN WE COULDN'T STOP LAUGHING.
THAT'S RIGHT.
THEY WERE GONE NOT LONG AFTER THAT.
YES. FIRST MAMA, THEN PAPA.
I DON'T REMEMBER THEM. BUT I MISS THEM.
I MISS THEM, TOO.
BUT I AM HERE, ISAAC. I WILL ALWAYS BE HERE.

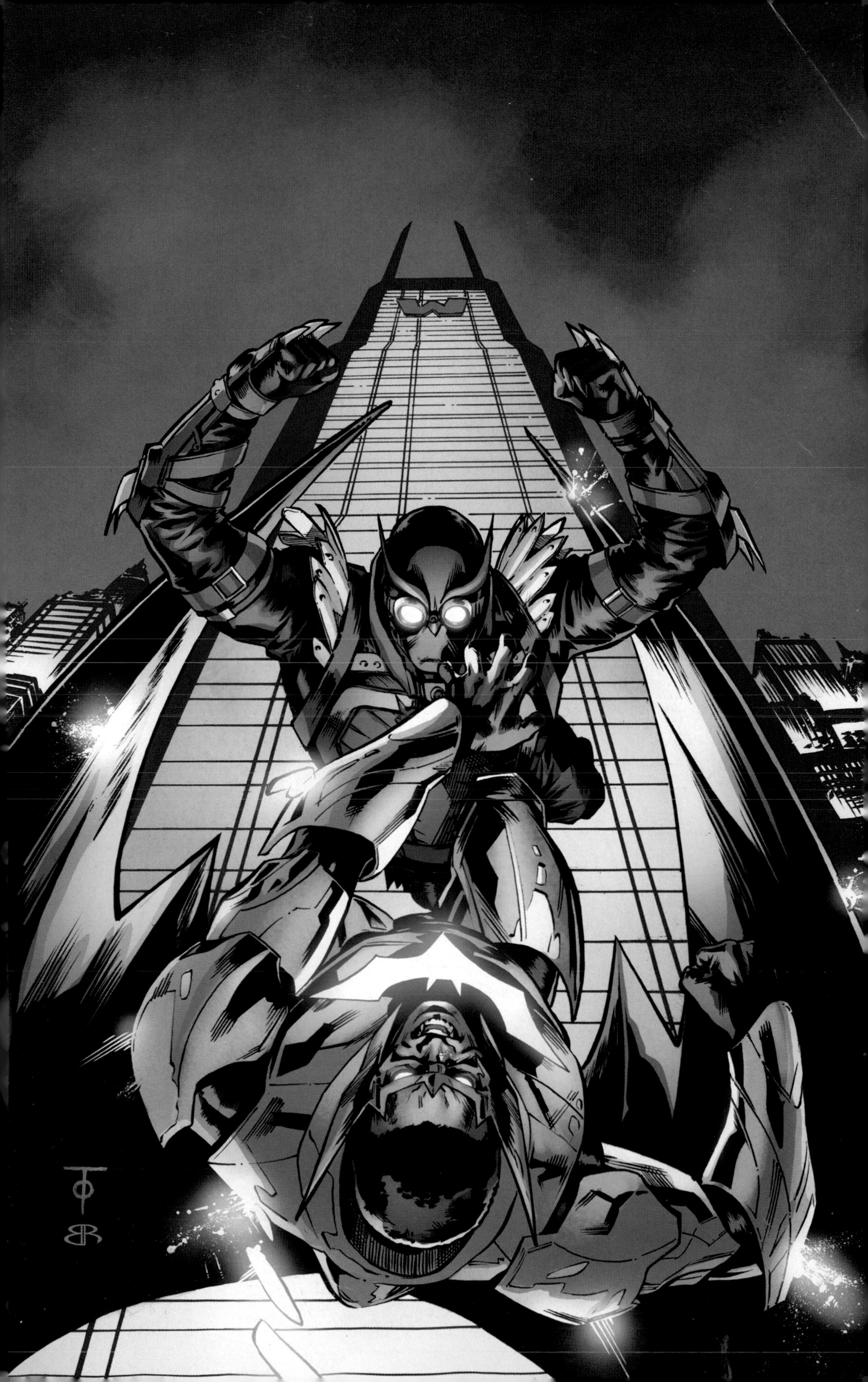

YOU HAVE BEEN JUDGED UNWORTHY

JUDD WINICK writer **MARCUS TO** penciller **RYAN WINN** inker cover art by **MARCUS TO & BRIAN REBER**

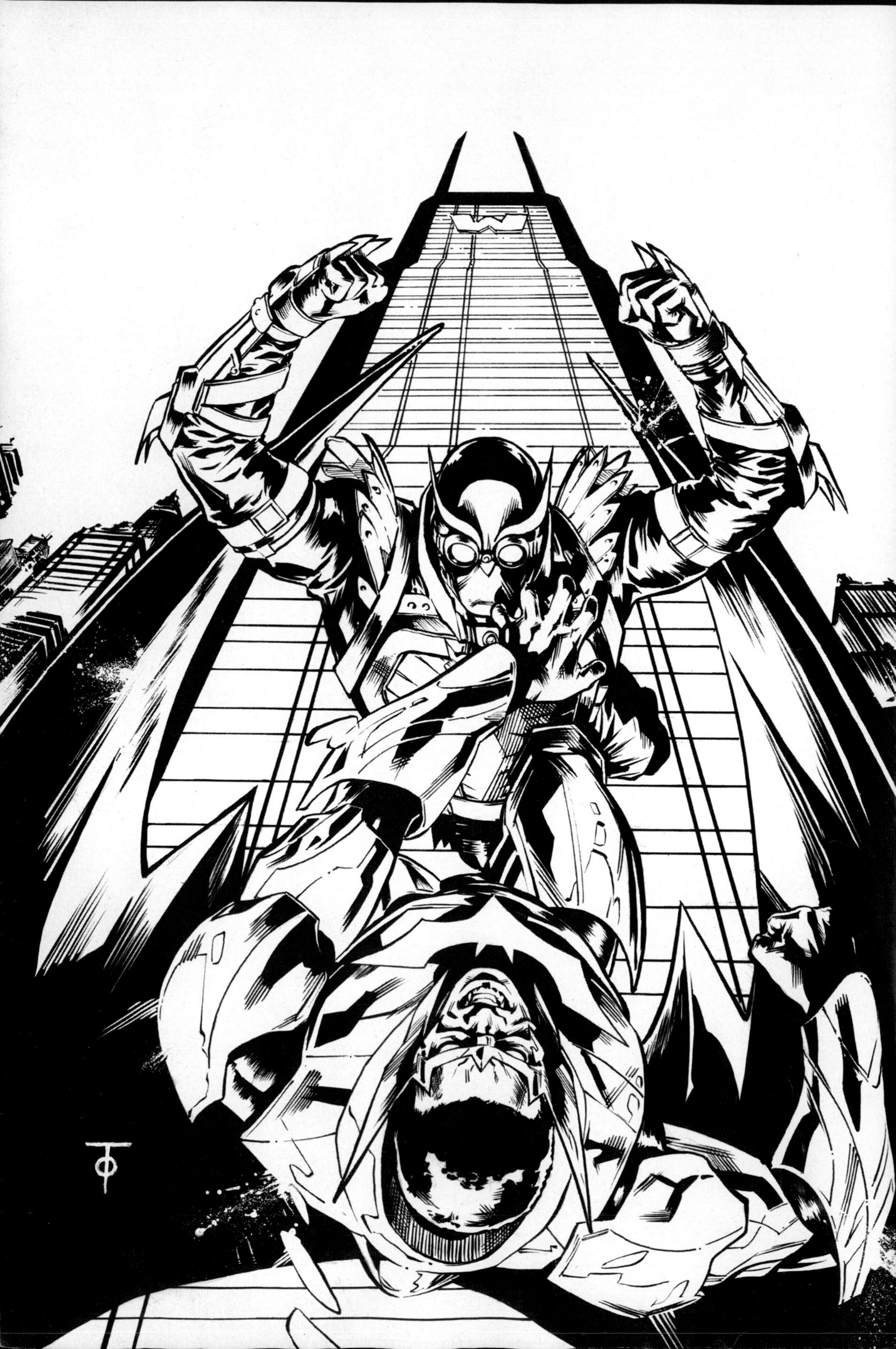

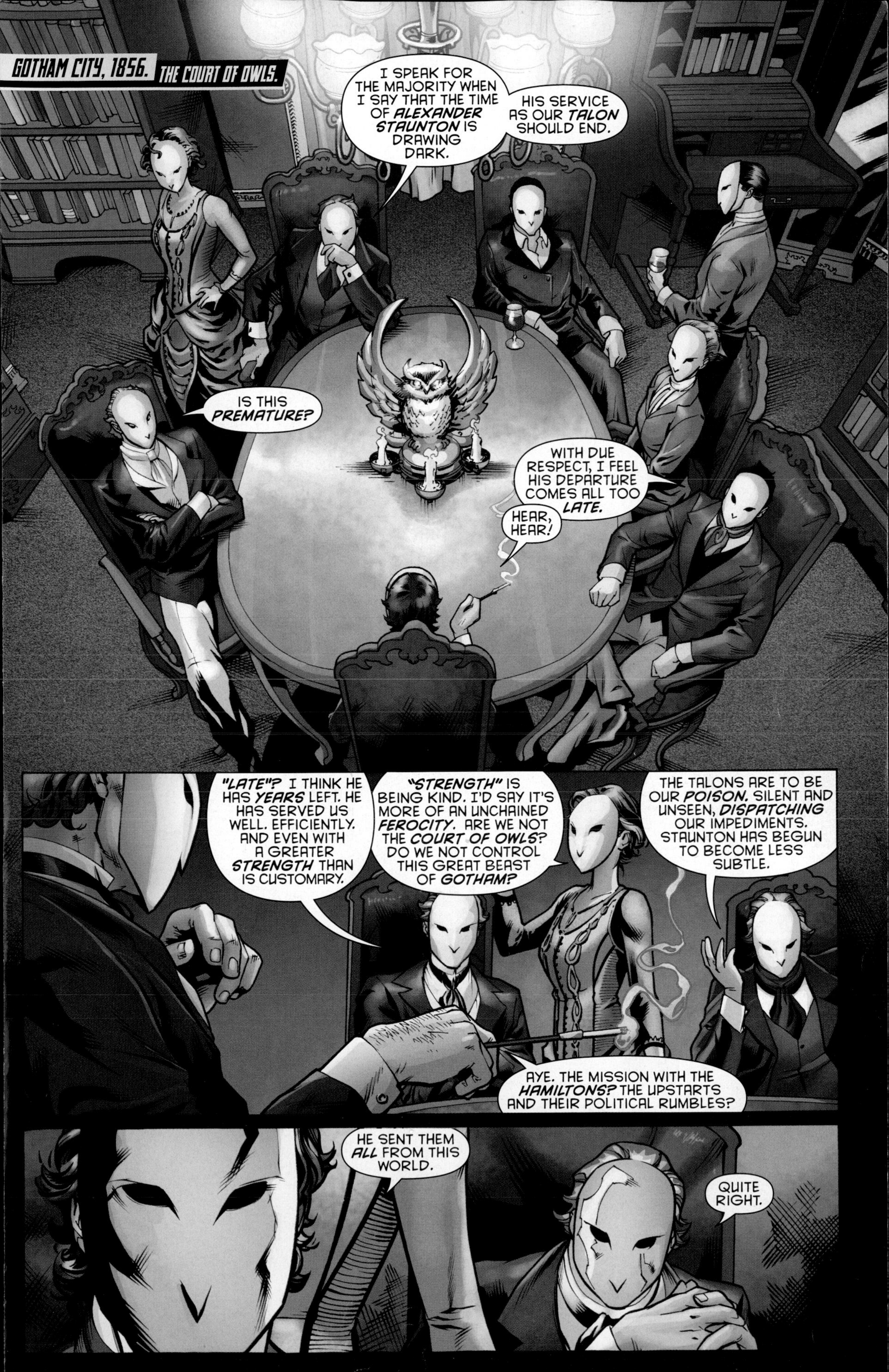
GOTHAM CITY, 1856. THE COURT OF OWLS.
I SPEAK FOR THE MAJORITY WHEN I SAY THAT THE TIME OF ALEXANDER STAUNTON IS DRAWING DARK.
HIS SERVICE AS OUR TALON SHOULD END.
IS THIS PREMATURE?
WITH DUE RESPECT, I FEEL HIS DEPARTURE COMES ALL TOO LATE.
HEAR, HEAR!
"LATE"? I THINK HE HAS YEARS LEFT. HE HAS SERVED US WELL. EFFICIENTLY. AND EVEN WITH A GREATER STRENGTH THAN IS CUSTOMARY.
"STRENGTH" IS BEING KIND. I'D SAY IT'S MORE OF AN UNCHAINED FEROCITY. ARE WE NOT THE COURT OF OWLS? DO WE NOT CONTROL THIS GREAT BEAST OF GOTHAM?
THE TALONS ARE TO BE OUR POISON. SILENT AND UNSEEN, DISPATCHING OUR IMPEDIMENTS. STAUNTON HAS BEGUN TO BECOME LESS SUBTLE.
AYE. THE MISSION WITH THE HAMILTONS? THE UPSTARTS AND THEIR POLITICAL RUMBLES?
HE SENT THEM ALL FROM THIS WORLD.
QUITE RIGHT.

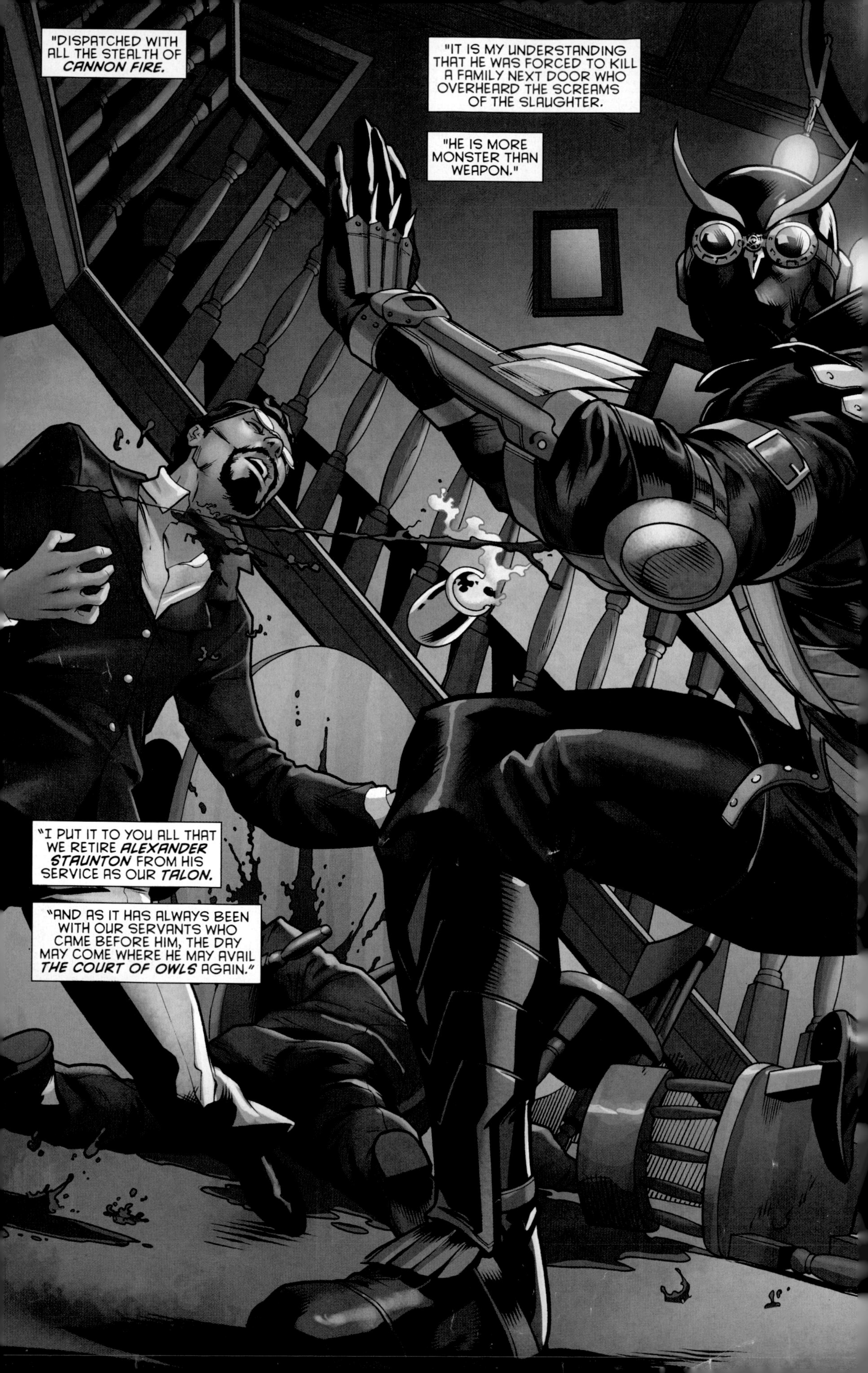
"DISPATCHED WITH ALL THE STEALTH OF *CANNON FIRE.*
"IT IS MY UNDERSTANDING THAT HE WAS FORCED TO KILL A FAMILY NEXT DOOR WHO OVERHEARD THE SCREAMS OF THE SLAUGHTER.
"HE IS MORE MONSTER THAN WEAPON."
"I PUT IT TO YOU ALL THAT WE RETIRE *ALEXANDER STAUNTON* FROM HIS SERVICE AS OUR *TALON.*
"AND AS IT HAS ALWAYS BEEN WITH OUR SERVANTS WHO CAME BEFORE HIM, THE DAY MAY COME WHERE HE MAY AVAIL *THE COURT OF OWLS* AGAIN."

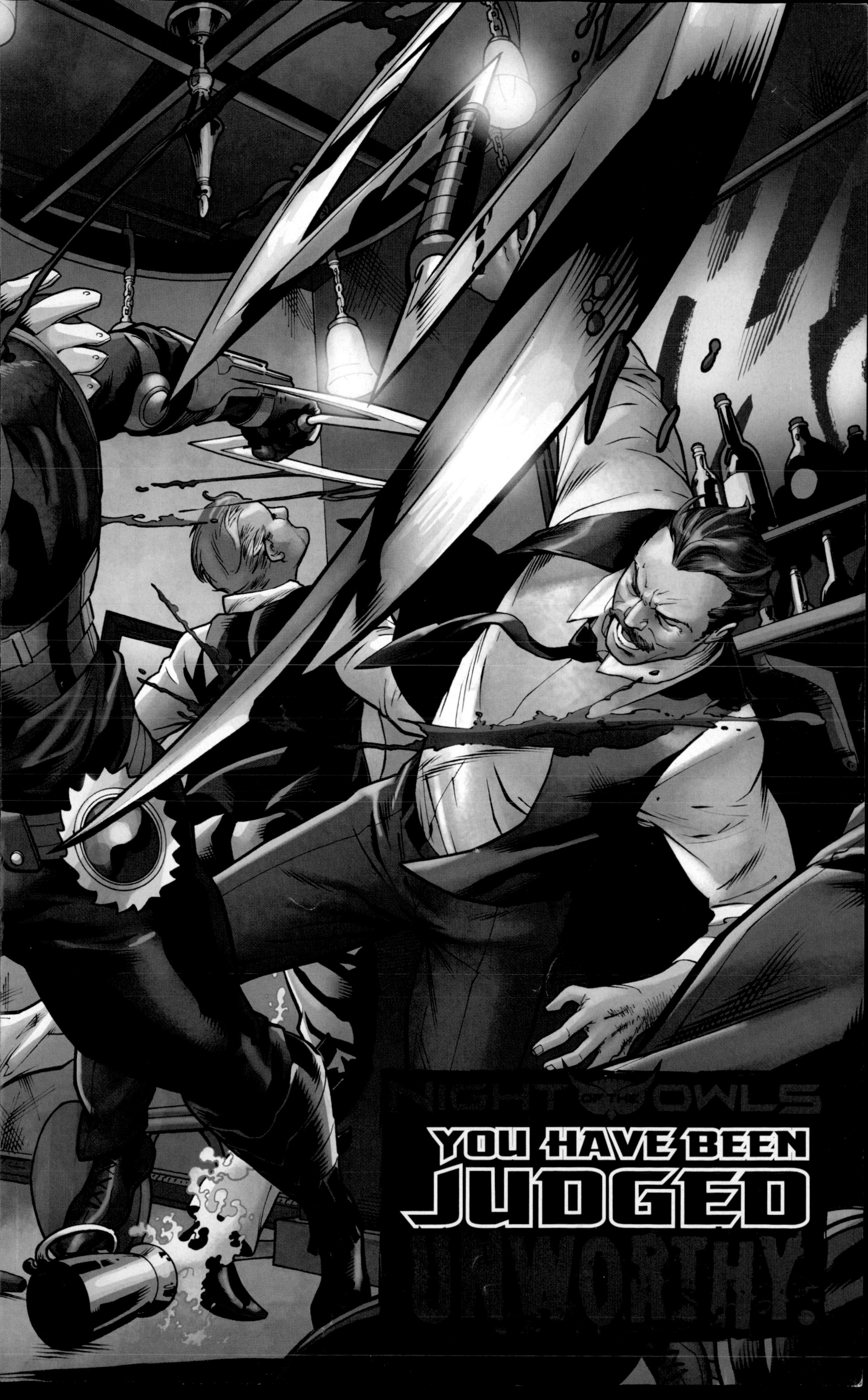
NIGHT OF THE OWLS
YOU HAVE BEEN
JUDGED
UNWORTHY!

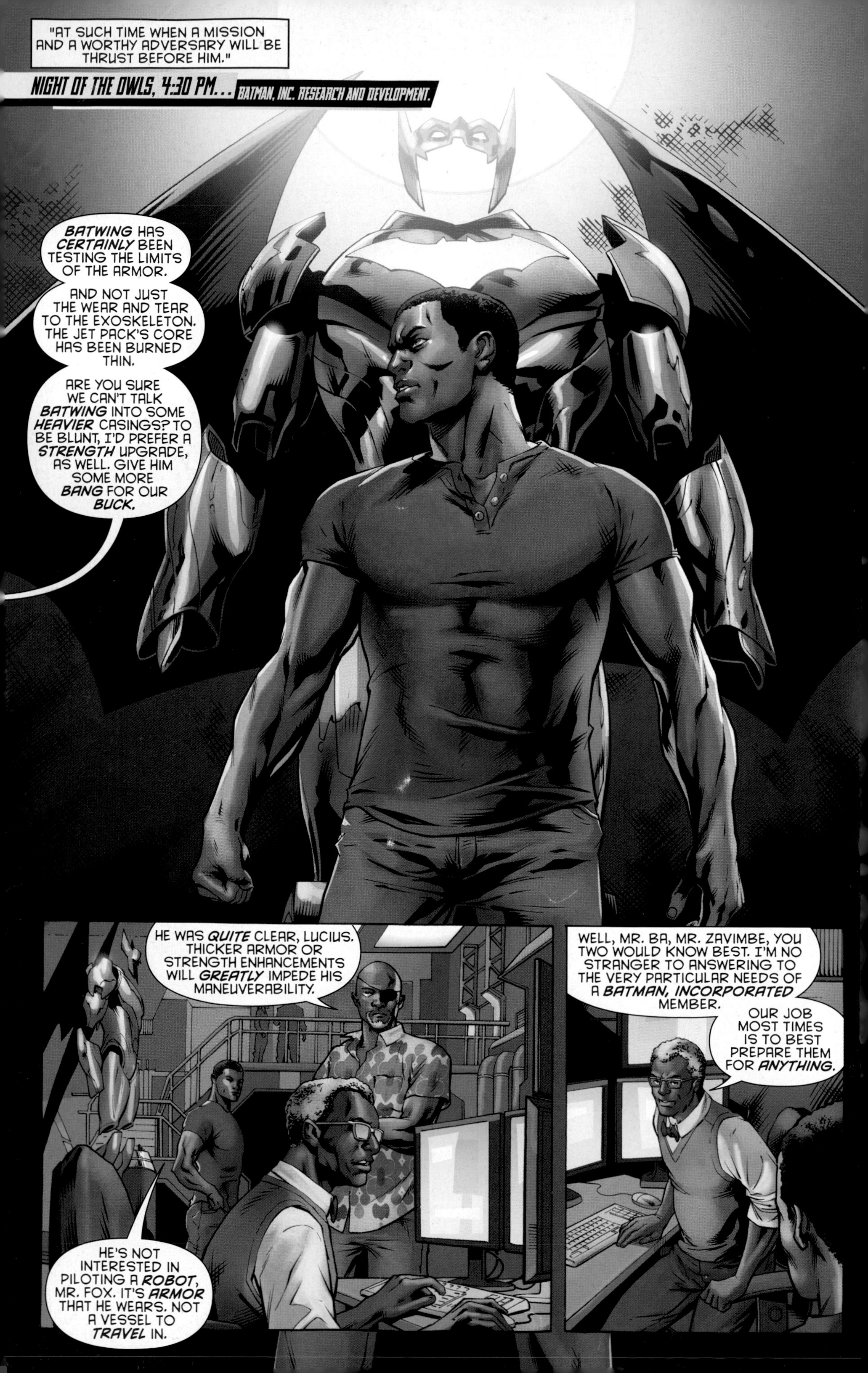
"AT SUCH TIME WHEN A MISSION AND A WORTHY ADVERSARY WILL BE THRUST BEFORE HIM."
NIGHT OF THE OWLS, 4:30 PM... BATMAN, INC. RESEARCH AND DEVELOPMENT.
BATWING HAS CERTAINLY BEEN TESTING THE LIMITS OF THE ARMOR.
AND NOT JUST THE WEAR AND TEAR TO THE EXOSKELETON. THE JET PACK'S CORE HAS BEEN BURNED THIN.
ARE YOU SURE WE CAN'T TALK BATWING INTO SOME HEAVIER CASINGS? TO BE BLUNT, I'D PREFER A STRENGTH UPGRADE, AS WELL. GIVE HIM SOME MORE BANG FOR OUR BUCK.
HE WAS QUITE CLEAR, LUCIUS. THICKER ARMOR OR STRENGTH ENHANCEMENTS WILL GREATLY IMPEDE HIS MANEUVERABILITY.
HE'S NOT INTERESTED IN PILOTING A ROBOT, MR. FOX. IT'S ARMOR THAT HE WEARS. NOT A VESSEL TO TRAVEL IN.
WELL, MR. BA, MR. ZAVIMBE, YOU TWO WOULD KNOW BEST. I'M NO STRANGER TO ANSWERING TO THE VERY PARTICULAR NEEDS OF A BATMAN, INCORPORATED MEMBER.
OUR JOB MOST TIMES IS TO BEST PREPARE THEM FOR ANYTHING.

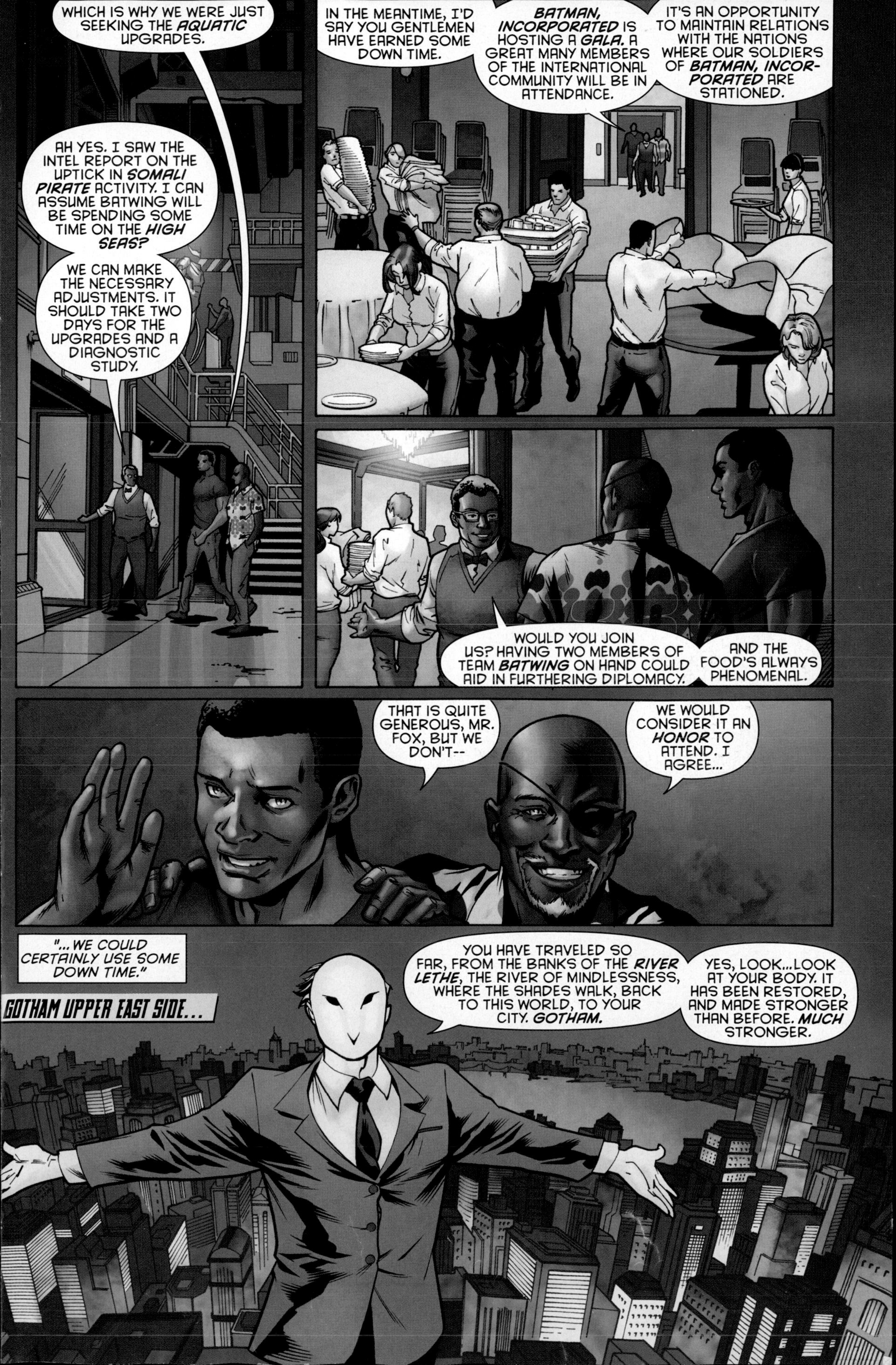
WHICH IS WHY WE WERE JUST SEEKING THE AQUATIC UPGRADES.
AH YES. I SAW THE INTEL REPORT ON THE UPTICK IN SOMALI PIRATE ACTIVITY. I CAN ASSUME BATWING WILL BE SPENDING SOME TIME ON THE HIGH SEAS?
WE CAN MAKE THE NECESSARY ADJUSTMENTS. IT SHOULD TAKE TWO DAYS FOR THE UPGRADES AND A DIAGNOSTIC STUDY.
IN THE MEANTIME, I'D SAY YOU GENTLEMEN HAVE EARNED SOME DOWN TIME.
BATMAN, INCORPORATED IS HOSTING A GALA. A GREAT MANY MEMBERS OF THE INTERNATIONAL COMMUNITY WILL BE IN ATTENDANCE.
IT'S AN OPPORTUNITY TO MAINTAIN RELATIONS WITH THE NATIONS WHERE OUR SOLDIERS OF BATMAN, INCORPORATED ARE STATIONED.
WOULD YOU JOIN US? HAVING TWO MEMBERS OF TEAM BATWING ON HAND COULD AID IN FURTHERING DIPLOMACY.
AND THE FOOD'S ALWAYS PHENOMENAL.
THAT IS QUITE GENEROUS, MR. FOX, BUT WE DON'T--
WE WOULD CONSIDER IT AN HONOR TO ATTEND. I AGREE...
"...WE COULD CERTAINLY USE SOME DOWN TIME."
GOTHAM UPPER EAST SIDE...
YOU HAVE TRAVELED SO FAR, FROM THE BANKS OF THE RIVER LETHE, THE RIVER OF MINDLESSNESS, WHERE THE SHADES WALK, BACK TO THIS WORLD, TO YOUR CITY. GOTHAM.
YES, LOOK...LOOK AT YOUR BODY. IT HAS BEEN RESTORED, AND MADE STRONGER THAN BEFORE. MUCH STRONGER.

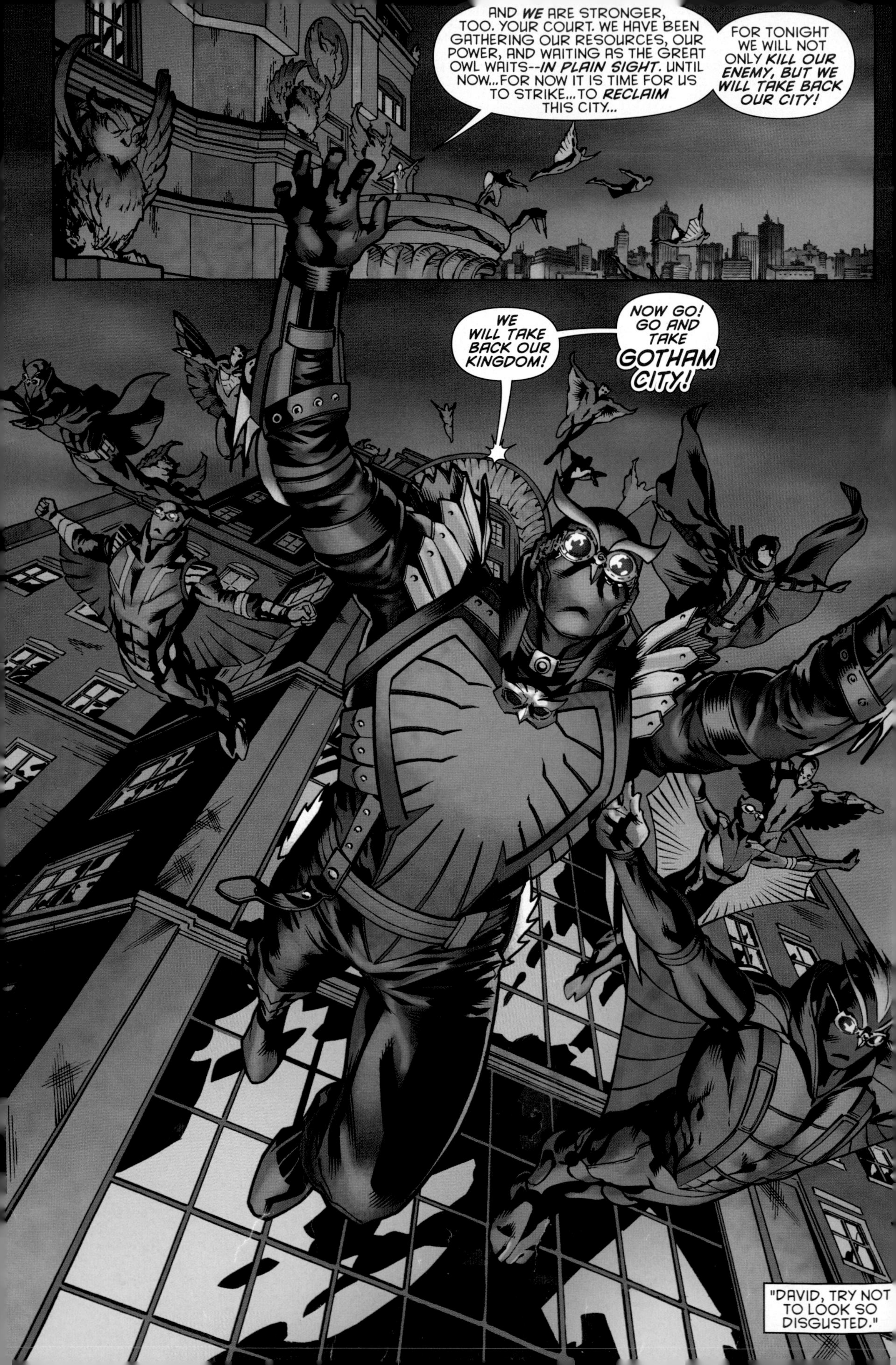
AND WE ARE STRONGER, TOO. YOUR COURT. WE HAVE BEEN GATHERING OUR RESOURCES, OUR POWER, AND WAITING AS THE GREAT OWL WAITS--IN PLAIN SIGHT. UNTIL NOW...FOR NOW IT IS TIME FOR US TO STRIKE...TO RECLAIM THIS CITY...
FOR TONIGHT WE WILL NOT ONLY KILL OUR ENEMY, BUT WE WILL TAKE BACK OUR CITY!
WE WILL TAKE BACK OUR KINGDOM!
NOW GO! GO AND TAKE GOTHAM CITY!
"DAVID, TRY NOT TO LOOK SO DISGUSTED."

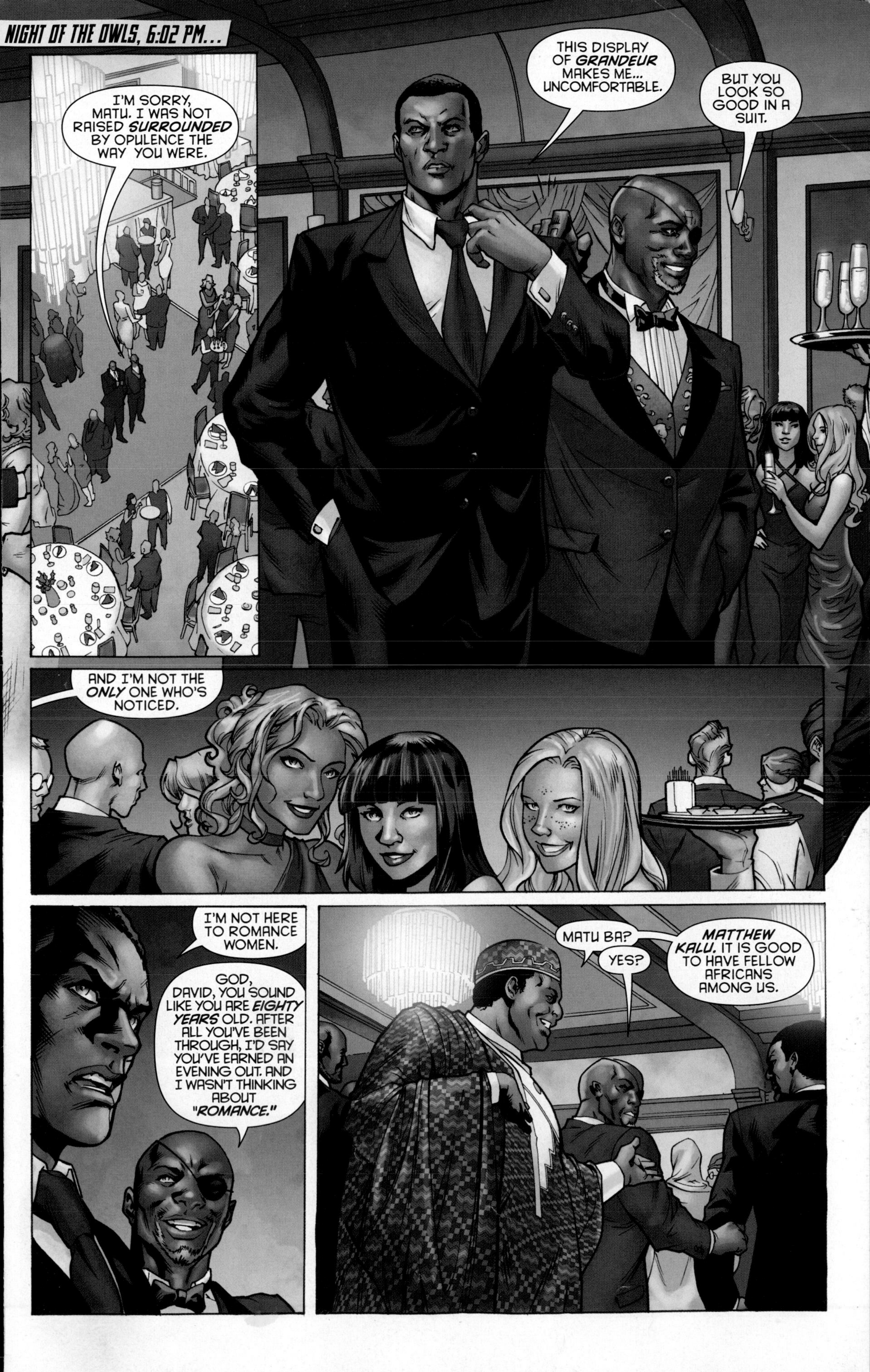
NIGHT OF THE OWLS, 6:02 PM...
THIS DISPLAY OF GRANDEUR MAKES ME... UNCOMFORTABLE.
BUT YOU LOOK SO GOOD IN A SUIT.
I'M SORRY, MATU. I WAS NOT RAISED SURROUNDED BY OPULENCE THE WAY YOU WERE.
AND I'M NOT THE ONLY ONE WHO'S NOTICED.
I'M NOT HERE TO ROMANCE WOMEN.
GOD, DAVID, YOU SOUND LIKE YOU ARE EIGHTY YEARS OLD. AFTER ALL YOU'VE BEEN THROUGH, I'D SAY YOU'VE EARNED AN EVENING OUT. AND I WASN'T THINKING ABOUT "ROMANCE."
MATU BA?
YES?
MATTHEW KALU. IT IS GOOD TO HAVE FELLOW AFRICANS AMONG US.

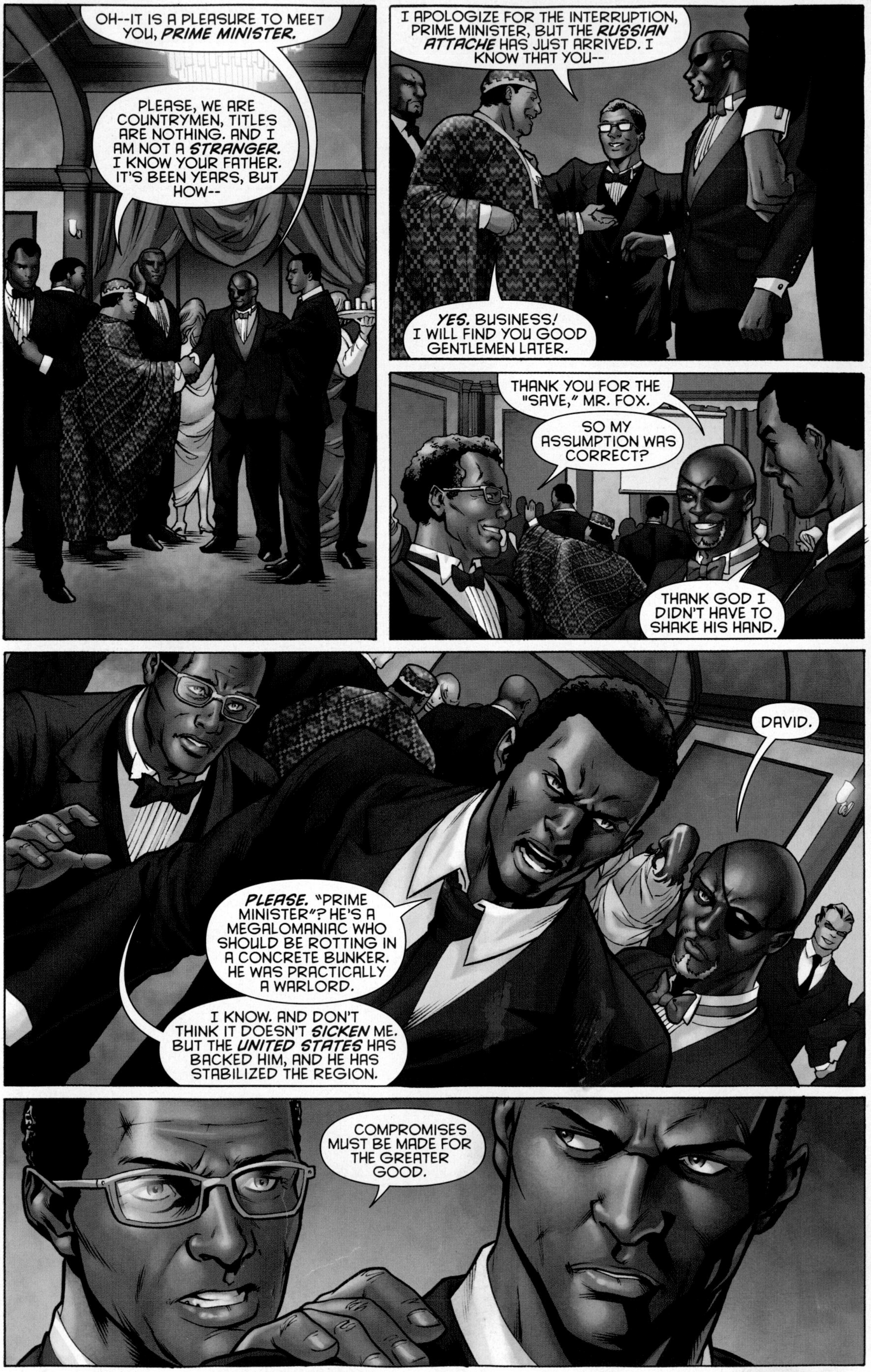
OH--IT IS A PLEASURE TO MEET YOU, PRIME MINISTER.
PLEASE, WE ARE COUNTRYMEN, TITLES ARE NOTHING. AND I AM NOT A STRANGER. I KNOW YOUR FATHER. IT'S BEEN YEARS, BUT HOW--
I APOLOGIZE FOR THE INTERRUPTION, PRIME MINISTER, BUT THE RUSSIAN ATTACHE HAS JUST ARRIVED. I KNOW THAT YOU--
YES. BUSINESS! I WILL FIND YOU GOOD GENTLEMEN LATER.
THANK YOU FOR THE "SAVE," MR. FOX.
SO MY ASSUMPTION WAS CORRECT?
THANK GOD I DIDN'T HAVE TO SHAKE HIS HAND.
DAVID.
PLEASE. "PRIME MINISTER"? HE'S A MEGALOMANIAC WHO SHOULD BE ROTTING IN A CONCRETE BUNKER. HE WAS PRACTICALLY A WARLORD.
I KNOW. AND DON'T THINK IT DOESN'T SICKEN ME. BUT THE UNITED STATES HAS BACKED HIM, AND HE HAS STABILIZED THE REGION.
COMPROMISES MUST BE MADE FOR THE GREATER GOOD.

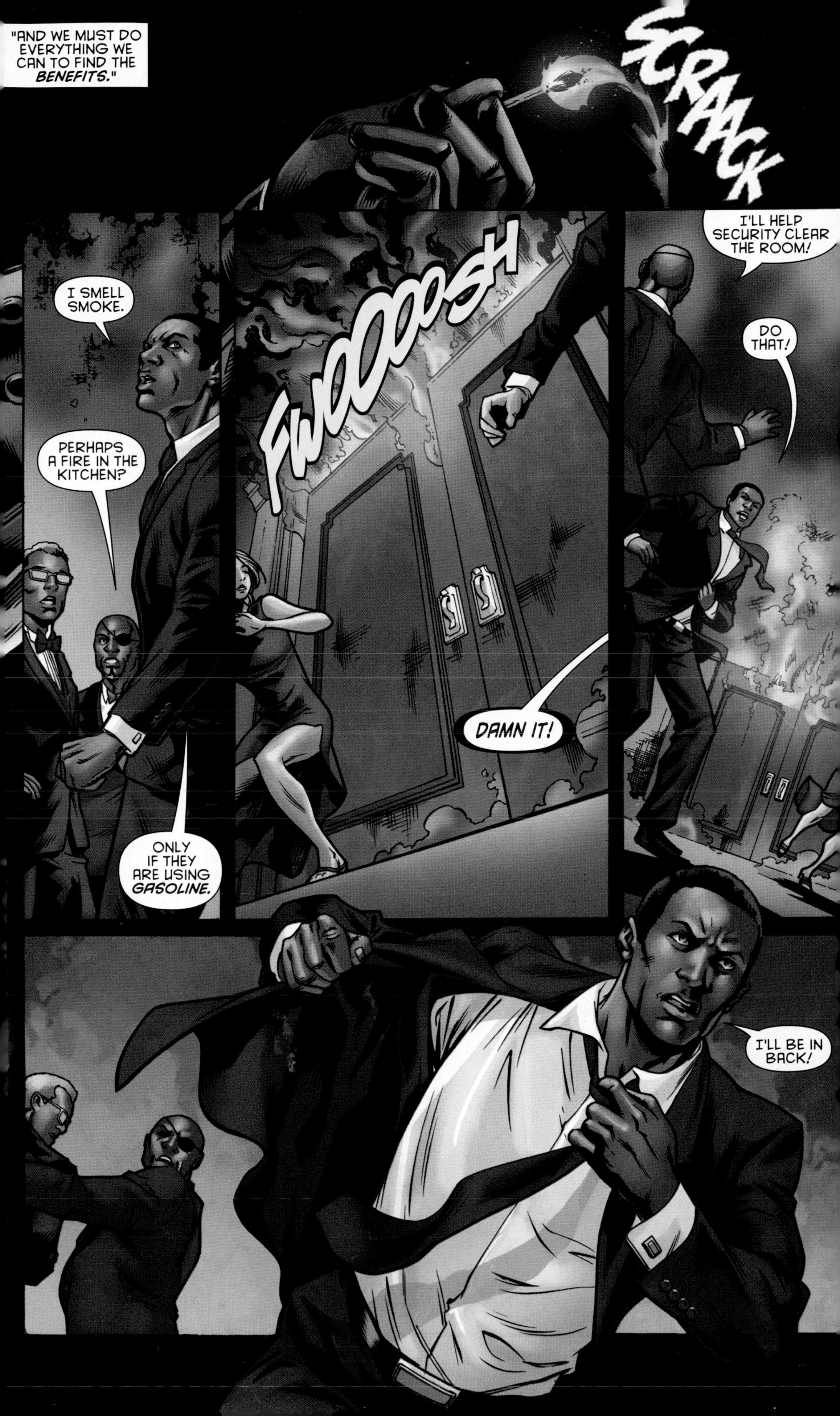
"AND WE MUST DO EVERYTHING WE CAN TO FIND THE *BENEFITS.*"
SCRAACK
I SMELL SMOKE.
PERHAPS A FIRE IN THE KITCHEN?
ONLY IF THEY ARE USING *GASOLINE.*
FWOOOOSH
DAMN IT!
I'LL HELP SECURITY CLEAR THE ROOM!
DO THAT!
I'LL BE IN BACK!

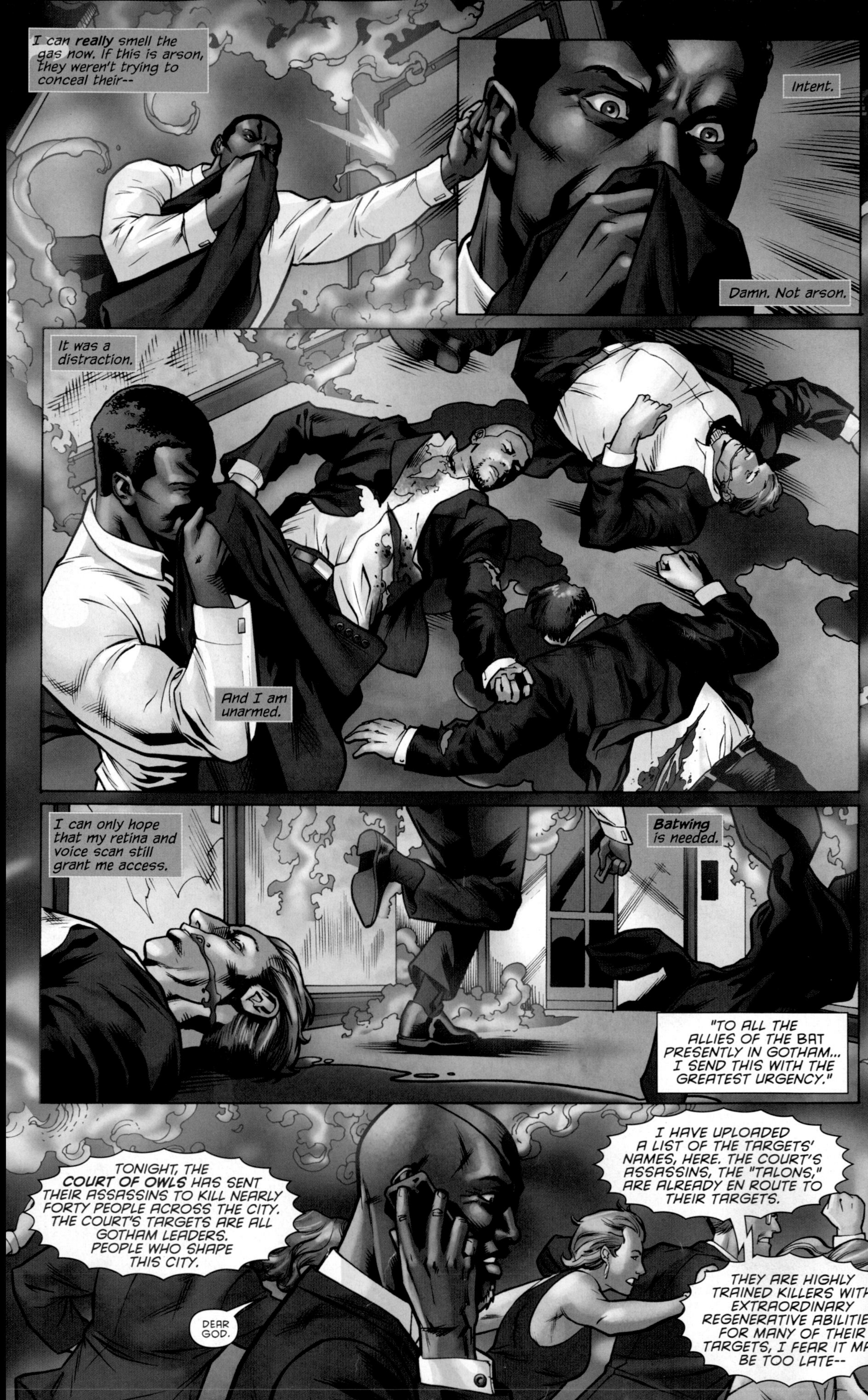
I can really smell the gas now. If this is arson, they weren't trying to conceal their--
Intent.
Damn. Not arson.
It was a distraction.
And I am unarmed.
I can only hope that my retina and voice scan still grant me access.
Batwing is needed.
"TO ALL THE ALLIES OF THE BAT PRESENTLY IN GOTHAM... I SEND THIS WITH THE GREATEST URGENCY."
TONIGHT, THE COURT OF OWLS HAS SENT THEIR ASSASSINS TO KILL NEARLY FORTY PEOPLE ACROSS THE CITY. THE COURT'S TARGETS ARE ALL GOTHAM LEADERS. PEOPLE WHO SHAPE THIS CITY.
DEAR GOD.
I HAVE UPLOADED A LIST OF THE TARGETS' NAMES, HERE. THE COURT'S ASSASSINS, THE "TALONS," ARE ALREADY EN ROUTE TO THEIR TARGETS.
THEY ARE HIGHLY TRAINED KILLERS WITH EXTRAORDINARY REGENERATIVE ABILITIE FOR MANY OF THEIR TARGETS, I FEAR IT MA BE TOO LATE--

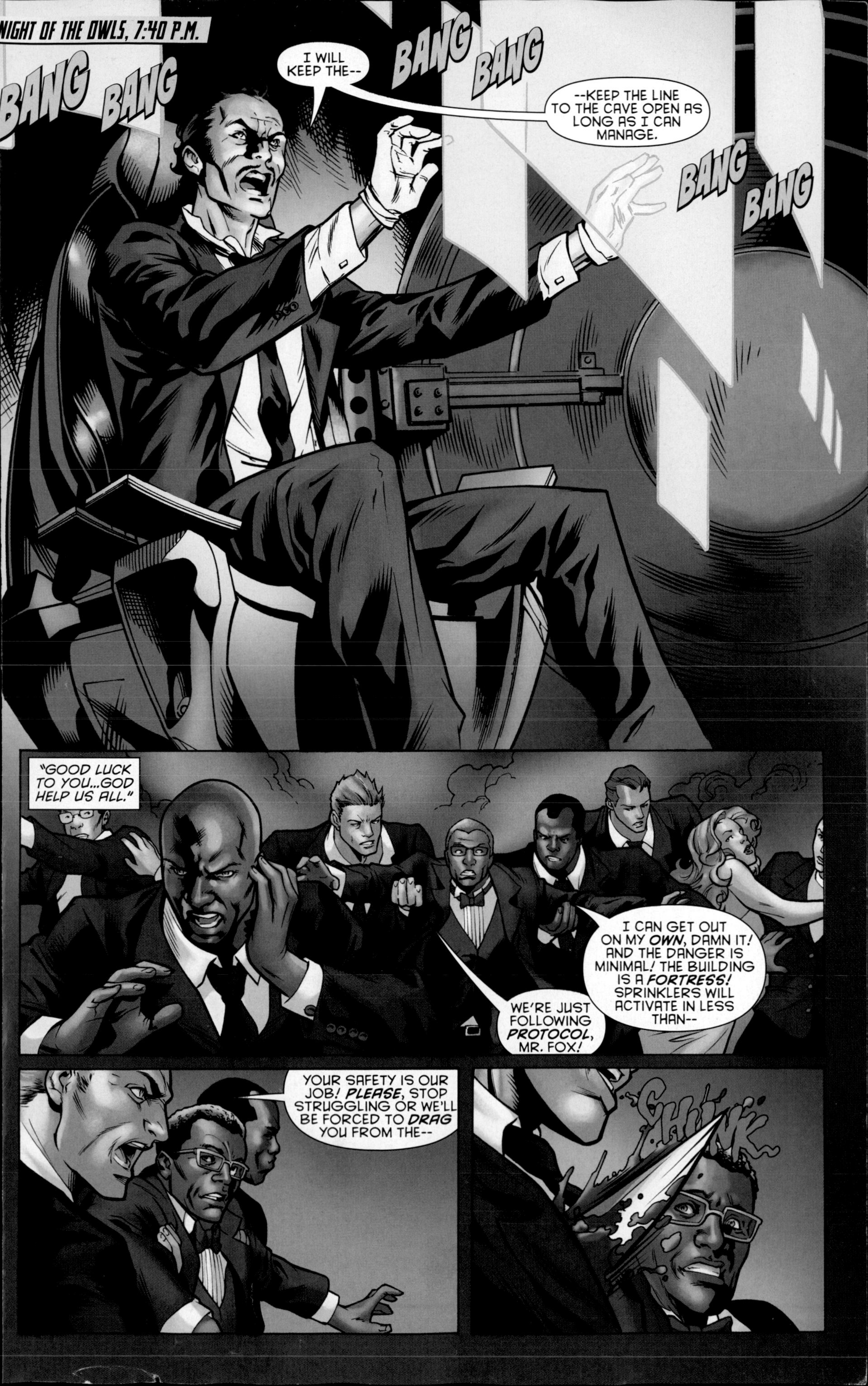
NIGHT OF THE OWLS, 7:40 P.M.
BANG BANG
I WILL KEEP THE--
BANG BANG
--KEEP THE LINE TO THE CAVE OPEN AS LONG AS I CAN MANAGE.
BANG BANG
"GOOD LUCK TO YOU...GOD HELP US ALL."
I CAN GET OUT ON MY OWN, DAMN IT! AND THE DANGER IS MINIMAL! THE BUILDING IS A FORTRESS! SPRINKLERS WILL ACTIVATE IN LESS THAN--
WE'RE JUST FOLLOWING PROTOCOL, MR. FOX!
YOUR SAFETY IS OUR JOB! PLEASE, STOP STRUGGLING OR WE'LL BE FORCED TO DRAG YOU FROM THE--
CHUNK

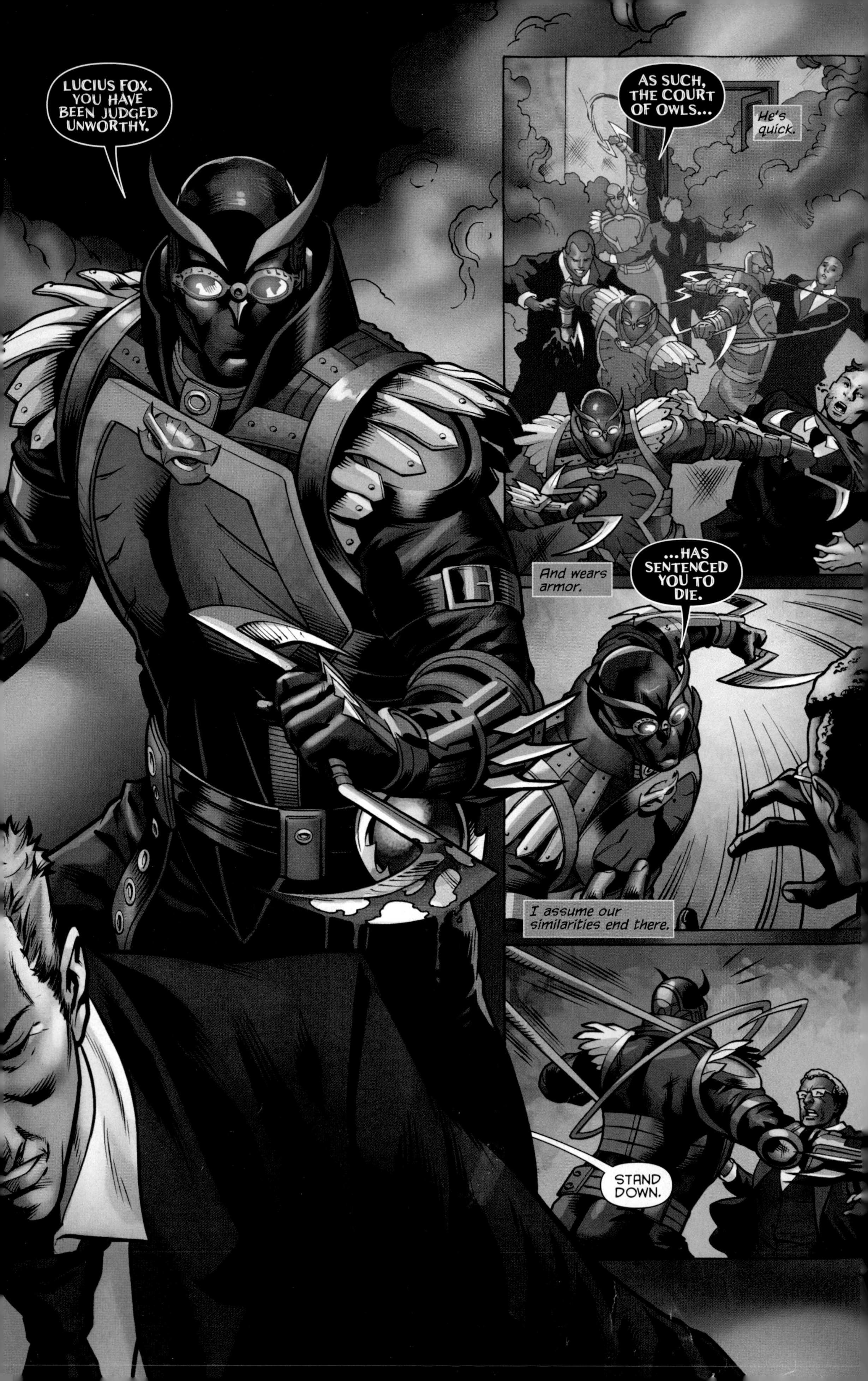
LUCIUS FOX. YOU HAVE BEEN JUDGED UNWORTHY.
AS SUCH, THE COURT OF OWLS...
He's quick.
And wears armor.
...HAS SENTENCED YOU TO DIE.
I assume our similarities end there.
STAND DOWN.

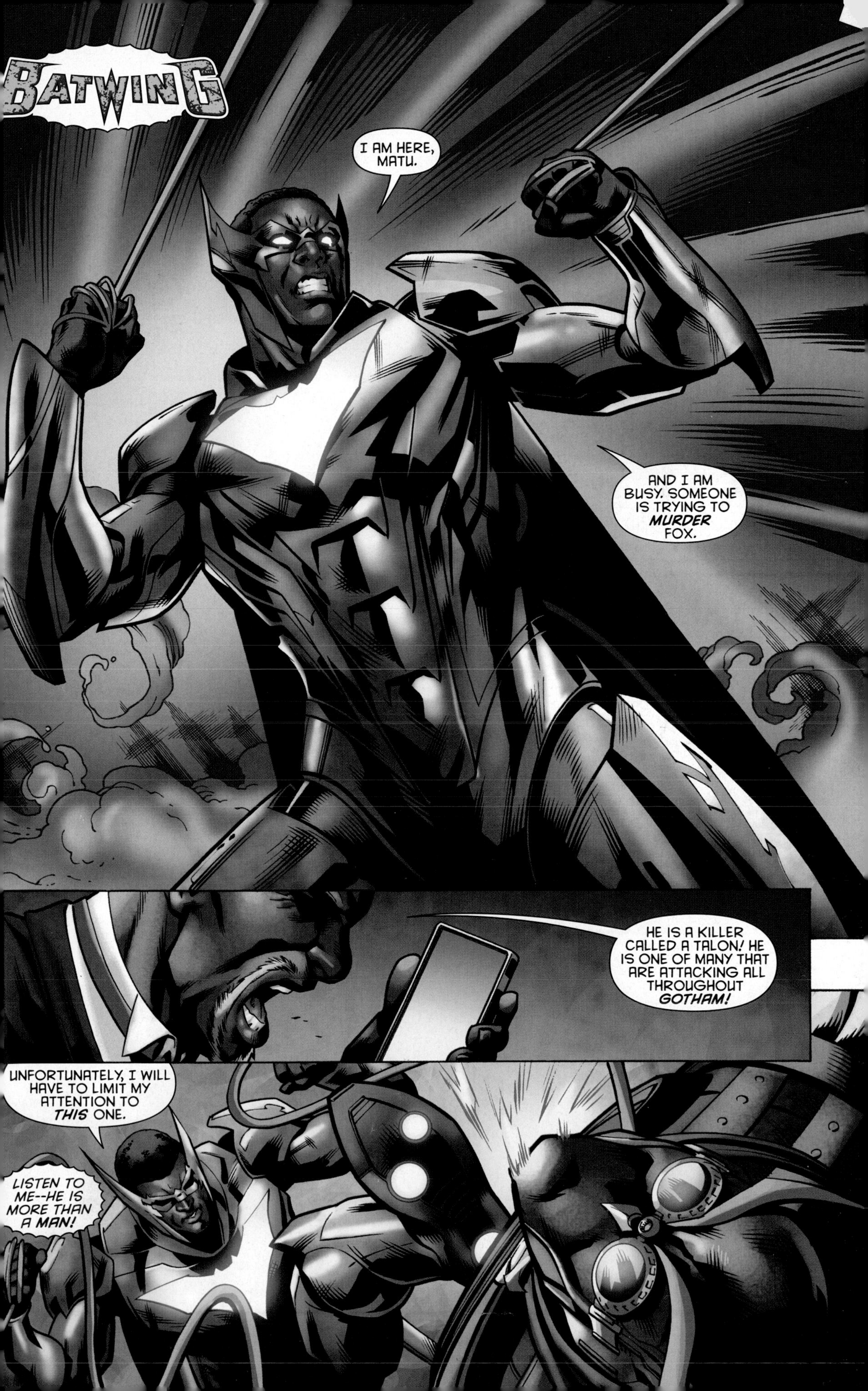
BATWING
I AM HERE, MATU.
AND I AM BUSY. SOMEONE IS TRYING TO MURDER FOX.
HE IS A KILLER CALLED A TALON! HE IS ONE OF MANY THAT ARE ATTACKING ALL THROUGHOUT GOTHAM!
UNFORTUNATELY, I WILL HAVE TO LIMIT MY ATTENTION TO THIS ONE.
LISTEN TO ME--HE IS MORE THAN A MAN!

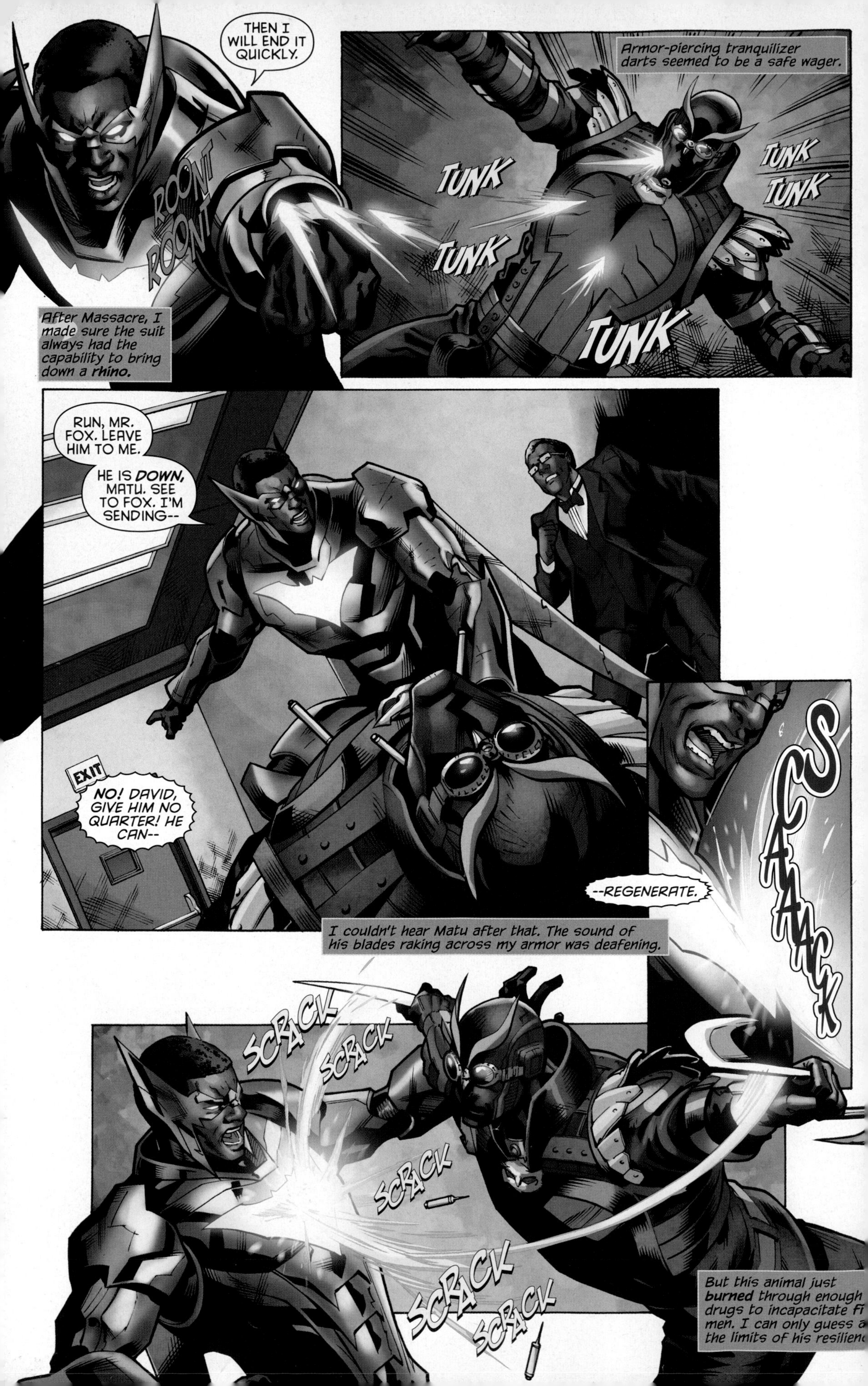
THEN I WILL END IT QUICKLY.
ROONT ROONT
After Massacre, I made sure the suit always had the capability to bring down a rhino.
Armor-piercing tranquilizer darts seemed to be a safe wager.
TUNK
TUNK TUNK
TUNK
TUNK
RUN, MR. FOX. LEAVE HIM TO ME.
HE IS DOWN, MATU. SEE TO FOX. I'M SENDING--
EXIT
NO! DAVID, GIVE HIM NO QUARTER! HE CAN--
--REGENERATE.
SCCAAACK
I couldn't hear Matu after that. The sound of his blades raking across my armor was deafening.
SCRACK
SCRACK
SCRACK
SCRACK
SCRACK

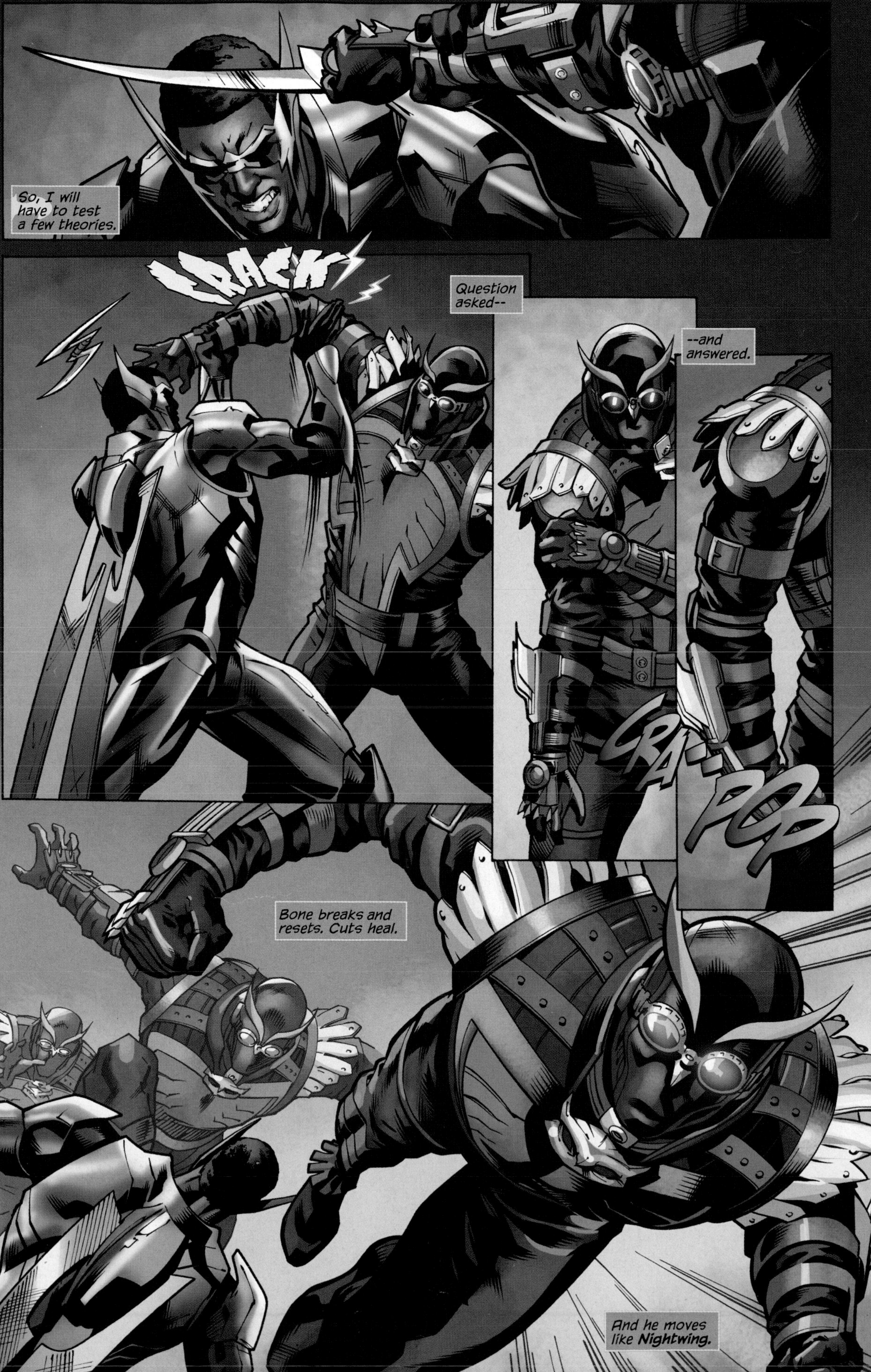
So, I will have to test a few theories.
CRACK
Question asked--
--and answered.
CRA--POP
Bone breaks and resets. Cuts heal.
And he moves like **Nightwing.**

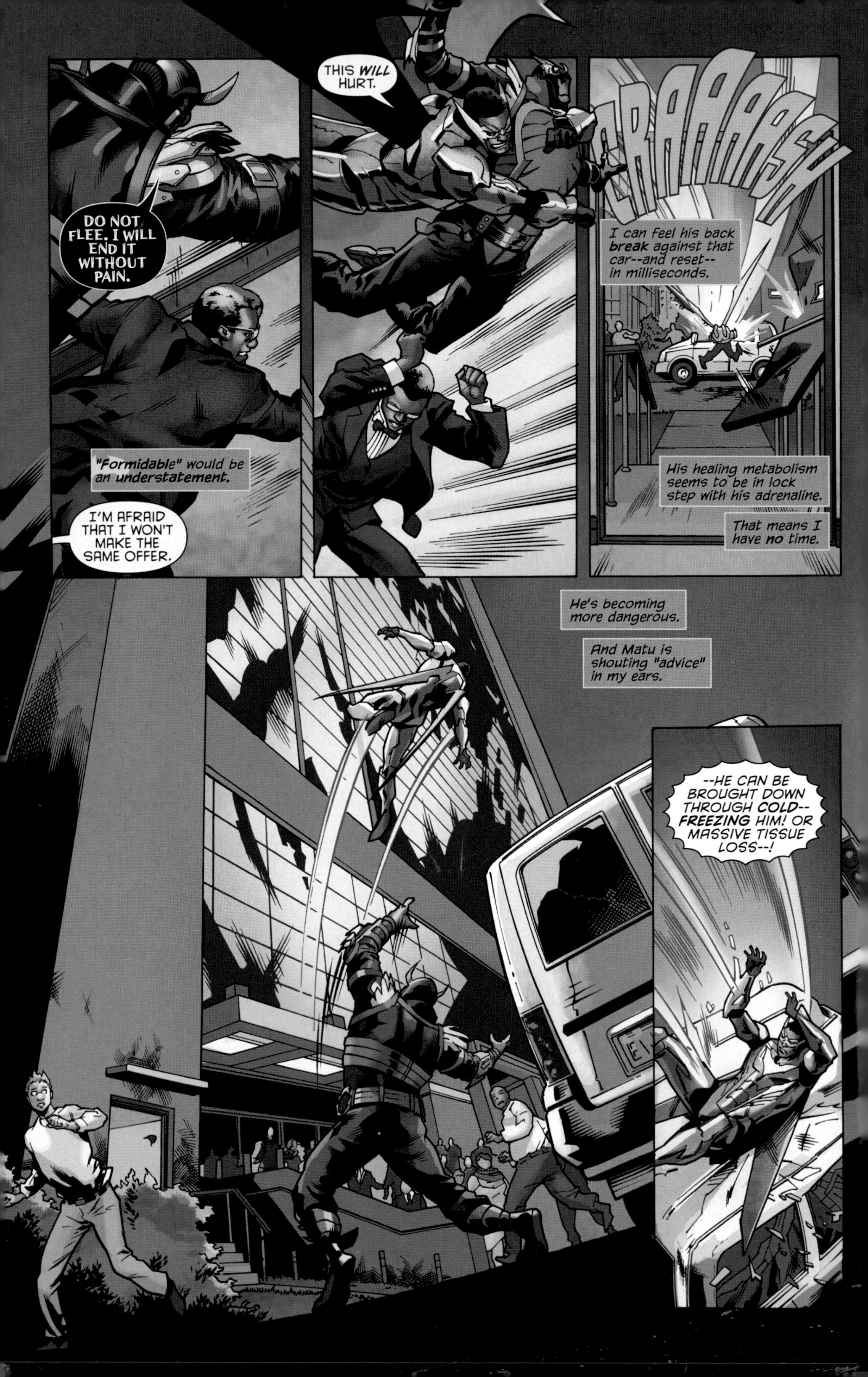
DO NOT FLEE. I WILL END IT WITHOUT PAIN.
"Formidable" would be an understatement.
I'M AFRAID THAT I WON'T MAKE THE SAME OFFER.
THIS WILL HURT.
CRAAAAASH
I can feel his back break against that car--and reset--in milliseconds.
His healing metabolism seems to be in lock step with his adrenaline.
That means I have no time.
He's becoming more dangerous.
And Matu is shouting "advice" in my ears.
--HE CAN BE BROUGHT DOWN THROUGH COLD--FREEZING HIM! OR MASSIVE TISSUE LOSS--!

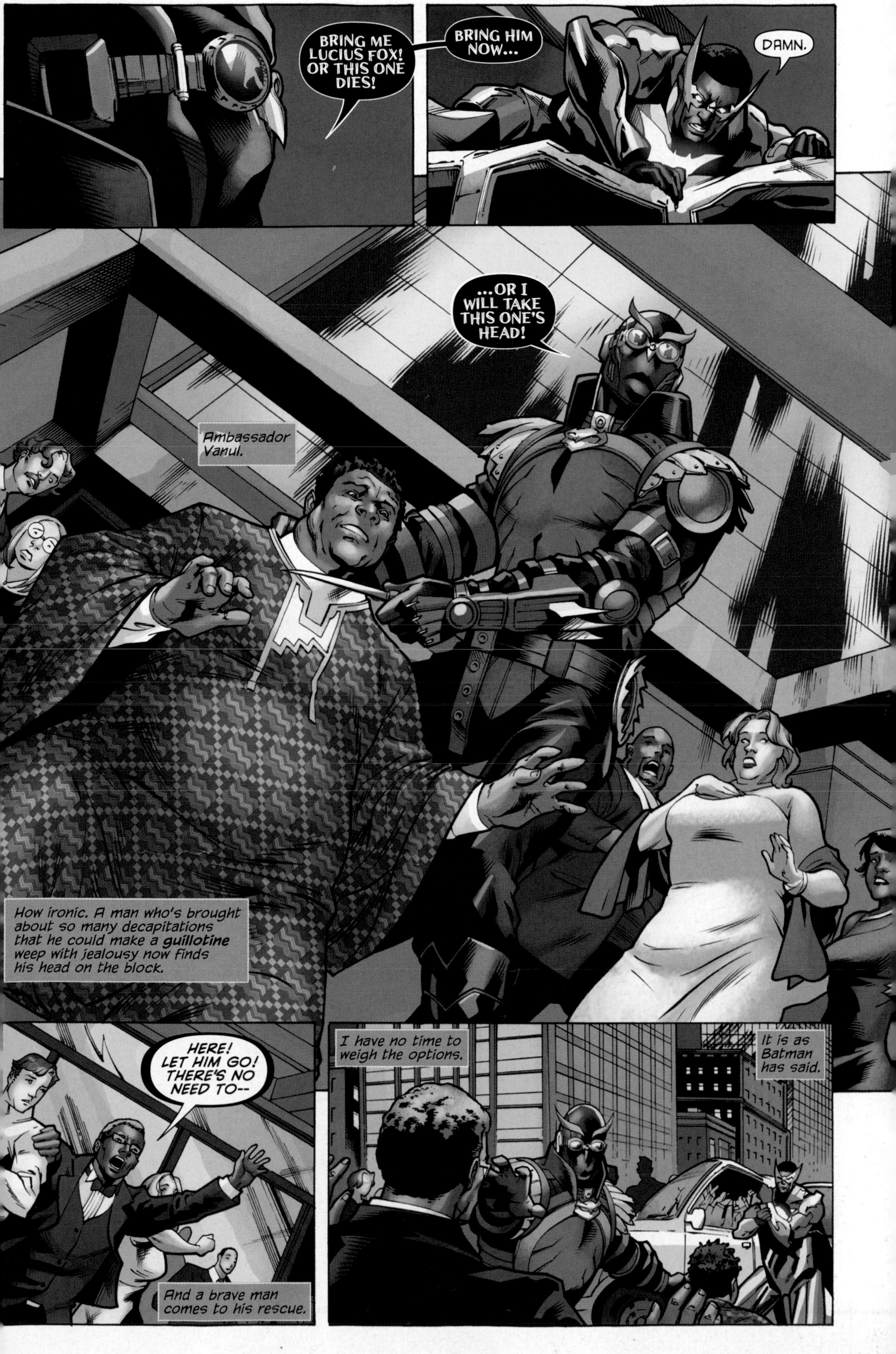
BRING ME LUCIUS FOX! OR THIS ONE DIES!
BRING HIM NOW...
DAMN.
...OR I WILL TAKE THIS ONE'S HEAD!
Ambassador Vanul.
How ironic. A man who's brought about so many decapitations that he could make a **guillotine** weep with jealousy now finds his head on the block.
HERE! LET HIM GO! THERE'S NO NEED TO--
And a brave man comes to his rescue.
I have no time to weigh the options.
It is as Batman has said.

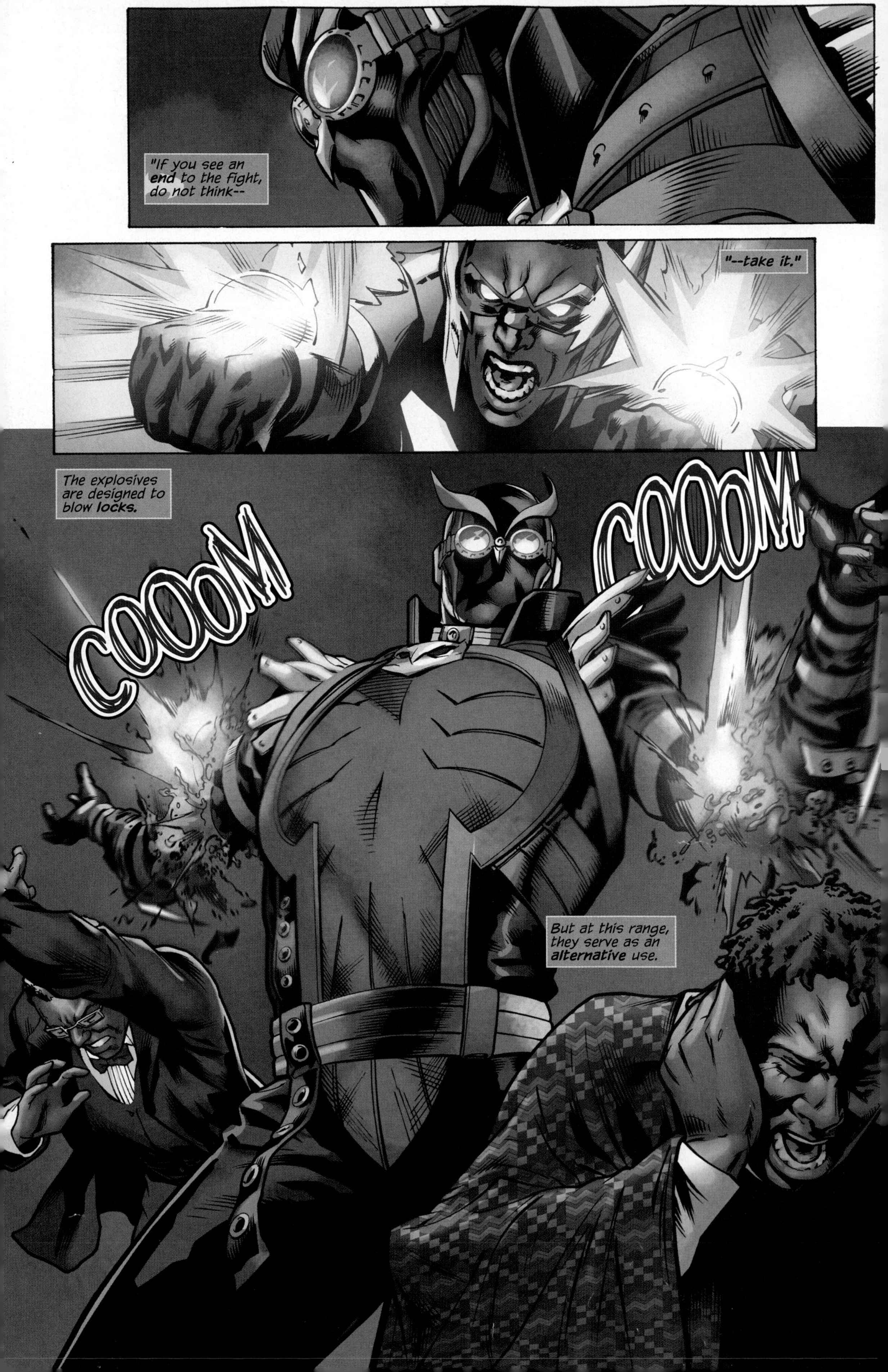
"If you see an end to the fight, do not think--
"--take it."
The explosives are designed to blow locks.
COOOM
COOOM
But at this range, they serve as an alternative use.

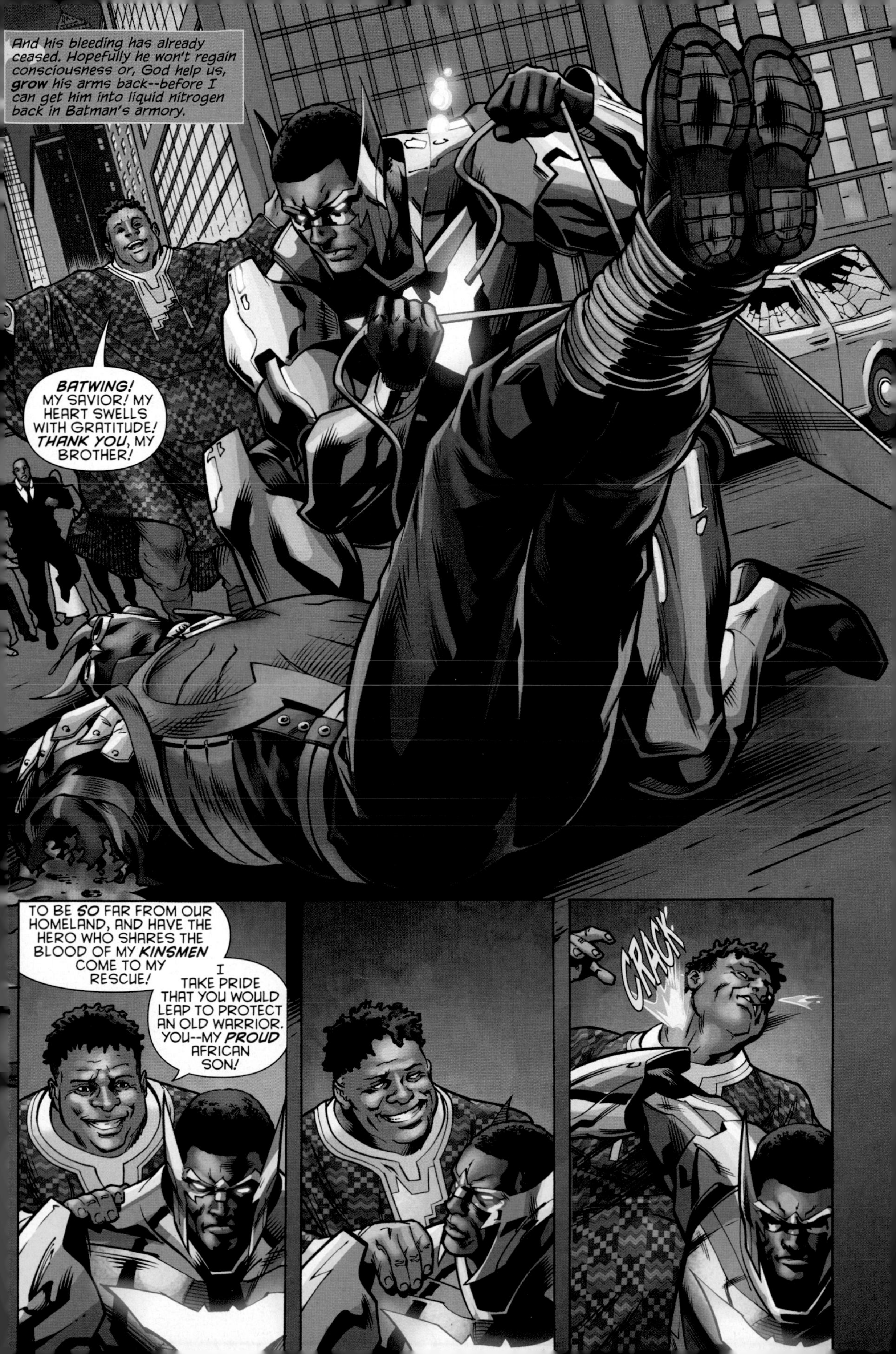
And his bleeding has already ceased. Hopefully he won't regain consciousness or, God help us, **grow** his arms back--before I can get him into liquid nitrogen back in Batman's armory.
BATWING! MY SAVIOR! MY HEART SWELLS WITH GRATITUDE! ***THANK YOU***, MY BROTHER!
TO BE ***SO*** FAR FROM OUR HOMELAND, AND HAVE THE HERO WHO SHARES THE BLOOD OF MY ***KINSMEN*** COME TO MY RESCUE!
I TAKE PRIDE THAT YOU WOULD LEAP TO PROTECT AN OLD WARRIOR. YOU--MY ***PROUD*** AFRICAN SON!
CRACK

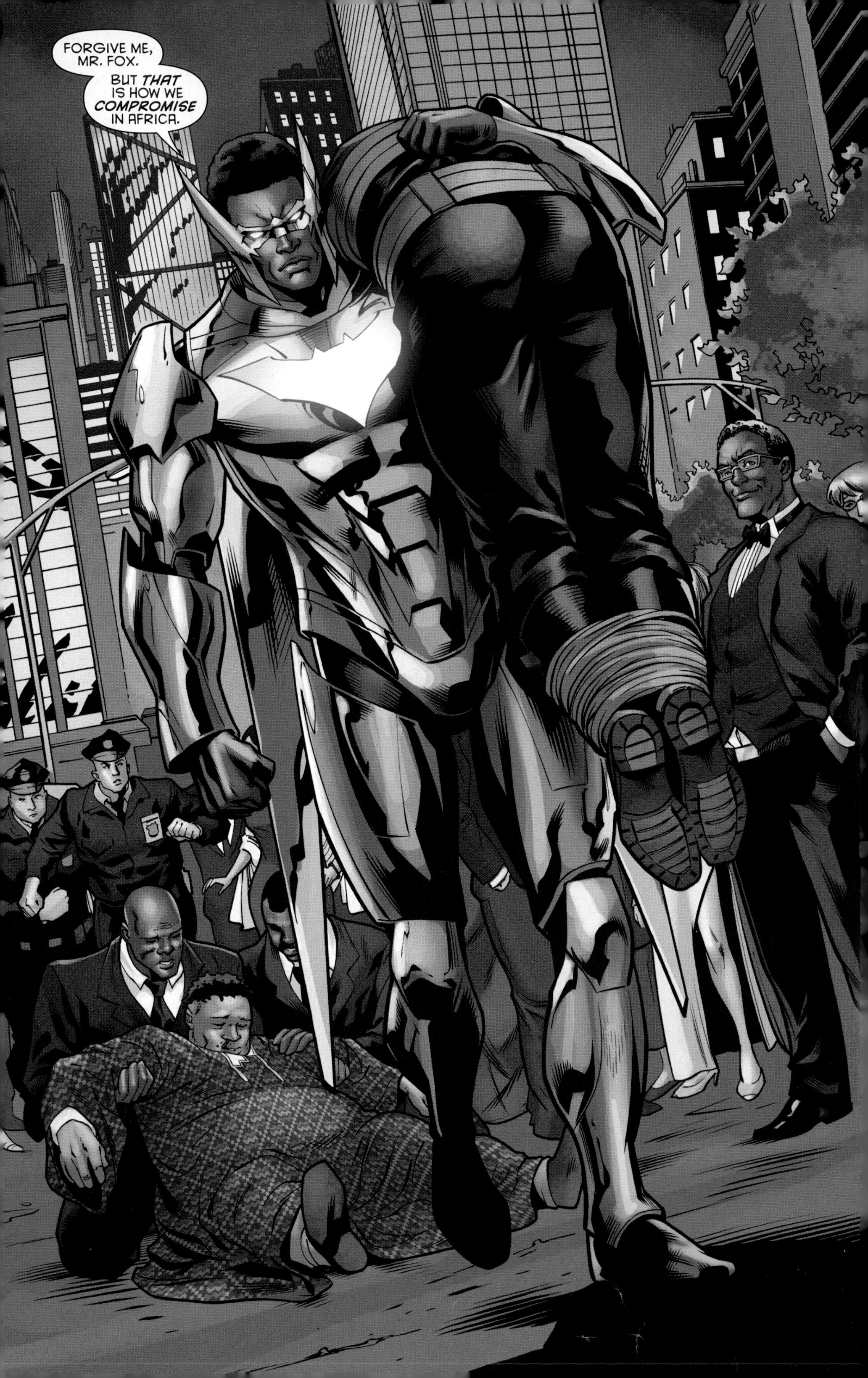
FORGIVE ME, MR. FOX. BUT *THAT* IS HOW WE ***COMPROMISE*** IN AFRICA.

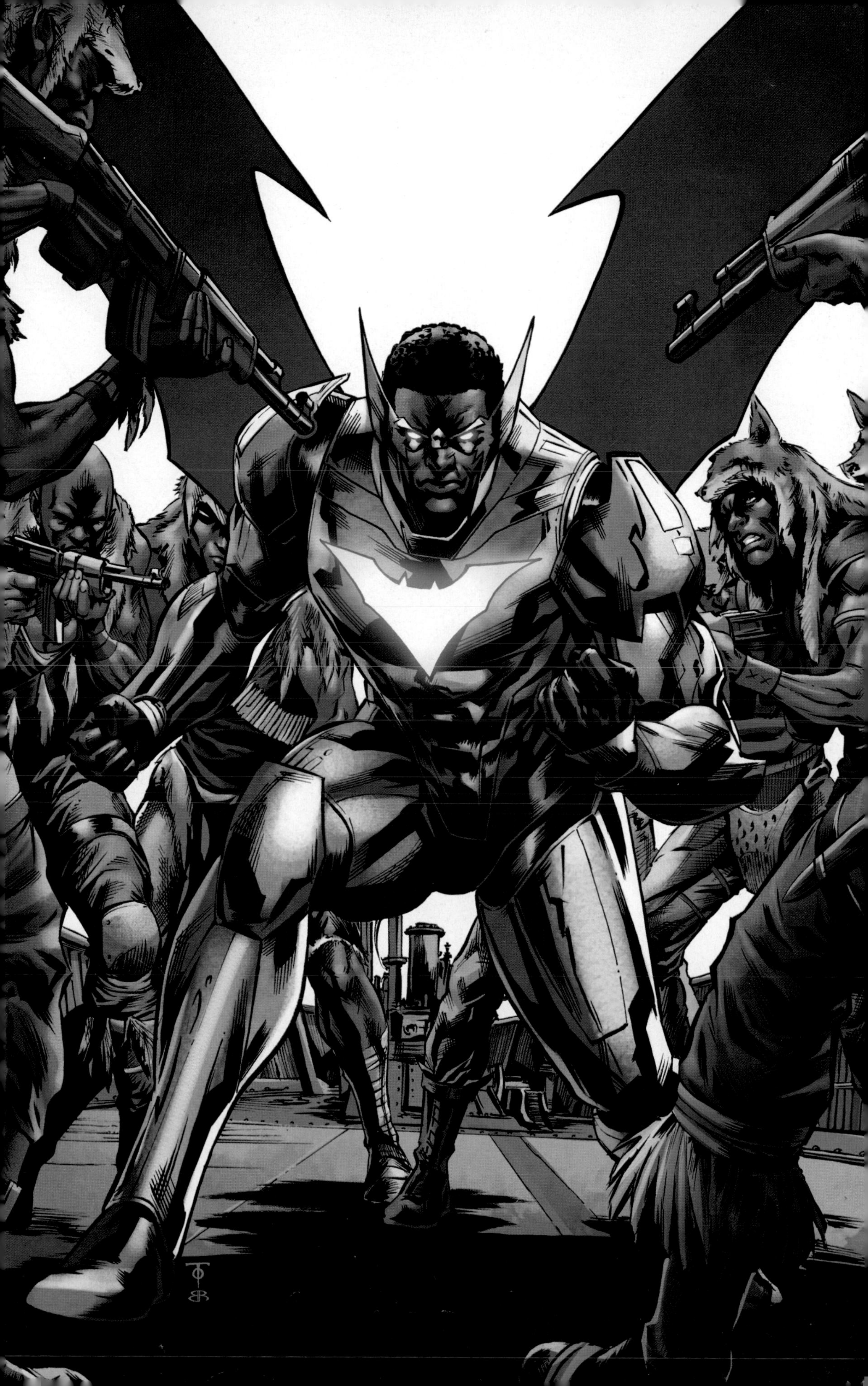

FIGHT OR FLIGHT

JUDD WINICK writer **MARCUS TO** penciller **RYAN WINN** inker cover art by **MARCUS TO & BRIAN REBER**

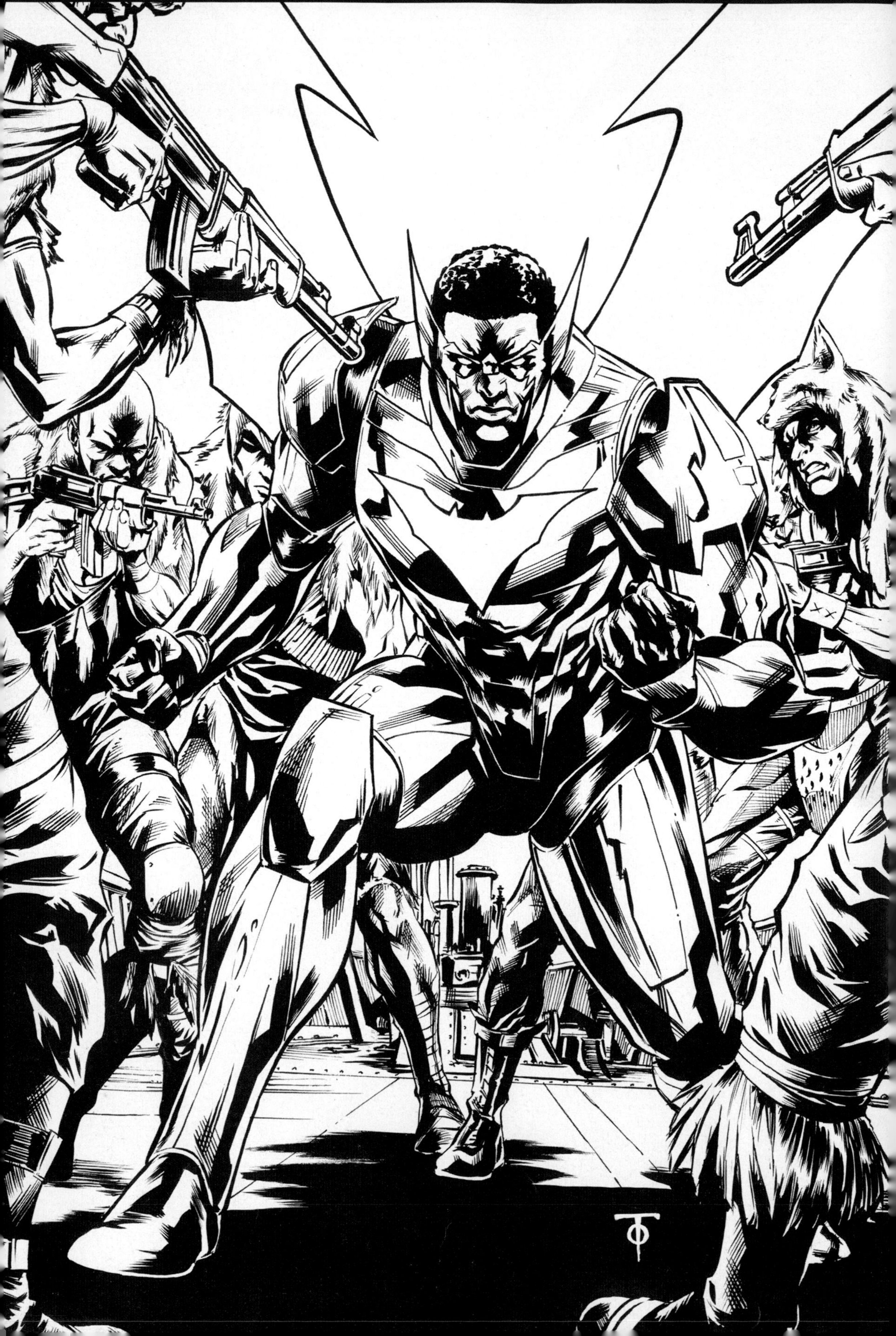

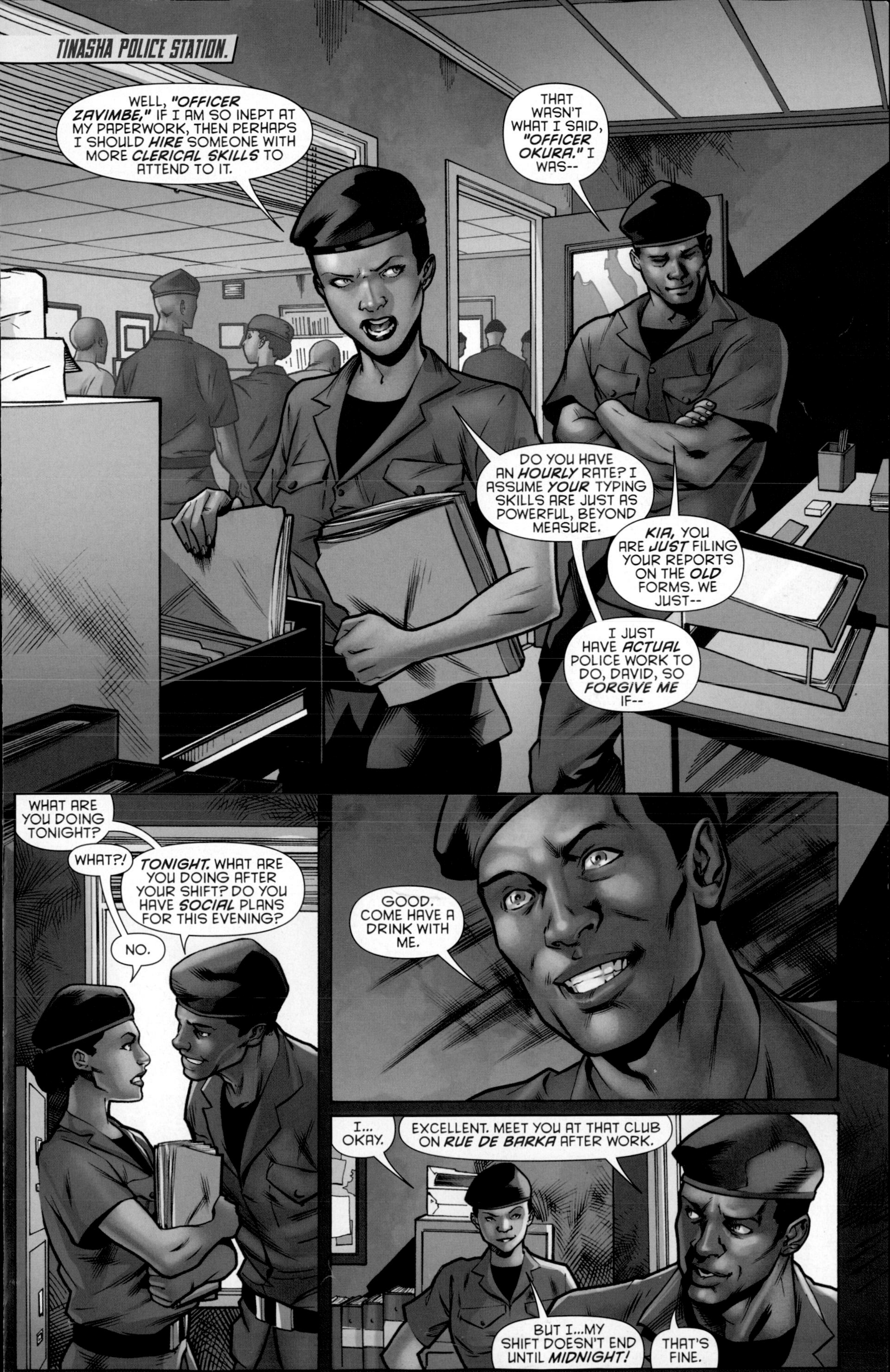
TINASHA POLICE STATION.
WELL, "OFFICER ZAVIMBE," IF I AM SO INEPT AT MY PAPERWORK, THEN PERHAPS I SHOULD HIRE SOMEONE WITH MORE CLERICAL SKILLS TO ATTEND TO IT.
THAT WASN'T WHAT I SAID, "OFFICER OKURA." I WAS--
DO YOU HAVE AN HOURLY RATE? I ASSUME YOUR TYPING SKILLS ARE JUST AS POWERFUL, BEYOND MEASURE.
KIA, YOU ARE JUST FILING YOUR REPORTS ON THE OLD FORMS. WE JUST--
I JUST HAVE ACTUAL POLICE WORK TO DO, DAVID, SO FORGIVE ME IF--
WHAT ARE YOU DOING TONIGHT?
WHAT?!
TONIGHT. WHAT ARE YOU DOING AFTER YOUR SHIFT? DO YOU HAVE SOCIAL PLANS FOR THIS EVENING?
NO.
GOOD. COME HAVE A DRINK WITH ME.
I... OKAY.
EXCELLENT. MEET YOU AT THAT CLUB ON RUE DE BARKA AFTER WORK.
BUT I...MY SHIFT DOESN'T END UNTIL MIDNIGHT!
THAT'S FINE.

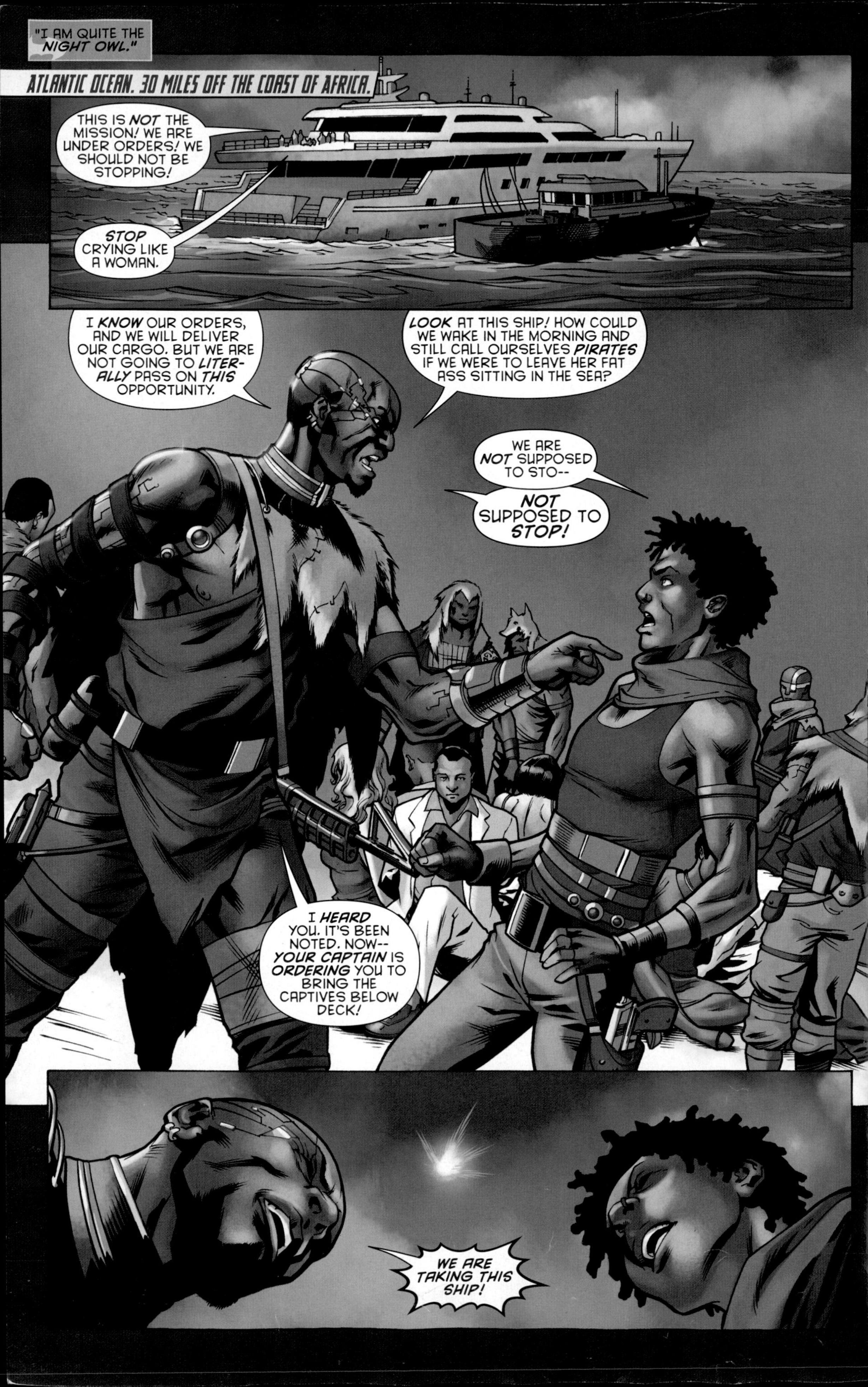
"I AM QUITE THE NIGHT OWL."
ATLANTIC OCEAN. 30 MILES OFF THE COAST OF AFRICA.
THIS IS NOT THE MISSION! WE ARE UNDER ORDERS! WE SHOULD NOT BE STOPPING!
STOP CRYING LIKE A WOMAN.
I KNOW OUR ORDERS, AND WE WILL DELIVER OUR CARGO. BUT WE ARE NOT GOING TO LITER-ALLY PASS ON THIS OPPORTUNITY.
LOOK AT THIS SHIP! HOW COULD WE WAKE IN THE MORNING AND STILL CALL OURSELVES PIRATES IF WE WERE TO LEAVE HER FAT ASS SITTING IN THE SEA?
WE ARE NOT SUPPOSED TO STO--
NOT SUPPOSED TO STOP!
I HEARD YOU. IT'S BEEN NOTED. NOW-- YOUR CAPTAIN IS ORDERING YOU TO BRING THE CAPTIVES BELOW DECK!
WE ARE TAKING THIS SHIP!

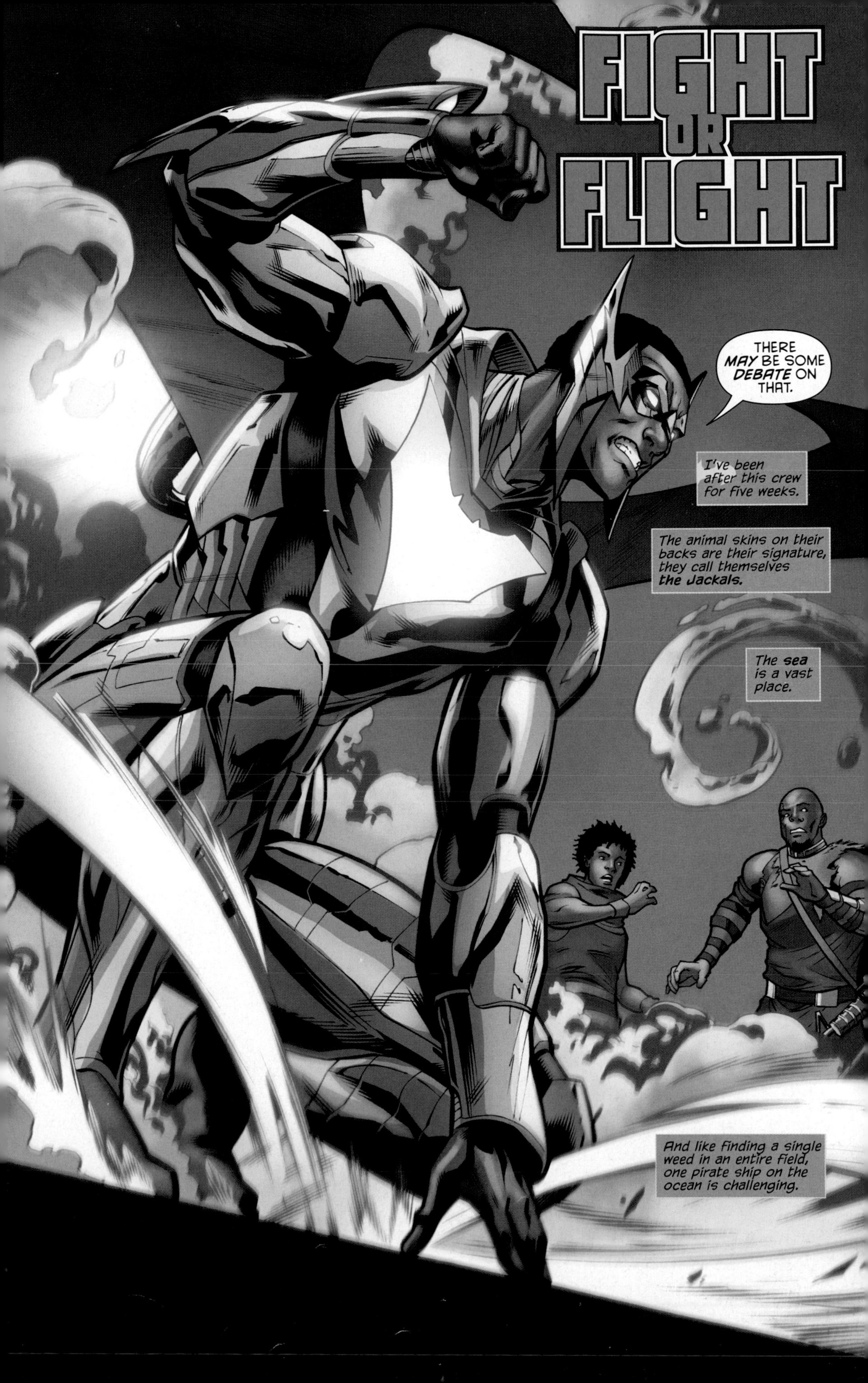
FIGHT OR FLIGHT
THERE MAY BE SOME DEBATE ON THAT.
I've been after this crew for five weeks.
The animal skins on their backs are their signature, they call themselves the Jackals.
The sea is a vast place.
And like finding a single weed in an entire field, one pirate ship on the ocean is challenging.

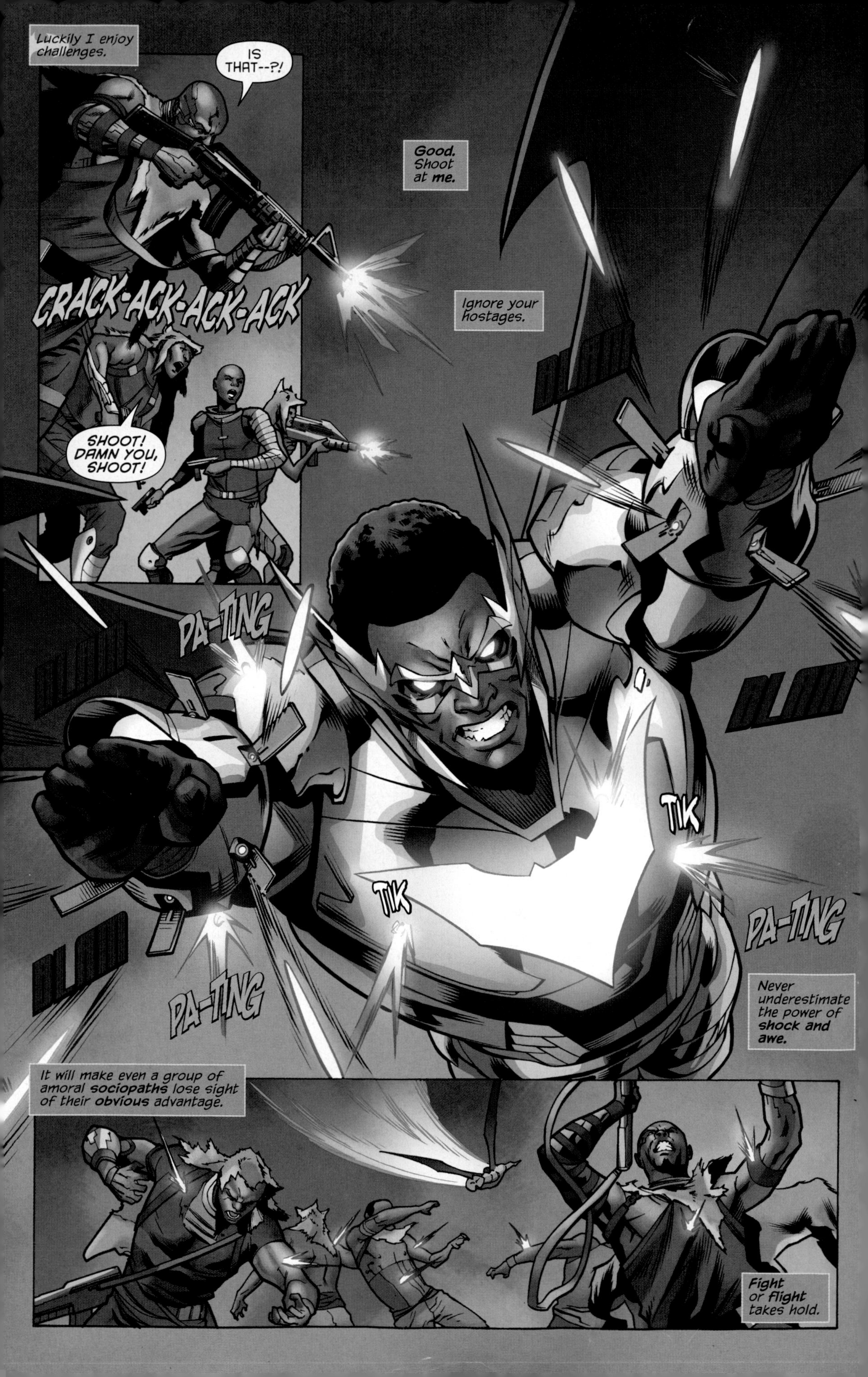
Luckily I enjoy challenges.
IS THAT--?!
Good. Shoot at me.
CRACK-ACK-ACK-ACK
Ignore your hostages.
SHOOT! DAMN YOU, SHOOT!
PA-TING
TIK
TIK
PA-TING
PA-TING
Never underestimate the power of shock and awe.
It will make even a group of amoral sociopaths lose sight of their obvious advantage.
Fight or flight takes hold.

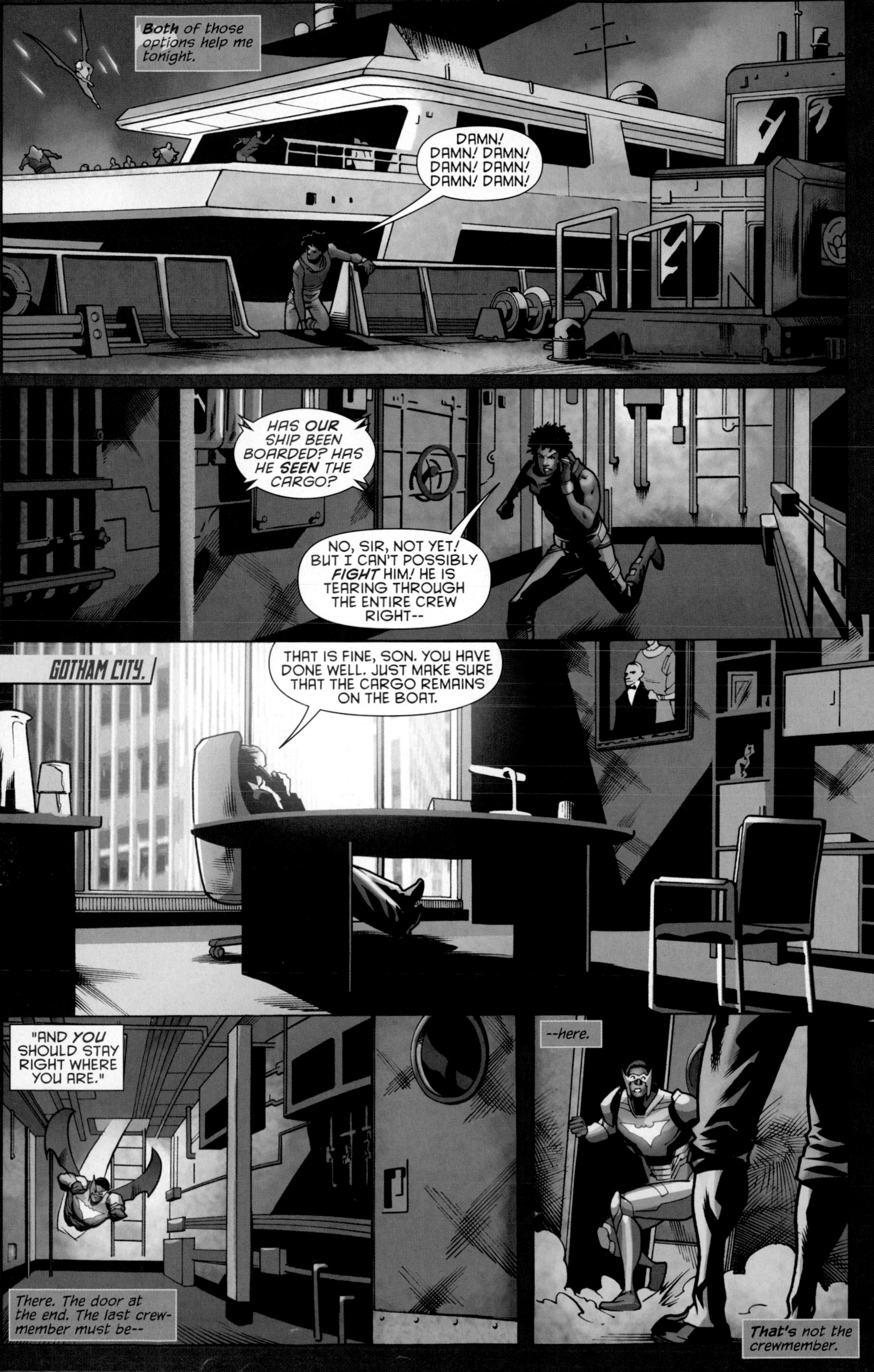
Both of those options help me tonight.
DAMN! DAMN! DAMN! DAMN! DAMN! DAMN! DAMN!
HAS OUR SHIP BEEN BOARDED? HAS HE SEEN THE CARGO?
NO, SIR, NOT YET! BUT I CAN'T POSSIBLY FIGHT HIM! HE IS TEARING THROUGH THE ENTIRE CREW RIGHT--
GOTHAM CITY.
THAT IS FINE, SON. YOU HAVE DONE WELL. JUST MAKE SURE THAT THE CARGO REMAINS ON THE BOAT.
"AND YOU SHOULD STAY RIGHT WHERE YOU ARE."
There. The door at the end. The last crew-member must be--
--here.
That's not the crewmember.

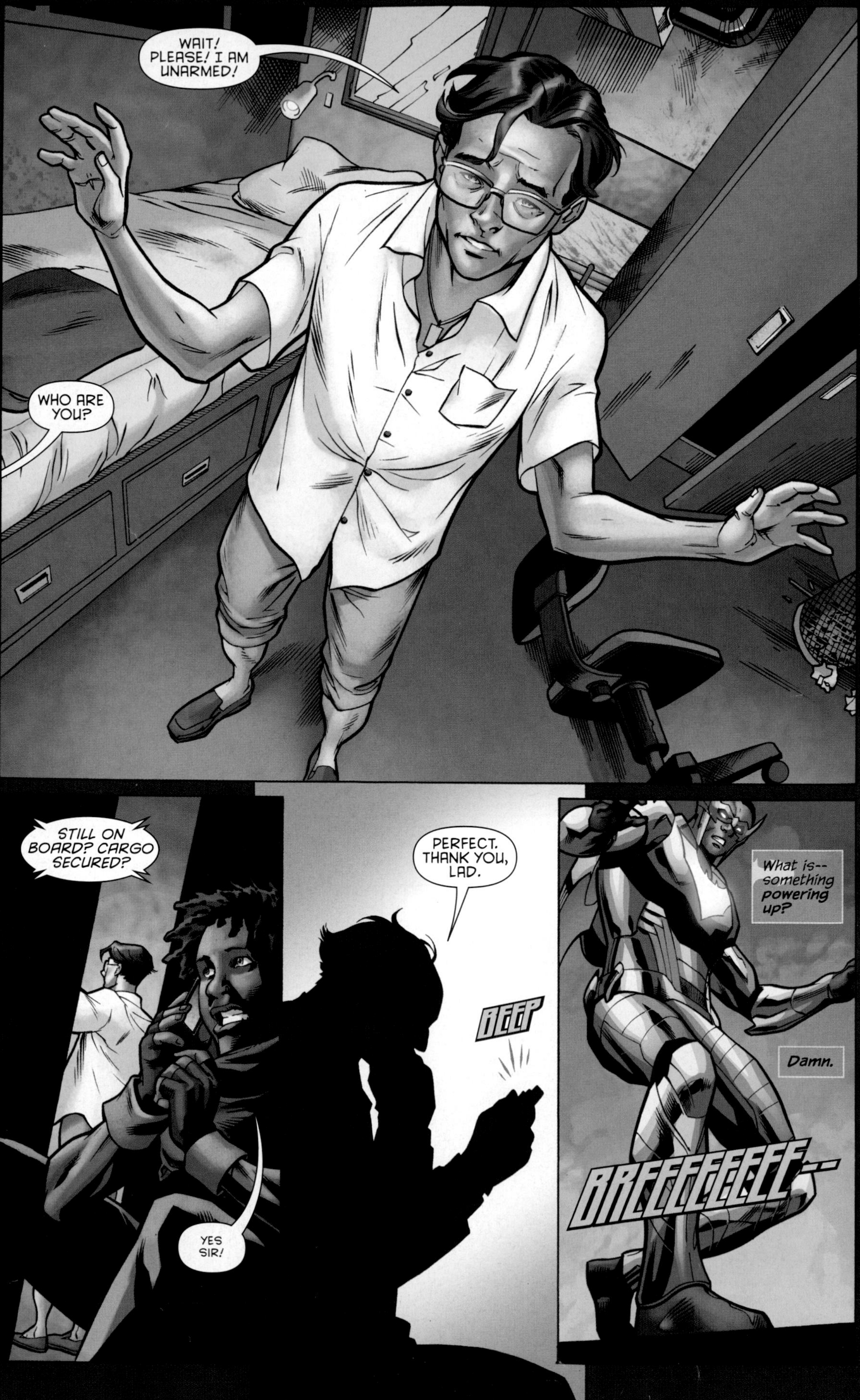
WAIT! PLEASE! I AM UNARMED!
WHO ARE YOU?
STILL ON BOARD? CARGO SECURED?
YES SIR!
PERFECT. THANK YOU, LAD.
BEEP
What is-- something powering up?
Damn.
BREEEEEEEE--

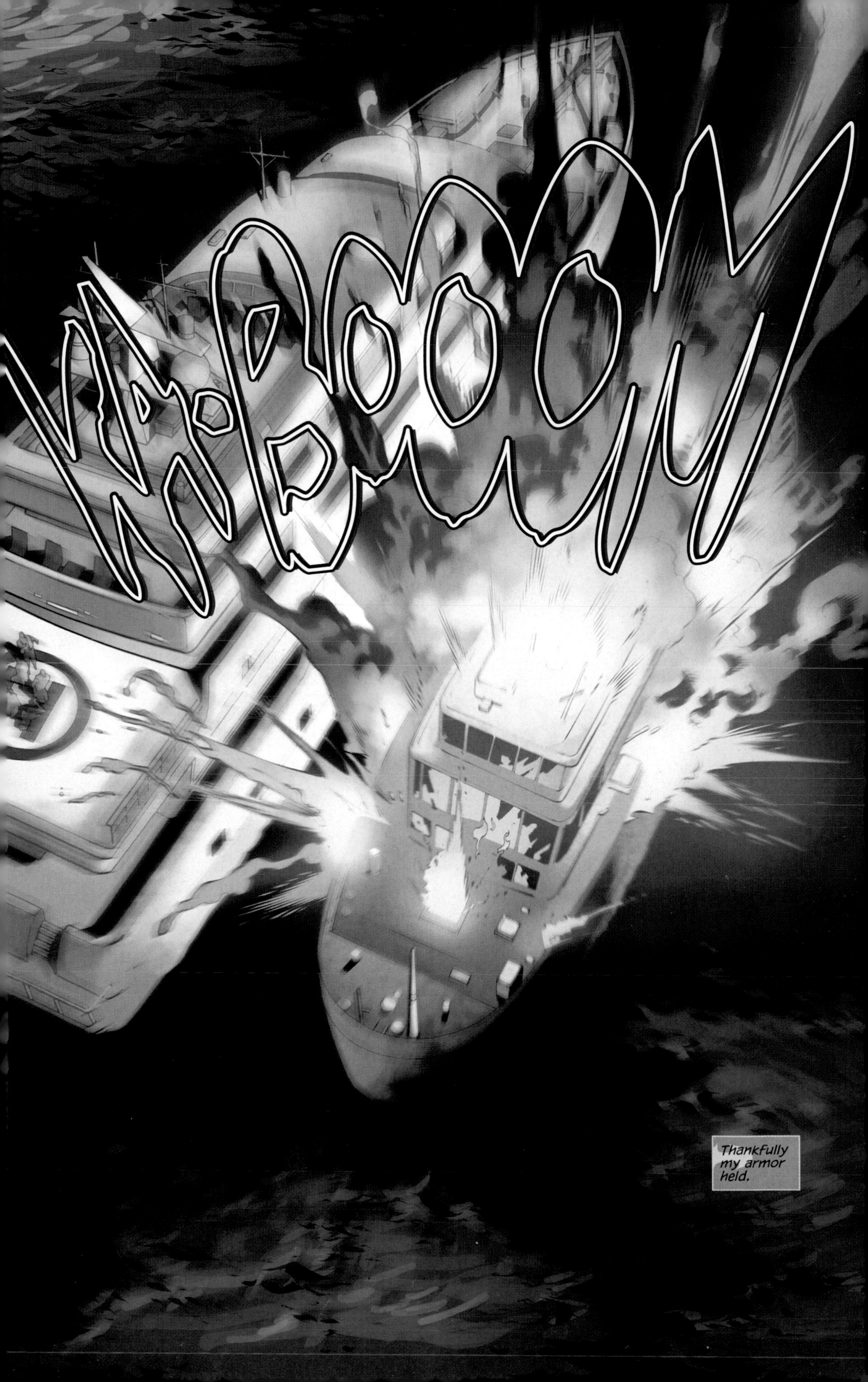
WHOOOM
KABOOM
Thankfully my armor held.

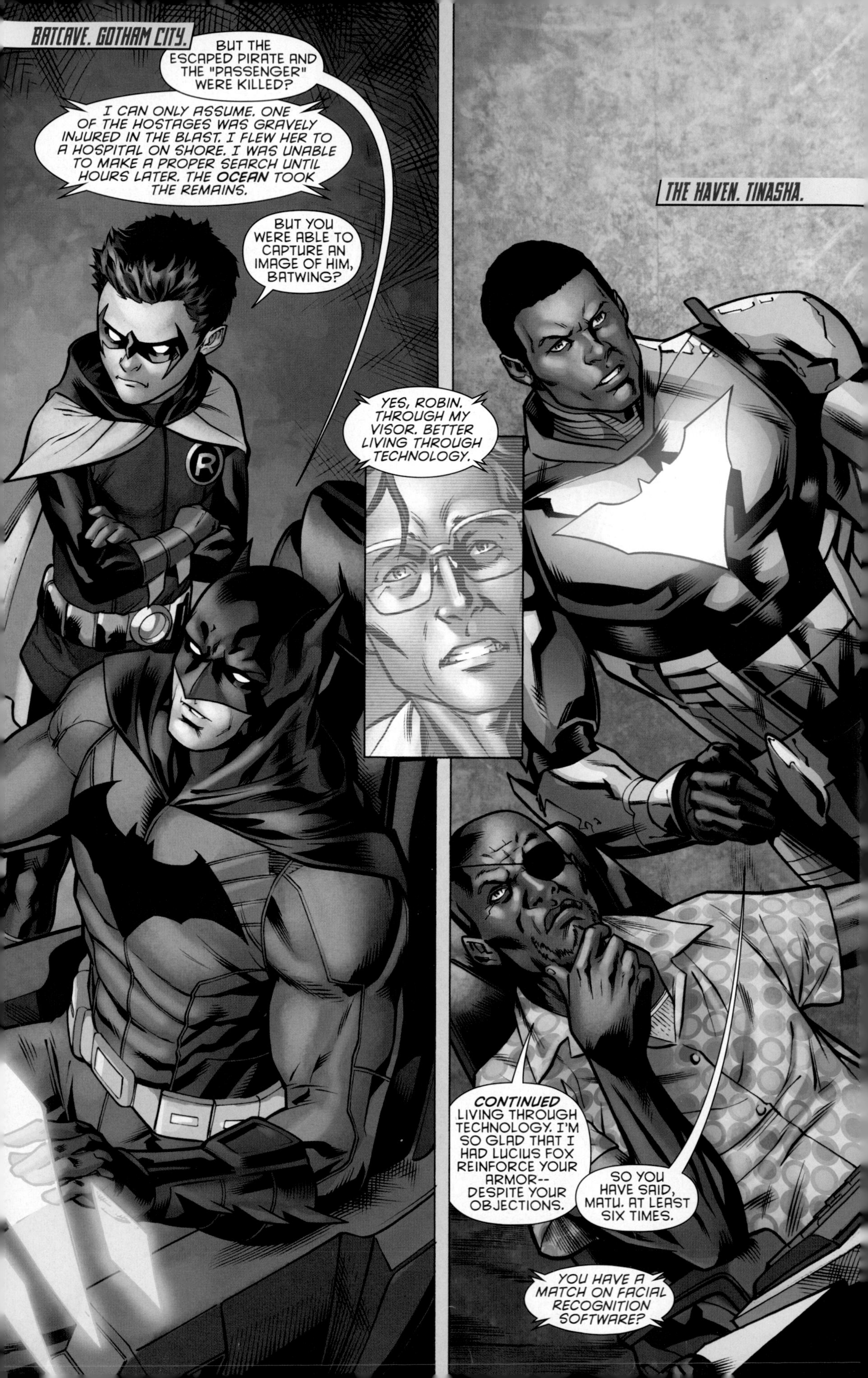
BATCAVE. GOTHAM CITY.
BUT THE ESCAPED PIRATE AND THE "PASSENGER" WERE KILLED?
I CAN ONLY ASSUME. ONE OF THE HOSTAGES WAS GRAVELY INJURED IN THE BLAST. I FLEW HER TO A HOSPITAL ON SHORE. I WAS UNABLE TO MAKE A PROPER SEARCH UNTIL HOURS LATER. THE OCEAN TOOK THE REMAINS.
BUT YOU WERE ABLE TO CAPTURE AN IMAGE OF HIM, BATWING?
YES, ROBIN. THROUGH MY VISOR. BETTER LIVING THROUGH TECHNOLOGY.
THE HAVEN. TINASHA.
CONTINUED LIVING THROUGH TECHNOLOGY. I'M SO GLAD THAT I HAD LUCIUS FOX REINFORCE YOUR ARMOR-- DESPITE YOUR OBJECTIONS.
SO YOU HAVE SAID, MATU. AT LEAST SIX TIMES.
YOU HAVE A MATCH ON FACIAL RECOGNITION SOFTWARE?

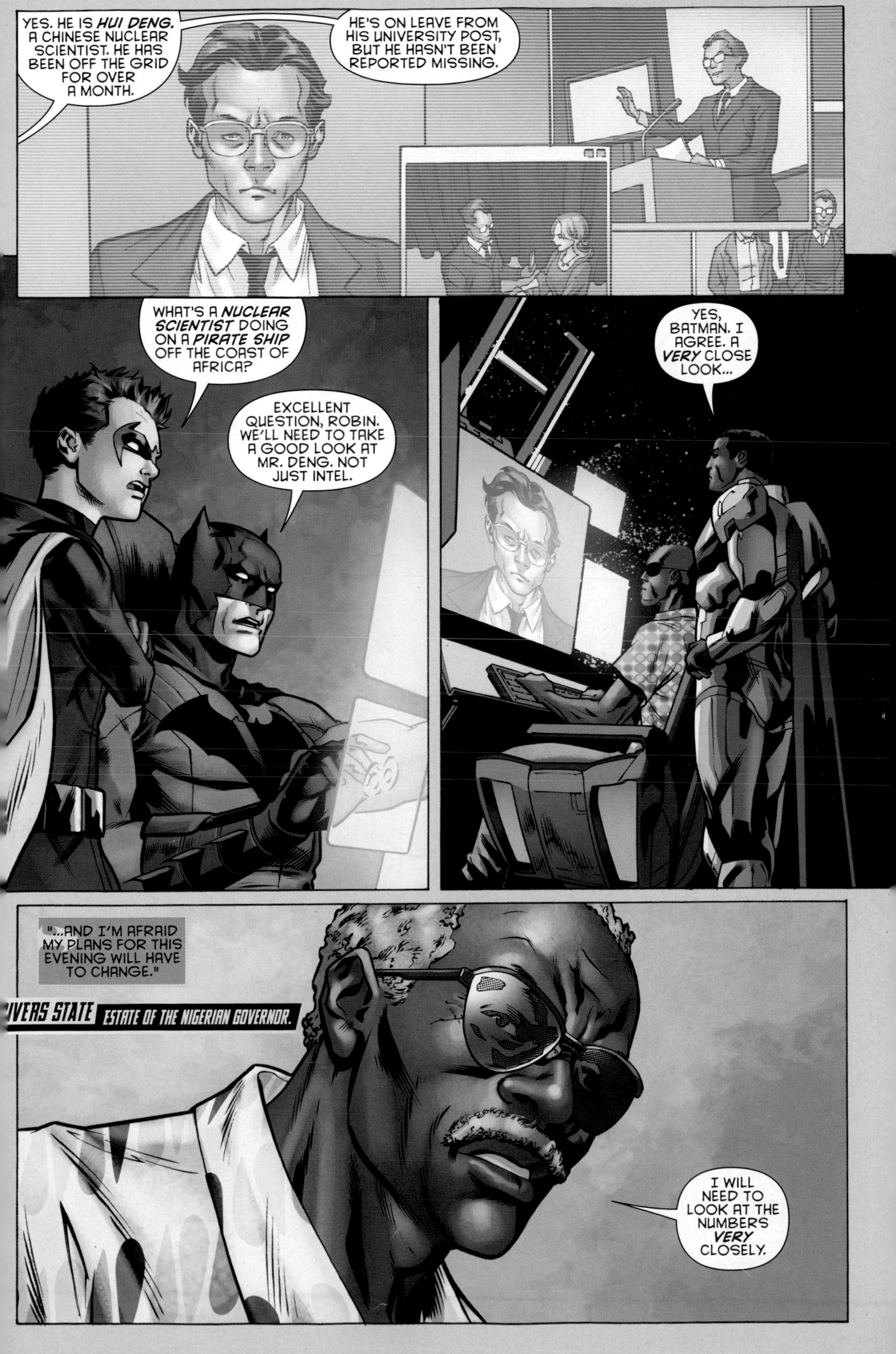
YES. HE IS HUI DENG. A CHINESE NUCLEAR SCIENTIST. HE HAS BEEN OFF THE GRID FOR OVER A MONTH.
HE'S ON LEAVE FROM HIS UNIVERSITY POST, BUT HE HASN'T BEEN REPORTED MISSING.
WHAT'S A NUCLEAR SCIENTIST DOING ON A PIRATE SHIP OFF THE COAST OF AFRICA?
EXCELLENT QUESTION, ROBIN. WE'LL NEED TO TAKE A GOOD LOOK AT MR. DENG. NOT JUST INTEL.
YES, BATMAN. I AGREE. A VERY CLOSE LOOK...
"...AND I'M AFRAID MY PLANS FOR THIS EVENING WILL HAVE TO CHANGE."
IVERS STATE
ESTATE OF THE NIGERIAN GOVERNOR.
I WILL NEED TO LOOK AT THE NUMBERS VERY CLOSELY.

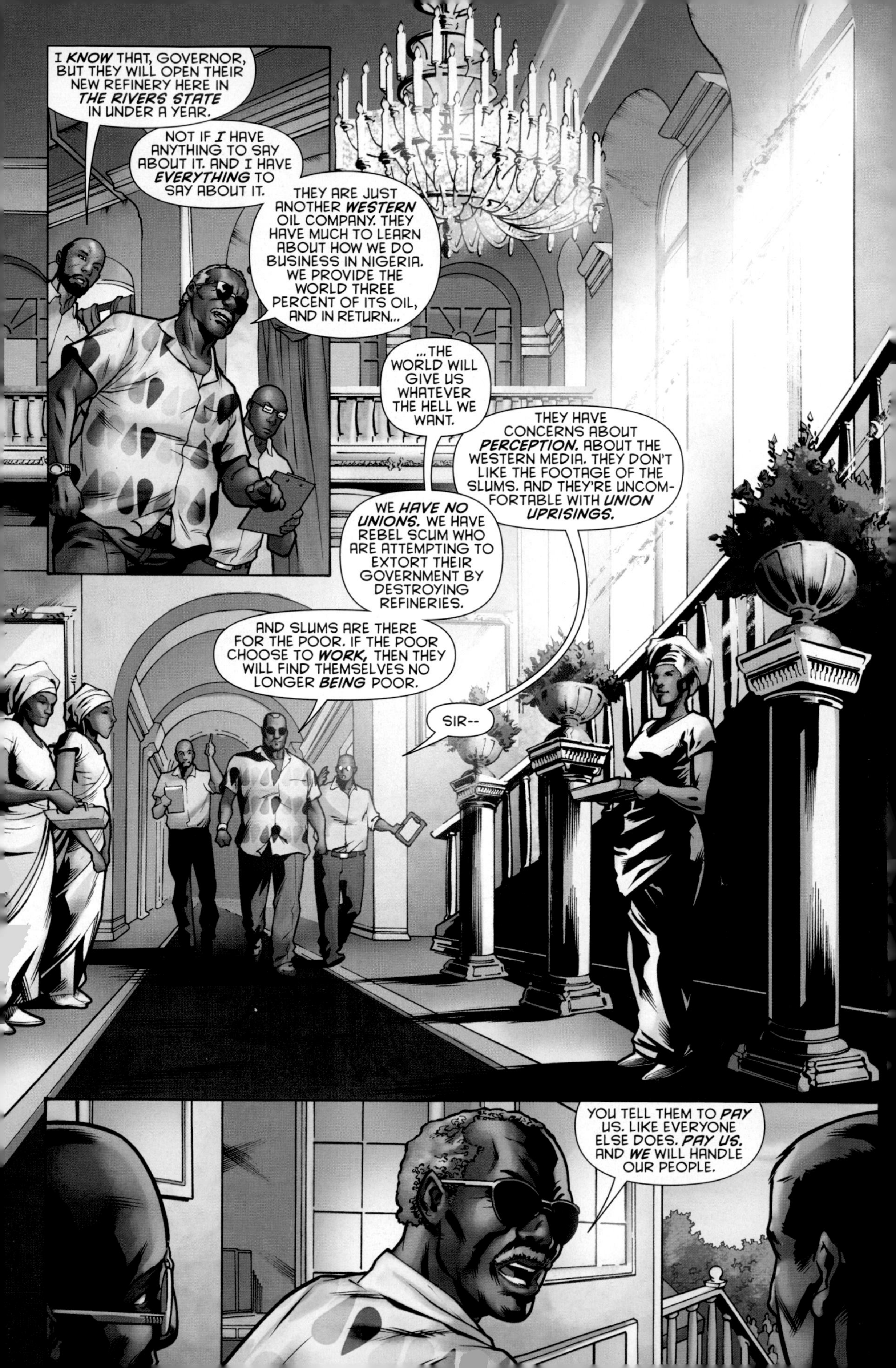
I KNOW THAT, GOVERNOR, BUT THEY WILL OPEN THEIR NEW REFINERY HERE IN THE RIVERS STATE IN UNDER A YEAR.
NOT IF I HAVE ANYTHING TO SAY ABOUT IT. AND I HAVE EVERYTHING TO SAY ABOUT IT.
THEY ARE JUST ANOTHER WESTERN OIL COMPANY. THEY HAVE MUCH TO LEARN ABOUT HOW WE DO BUSINESS IN NIGERIA. WE PROVIDE THE WORLD THREE PERCENT OF ITS OIL, AND IN RETURN...
...THE WORLD WILL GIVE US WHATEVER THE HELL WE WANT.
THEY HAVE CONCERNS ABOUT PERCEPTION. ABOUT THE WESTERN MEDIA. THEY DON'T LIKE THE FOOTAGE OF THE SLUMS. AND THEY'RE UNCOMFORTABLE WITH UNION UPRISINGS.
WE HAVE NO UNIONS. WE HAVE REBEL SCUM WHO ARE ATTEMPTING TO EXTORT THEIR GOVERNMENT BY DESTROYING REFINERIES.
AND SLUMS ARE THERE FOR THE POOR. IF THE POOR CHOOSE TO WORK, THEN THEY WILL FIND THEMSELVES NO LONGER BEING POOR.
SIR--
YOU TELL THEM TO PAY US. LIKE EVERYONE ELSE DOES. PAY US. AND WE WILL HANDLE OUR PEOPLE.

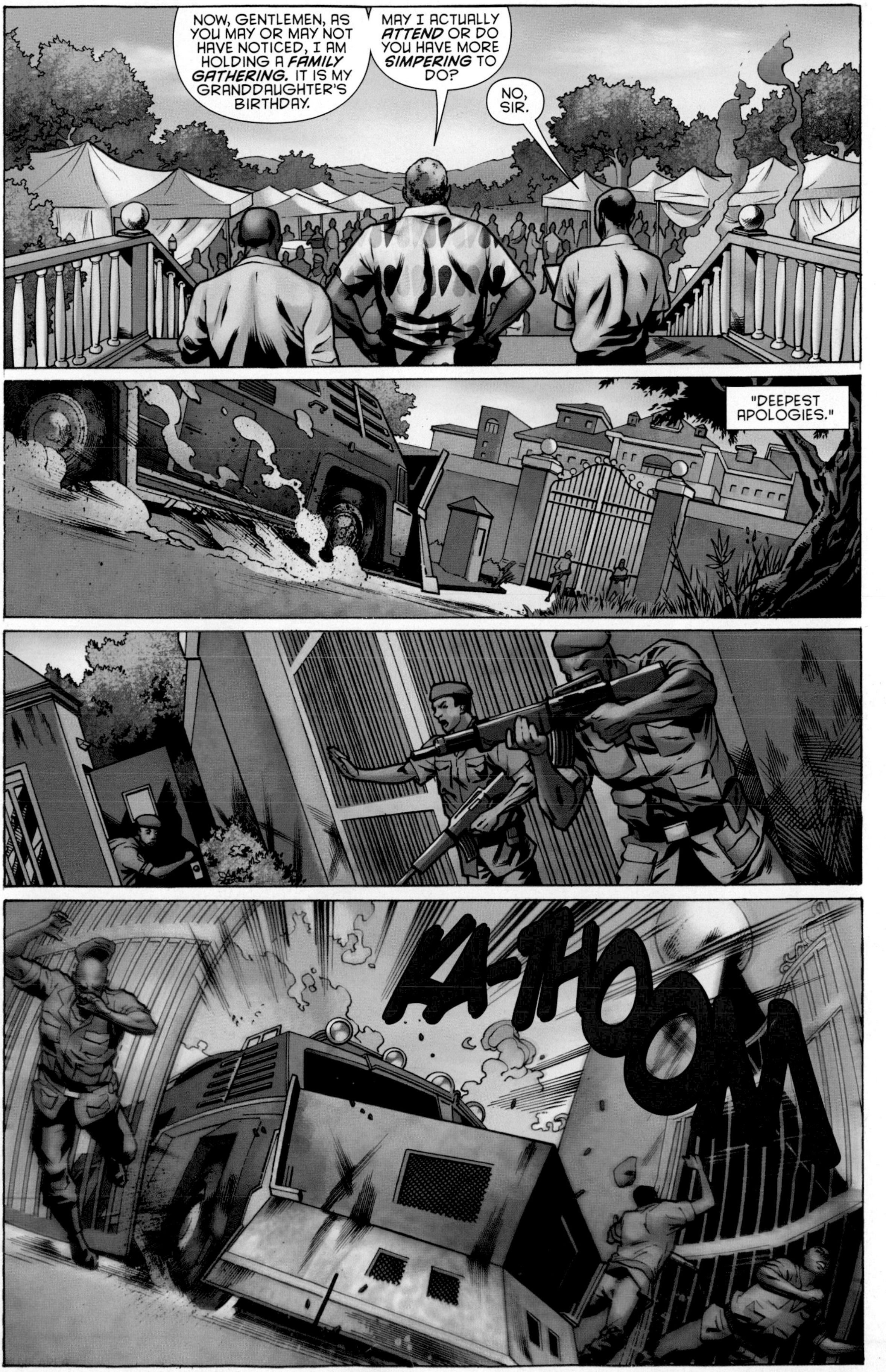
NOW, GENTLEMEN, AS YOU MAY OR MAY NOT HAVE NOTICED, I AM HOLDING A *FAMILY GATHERING.* IT IS MY GRANDDAUGHTER'S BIRTHDAY.
MAY I ACTUALLY *ATTEND* OR DO YOU HAVE MORE *SIMPERING* TO DO?
NO, SIR.
"DEEPEST APOLOGIES."
KA-THOOM

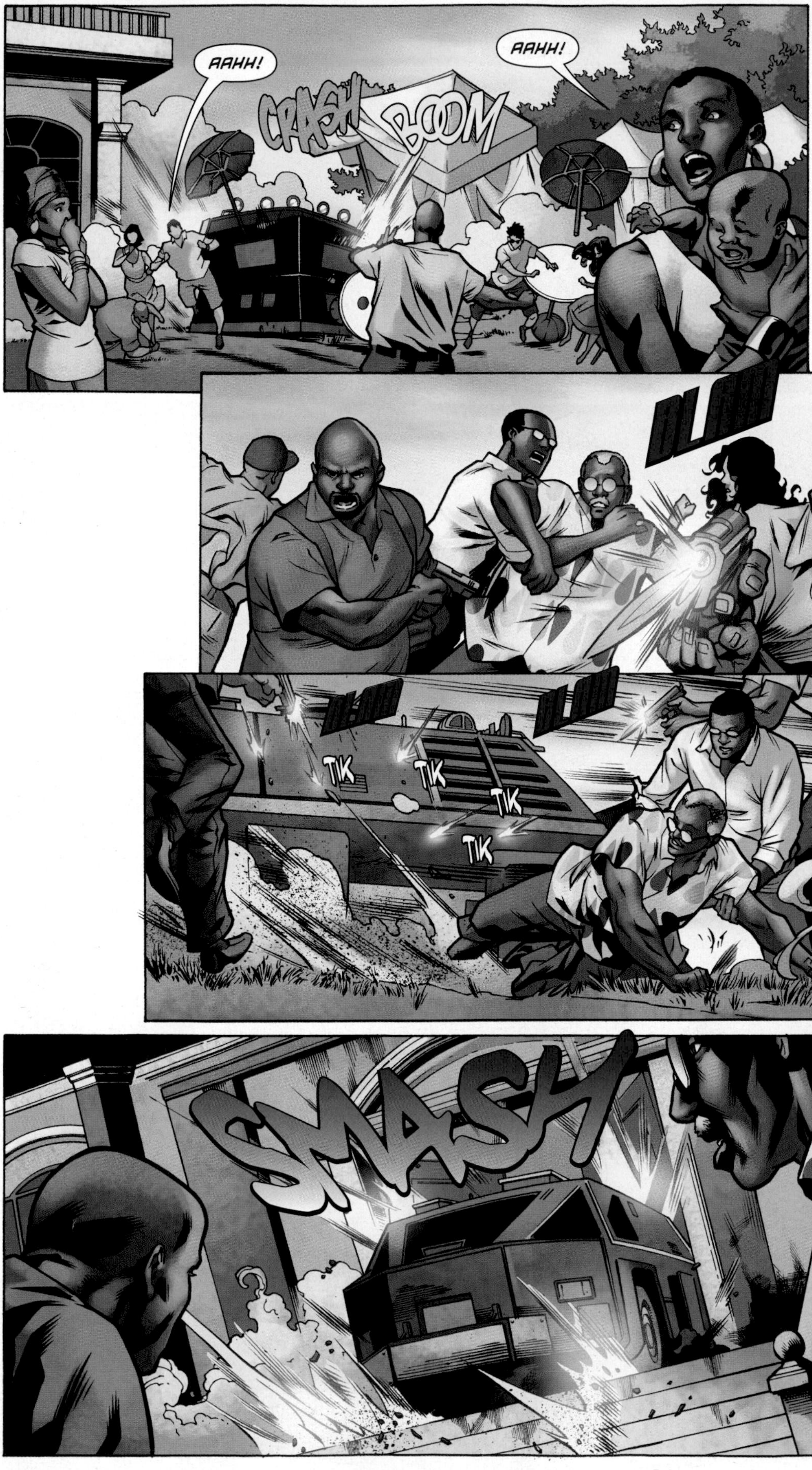
AAHH!
CRASH
BOOM
AAHH!
TIK
TIK
TIK
TIK
SMASH

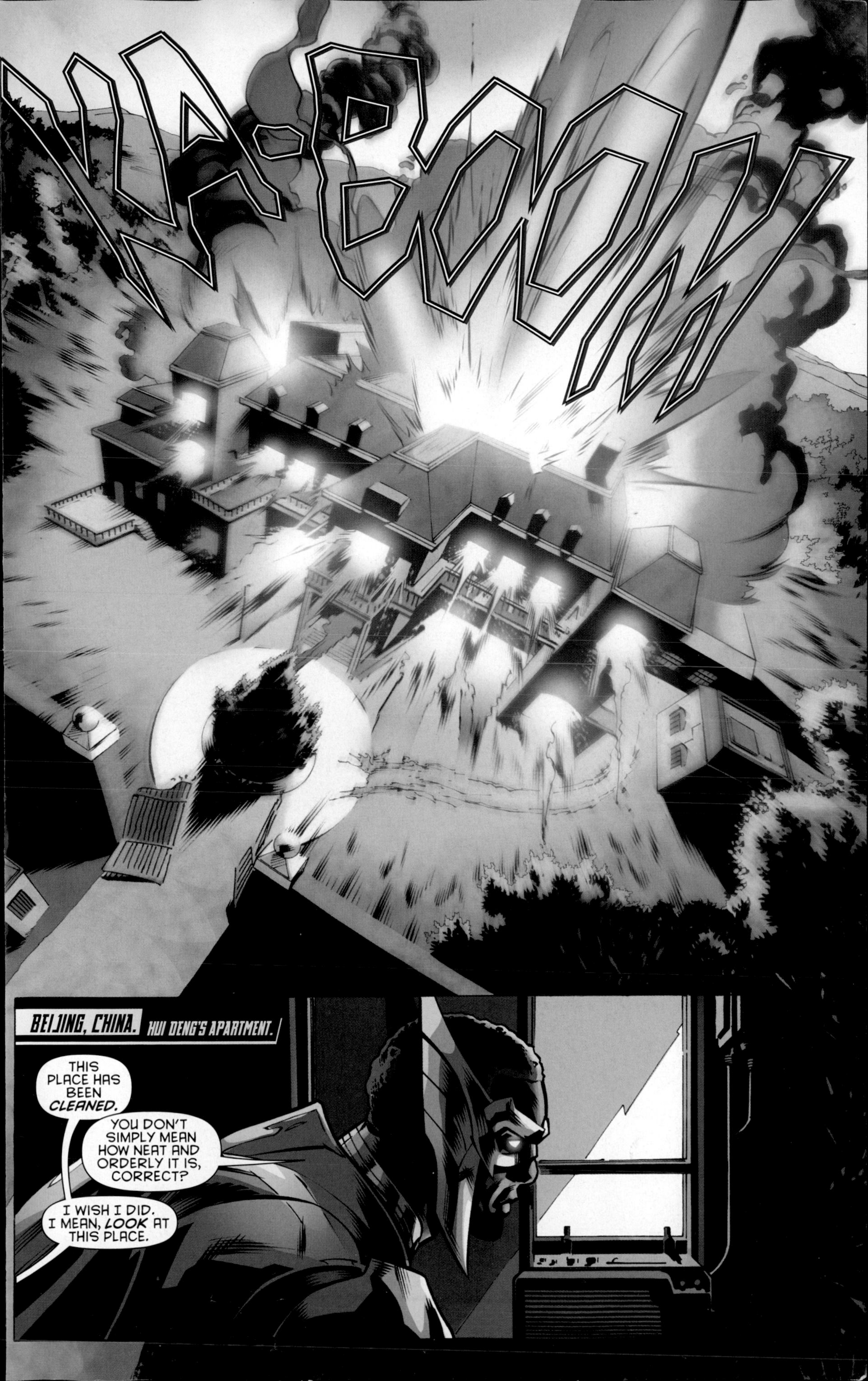
BEIJING, CHINA.
HUI DENG'S APARTMENT.
THIS PLACE HAS BEEN CLEANED.
YOU DON'T SIMPLY MEAN HOW NEAT AND ORDERLY IT IS, CORRECT?
I WISH I DID. I MEAN, LOOK AT THIS PLACE.

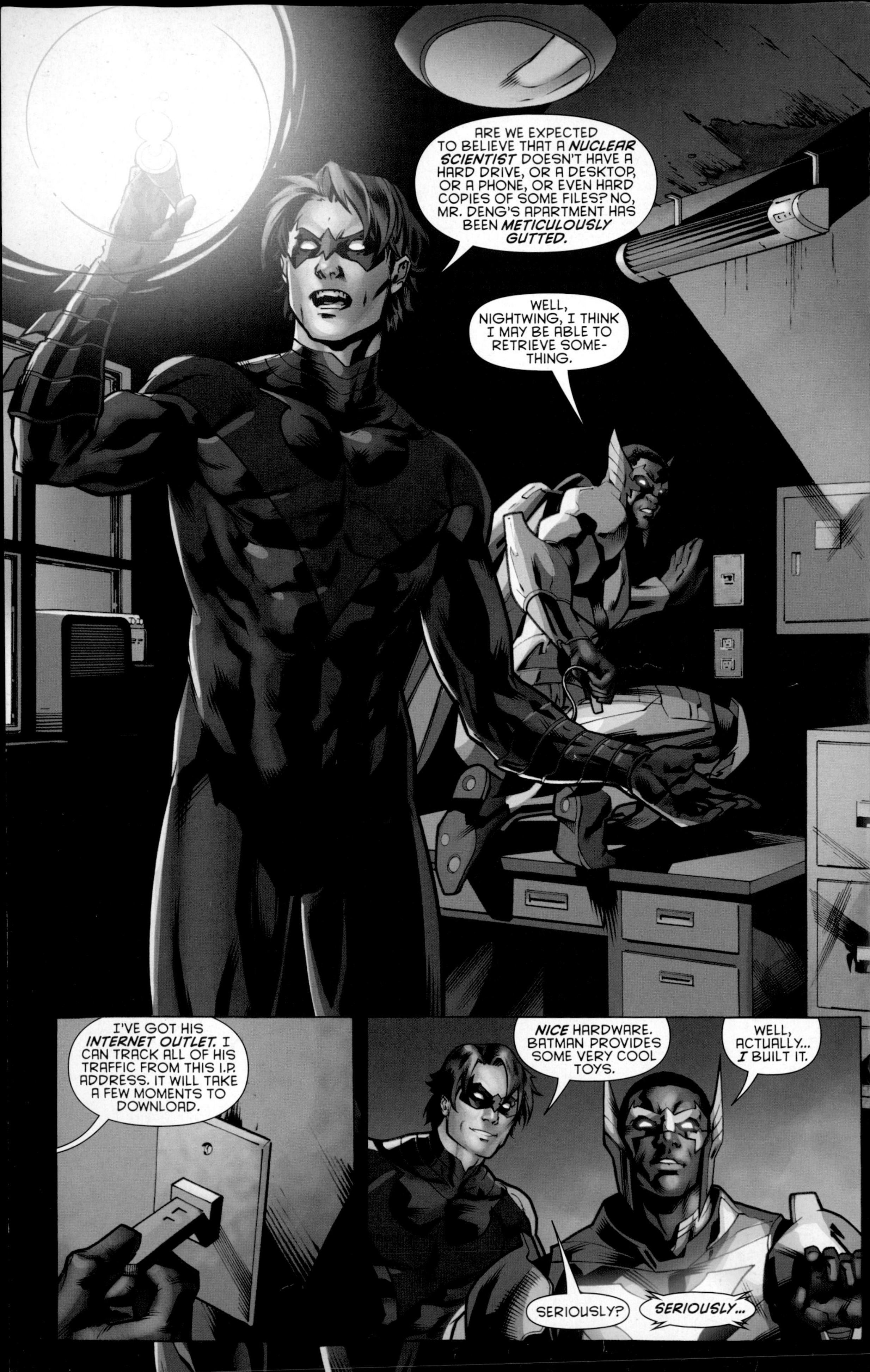
ARE WE EXPECTED TO BELIEVE THAT A NUCLEAR SCIENTIST DOESN'T HAVE A HARD DRIVE, OR A DESKTOP, OR A PHONE, OR EVEN HARD COPIES OF SOME FILES? NO, MR. DENG'S APARTMENT HAS BEEN METICULOUSLY GUTTED.
WELL, NIGHTWING, I THINK I MAY BE ABLE TO RETRIEVE SOME-THING.
I'VE GOT HIS INTERNET OUTLET. I CAN TRACK ALL OF HIS TRAFFIC FROM THIS I.P. ADDRESS. IT WILL TAKE A FEW MOMENTS TO DOWNLOAD.
NICE HARDWARE. BATMAN PROVIDES SOME VERY COOL TOYS.
WELL, ACTUALLY... I BUILT IT.
SERIOUSLY?
SERIOUSLY...

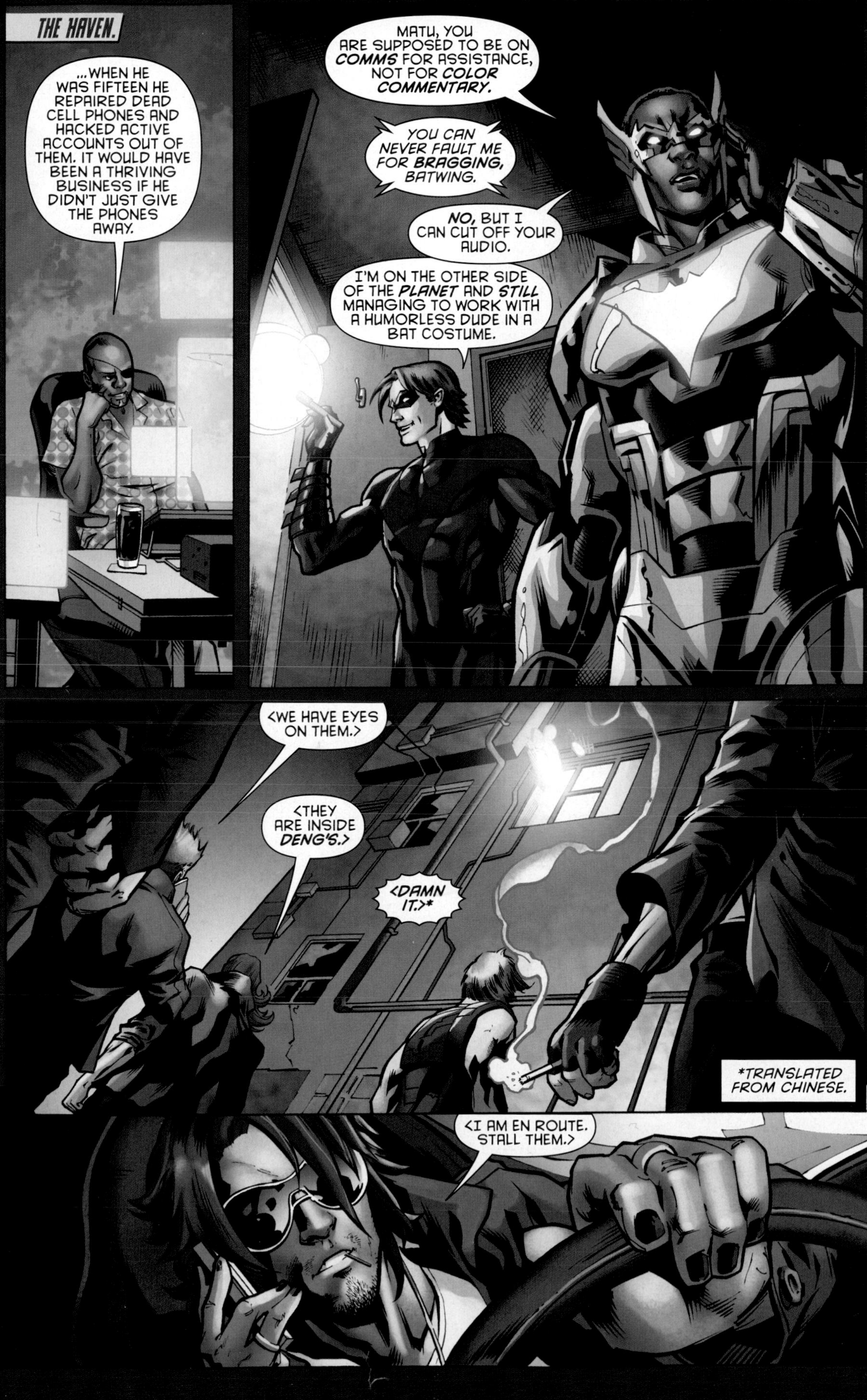
THE HAVEN.
...WHEN HE WAS FIFTEEN HE REPAIRED DEAD CELL PHONES AND HACKED ACTIVE ACCOUNTS OUT OF THEM. IT WOULD HAVE BEEN A THRIVING BUSINESS IF HE DIDN'T JUST GIVE THE PHONES AWAY.
MATU, YOU ARE SUPPOSED TO BE ON COMMS FOR ASSISTANCE, NOT FOR COLOR COMMENTARY.
YOU CAN NEVER FAULT ME FOR BRAGGING, BATWING.
NO, BUT I CAN CUT OFF YOUR AUDIO.
I'M ON THE OTHER SIDE OF THE PLANET AND STILL MANAGING TO WORK WITH A HUMORLESS DUDE IN A BAT COSTUME.
<WE HAVE EYES ON THEM.>
<THEY ARE INSIDE DENG'S.>
<DAMN IT.>*
*TRANSLATED FROM CHINESE.
<I AM EN ROUTE. STALL THEM.>

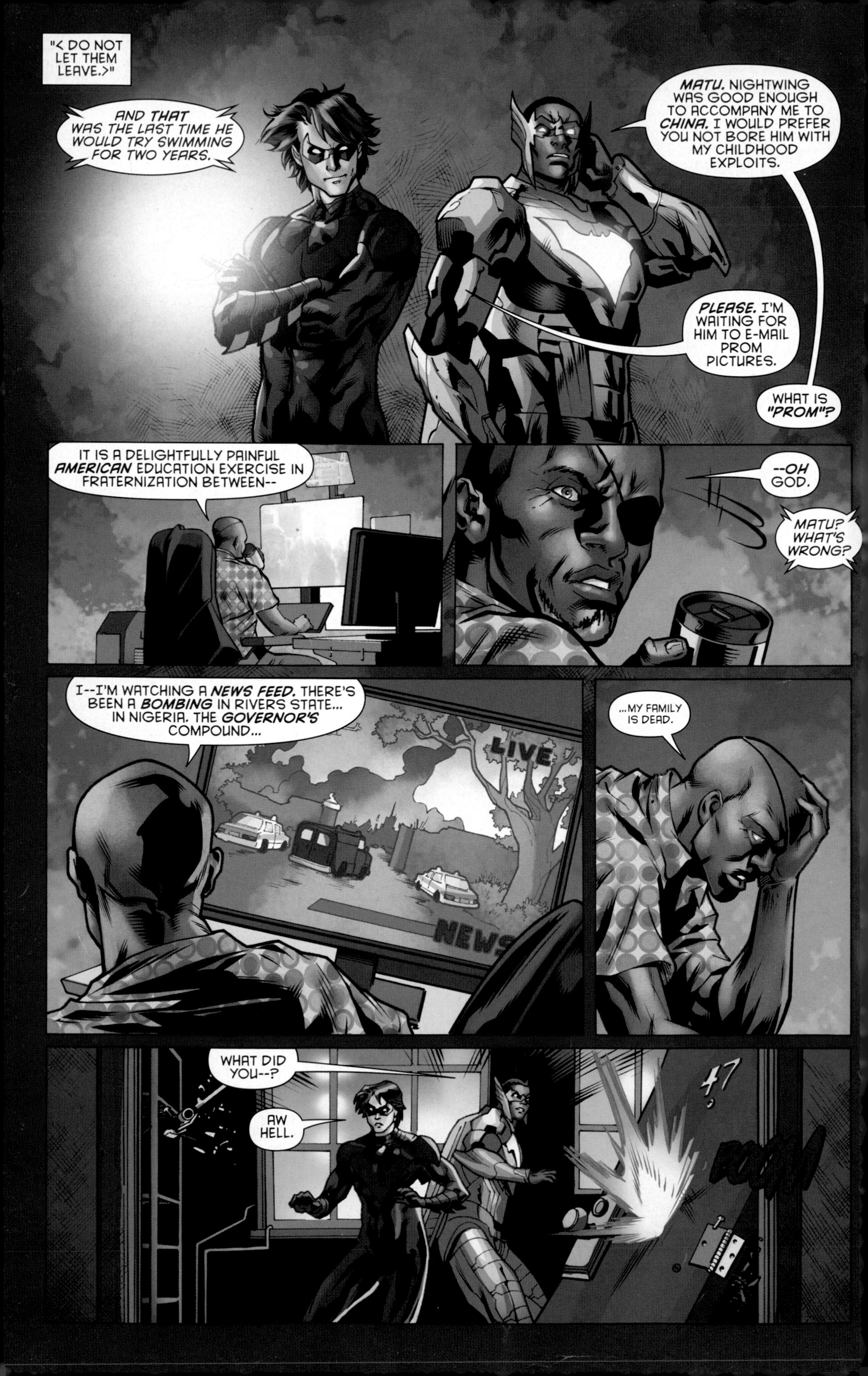
"< DO NOT LET THEM LEAVE.>"
AND THAT WAS THE LAST TIME HE WOULD TRY SWIMMING FOR TWO YEARS.
MATU. NIGHTWING WAS GOOD ENOUGH TO ACCOMPANY ME TO CHINA. I WOULD PREFER YOU NOT BORE HIM WITH MY CHILDHOOD EXPLOITS.
PLEASE. I'M WAITING FOR HIM TO E-MAIL PROM PICTURES.
WHAT IS "PROM"?
IT IS A DELIGHTFULLY PAINFUL AMERICAN EDUCATION EXERCISE IN FRATERNIZATION BETWEEN--
--OH GOD.
MATU? WHAT'S WRONG?
I--I'M WATCHING A NEWS FEED. THERE'S BEEN A BOMBING IN RIVERS STATE... IN NIGERIA. THE GOVERNOR'S COMPOUND...
LIVE
NEWS
...MY FAMILY IS DEAD.
WHAT DID YOU--?
AW HELL.
47

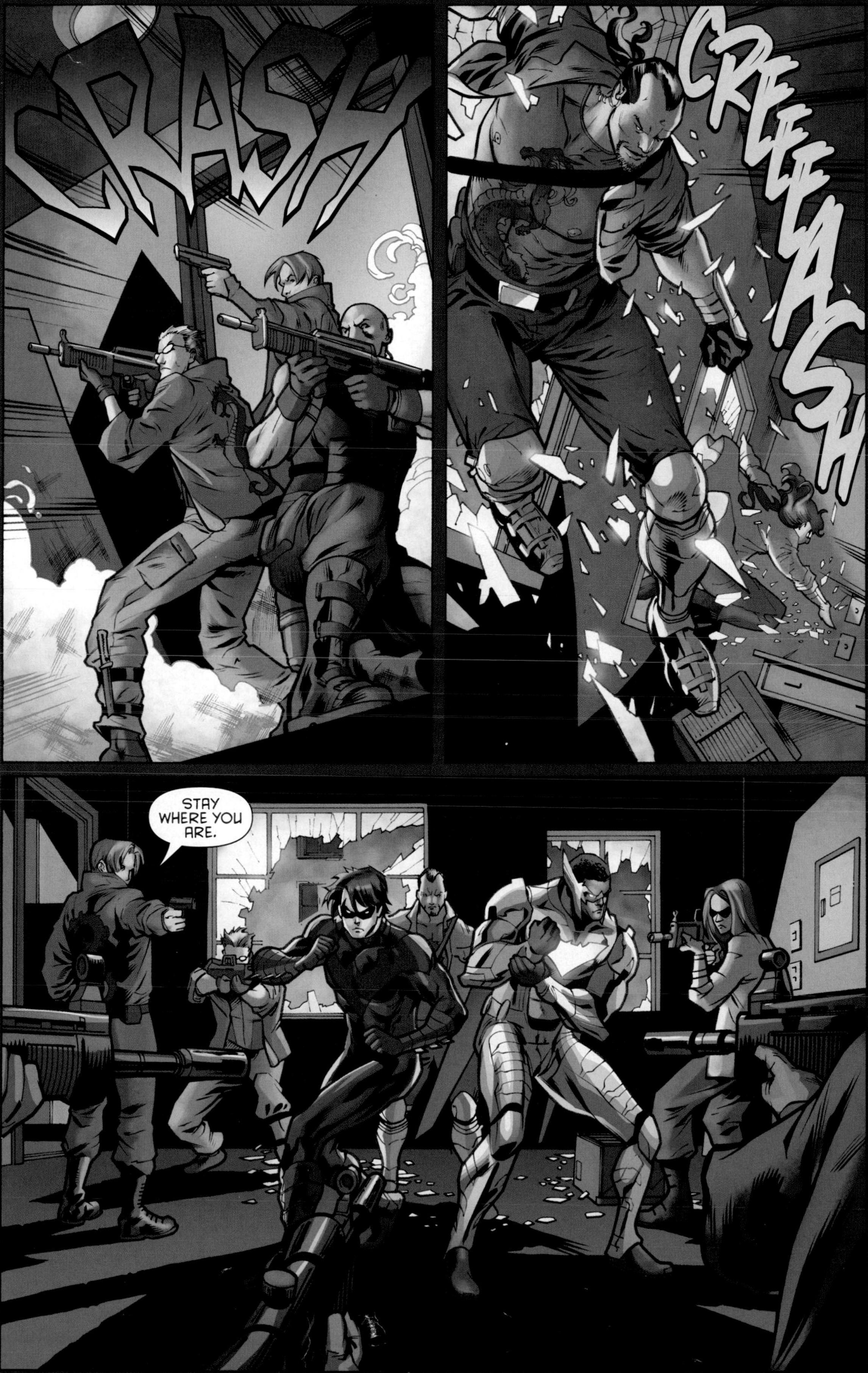
CRASH
CREEEASH
STAY WHERE YOU ARE.

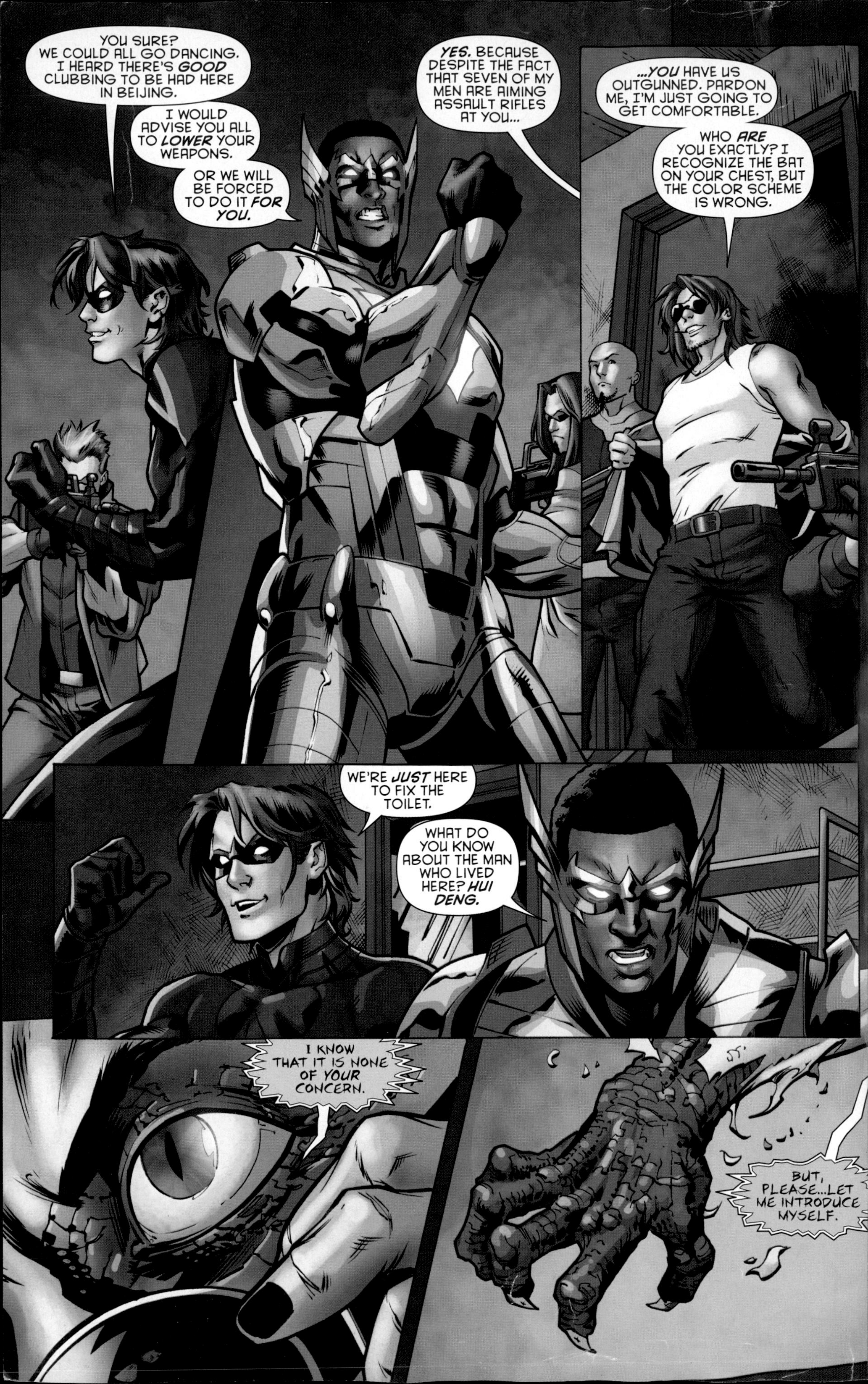
YOU SURE? WE COULD ALL GO DANCING. I HEARD THERE'S GOOD CLUBBING TO BE HAD HERE IN BEIJING.
I WOULD ADVISE YOU ALL TO LOWER YOUR WEAPONS.
OR WE WILL BE FORCED TO DO IT FOR YOU.
YES. BECAUSE DESPITE THE FACT THAT SEVEN OF MY MEN ARE AIMING ASSAULT RIFLES AT YOU...
...YOU HAVE US OUTGUNNED. PARDON ME, I'M JUST GOING TO GET COMFORTABLE.
WHO ARE YOU EXACTLY? I RECOGNIZE THE BAT ON YOUR CHEST, BUT THE COLOR SCHEME IS WRONG.
WE'RE JUST HERE TO FIX THE TOILET.
WHAT DO YOU KNOW ABOUT THE MAN WHO LIVED HERE? HUI DENG.
I KNOW THAT IT IS NONE OF YOUR CONCERN.
BUT, PLEASE...LET ME INTRODUCE MYSELF.

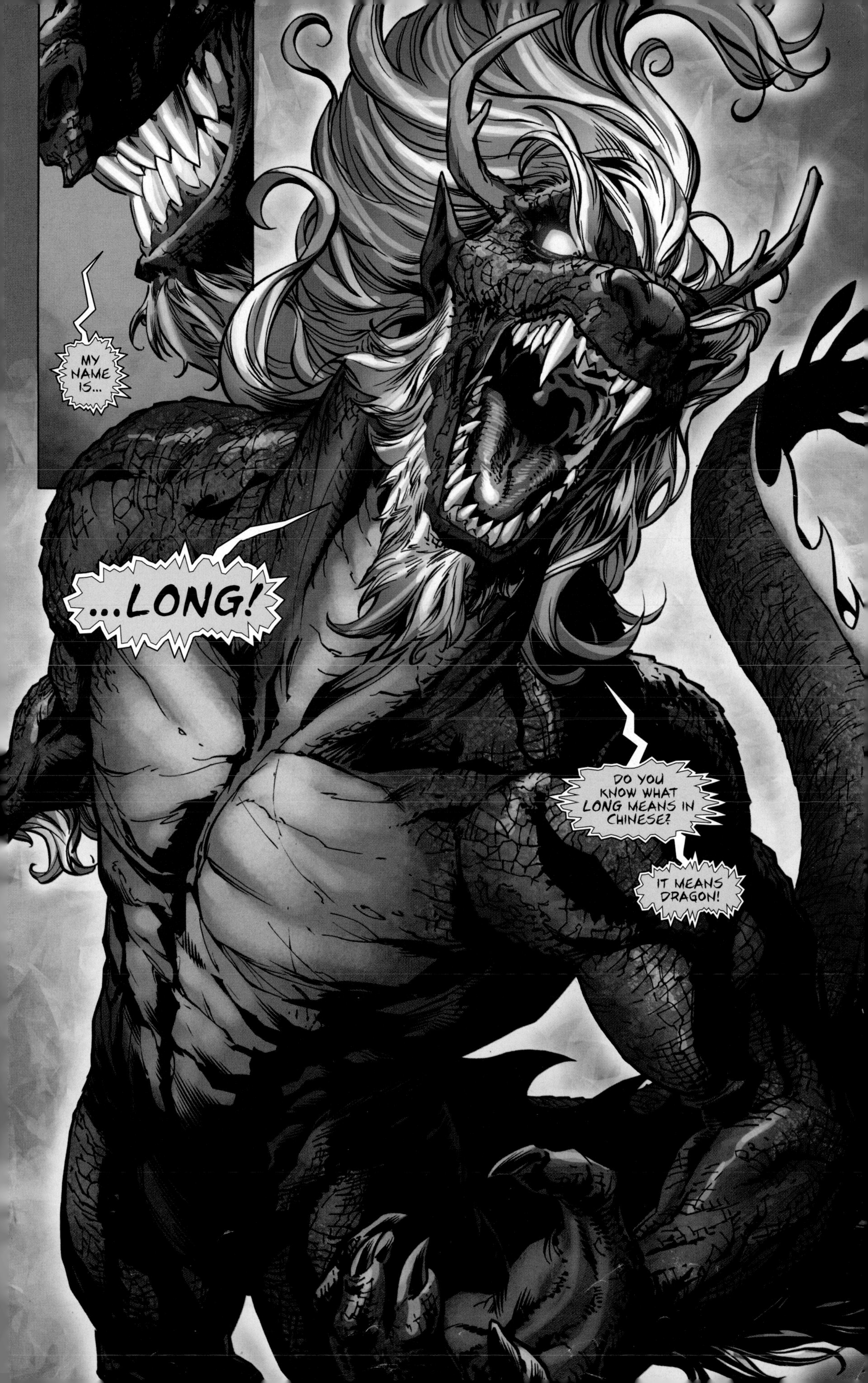
MY NAME IS...
...LONG!
DO YOU KNOW WHAT LONG MEANS IN CHINESE?
IT MEANS DRAGON!

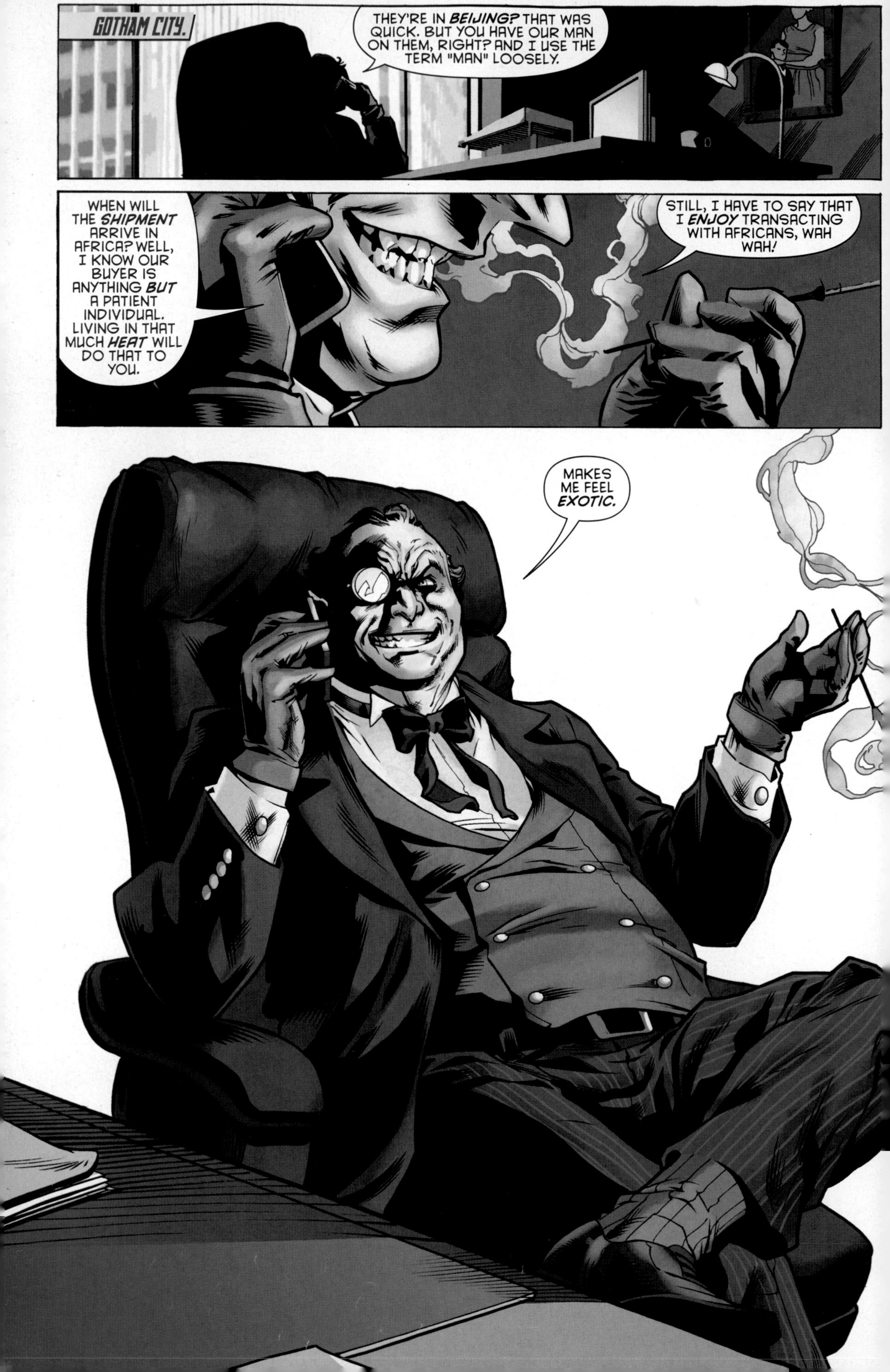
GOTHAM CITY.
THEY'RE IN BEIJING? THAT WAS QUICK. BUT YOU HAVE OUR MAN ON THEM, RIGHT? AND I USE THE TERM "MAN" LOOSELY.
WHEN WILL THE SHIPMENT ARRIVE IN AFRICA? WELL, I KNOW OUR BUYER IS ANYTHING BUT A PATIENT INDIVIDUAL. LIVING IN THAT MUCH HEAT WILL DO THAT TO YOU.
STILL, I HAVE TO SAY THAT I ENJOY TRANSACTING WITH AFRICANS, WAH WAH!
MAKES ME FEEL EXOTIC.

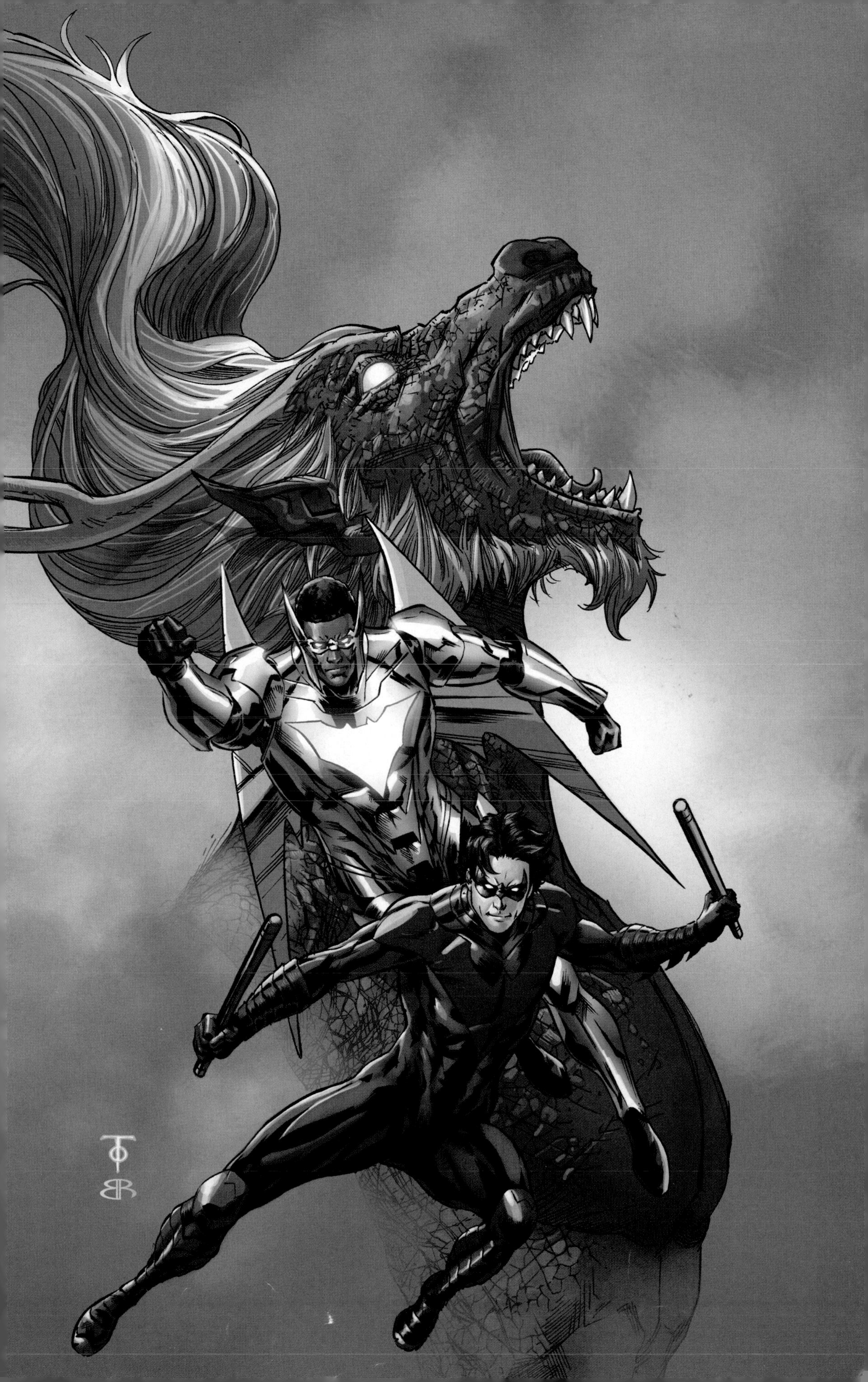

I SEE ALL OF IT NOW

JUDD WINICK writer **MARCUS TO** penciller **RYAN WINN & LE BEAU UNDERWOOD** inkers cover art by **MARCUS TO & BRIAN REBER**

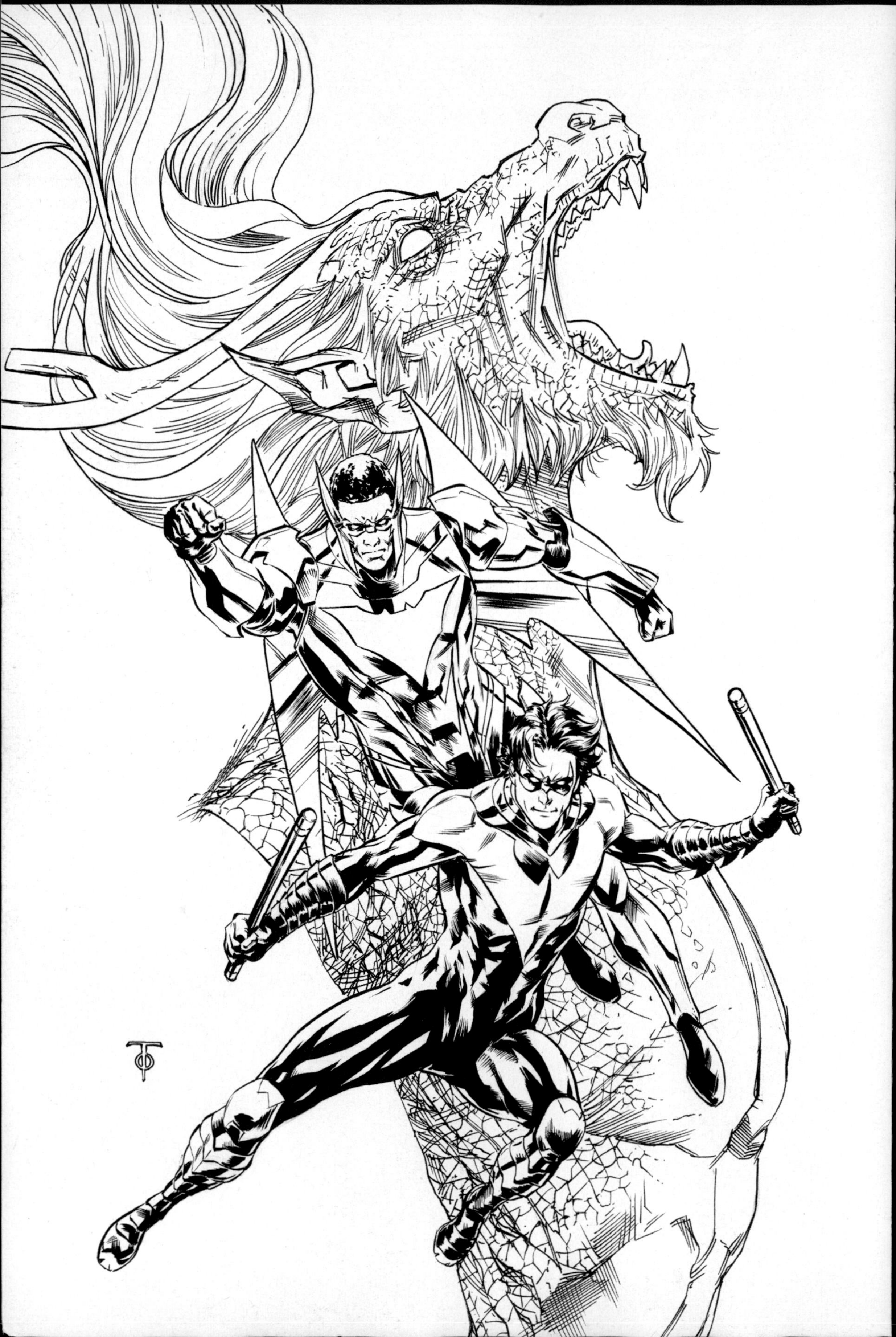

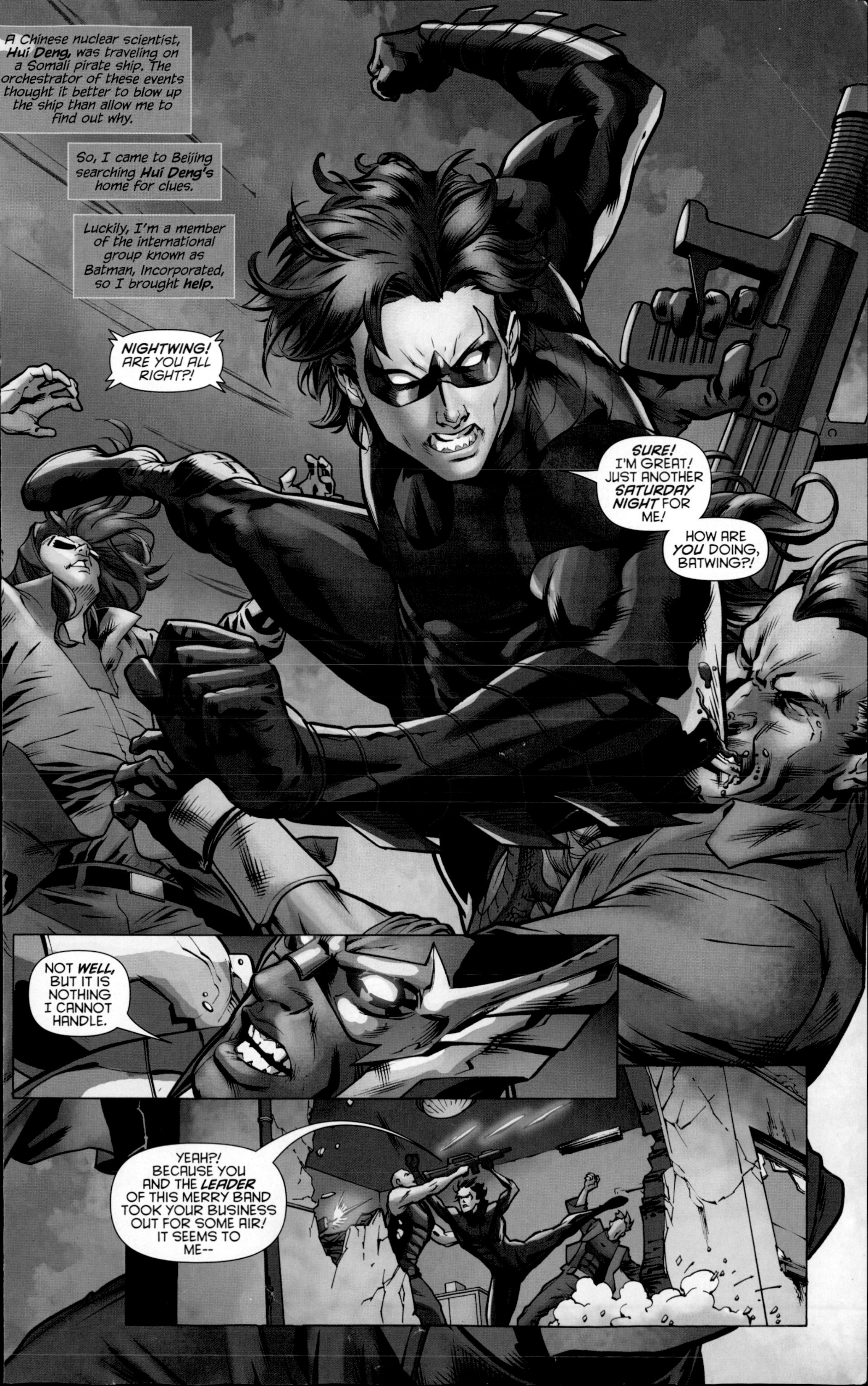
A Chinese nuclear scientist, Hui Deng, was traveling on a Somali pirate ship. The orchestrator of these events thought it better to blow up the ship than allow me to find out why.
So, I came to Beijing searching Hui Deng's home for clues.
Luckily, I'm a member of the international group known as Batman, Incorporated, so I brought help.
NIGHTWING! ARE YOU ALL RIGHT?!
SURE! I'M GREAT! JUST ANOTHER SATURDAY NIGHT FOR ME!
HOW ARE YOU DOING, BATWING?!
NOT WELL, BUT IT IS NOTHING I CANNOT HANDLE.
YEAH?! BECAUSE YOU AND THE LEADER OF THIS MERRY BAND TOOK YOUR BUSINESS OUT FOR SOME AIR! IT SEEMS TO ME--

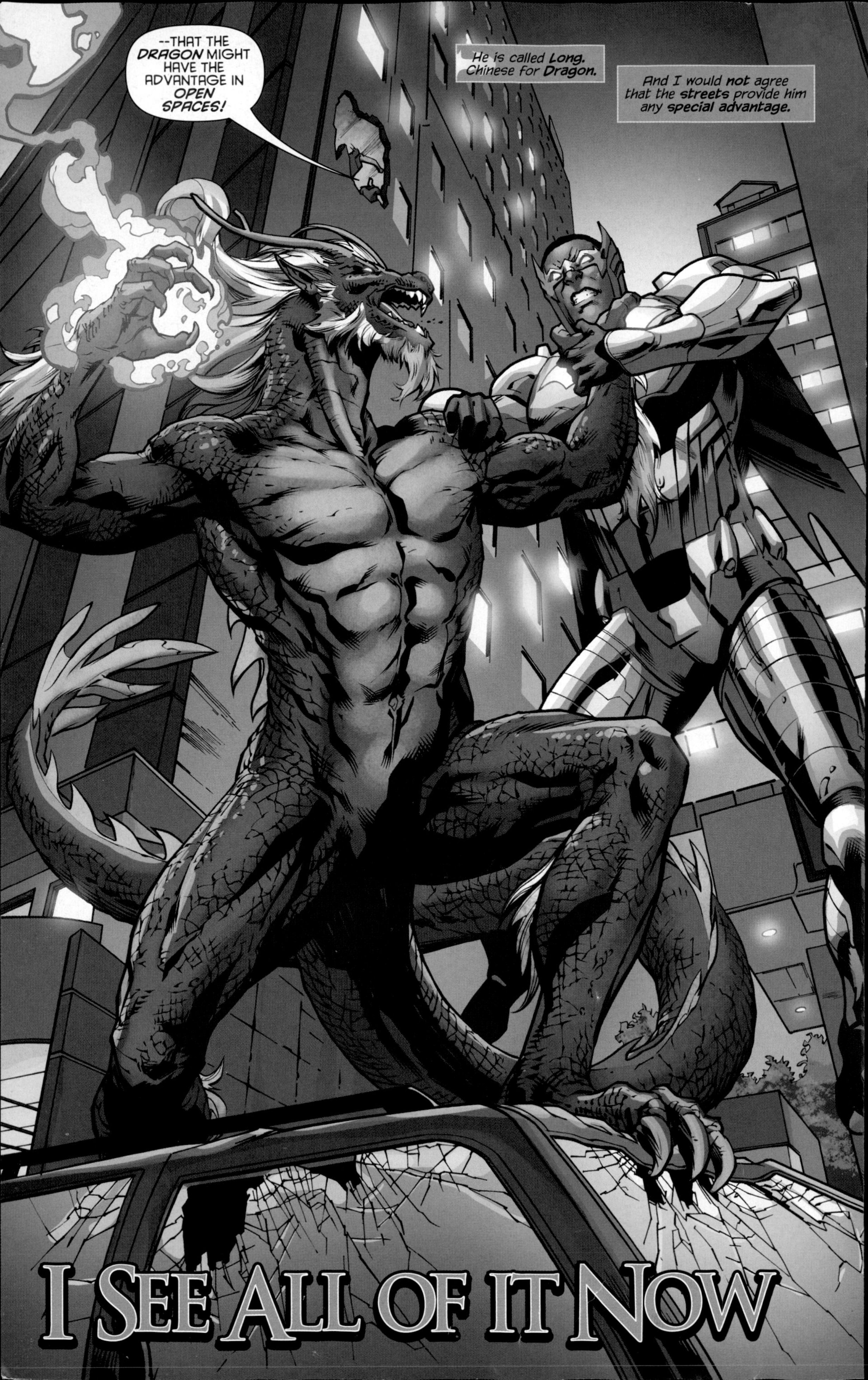
--THAT THE DRAGON MIGHT HAVE THE ADVANTAGE IN OPEN SPACES!
He is called Long. Chinese for Dragon.
And I would not agree that the streets provide him any special advantage.
I SEE ALL OF IT NOW

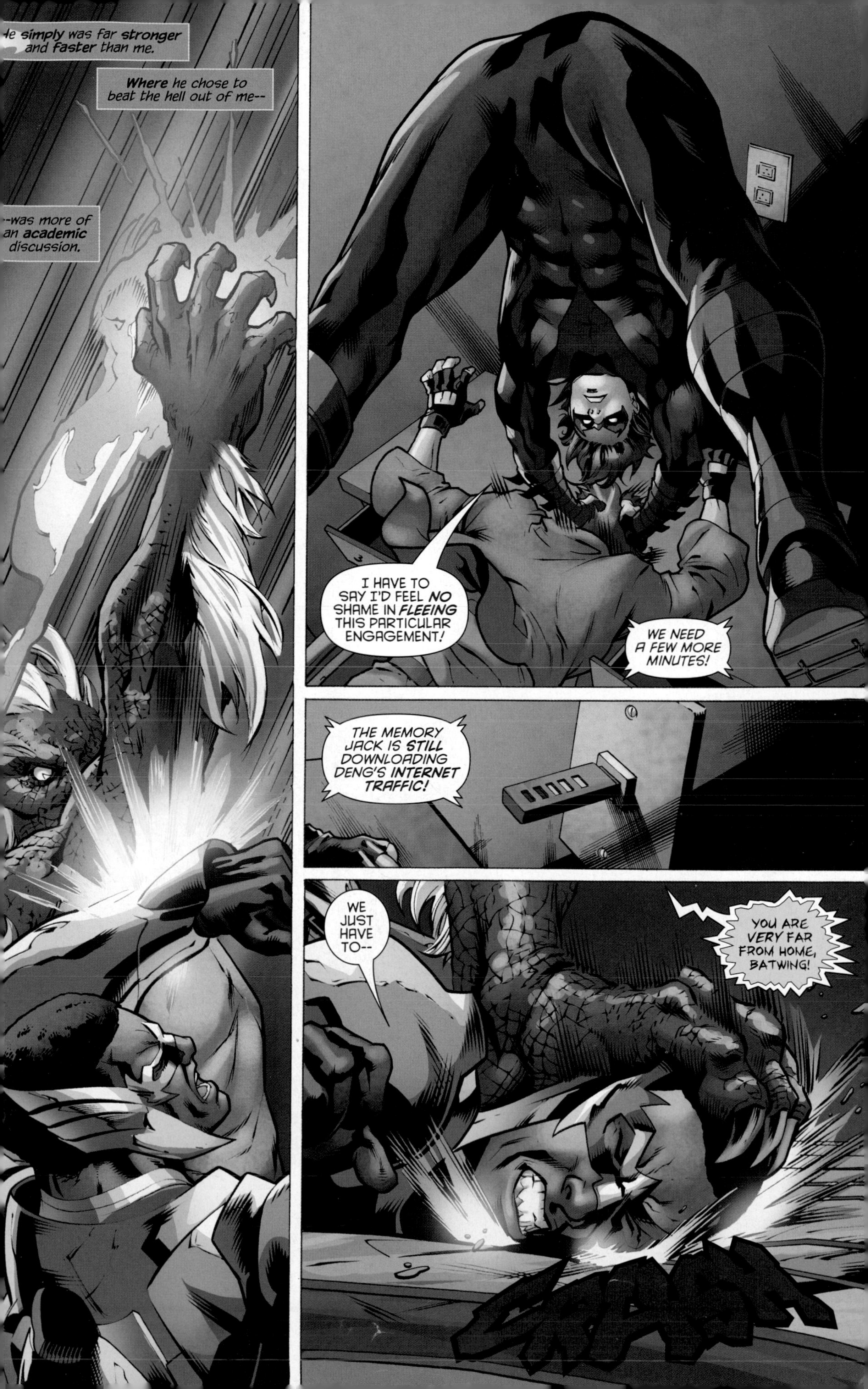

He simply was far stronger and faster than me.
Where he chose to beat the hell out of me--
--was more of an academic discussion.
I HAVE TO SAY I'D FEEL NO SHAME IN FLEEING THIS PARTICULAR ENGAGEMENT!
WE NEED A FEW MORE MINUTES!
THE MEMORY JACK IS STILL DOWNLOADING DENG'S INTERNET TRAFFIC!
WE JUST HAVE TO--
YOU ARE VERY FAR FROM HOME, BATWING!

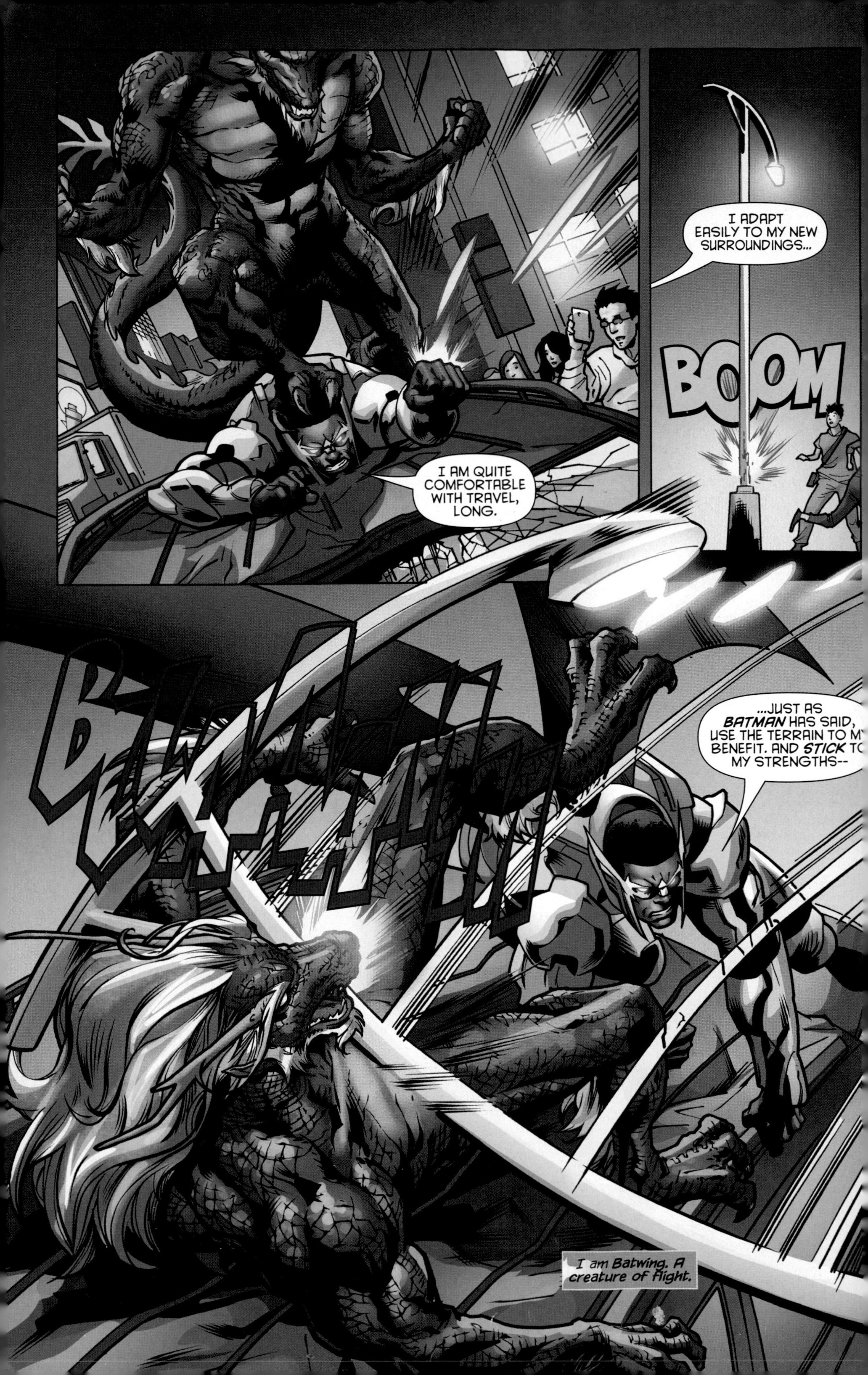
I AM QUITE COMFORTABLE WITH TRAVEL, LONG.
I ADAPT EASILY TO MY NEW SURROUNDINGS...
BOOM
...JUST AS BATMAN HAS SAID, USE THE TERRAIN TO MY BENEFIT. AND STICK TO MY STRENGTHS--
I am Batwing. A creature of flight.

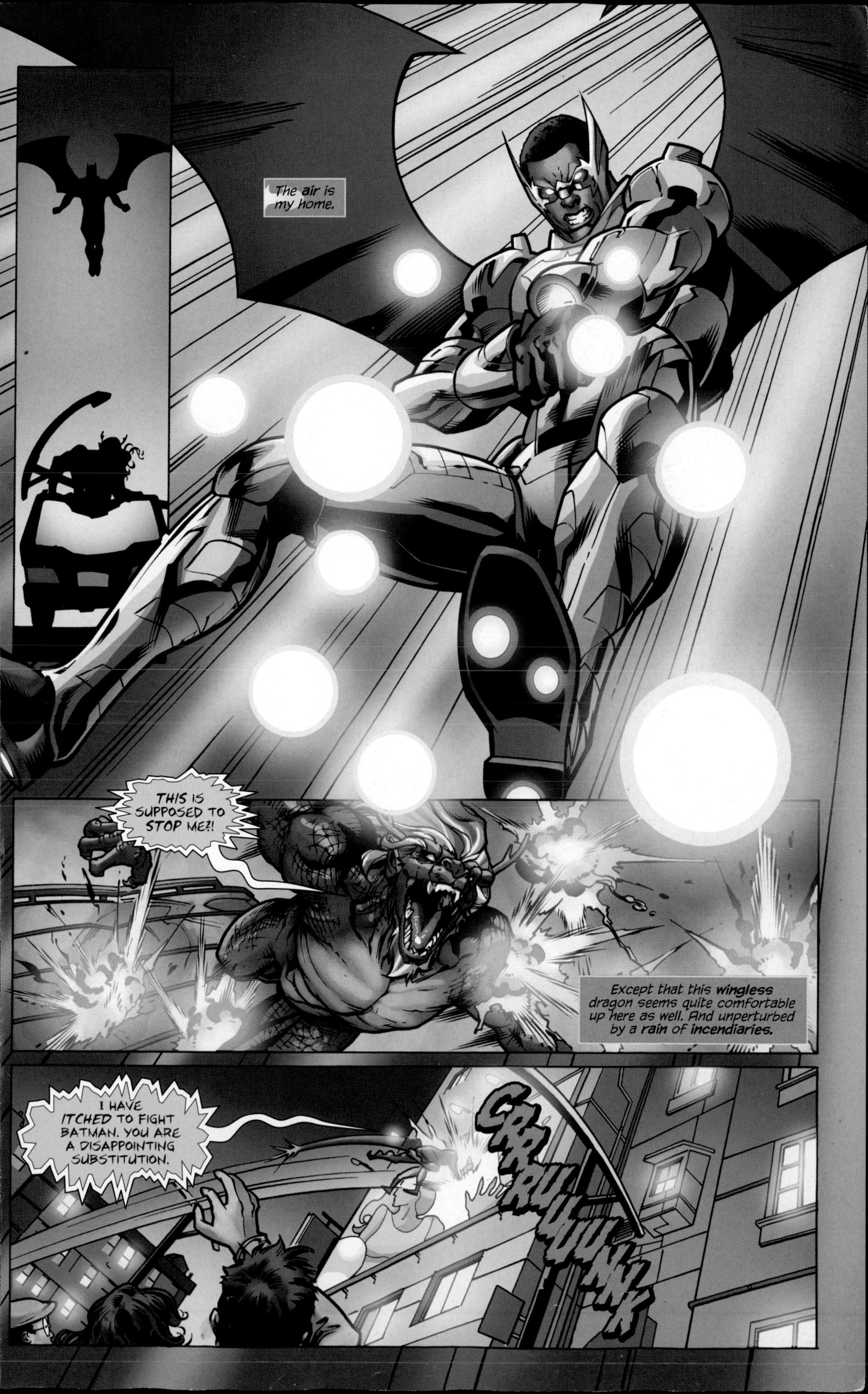
The air is my home.
THIS IS SUPPOSED TO STOP ME?!
Except that this wingless dragon seems quite comfortable up here as well. And unperturbed by a rain of incendiaries.
I HAVE ITCHED TO FIGHT BATMAN. YOU ARE A DISAPPOINTING SUBSTITUTION.
CRRRUUUNNK

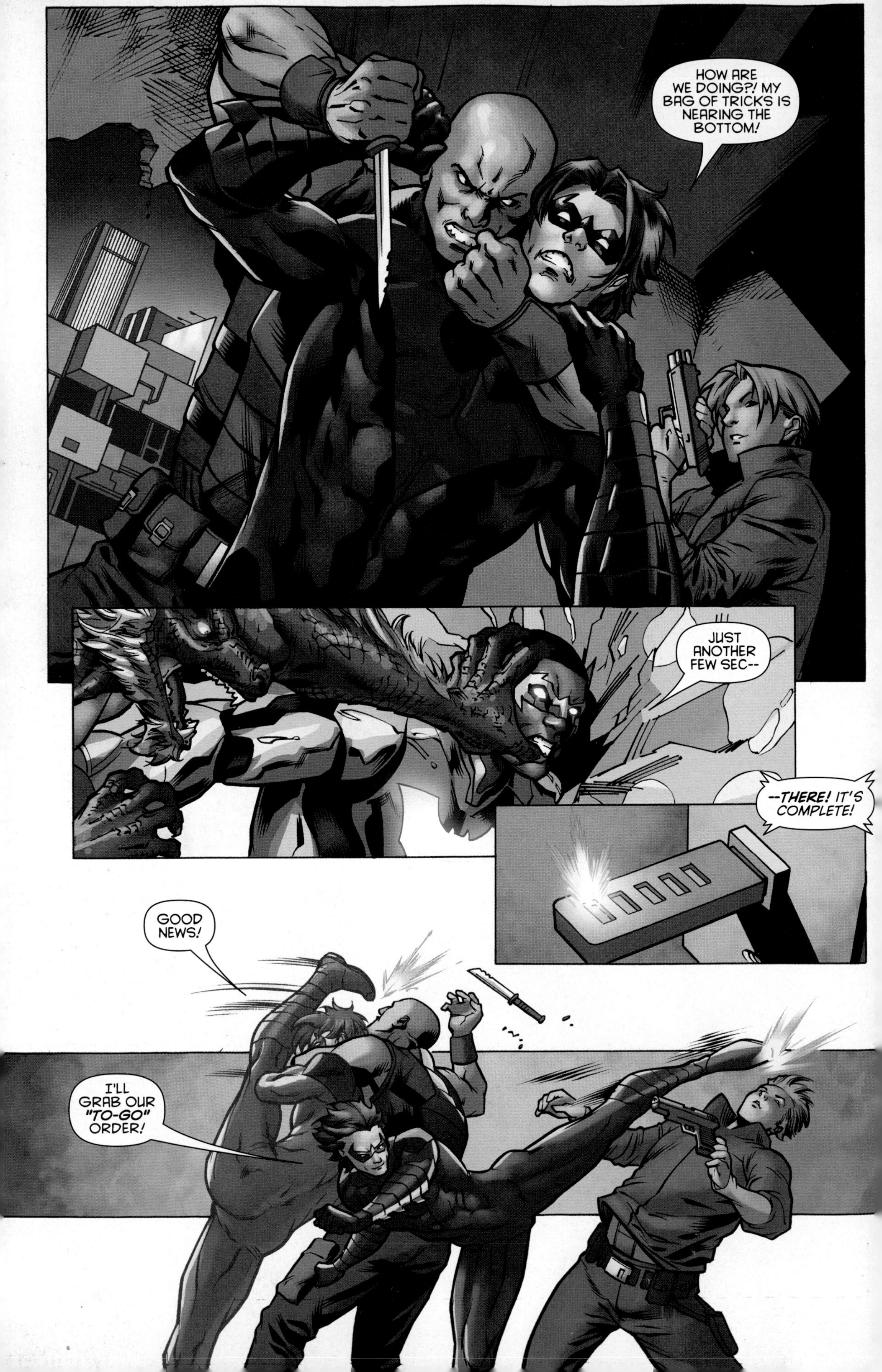
HOW ARE WE DOING?! MY BAG OF TRICKS IS NEARING THE BOTTOM!
JUST ANOTHER FEW SEC--
--THERE! IT'S COMPLETE!
GOOD NEWS!
I'LL GRAB OUR "TO-GO" ORDER!

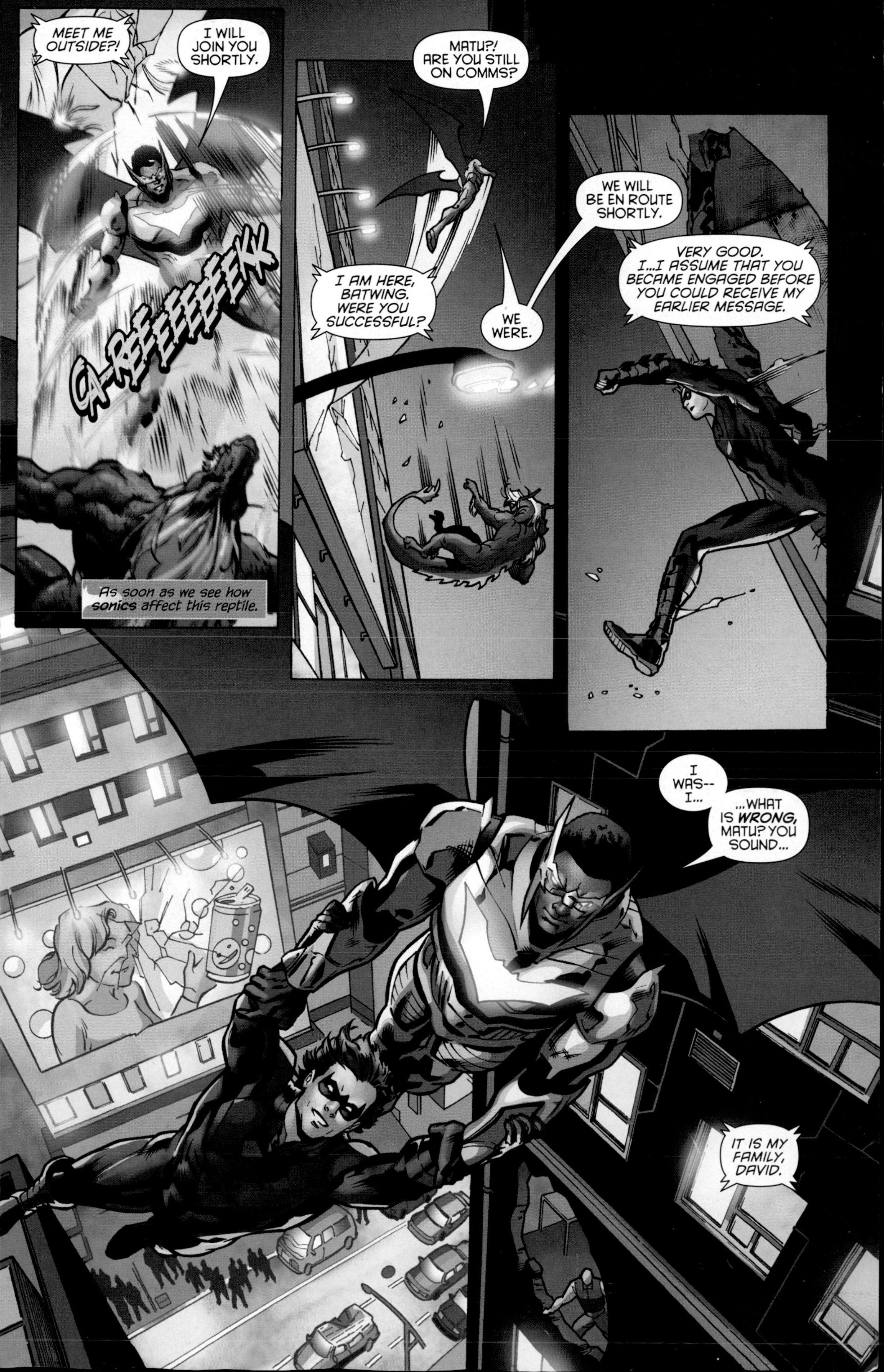
MEET ME OUTSIDE?!
I WILL JOIN YOU SHORTLY.
CA-REEEEEEEEK
As soon as we see how sonics affect this reptile.
MATU?! ARE YOU STILL ON COMMS?
I AM HERE, BATWING. WERE YOU SUCCESSFUL?
WE WERE.
WE WILL BE EN ROUTE SHORTLY.
VERY GOOD. I...I ASSUME THAT YOU BECAME ENGAGED BEFORE YOU COULD RECEIVE MY EARLIER MESSAGE.
I WAS-- I...
...WHAT IS WRONG, MATU? YOU SOUND...
IT IS MY FAMILY, DAVID.

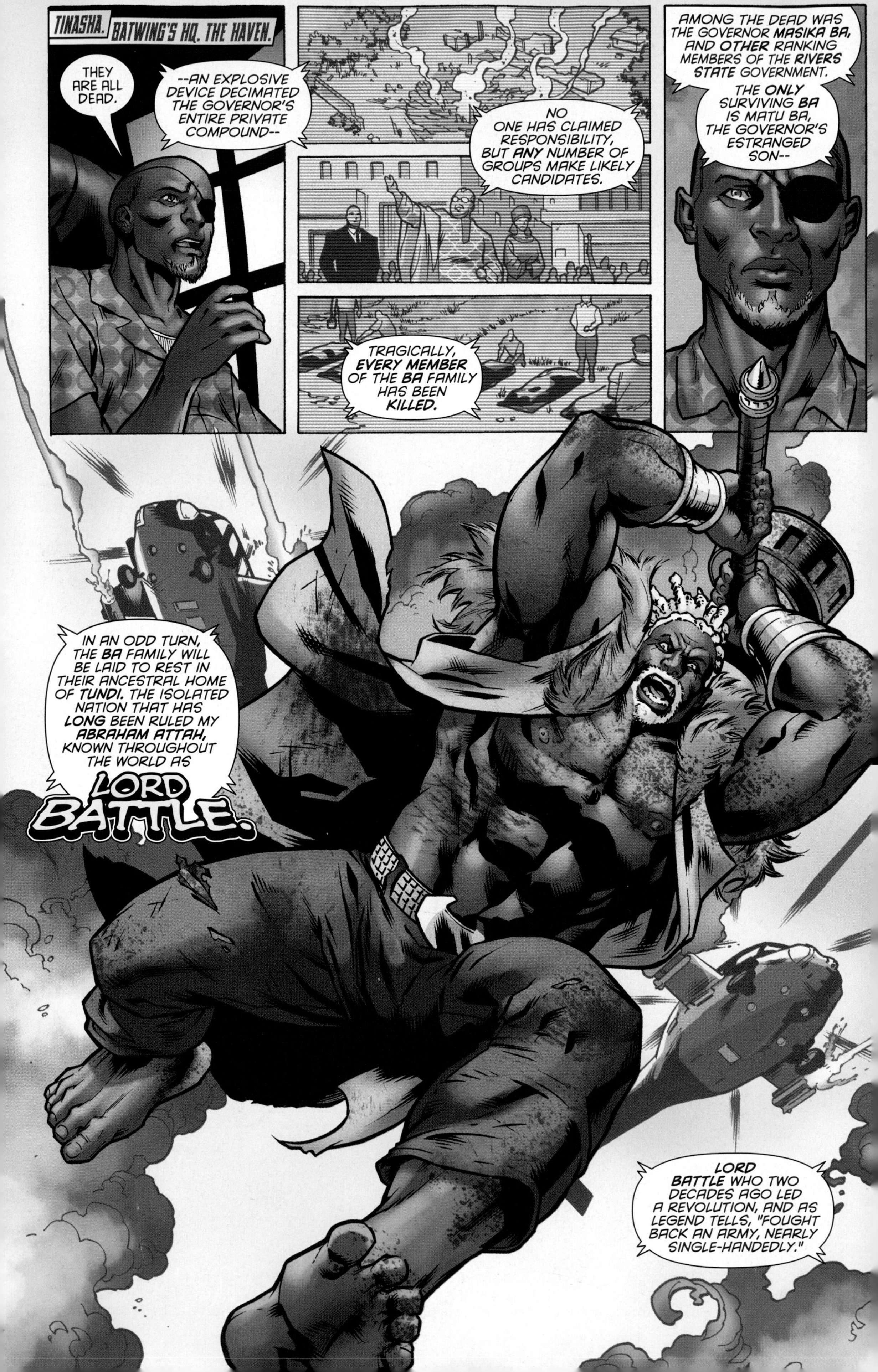
TINASHA. BATWING'S HQ. THE HAVEN.
THEY ARE ALL DEAD.
--AN EXPLOSIVE DEVICE DECIMATED THE GOVERNOR'S ENTIRE PRIVATE COMPOUND--
NO ONE HAS CLAIMED RESPONSIBILITY, BUT ANY NUMBER OF GROUPS MAKE LIKELY CANDIDATES.
TRAGICALLY, EVERY MEMBER OF THE BA FAMILY HAS BEEN KILLED.
AMONG THE DEAD WAS THE GOVERNOR MASIKA BA, AND OTHER RANKING MEMBERS OF THE RIVERS STATE GOVERNMENT.
THE ONLY SURVIVING BA IS MATU BA, THE GOVERNOR'S ESTRANGED SON--
IN AN ODD TURN, THE BA FAMILY WILL BE LAID TO REST IN THEIR ANCESTRAL HOME OF TUNDI. THE ISOLATED NATION THAT HAS LONG BEEN RULED MY ABRAHAM ATTAH, KNOWN THROUGHOUT THE WORLD AS
LORD BATTLE.
LORD BATTLE WHO TWO DECADES AGO LED A REVOLUTION, AND AS LEGEND TELLS, "FOUGHT BACK AN ARMY, NEARLY SINGLE-HANDEDLY."

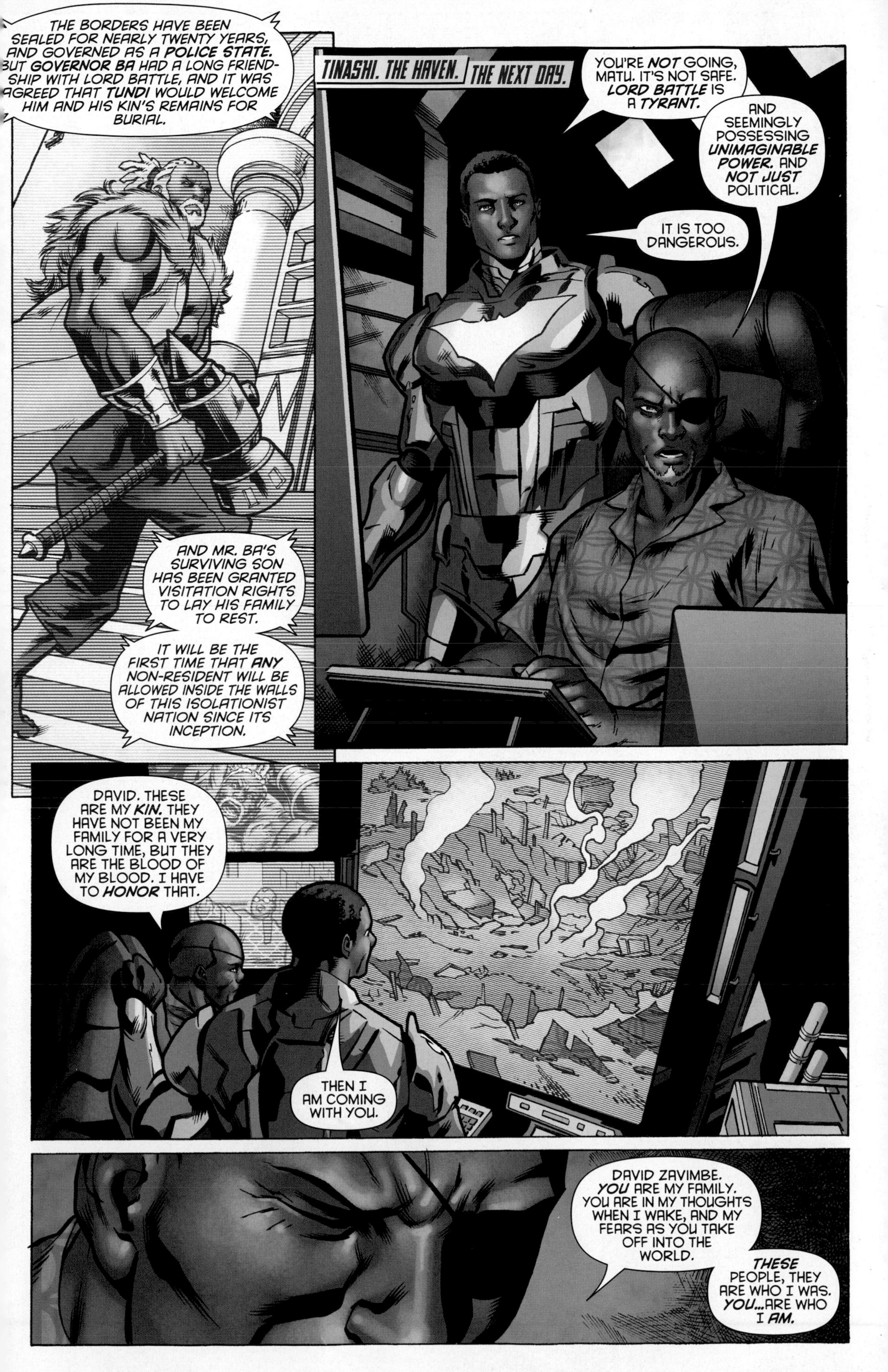
THE BORDERS HAVE BEEN SEALED FOR NEARLY TWENTY YEARS, AND GOVERNED AS A POLICE STATE. BUT GOVERNOR BA HAD A LONG FRIENDSHIP WITH LORD BATTLE, AND IT WAS AGREED THAT TUNDI WOULD WELCOME HIM AND HIS KIN'S REMAINS FOR BURIAL.
AND MR. BA'S SURVIVING SON HAS BEEN GRANTED VISITATION RIGHTS TO LAY HIS FAMILY TO REST.
IT WILL BE THE FIRST TIME THAT ANY NON-RESIDENT WILL BE ALLOWED INSIDE THE WALLS OF THIS ISOLATIONIST NATION SINCE ITS INCEPTION.
TINASHI. THE HAVEN.
THE NEXT DAY.
YOU'RE NOT GOING, MATU. IT'S NOT SAFE. LORD BATTLE IS A TYRANT.
AND SEEMINGLY POSSESSING UNIMAGINABLE POWER. AND NOT JUST POLITICAL.
IT IS TOO DANGEROUS.
DAVID. THESE ARE MY KIN. THEY HAVE NOT BEEN MY FAMILY FOR A VERY LONG TIME, BUT THEY ARE THE BLOOD OF MY BLOOD. I HAVE TO HONOR THAT.
THEN I AM COMING WITH YOU.
DAVID ZAVIMBE. YOU ARE MY FAMILY. YOU ARE IN MY THOUGHTS WHEN I WAKE, AND MY FEARS AS YOU TAKE OFF INTO THE WORLD.
THESE PEOPLE, THEY ARE WHO I WAS. YOU...ARE WHO I AM.

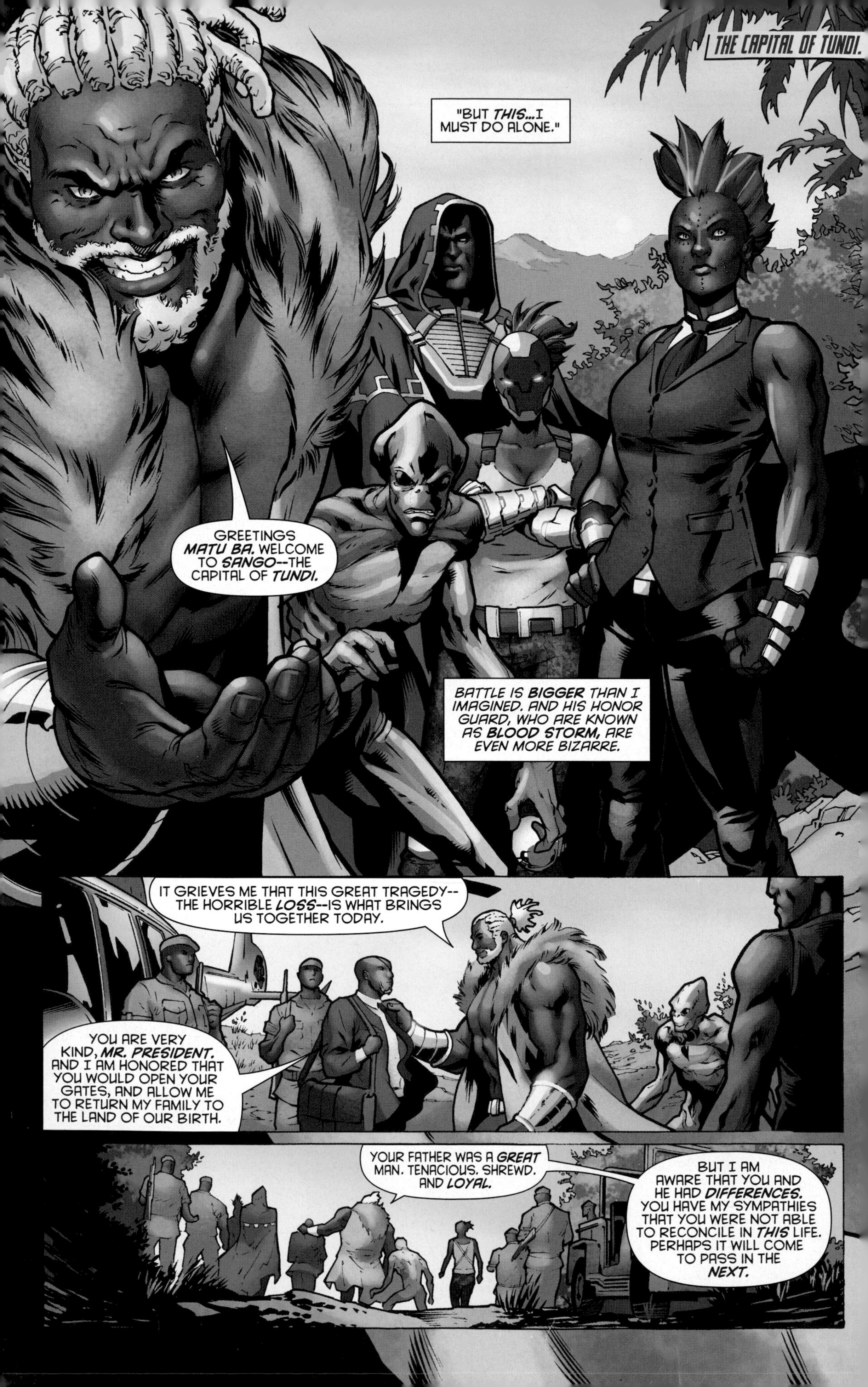
THE CAPITAL OF TUNDI.
"BUT THIS...I MUST DO ALONE."
GREETINGS MATU BA. WELCOME TO SANGO--THE CAPITAL OF TUNDI.
BATTLE IS BIGGER THAN I IMAGINED. AND HIS HONOR GUARD, WHO ARE KNOWN AS BLOOD STORM, ARE EVEN MORE BIZARRE.
IT GRIEVES ME THAT THIS GREAT TRAGEDY--THE HORRIBLE LOSS--IS WHAT BRINGS US TOGETHER TODAY.
YOU ARE VERY KIND, MR. PRESIDENT. AND I AM HONORED THAT YOU WOULD OPEN YOUR GATES, AND ALLOW ME TO RETURN MY FAMILY TO THE LAND OF OUR BIRTH.
YOUR FATHER WAS A GREAT MAN. TENACIOUS. SHREWD. AND LOYAL.
BUT I AM AWARE THAT YOU AND HE HAD DIFFERENCES. YOU HAVE MY SYMPATHIES THAT YOU WERE NOT ABLE TO RECONCILE IN THIS LIFE. PERHAPS IT WILL COME TO PASS IN THE NEXT.

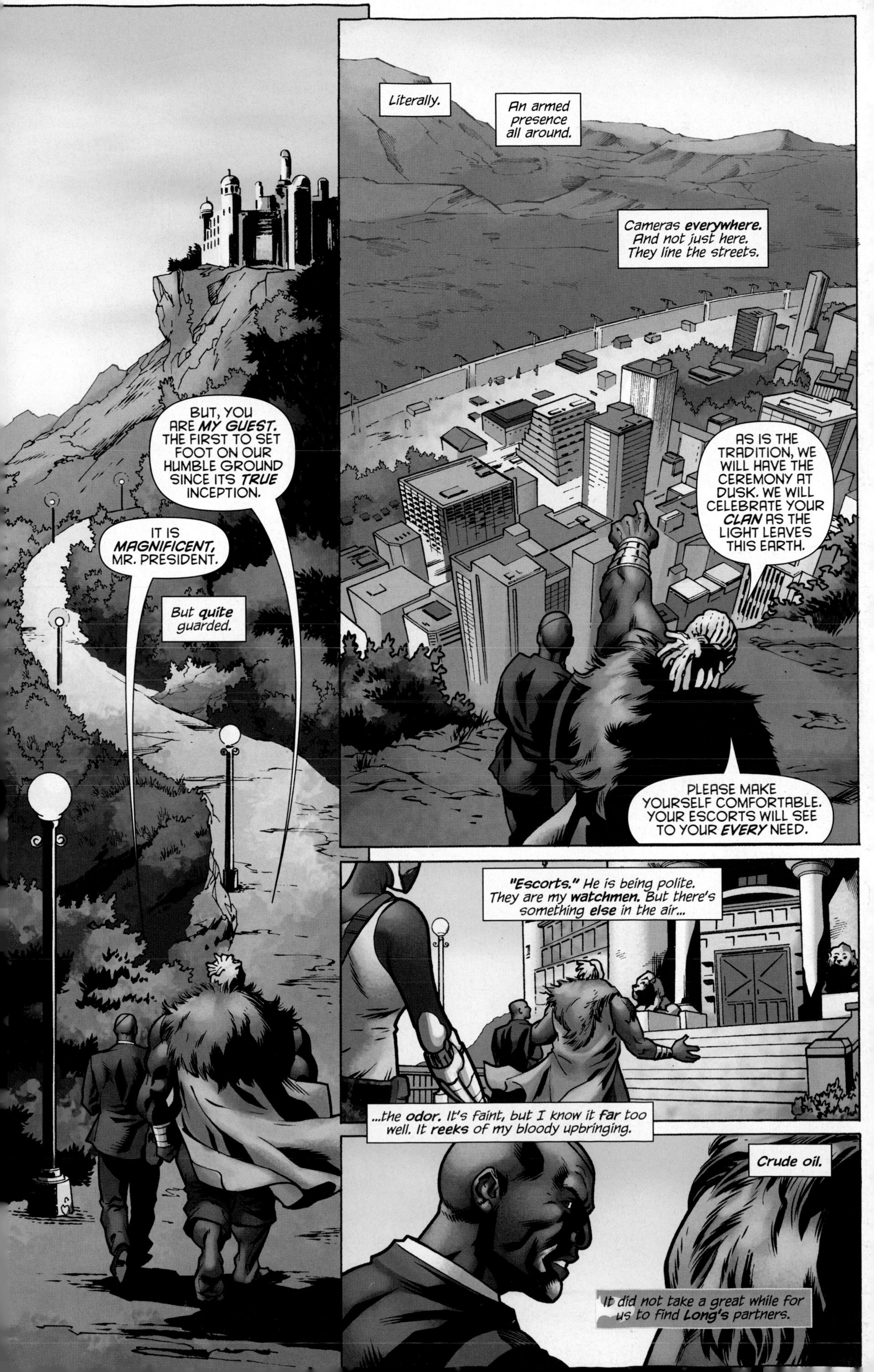

BUT, YOU ARE MY GUEST. THE FIRST TO SET FOOT ON OUR HUMBLE GROUND SINCE ITS TRUE INCEPTION.
IT IS MAGNIFICENT, MR. PRESIDENT.
But quite guarded.
Literally.
An armed presence all around.
Cameras everywhere. And not just here. They line the streets.
AS IS THE TRADITION, WE WILL HAVE THE CEREMONY AT DUSK. WE WILL CELEBRATE YOUR CLAN AS THE LIGHT LEAVES THIS EARTH.
PLEASE MAKE YOURSELF COMFORTABLE. YOUR ESCORTS WILL SEE TO YOUR EVERY NEED.
"Escorts." He is being polite. They are my watchmen. But there's something else in the air...
...the odor. It's faint, but I know it far too well. It reeks of my bloody upbringing.
Crude oil.
It did not take a great while for us to find Long's partners.

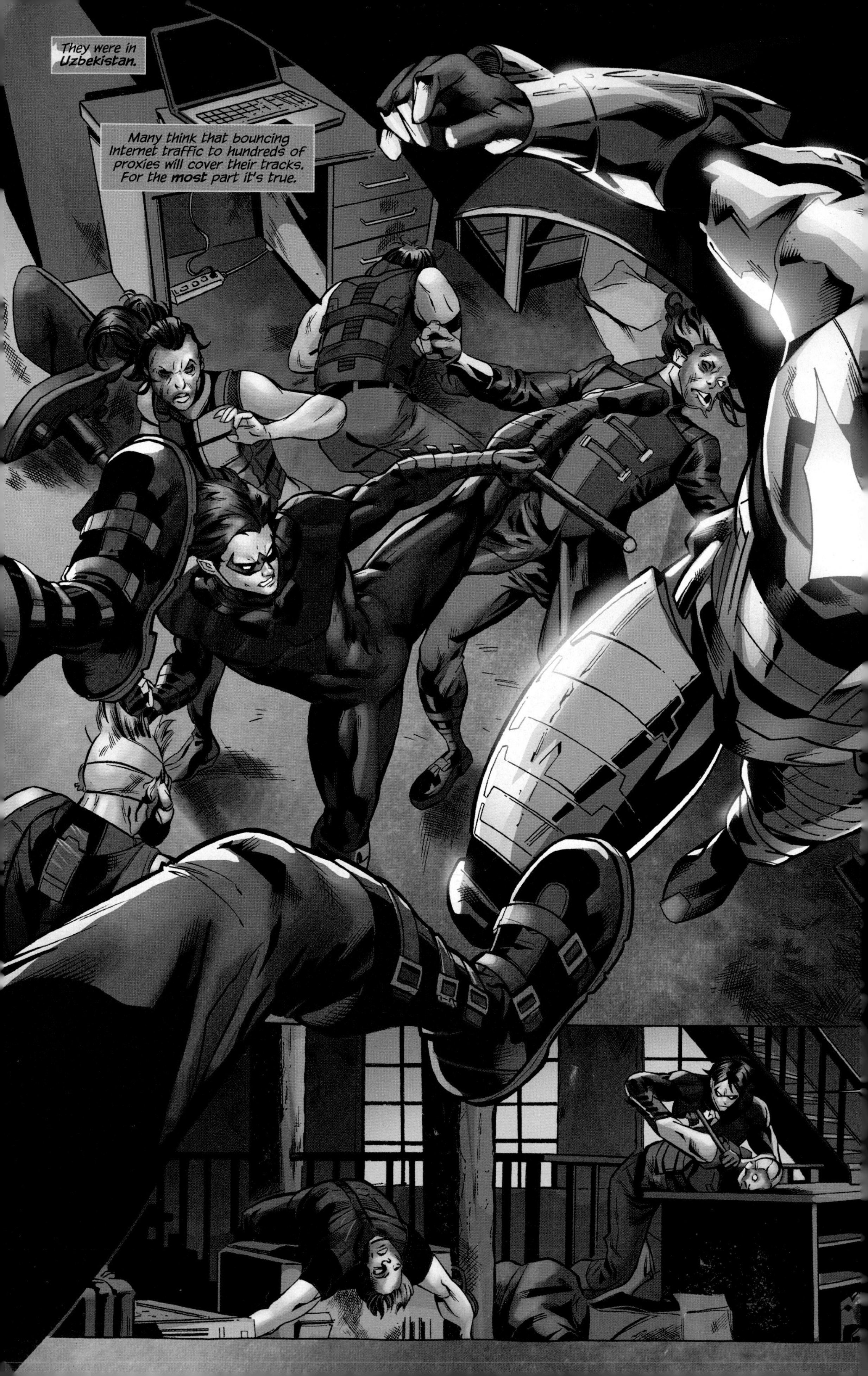
They were in Uzbekistan.
Many think that bouncing Internet traffic to hundreds of proxies will cover their tracks. For the most part it's true.

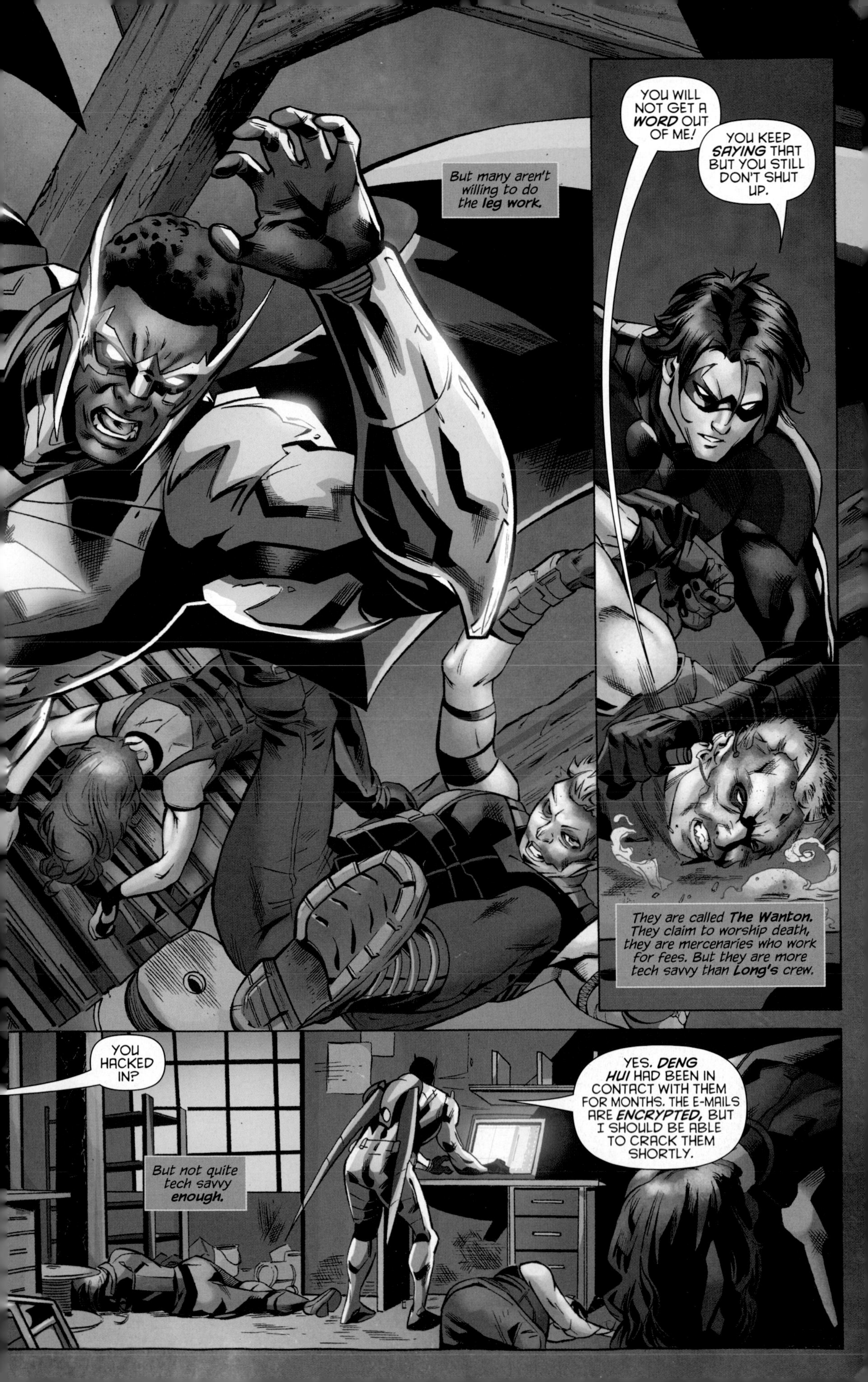

But many aren't willing to do the leg work.
YOU WILL NOT GET A WORD OUT OF ME!
YOU KEEP SAYING THAT BUT YOU STILL DON'T SHUT UP.
They are called The Wanton. They claim to worship death, they are mercenaries who work for fees. But they are more tech savvy than Long's crew.
YOU HACKED IN?
But not quite tech savvy enough.
YES. DENG HUI HAD BEEN IN CONTACT WITH THEM FOR MONTHS. THE E-MAILS ARE ENCRYPTED, BUT I SHOULD BE ABLE TO CRACK THEM SHORTLY.

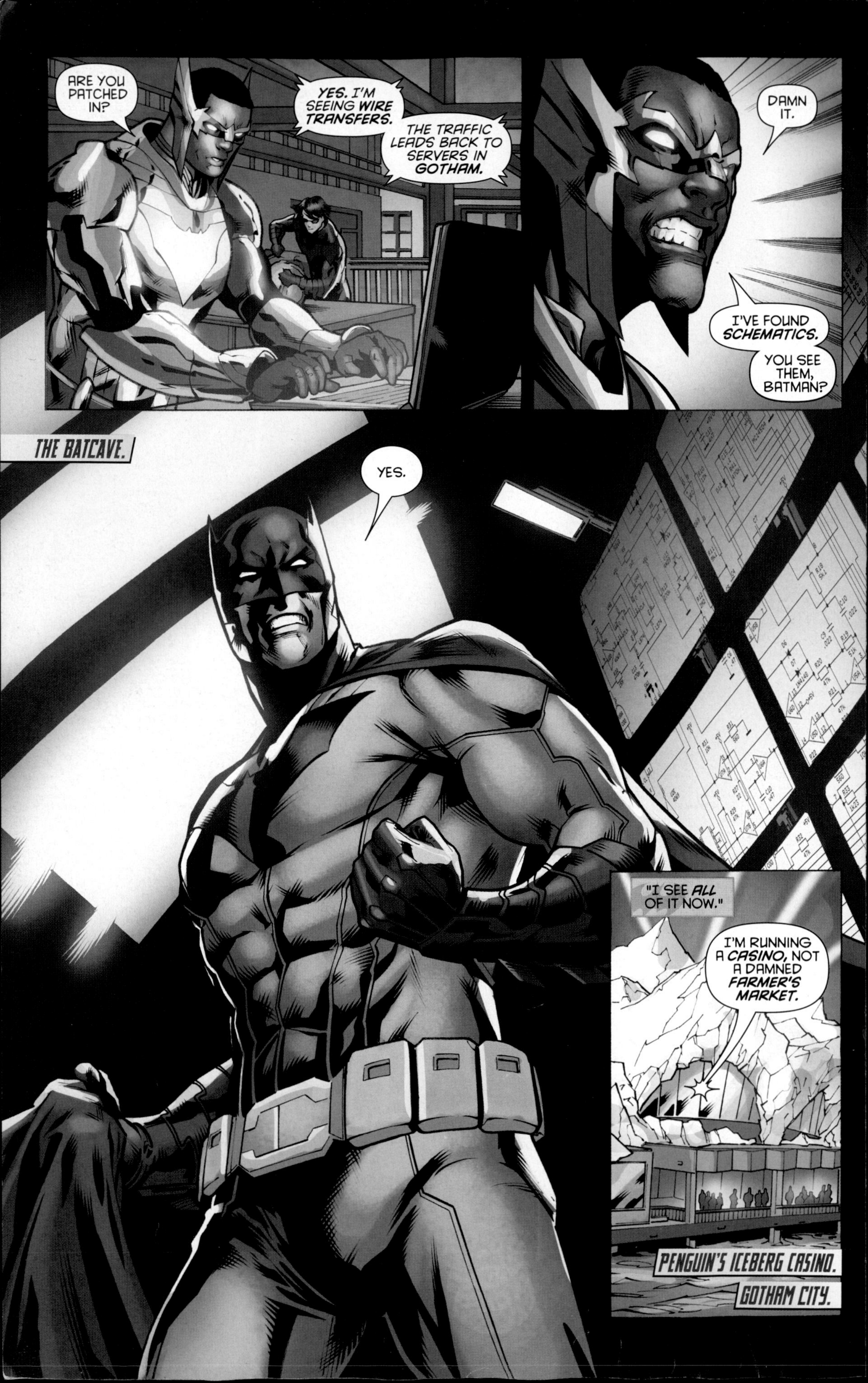
ARE YOU PATCHED IN?
YES. I'M SEEING WIRE TRANSFERS.
THE TRAFFIC LEADS BACK TO SERVERS IN GOTHAM.
DAMN IT.
I'VE FOUND SCHEMATICS.
YOU SEE THEM, BATMAN?
THE BATCAVE.
YES.
"I SEE ALL OF IT NOW."
I'M RUNNING A CASINO, NOT A DAMNED FARMER'S MARKET.
PENGUIN'S ICEBERG CASINO.
GOTHAM CITY.

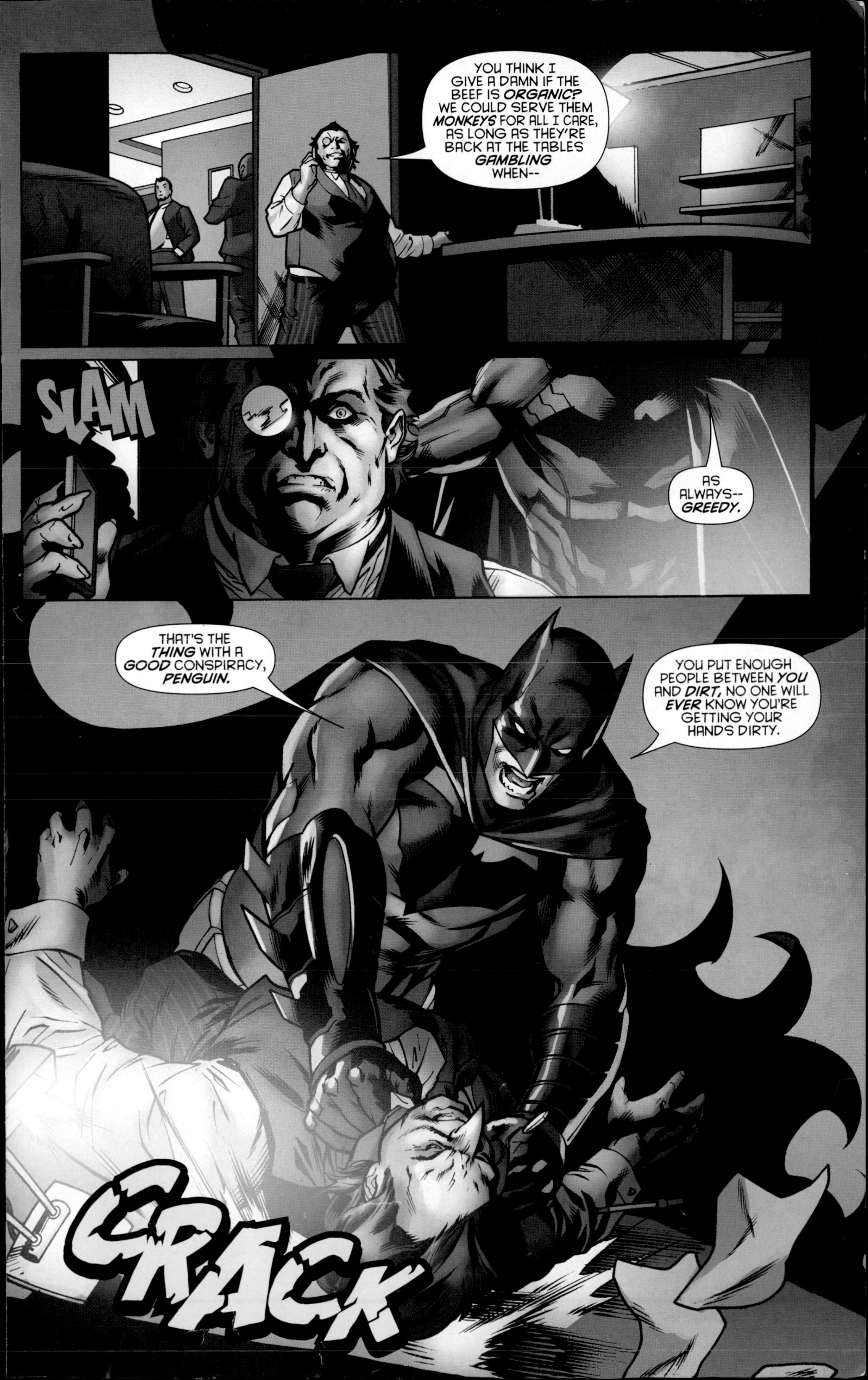
YOU THINK I GIVE A DAMN IF THE BEEF IS ORGANIC? WE COULD SERVE THEM MONKEYS FOR ALL I CARE, AS LONG AS THEY'RE BACK AT THE TABLES GAMBLING WHEN--
SLAM
AS ALWAYS-- GREEDY.
THAT'S THE THING WITH A GOOD CONSPIRACY, PENGUIN.
YOU PUT ENOUGH PEOPLE BETWEEN YOU AND DIRT, NO ONE WILL EVER KNOW YOU'RE GETTING YOUR HANDS DIRTY.
CRACK

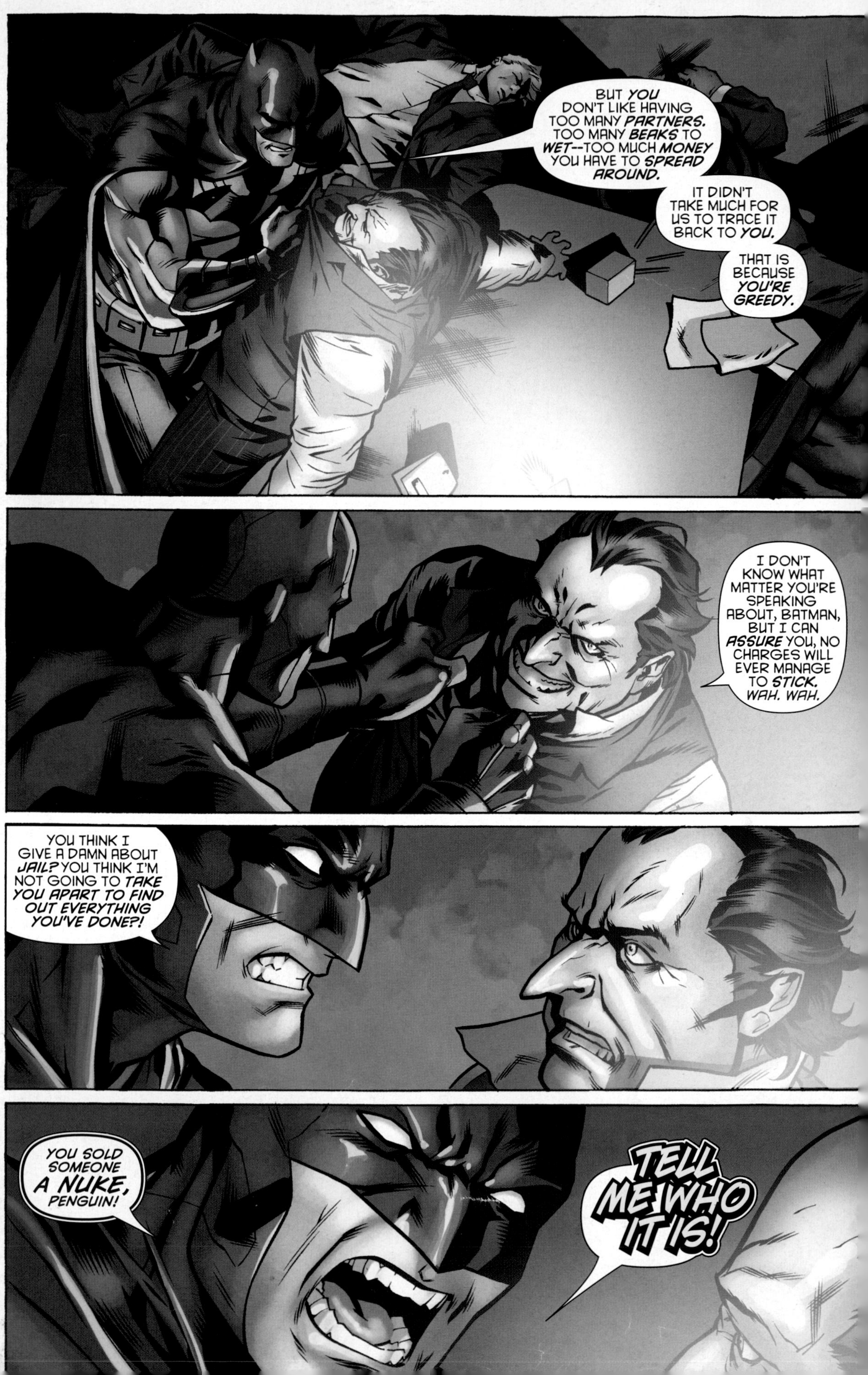
BUT *YOU* DON'T LIKE HAVING TOO MANY *PARTNERS.* TOO MANY *BEAKS* TO *WET*--TOO MUCH *MONEY* YOU HAVE TO *SPREAD AROUND.*
IT DIDN'T TAKE MUCH FOR US TO TRACE IT BACK TO *YOU.*
THAT IS BECAUSE *YOU'RE GREEDY.*
I DON'T KNOW WHAT MATTER YOU'RE SPEAKING ABOUT, BATMAN, BUT I CAN *ASSURE* YOU, NO CHARGES WILL EVER MANAGE TO *STICK.* WAH. WAH.
YOU THINK I GIVE A DAMN ABOUT *JAIL?* YOU THINK I'M NOT GOING TO *TAKE YOU APART TO FIND OUT EVERYTHING YOU'VE DONE?!*
YOU SOLD SOMEONE A NUKE, PENGUIN!
TELL ME WHO IT IS!

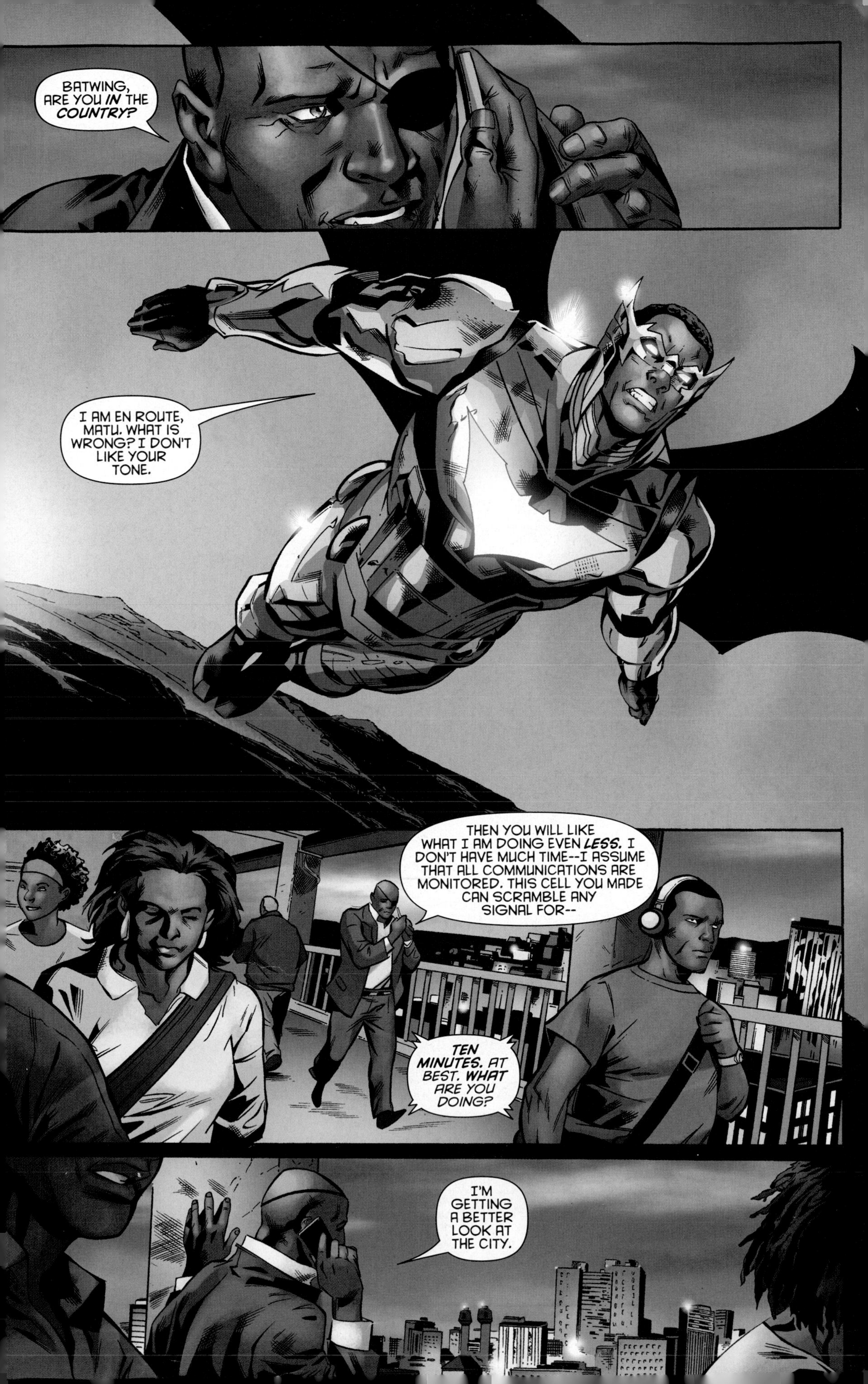
BATWING, ARE YOU *IN* THE *COUNTRY?*
I AM EN ROUTE, MATU. WHAT IS WRONG? I DON'T LIKE YOUR TONE.
THEN YOU WILL LIKE WHAT I AM DOING EVEN *LESS.* I DON'T HAVE MUCH TIME--I ASSUME THAT ALL COMMUNICATIONS ARE MONITORED. THIS CELL YOU MADE CAN SCRAMBLE ANY SIGNAL FOR--
TEN MINUTES. AT BEST. *WHAT* ARE YOU DOING?
I'M GETTING A BETTER LOOK AT THE CITY.

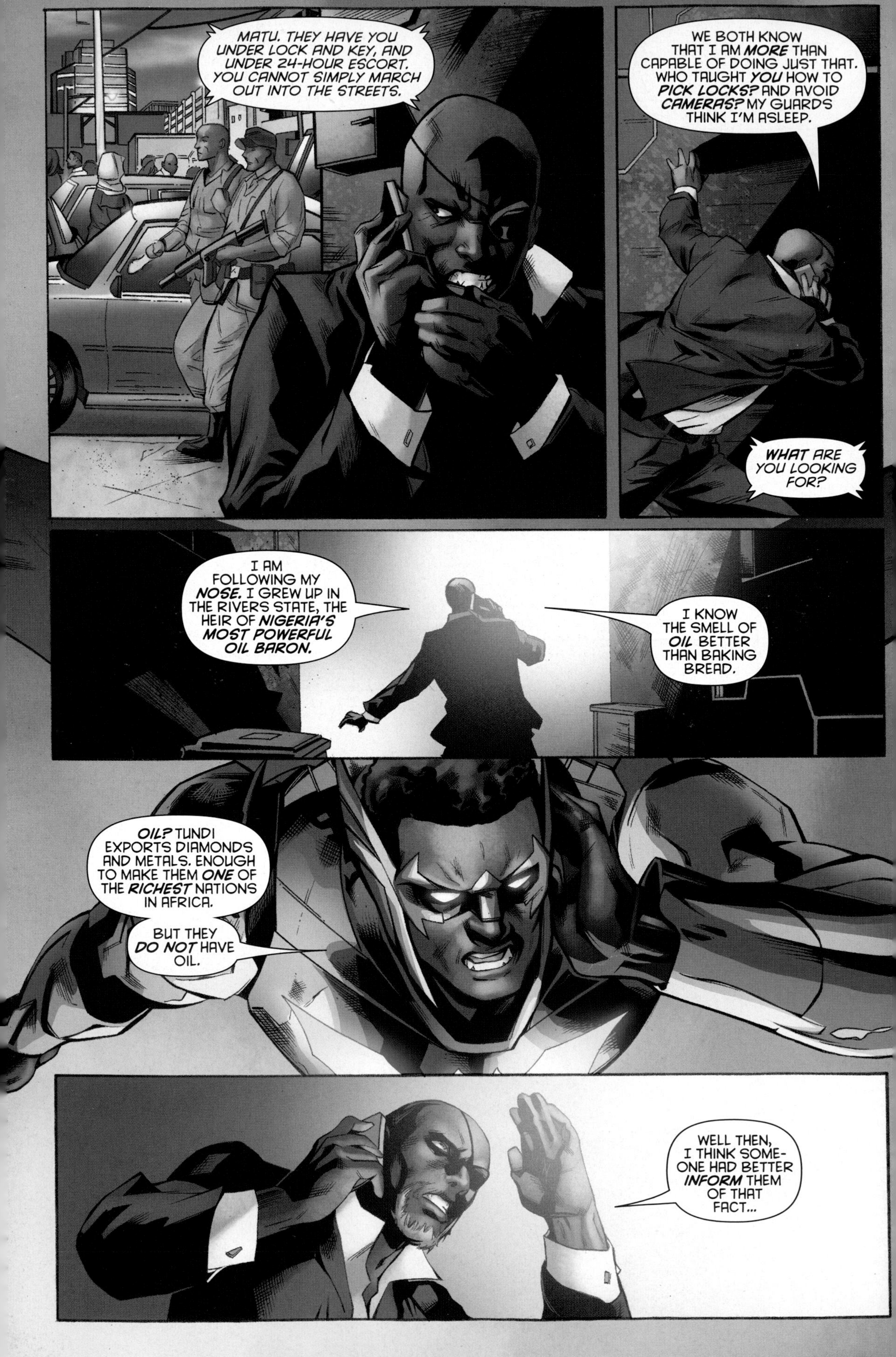
MATU. THEY HAVE YOU UNDER LOCK AND KEY, AND UNDER 24-HOUR ESCORT. YOU CANNOT SIMPLY MARCH OUT INTO THE STREETS.
WE BOTH KNOW THAT I AM MORE THAN CAPABLE OF DOING JUST THAT. WHO TAUGHT YOU HOW TO PICK LOCKS? AND AVOID CAMERAS? MY GUARDS THINK I'M ASLEEP.
WHAT ARE YOU LOOKING FOR?
I AM FOLLOWING MY NOSE. I GREW UP IN THE RIVERS STATE, THE HEIR OF NIGERIA'S MOST POWERFUL OIL BARON.
I KNOW THE SMELL OF OIL BETTER THAN BAKING BREAD.
OIL? TUNDI EXPORTS DIAMONDS AND METALS. ENOUGH TO MAKE THEM ONE OF THE RICHEST NATIONS IN AFRICA.
BUT THEY DO NOT HAVE OIL.
WELL THEN, I THINK SOME-ONE HAD BETTER INFORM THEM OF THAT FACT...

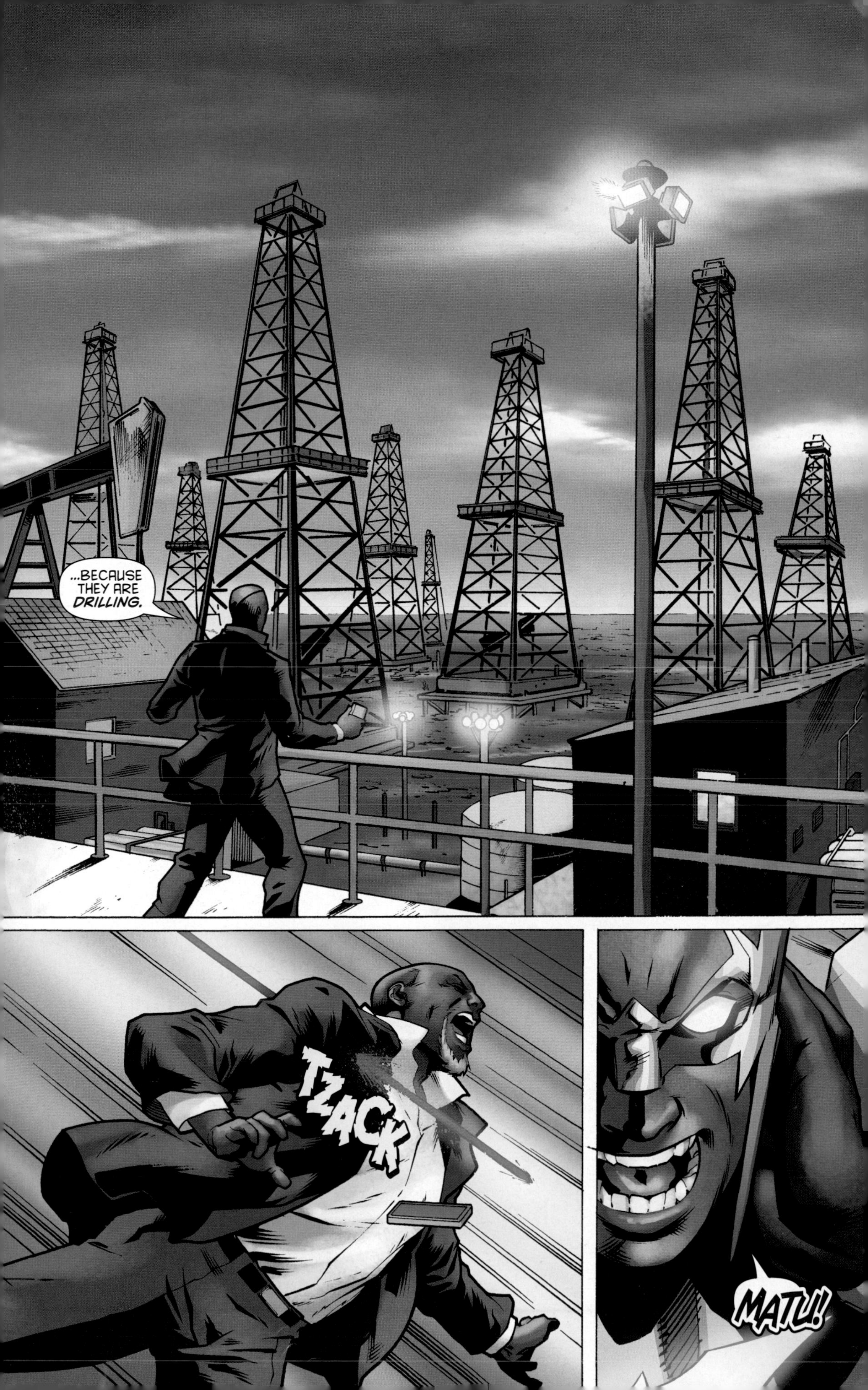
...BECAUSE THEY ARE DRILLING.
TZACK
MATU!

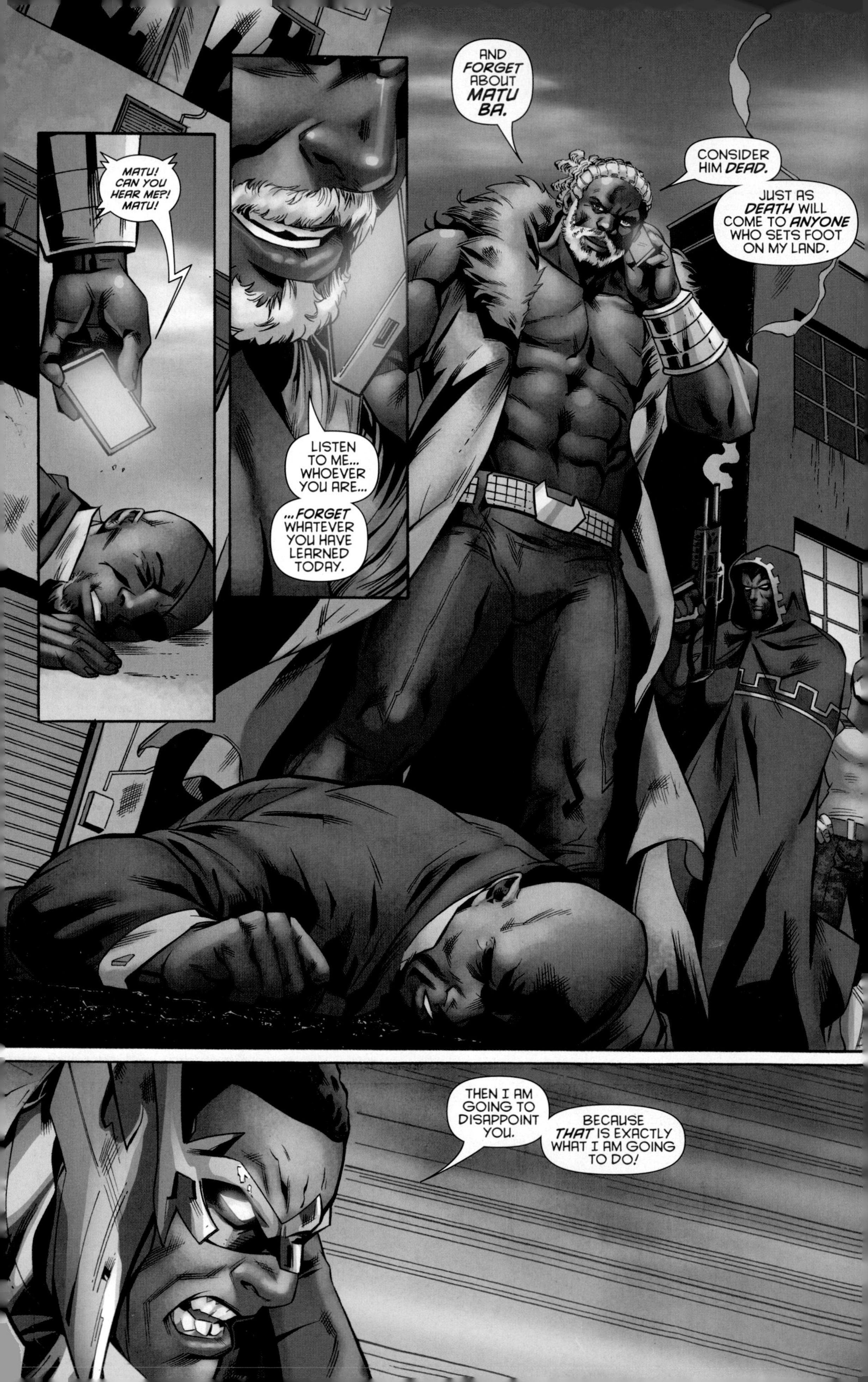
MATU! CAN YOU HEAR ME?! MATU!
LISTEN TO ME... WHOEVER YOU ARE...
...FORGET WHATEVER YOU HAVE LEARNED TODAY.
AND FORGET ABOUT MATU BA.
CONSIDER HIM DEAD.
JUST AS DEATH WILL COME TO ANYONE WHO SETS FOOT ON MY LAND.
THEN I AM GOING TO DISAPPOINT YOU.
BECAUSE THAT IS EXACTLY WHAT I AM GOING TO DO!

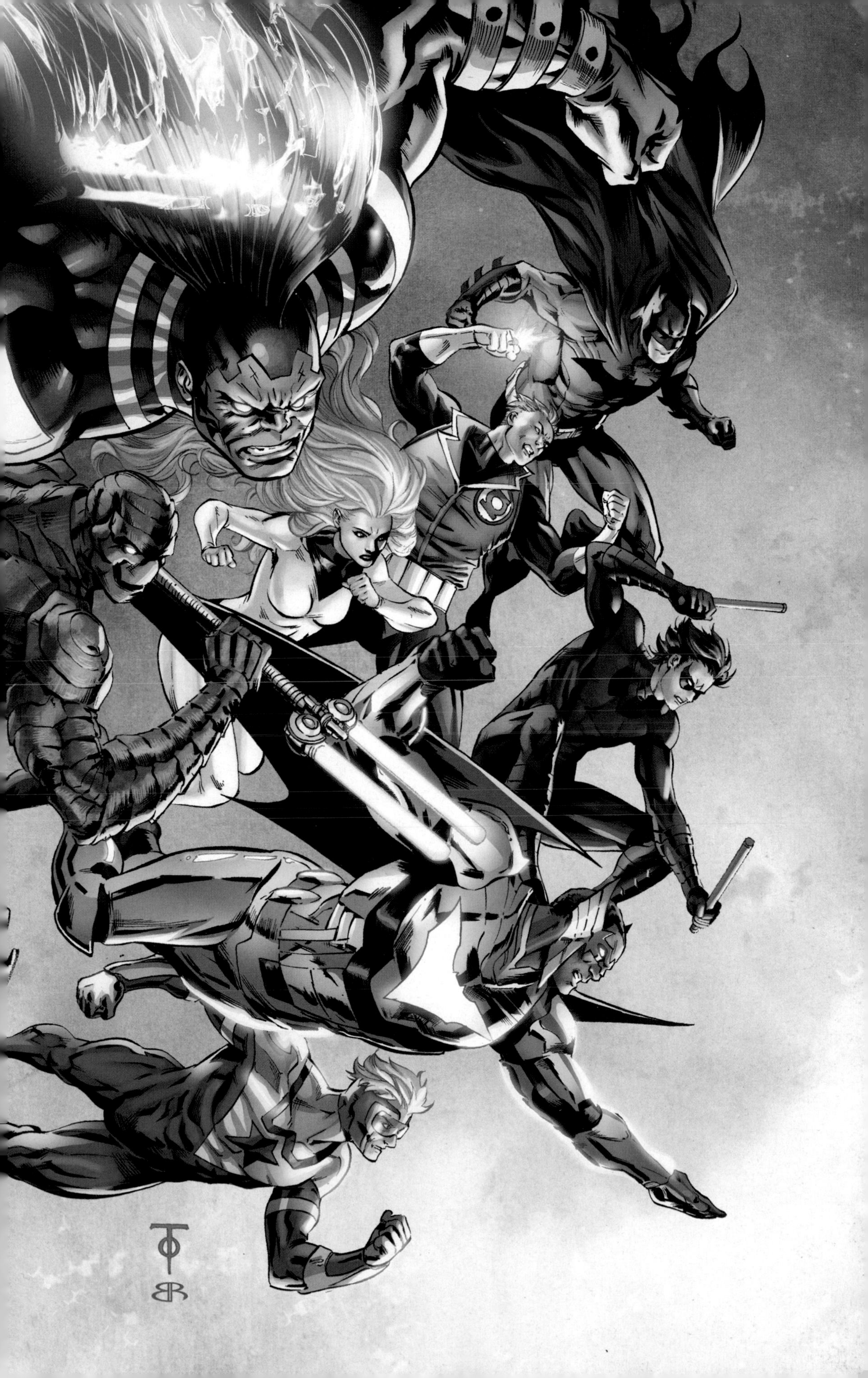

I AM ONE WITH THIS LAND

JUDD WINICK writer MARCUS TO penciller RYAN WINN, RICHARD ZAJAC & LE BEAU UNDERWOOD inkers cover art by MARCUS TO & BRIAN REBE

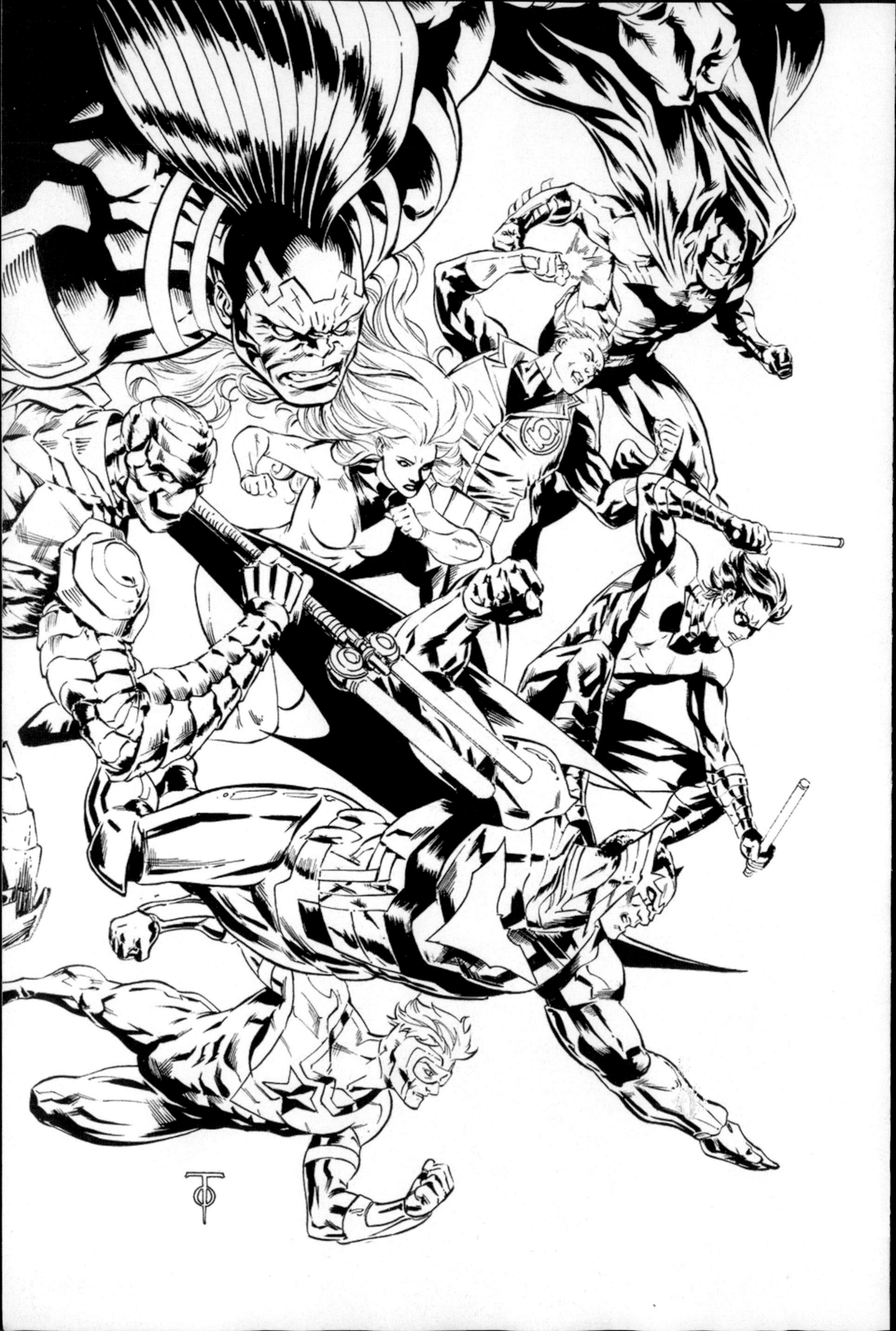

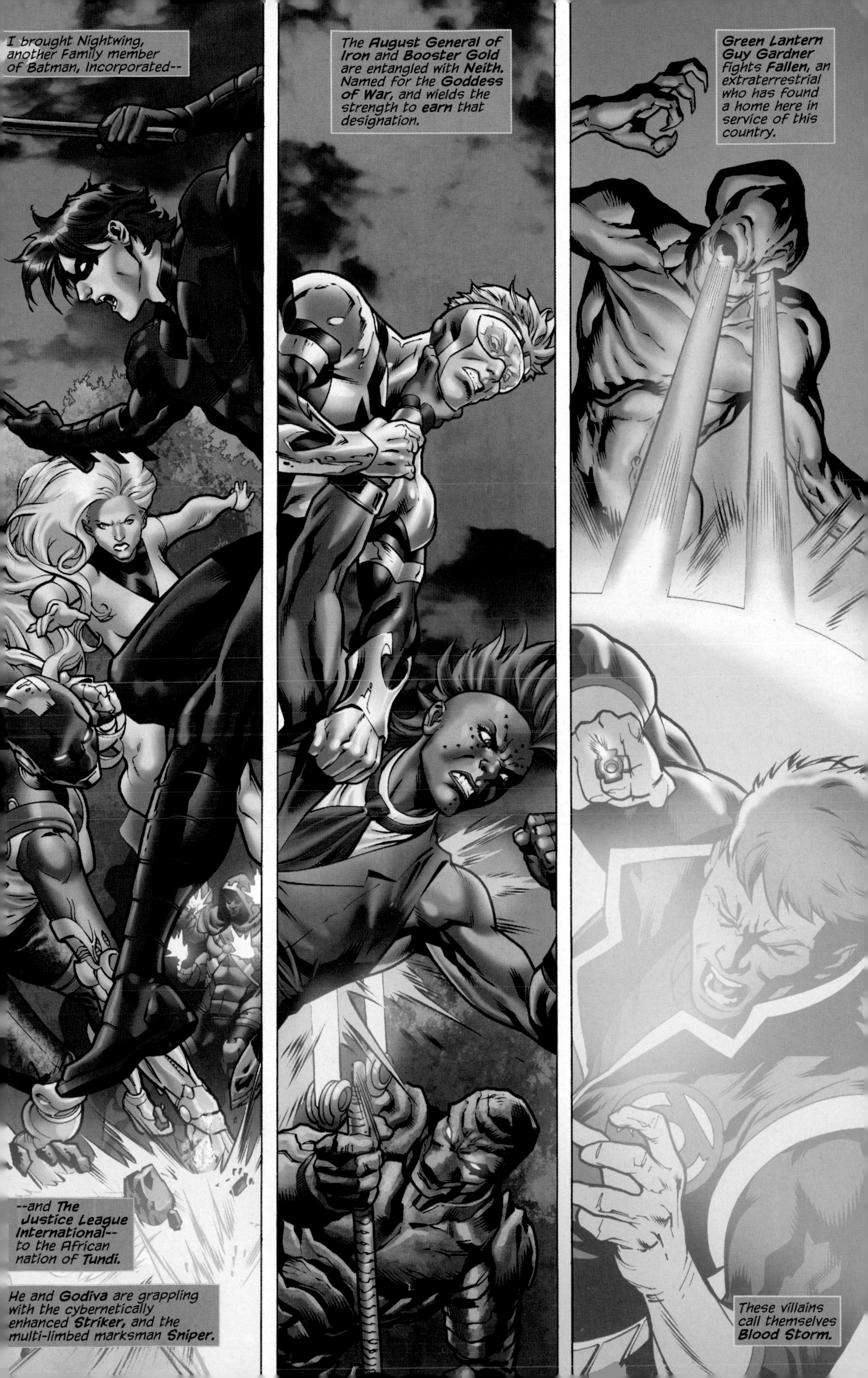

I brought Nightwing, another Family member of Batman, Incorporated--
--and The Justice League International-- to the African nation of Tundi.
He and Godiva are grappling with the cybernetically enhanced Striker, and the multi-limbed marksman Sniper.
The August General of Iron and Booster Gold are entangled with Neith. Named for the Goddess of War, and wields the strength to earn that designation.
Green Lantern Guy Gardner fights Fallen, an extraterrestrial who has found a home here in service of this country.
These villains call themselves Blood Storm.

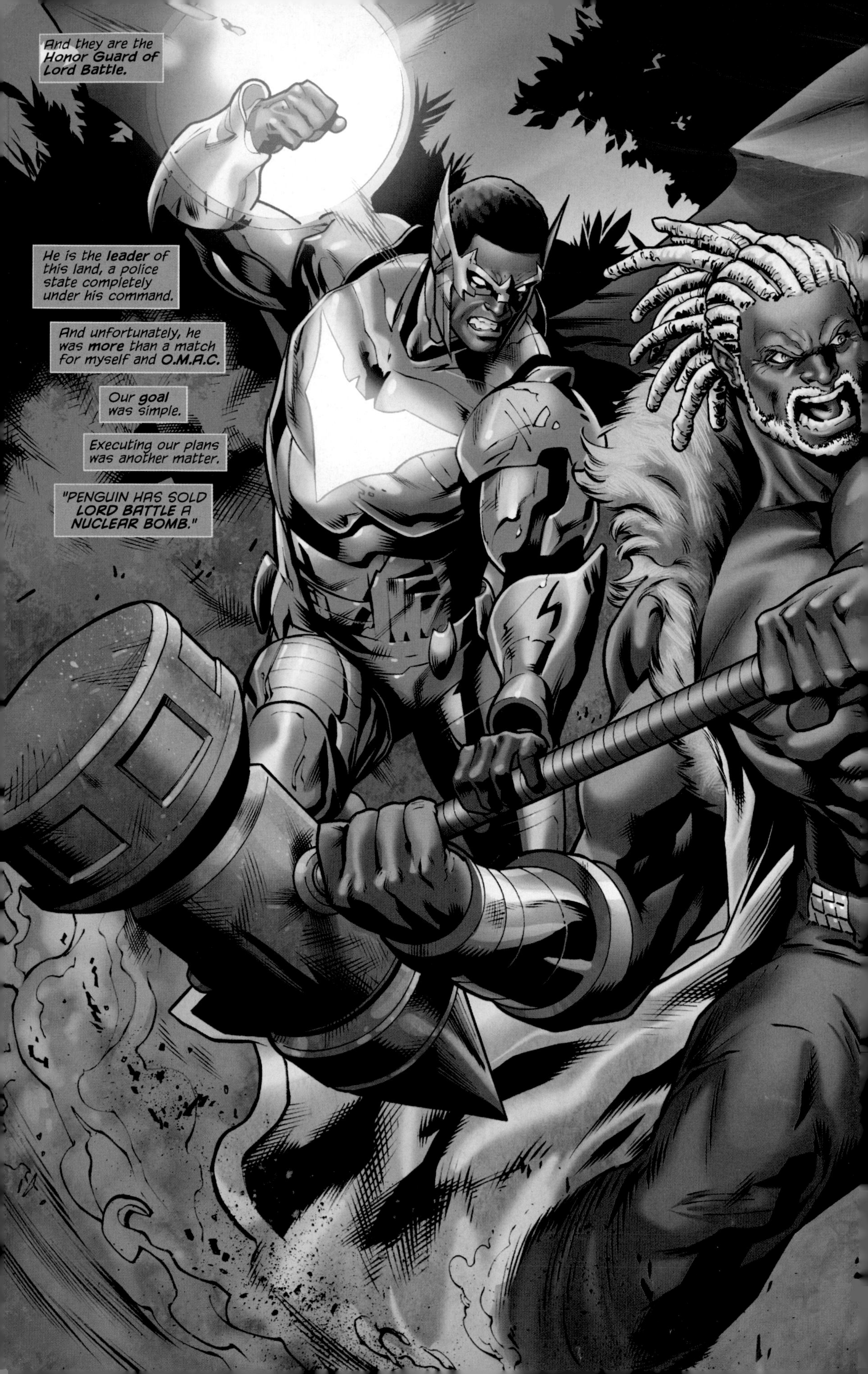
And they are the Honor Guard of Lord Battle.
He is the leader of this land, a police state completely under his command.
And unfortunately, he was more than a match for myself and O.M.A.C.
Our goal was simple.
Executing our plans was another matter.
"PENGUIN HAS SOLD LORD BATTLE A NUCLEAR BOMB."

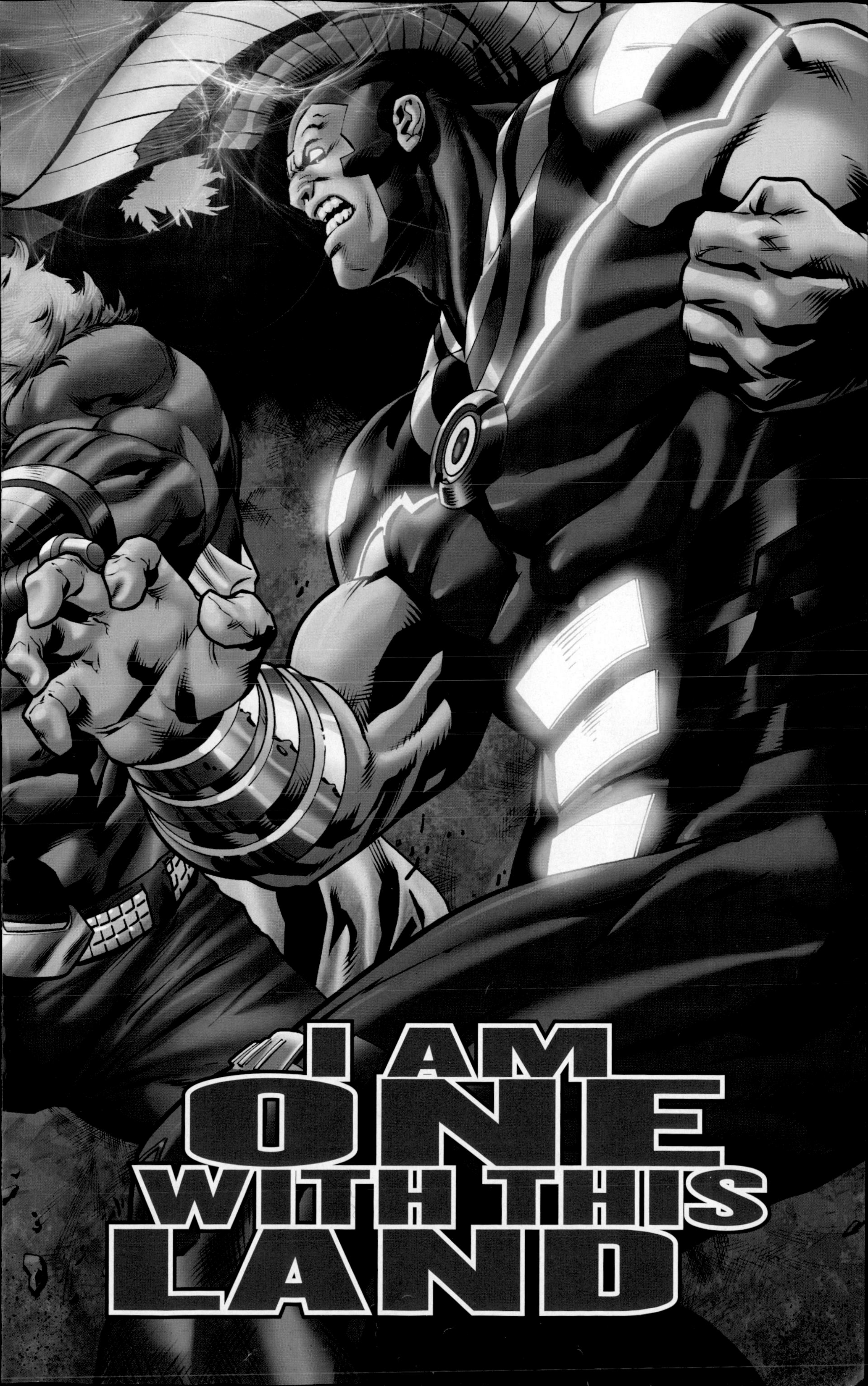
I AM
ONE
WITH THIS
LAND

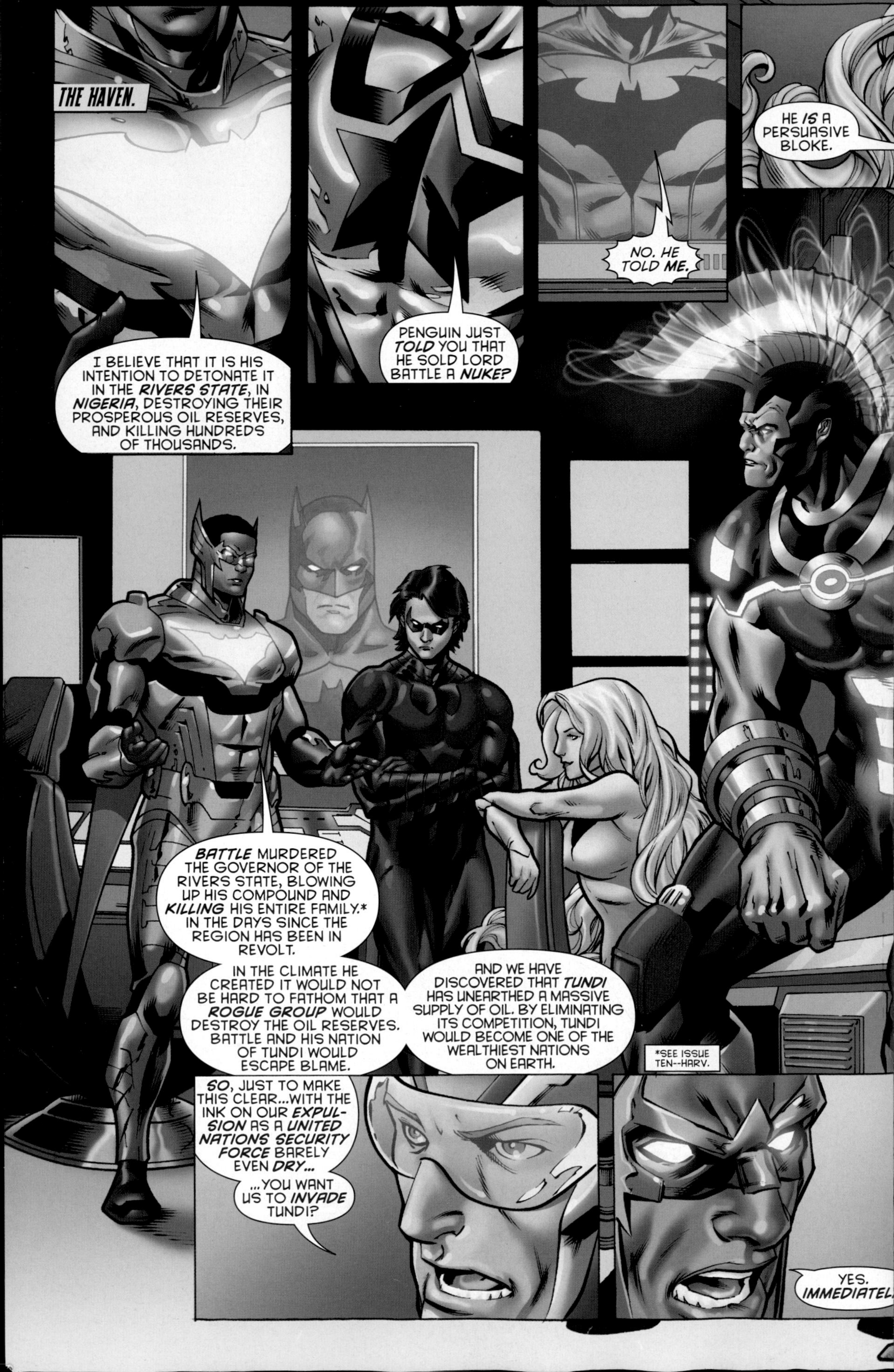
THE HAVEN.
I BELIEVE THAT IT IS HIS INTENTION TO DETONATE IT IN THE RIVERS STATE, IN NIGERIA, DESTROYING THEIR PROSPEROUS OIL RESERVES, AND KILLING HUNDREDS OF THOUSANDS.
PENGUIN JUST TOLD YOU THAT HE SOLD LORD BATTLE A NUKE?
NO. HE TOLD ME.
HE IS A PERSUASIVE BLOKE.
BATTLE MURDERED THE GOVERNOR OF THE RIVERS STATE, BLOWING UP HIS COMPOUND AND KILLING HIS ENTIRE FAMILY.* IN THE DAYS SINCE THE REGION HAS BEEN IN REVOLT.
IN THE CLIMATE HE CREATED IT WOULD NOT BE HARD TO FATHOM THAT A ROGUE GROUP WOULD DESTROY THE OIL RESERVES. BATTLE AND HIS NATION OF TUNDI WOULD ESCAPE BLAME.
AND WE HAVE DISCOVERED THAT TUNDI HAS UNEARTHED A MASSIVE SUPPLY OF OIL. BY ELIMINATING ITS COMPETITION, TUNDI WOULD BECOME ONE OF THE WEALTHIEST NATIONS ON EARTH.
*SEE ISSUE TEN--HARV.
SO, JUST TO MAKE THIS CLEAR...WITH THE INK ON OUR EXPULSION AS A UNITED NATIONS SECURITY FORCE BARELY EVEN DRY...
...YOU WANT US TO INVADE TUNDI?
YES. IMMEDIATEL

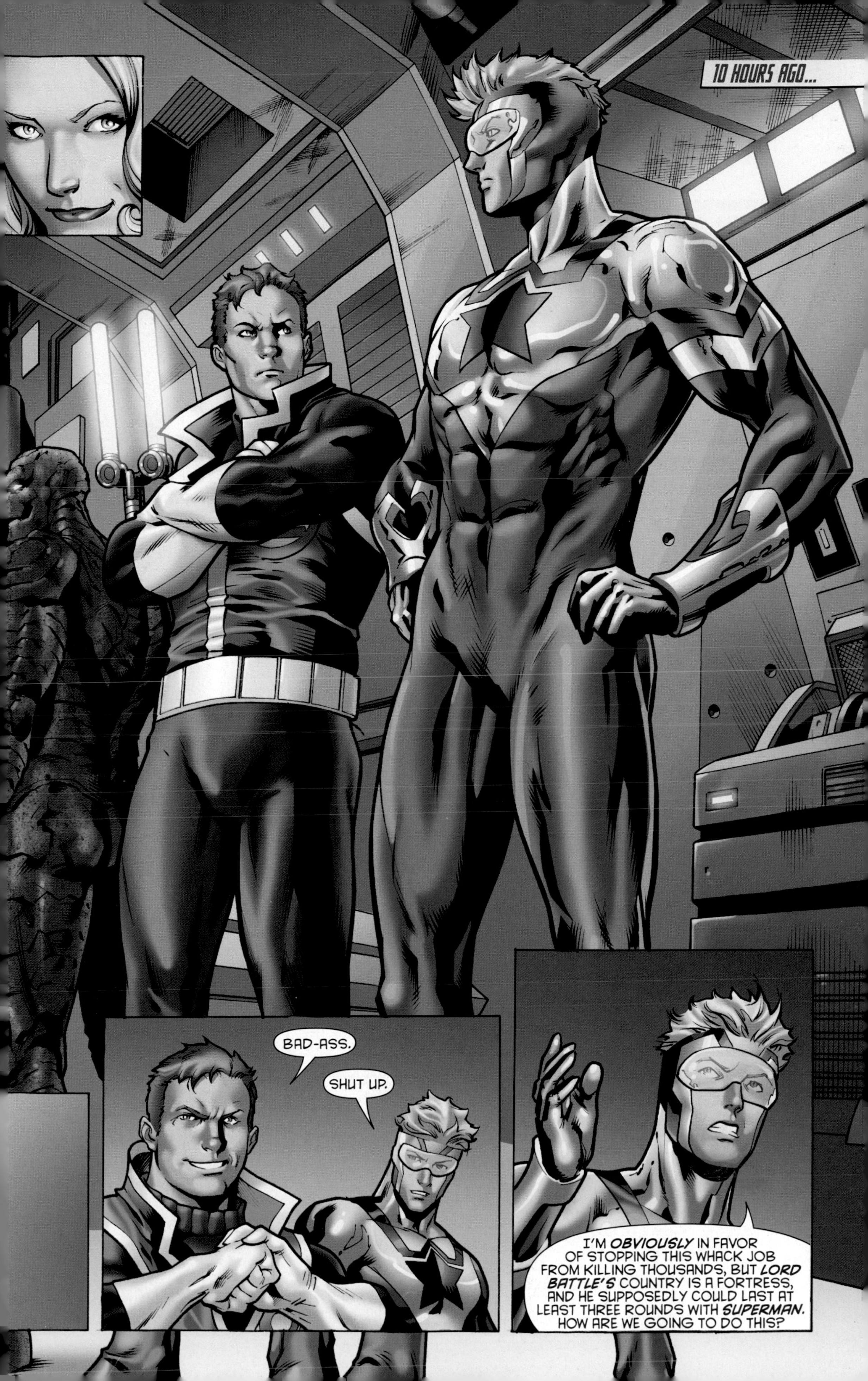
10 HOURS AGO...
BAD-ASS.
SHUT UP.
I'M OBVIOUSLY IN FAVOR OF STOPPING THIS WHACK JOB FROM KILLING THOUSANDS, BUT LORD BATTLE'S COUNTRY IS A FORTRESS, AND HE SUPPOSEDLY COULD LAST AT LEAST THREE ROUNDS WITH SUPERMAN. HOW ARE WE GOING TO DO THIS?

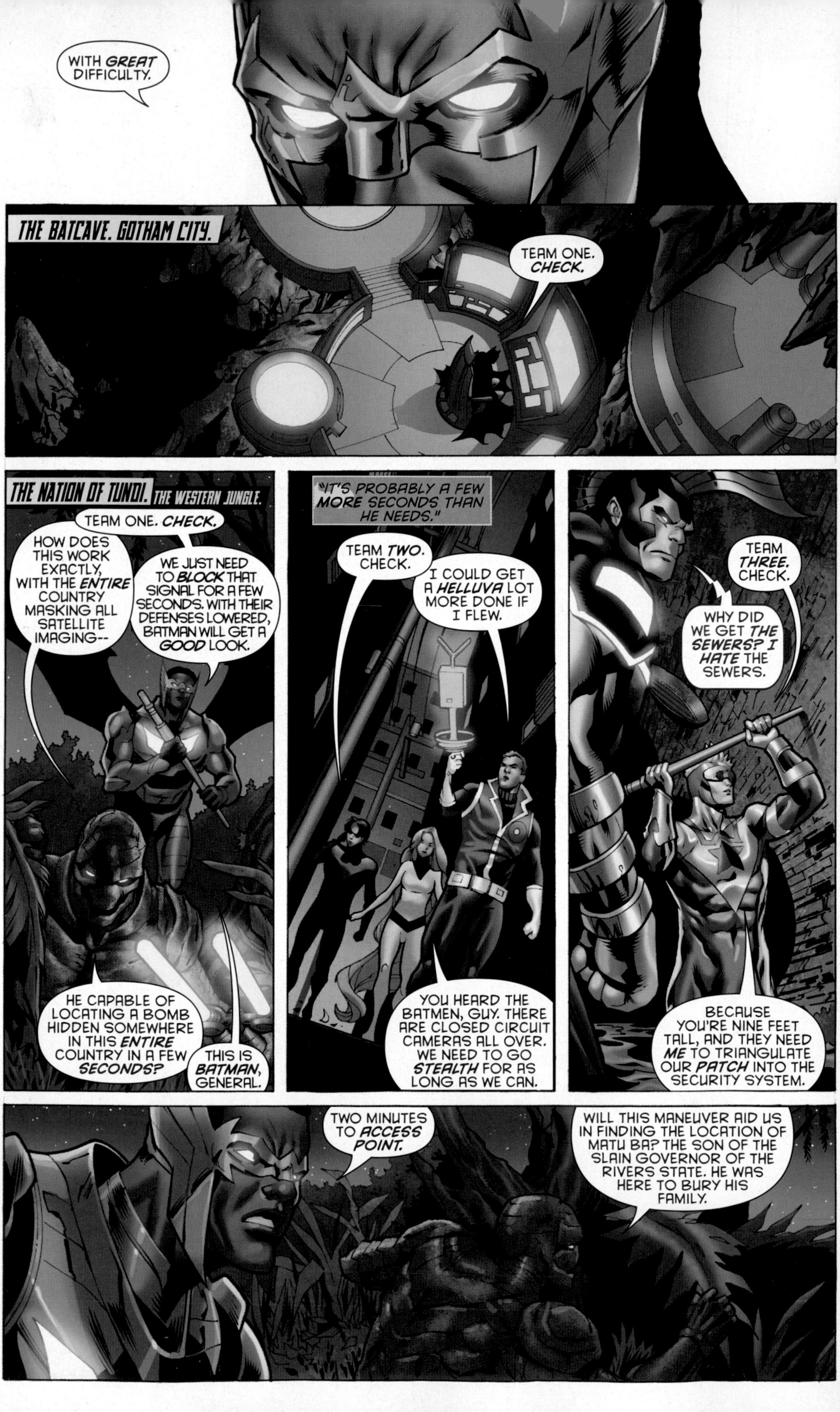
WITH GREAT DIFFICULTY.
THE BATCAVE. GOTHAM CITY.
TEAM ONE. CHECK.
THE NATION OF TUNDI. THE WESTERN JUNGLE.
TEAM ONE. CHECK.
HOW DOES THIS WORK EXACTLY, WITH THE ENTIRE COUNTRY MASKING ALL SATELLITE IMAGING--
WE JUST NEED TO BLOCK THAT SIGNAL FOR A FEW SECONDS. WITH THEIR DEFENSES LOWERED, BATMAN WILL GET A GOOD LOOK.
HE CAPABLE OF LOCATING A BOMB HIDDEN SOMEWHERE IN THIS ENTIRE COUNTRY IN A FEW SECONDS?
THIS IS BATMAN, GENERAL.
"IT'S PROBABLY A FEW MORE SECONDS THAN HE NEEDS."
TEAM TWO. CHECK.
I COULD GET A HELLUVA LOT MORE DONE IF I FLEW.
YOU HEARD THE BATMEN, GUY. THERE ARE CLOSED CIRCUIT CAMERAS ALL OVER. WE NEED TO GO STEALTH FOR AS LONG AS WE CAN.
TEAM THREE. CHECK.
WHY DID WE GET THE SEWERS? I HATE THE SEWERS.
BECAUSE YOU'RE NINE FEET TALL, AND THEY NEED ME TO TRIANGULATE OUR PATCH INTO THE SECURITY SYSTEM.
TWO MINUTES TO ACCESS POINT.
WILL THIS MANEUVER AID US IN FINDING THE LOCATION OF MATU BA? THE SON OF THE SLAIN GOVERNOR OF THE RIVERS STATE. HE WAS HERE TO BURY HIS FAMILY.

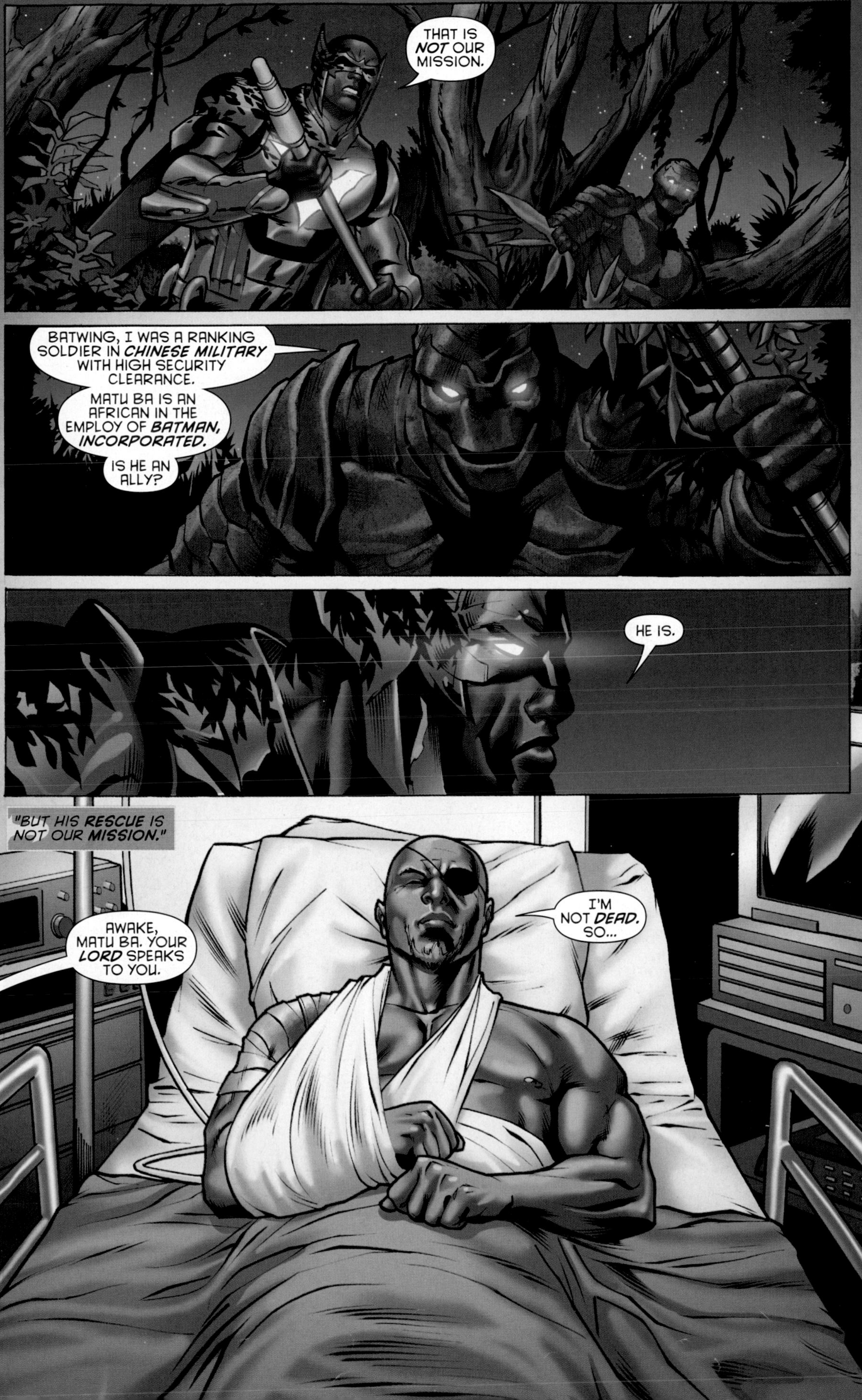
THAT IS NOT OUR MISSION.
BATWING, I WAS A RANKING SOLDIER IN CHINESE MILITARY WITH HIGH SECURITY CLEARANCE.
MATU BA IS AN AFRICAN IN THE EMPLOY OF BATMAN, INCORPORATED.
IS HE AN ALLY?
HE IS.
"BUT HIS RESCUE IS NOT OUR MISSION."
AWAKE, MATU BA. YOUR LORD SPEAKS TO YOU.
I'M NOT DEAD. SO...

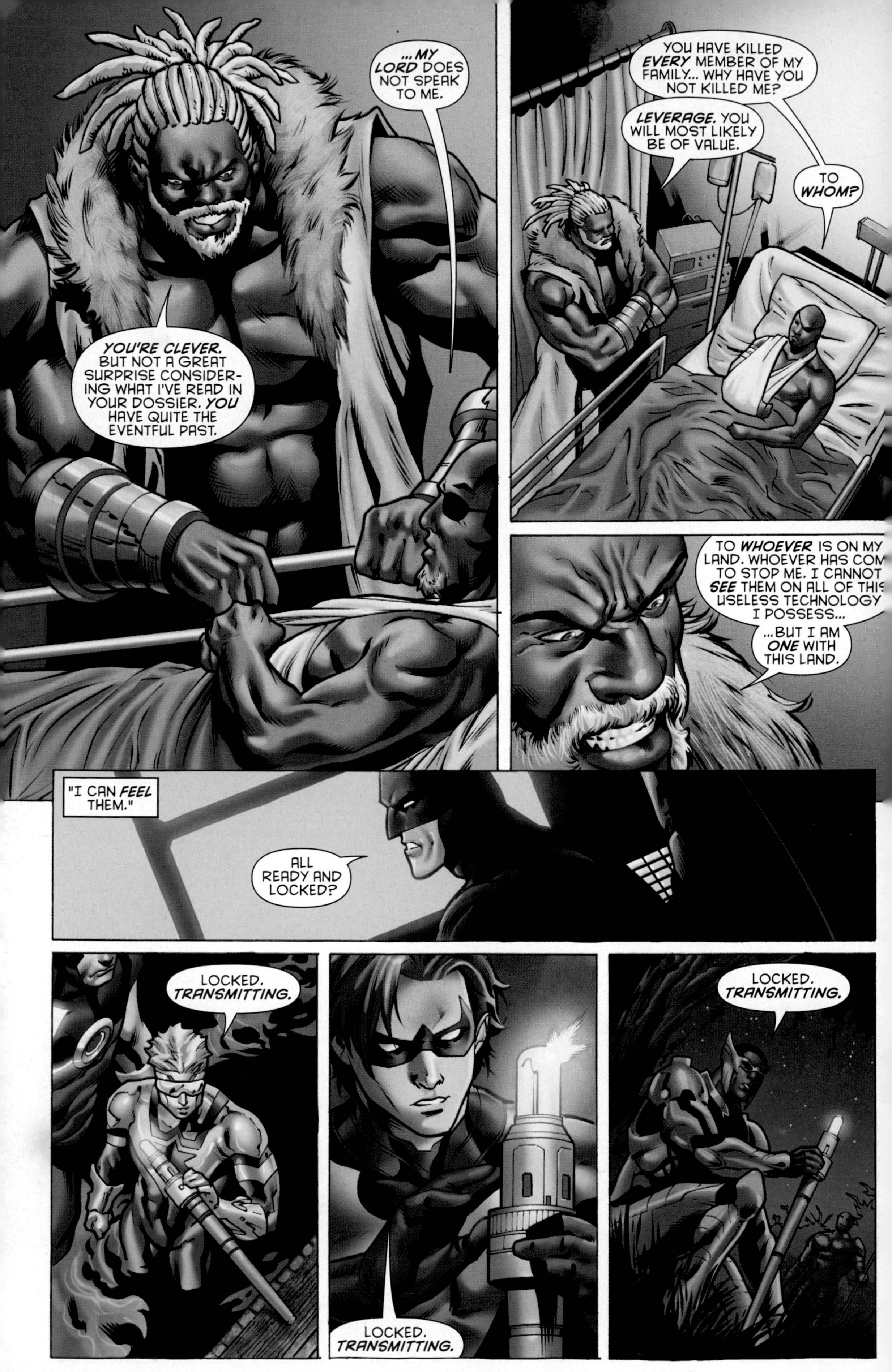
...MY LORD DOES NOT SPEAK TO ME.
YOU'RE CLEVER. BUT NOT A GREAT SURPRISE CONSIDERING WHAT I'VE READ IN YOUR DOSSIER. YOU HAVE QUITE THE EVENTFUL PAST.
YOU HAVE KILLED EVERY MEMBER OF MY FAMILY... WHY HAVE YOU NOT KILLED ME?
LEVERAGE. YOU WILL MOST LIKELY BE OF VALUE.
TO WHOM?
TO WHOEVER IS ON MY LAND. WHOEVER HAS COM TO STOP ME. I CANNOT SEE THEM ON ALL OF THIS USELESS TECHNOLOGY I POSSESS...
...BUT I AM ONE WITH THIS LAND.
"I CAN FEEL THEM."
ALL READY AND LOCKED?
LOCKED. TRANSMITTING.
LOCKED. TRANSMITTING.
LOCKED. TRANSMITTING.

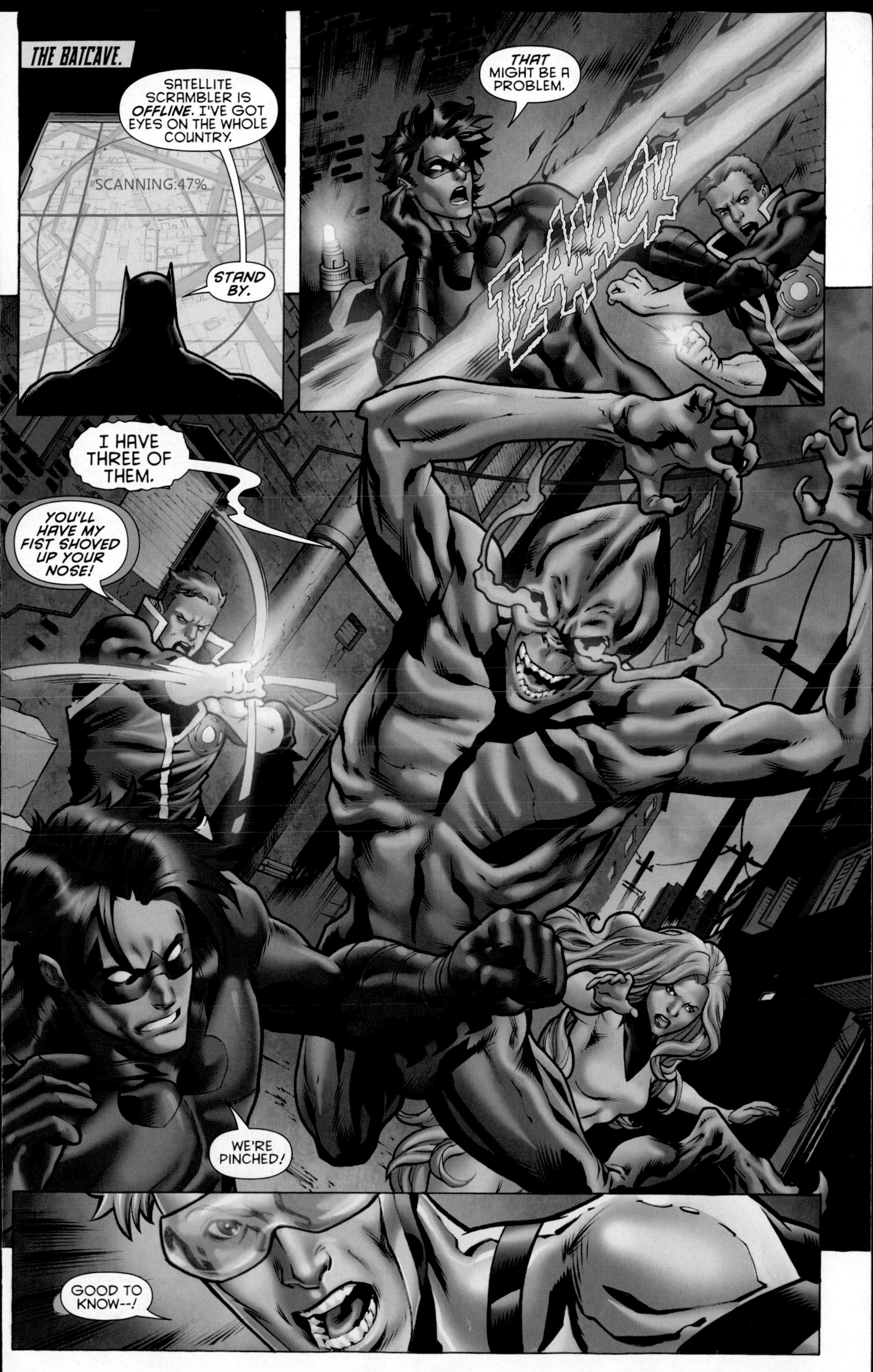
THE BATCAVE.
SATELLITE SCRAMBLER IS OFFLINE. I'VE GOT EYES ON THE WHOLE COUNTRY.
SCANNING:47%
STAND BY.
THAT MIGHT BE A PROBLEM.
TZZAAACK!
I HAVE THREE OF THEM.
YOU'LL HAVE MY FIST SHOVED UP YOUR NOSE!
WE'RE PINCHED!
GOOD TO KNOW--!

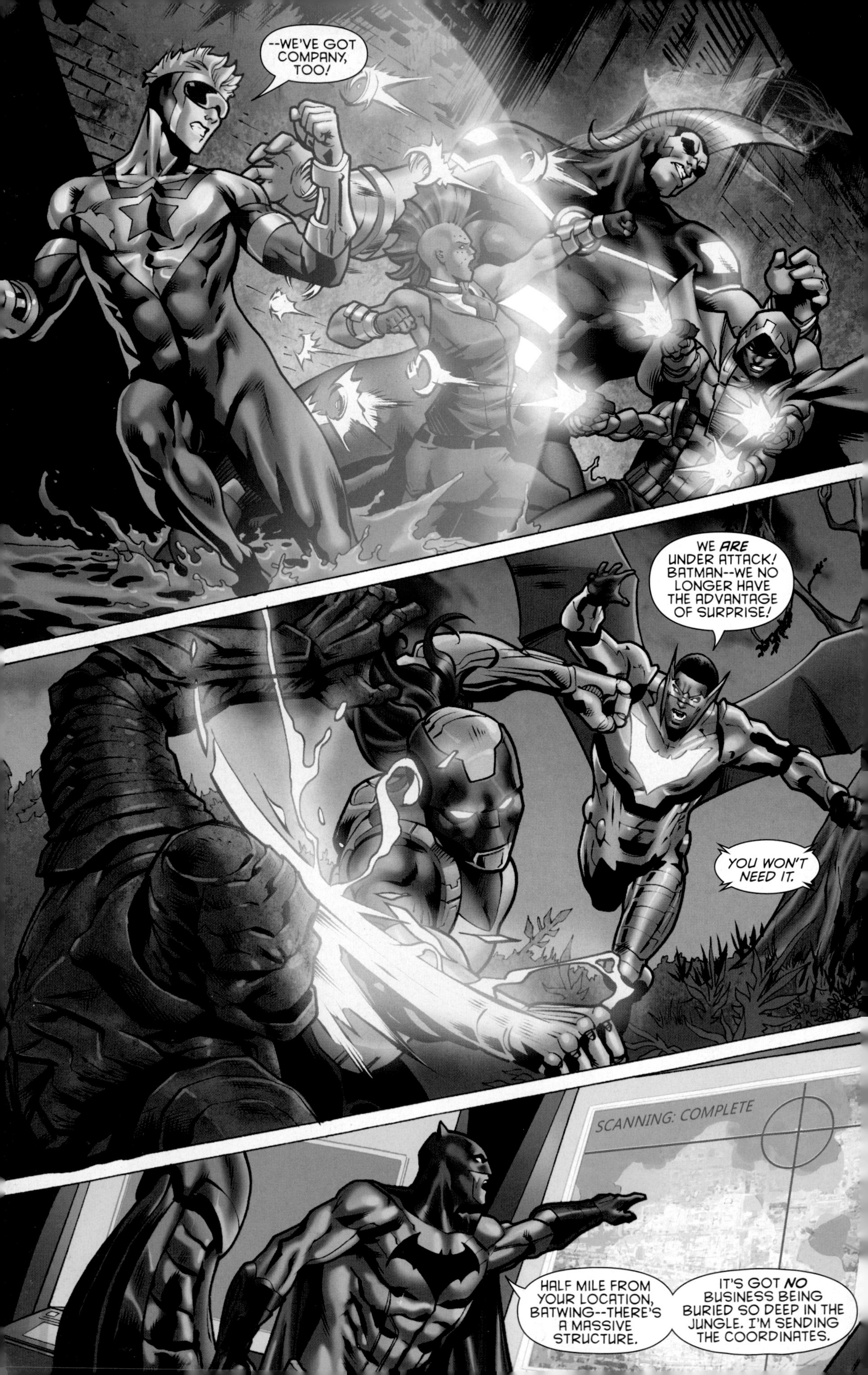

--WE'VE GOT COMPANY, TOO!
WE *ARE* UNDER ATTACK! BATMAN--WE NO LONGER HAVE THE ADVANTAGE OF SURPRISE!
YOU WON'T NEED IT.
SCANNING: COMPLETE
HALF MILE FROM YOUR LOCATION, BATWING--THERE'S A MASSIVE STRUCTURE.
IT'S GOT *NO* BUSINESS BEING BURIED SO DEEP IN THE JUNGLE. I'M SENDING THE COORDINATES.

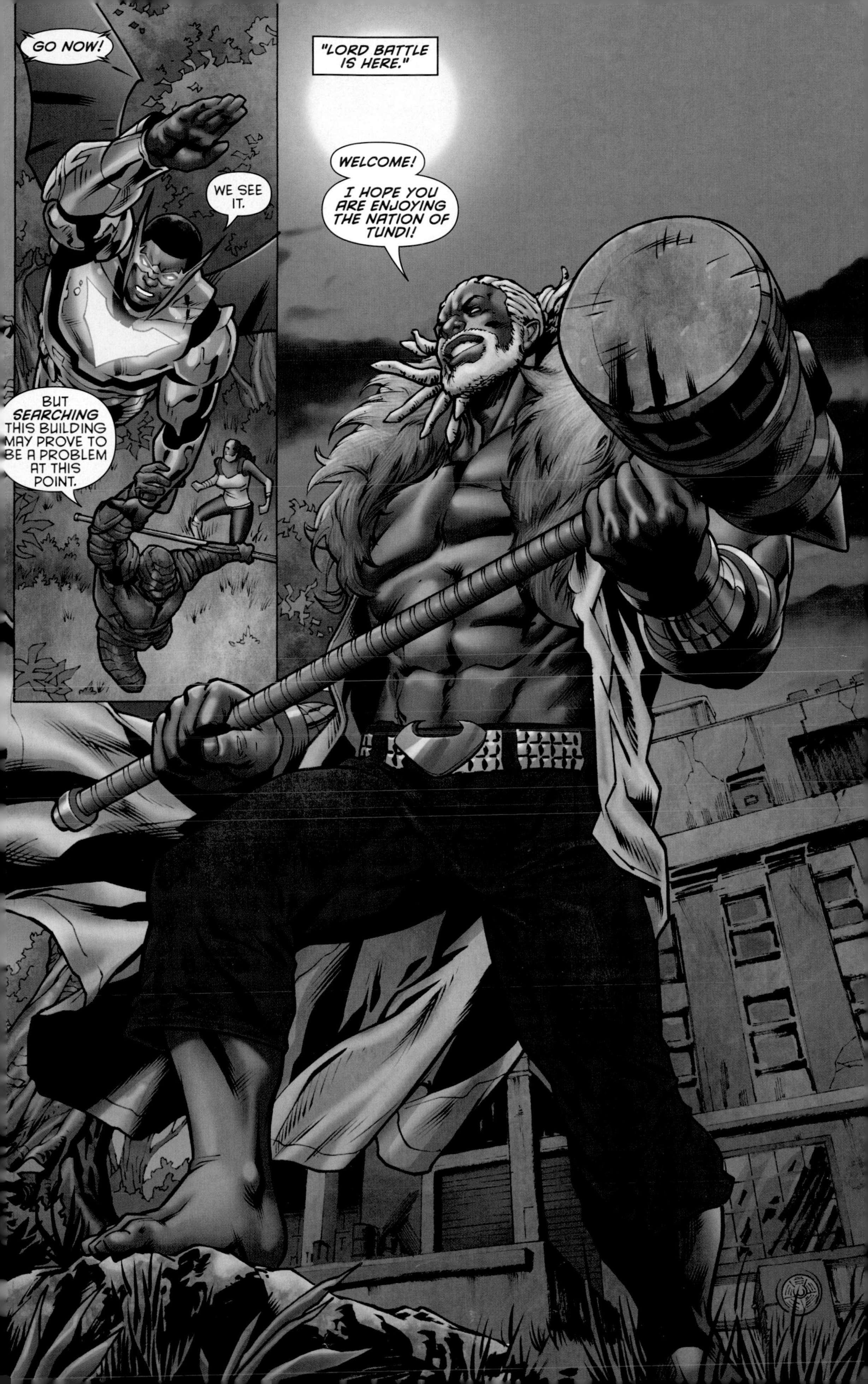
GO NOW!
WE SEE IT.
BUT SEARCHING THIS BUILDING MAY PROVE TO BE A PROBLEM AT THIS POINT.
"LORD BATTLE IS HERE."
WELCOME!
I HOPE YOU ARE ENJOYING THE NATION OF TUNDI!

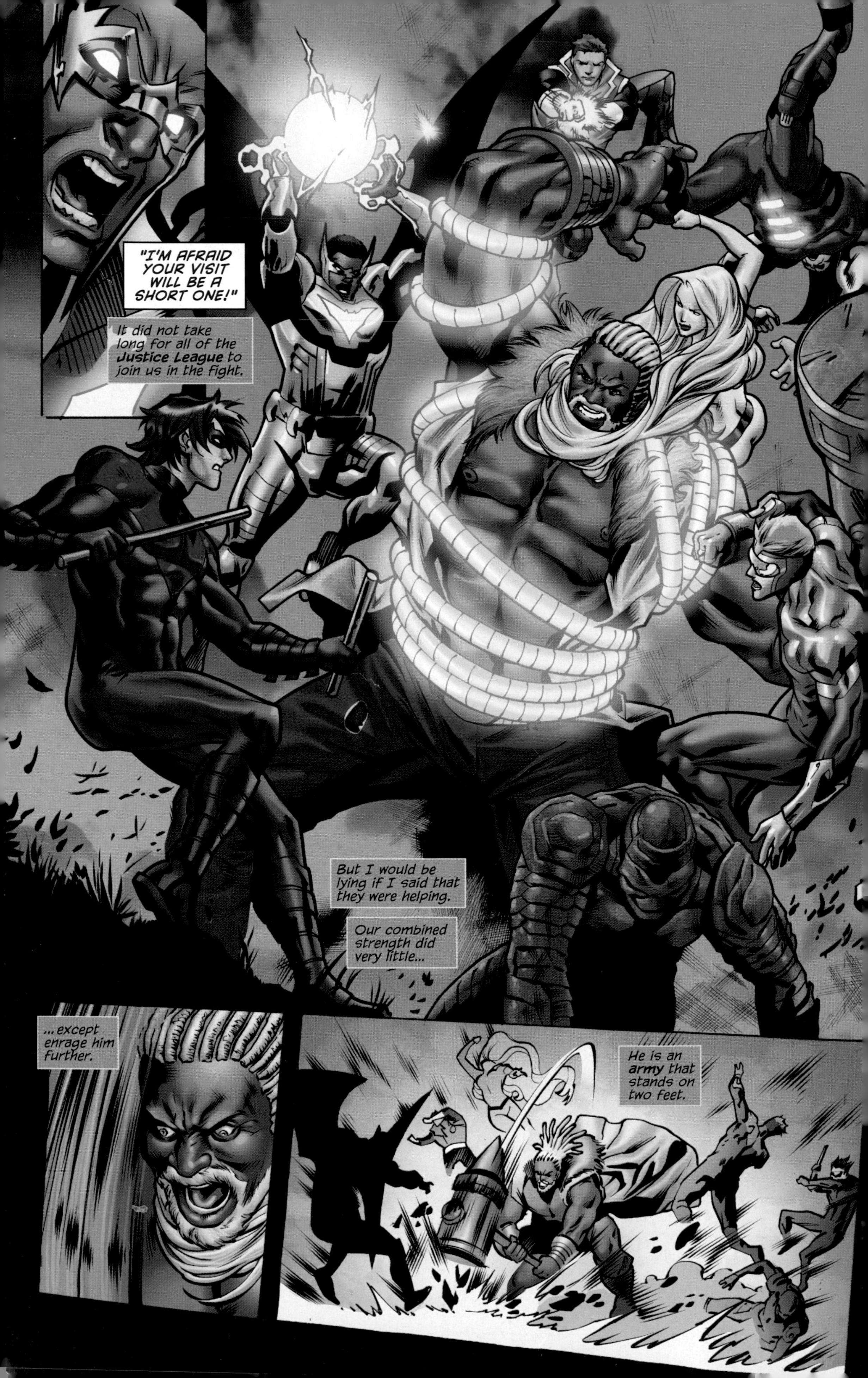

"I'M AFRAID YOUR VISIT WILL BE A SHORT ONE!"
It did not take long for all of the **Justice League** to join us in the fight.
But I would be lying if I said that they were helping.
Our combined strength did very little...
...except enrage him further.
He is an **army** that stands on two feet.

I am sorry, Matu. You will not be avenged. You will not be saved.

And I fear **many** more will die.

WHAT ARE YOU TRYING TO SAY?

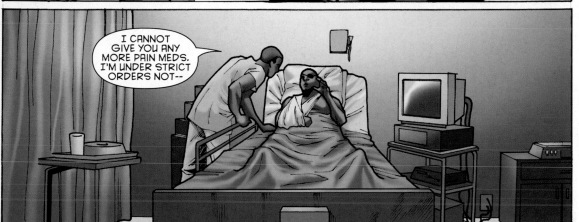

I CANNOT GIVE YOU ANY MORE PAIN MEDS. I'M UNDER STRICT ORDERS NOT--

CRACK

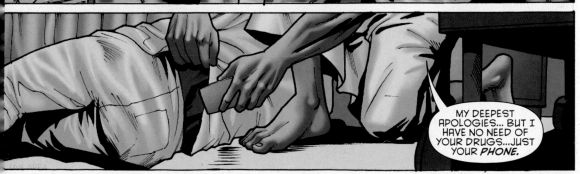

MY DEEPEST APOLOGIES... BUT I HAVE NO NEED OF YOUR DRUGS...JUST YOUR **PHONE**.

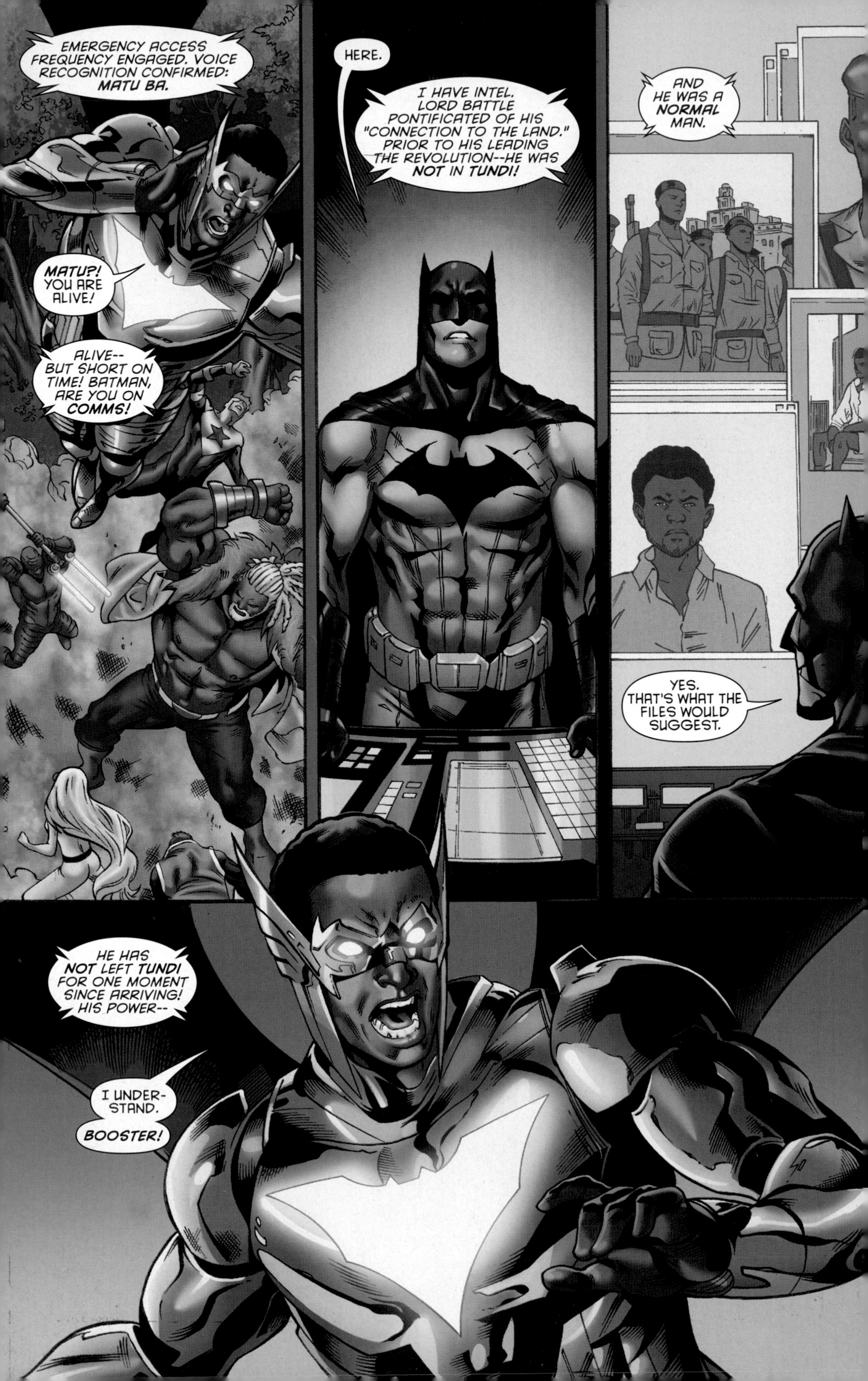
EMERGENCY ACCESS FREQUENCY ENGAGED. VOICE RECOGNITION CONFIRMED: MATU BA.
MATU?! YOU ARE ALIVE!
ALIVE-- BUT SHORT ON TIME! BATMAN, ARE YOU ON COMMS!
HERE.
I HAVE INTEL. LORD BATTLE PONTIFICATED OF HIS "CONNECTION TO THE LAND." PRIOR TO HIS LEADING THE REVOLUTION--HE WAS NOT IN TUNDI!
AND HE WAS A NORMAL MAN.
YES. THAT'S WHAT THE FILES WOULD SUGGEST.
HE HAS NOT LEFT TUNDI FOR ONE MOMENT SINCE ARRIVING! HIS POWER--
I UNDER-STAND. BOOSTER!

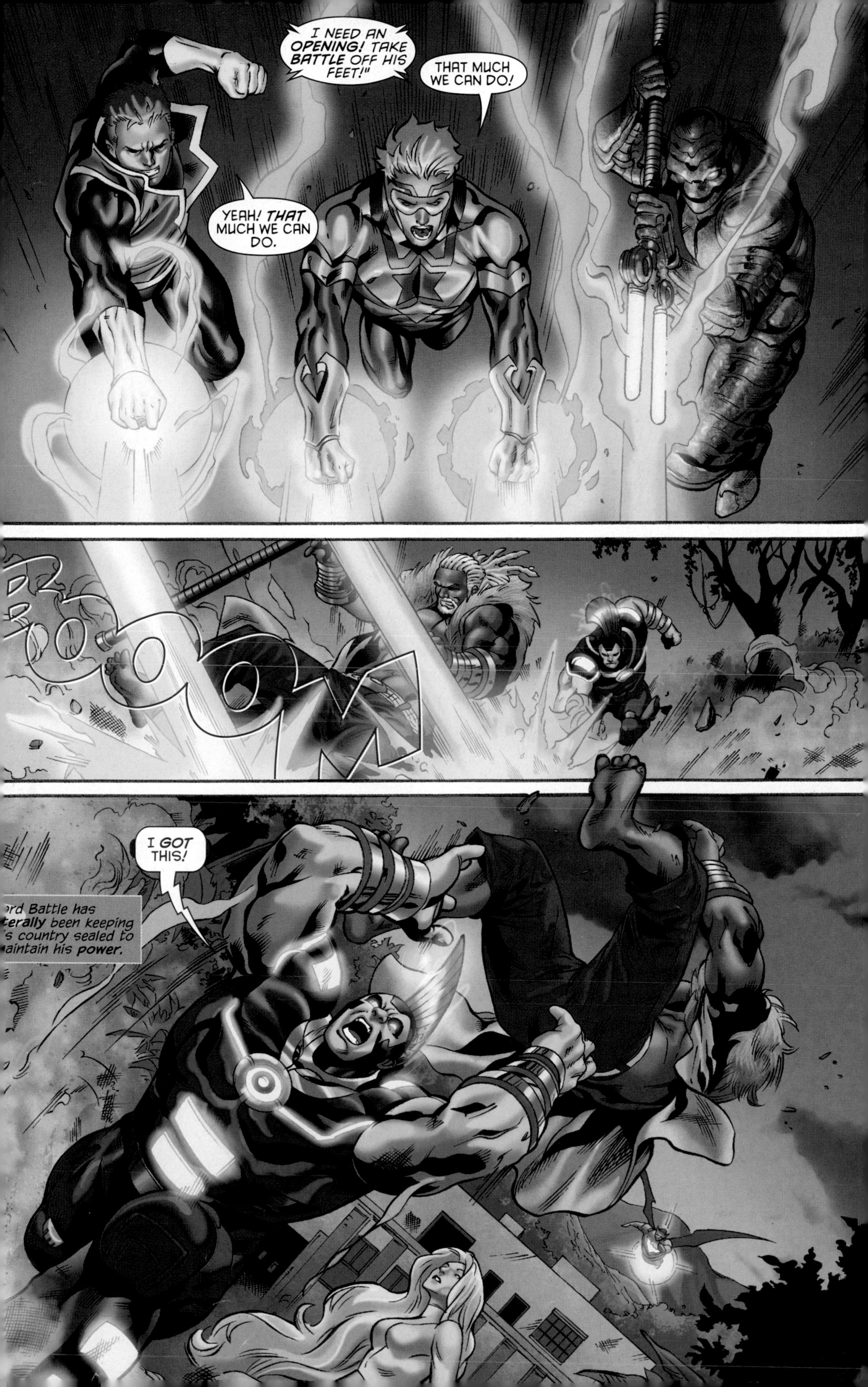
I NEED AN OPENING! TAKE BATTLE OFF HIS FEET!"
THAT MUCH WE CAN DO!
YEAH! THAT MUCH WE CAN DO.
I GOT THIS!
ord Battle has
terally been keeping
's country sealed to
aintain his power.

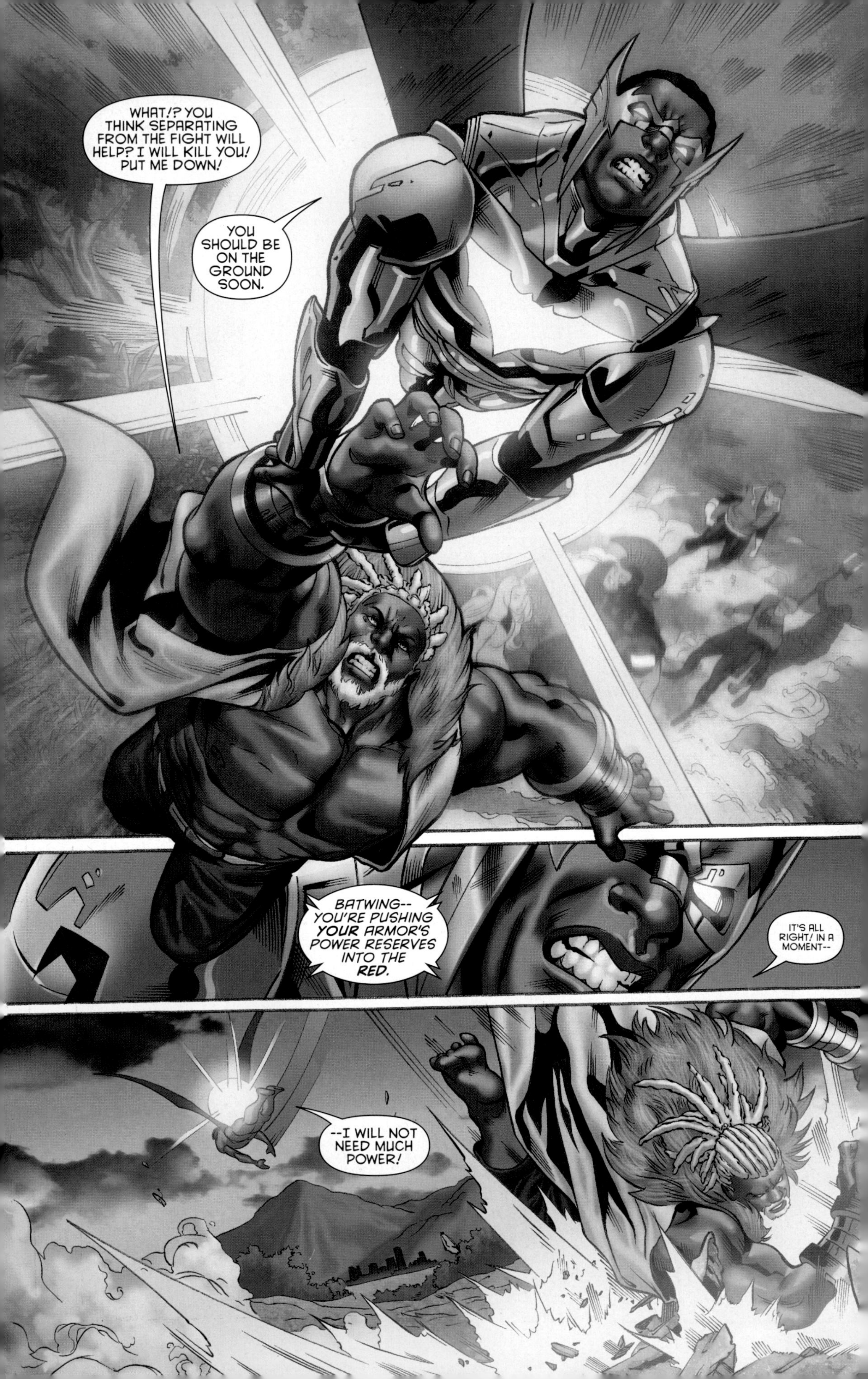
WHAT!? YOU THINK SEPARATING FROM THE FIGHT WILL HELP? I WILL KILL YOU! PUT ME DOWN!
YOU SHOULD BE ON THE GROUND SOON.
BATWING-- YOU'RE PUSHING YOUR ARMOR'S POWER RESERVES INTO THE RED.
IT'S ALL RIGHT! IN A MOMENT--
--I WILL NOT NEED MUCH POWER!

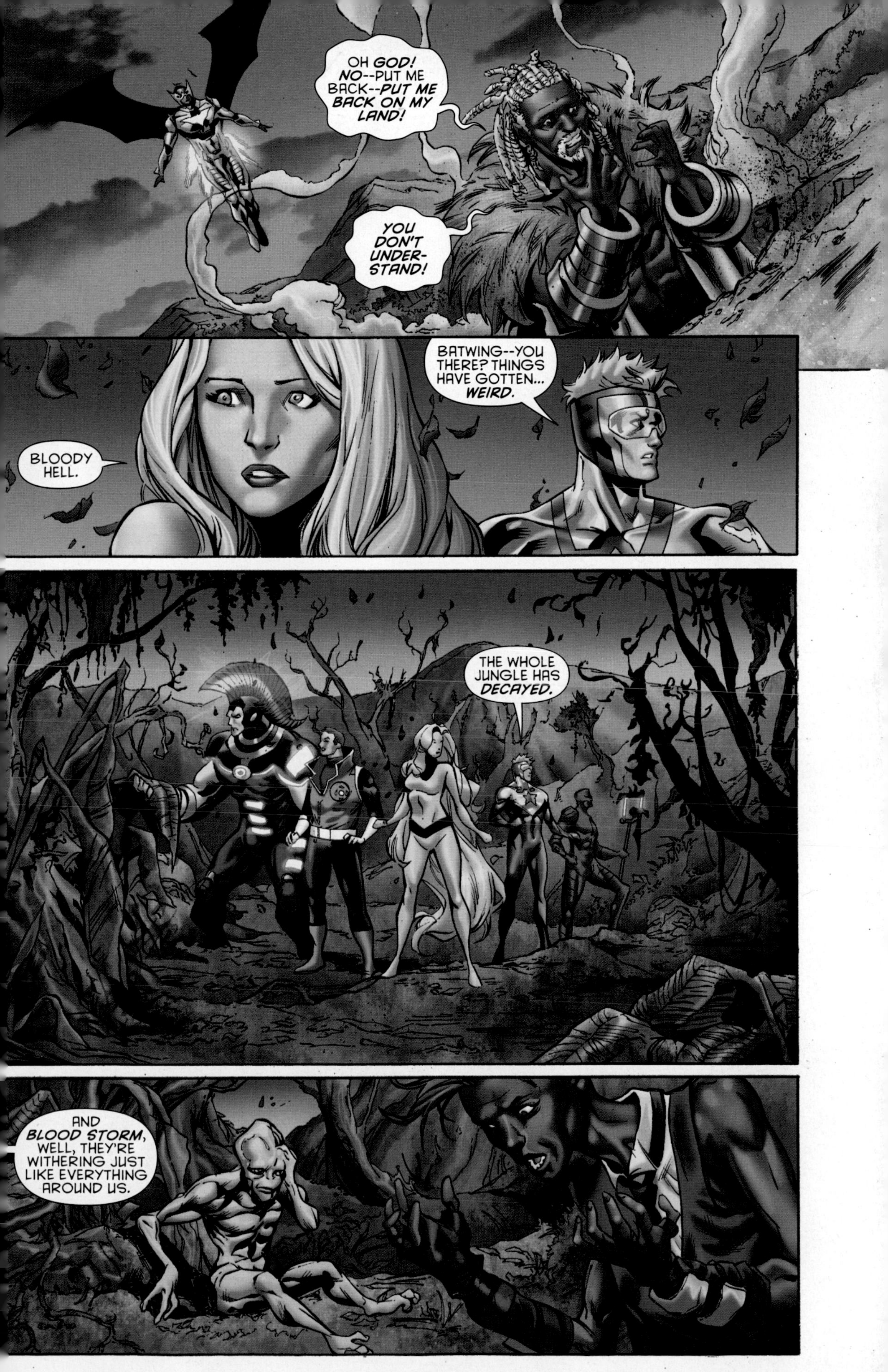
OH GOD! NO--PUT ME BACK--PUT ME BACK ON MY LAND!
YOU DON'T UNDER-STAND!
BATWING--YOU THERE? THINGS HAVE GOTTEN... WEIRD.
BLOODY HELL.
THE WHOLE JUNGLE HAS DECAYED.
AND BLOOD STORM, WELL, THEY'RE WITHERING JUST LIKE EVERYTHING AROUND US.

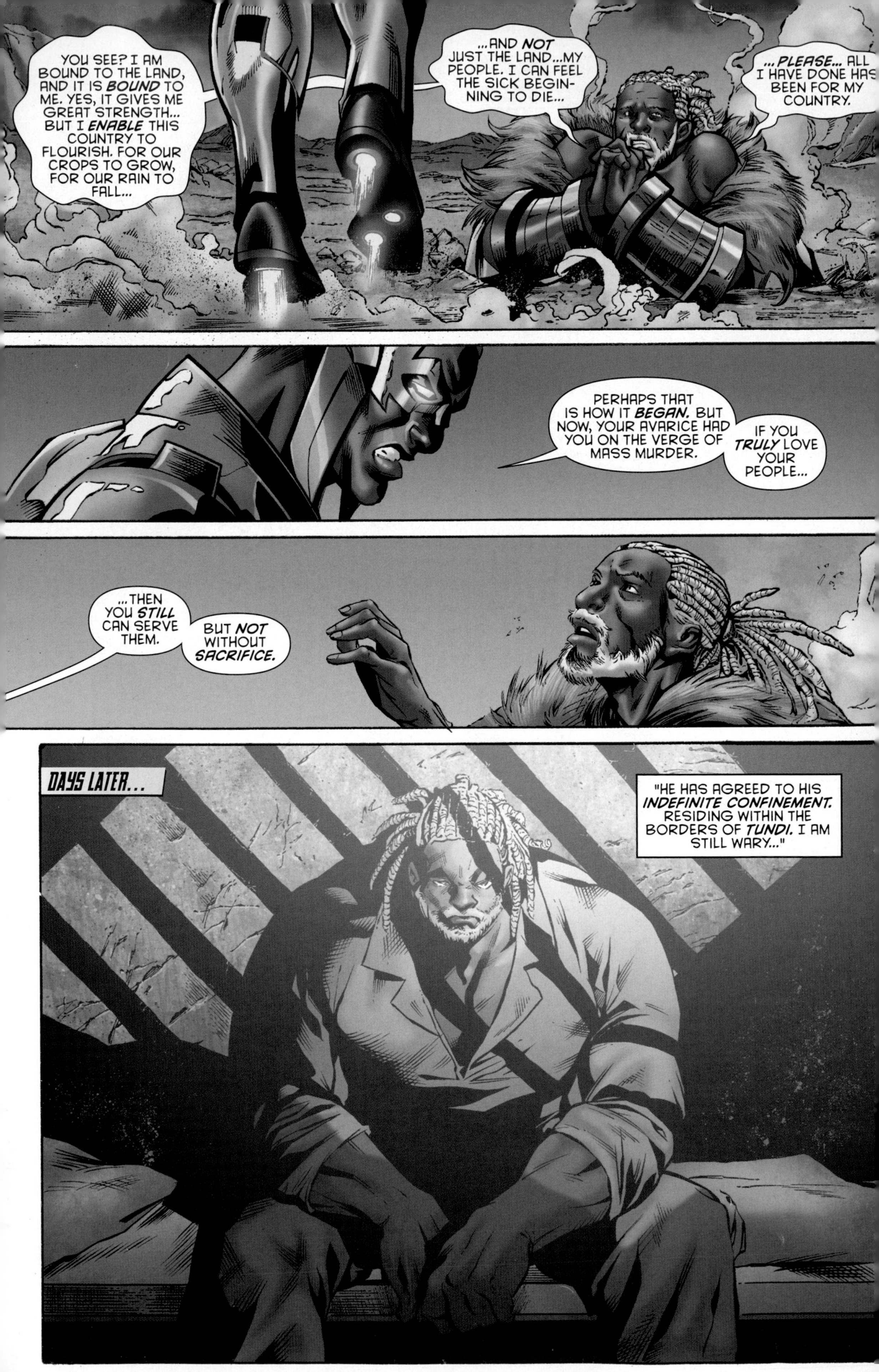
YOU SEE? I AM BOUND TO THE LAND, AND IT IS BOUND TO ME. YES, IT GIVES ME GREAT STRENGTH... BUT I ENABLE THIS COUNTRY TO FLOURISH. FOR OUR CROPS TO GROW, FOR OUR RAIN TO FALL...
...AND NOT JUST THE LAND...MY PEOPLE. I CAN FEEL THE SICK BEGINNING TO DIE...
...PLEASE... ALL I HAVE DONE HAS BEEN FOR MY COUNTRY.
PERHAPS THAT IS HOW IT BEGAN. BUT NOW, YOUR AVARICE HAD YOU ON THE VERGE OF MASS MURDER.
IF YOU TRULY LOVE YOUR PEOPLE...
...THEN YOU STILL CAN SERVE THEM.
BUT NOT WITHOUT SACRIFICE.
DAYS LATER...
"HE HAS AGREED TO HIS INDEFINITE CONFINEMENT. RESIDING WITHIN THE BORDERS OF TUNDI. I AM STILL WARY..."

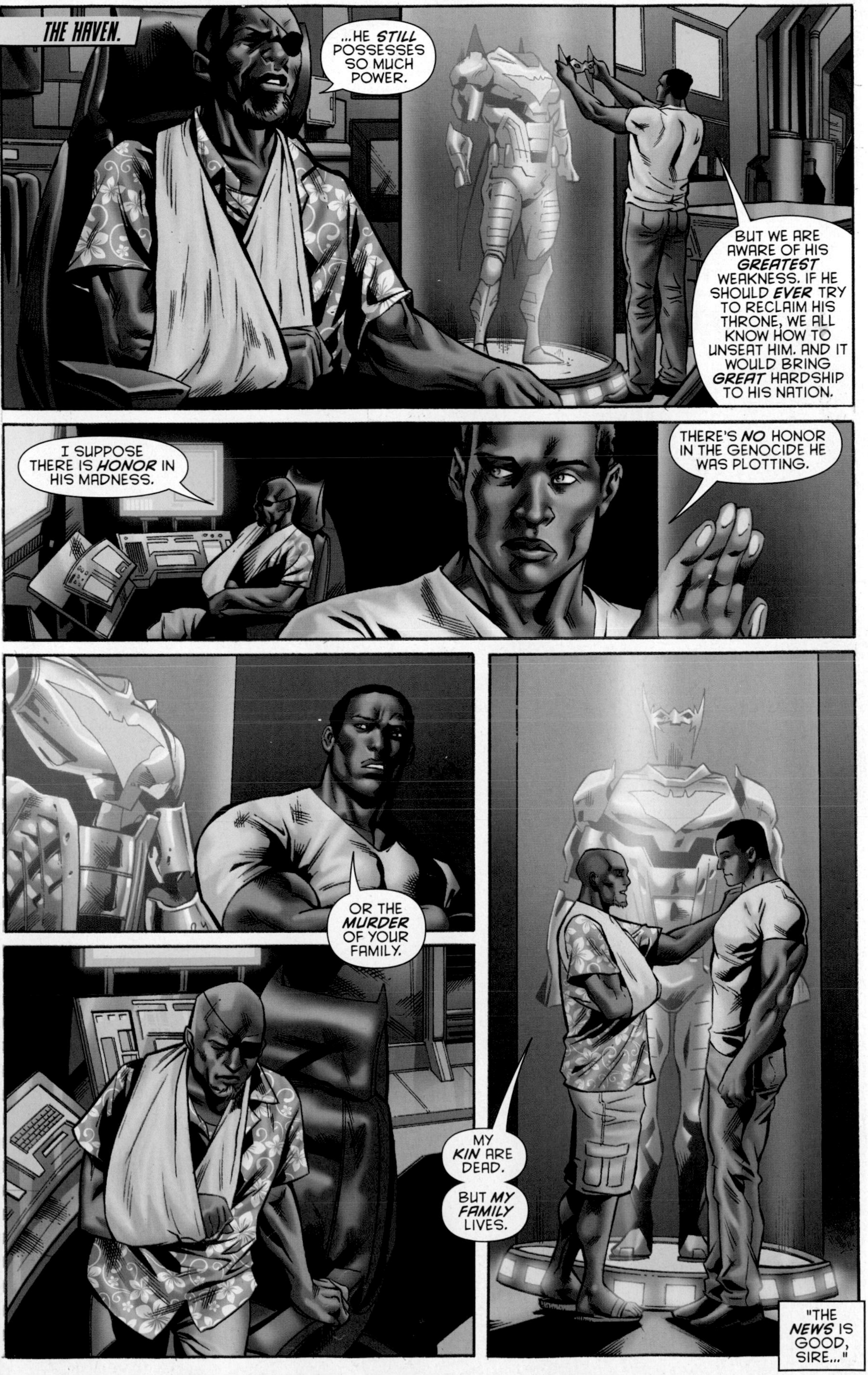
THE HAVEN.
...HE STILL POSSESSES SO MUCH POWER.
BUT WE ARE AWARE OF HIS GREATEST WEAKNESS. IF HE SHOULD EVER TRY TO RECLAIM HIS THRONE, WE ALL KNOW HOW TO UNSEAT HIM. AND IT WOULD BRING GREAT HARDSHIP TO HIS NATION.
I SUPPOSE THERE IS HONOR IN HIS MADNESS.
THERE'S NO HONOR IN THE GENOCIDE HE WAS PLOTTING.
OR THE MURDER OF YOUR FAMILY.
MY KIN ARE DEAD.
BUT MY FAMILY LIVES.
"THE NEWS IS GOOD, SIRE..."

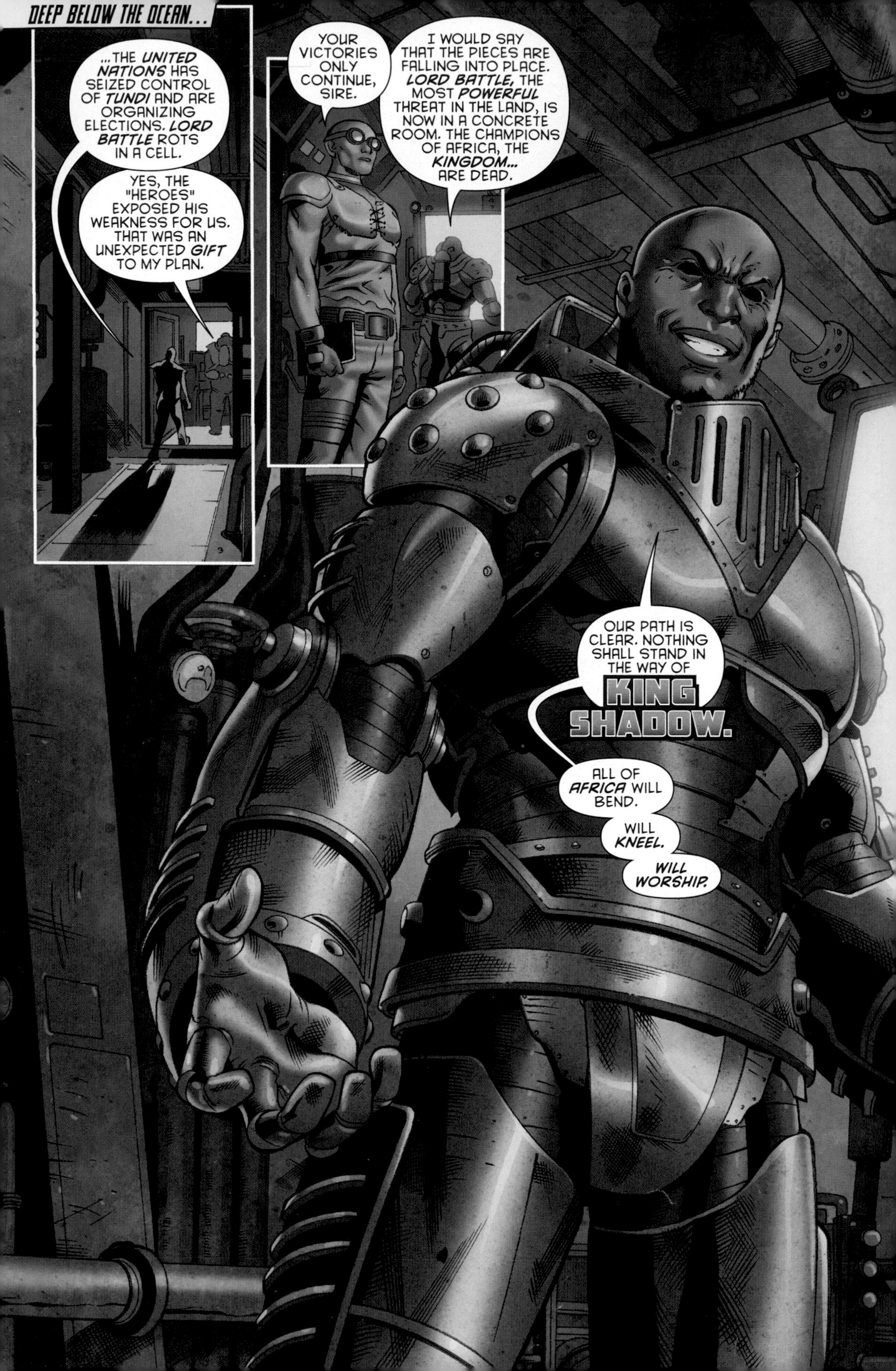
DEEP BELOW THE OCEAN...
...THE UNITED NATIONS HAS SEIZED CONTROL OF TUNDI AND ARE ORGANIZING ELECTIONS. LORD BATTLE ROTS IN A CELL.
YES, THE "HEROES" EXPOSED HIS WEAKNESS FOR US. THAT WAS AN UNEXPECTED GIFT TO MY PLAN.
YOUR VICTORIES ONLY CONTINUE, SIRE.
I WOULD SAY THAT THE PIECES ARE FALLING INTO PLACE. LORD BATTLE, THE MOST POWERFUL THREAT IN THE LAND, IS NOW IN A CONCRETE ROOM. THE CHAMPIONS OF AFRICA, THE KINGDOM... ARE DEAD.
OUR PATH IS CLEAR. NOTHING SHALL STAND IN THE WAY OF
KING SHADOW.
ALL OF AFRICA WILL BEND.
WILL KNEEL.
WILL WORSHIP.

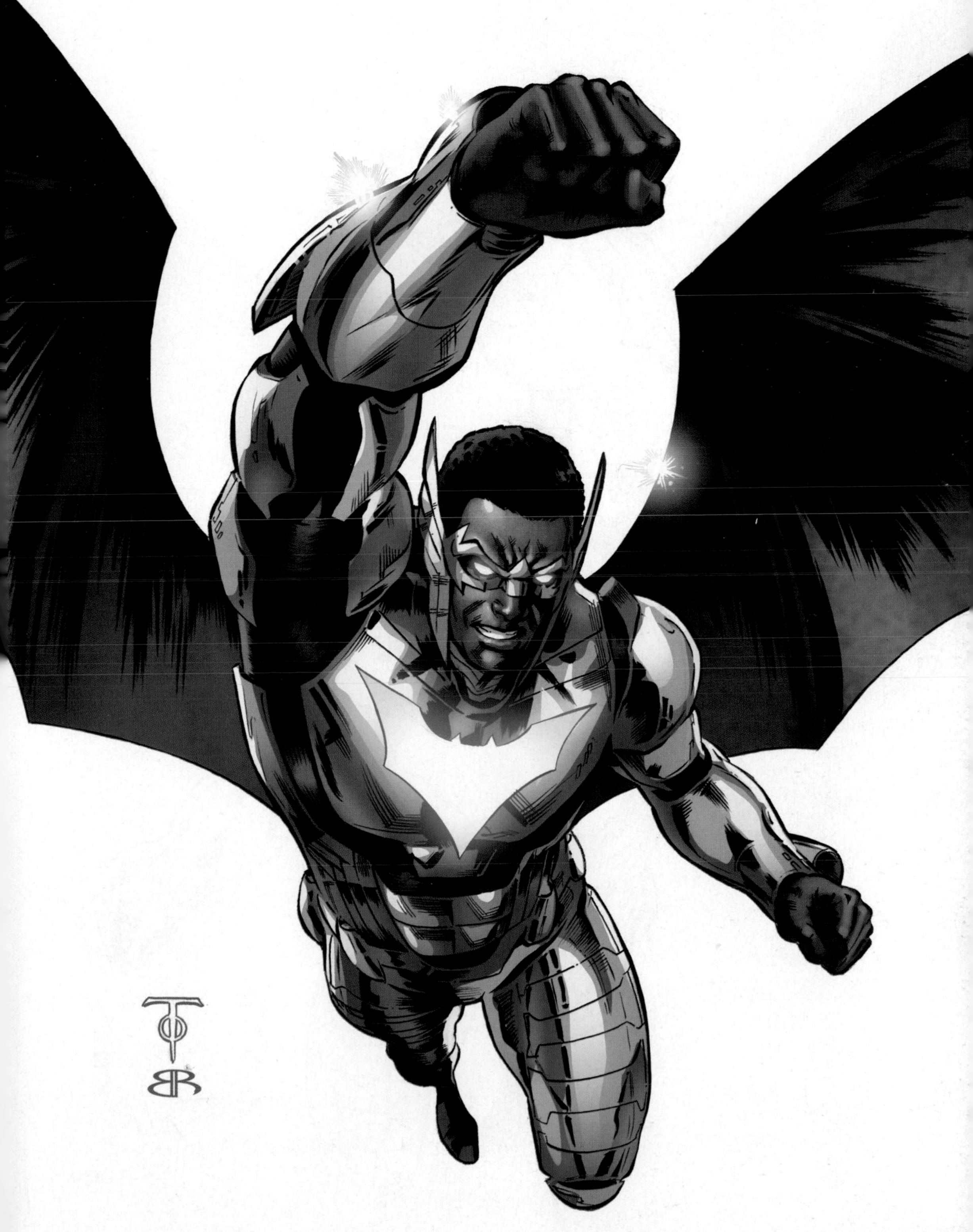

THEY WILL PAY FOR WHAT THEY'VE GIVEN BIRTH TO

JUDD WINICK writer MARCUS TO penciller RYAN WINN & RICHARD ZAJAC inkers cover art by MARCUS TO & BRIAN REBER

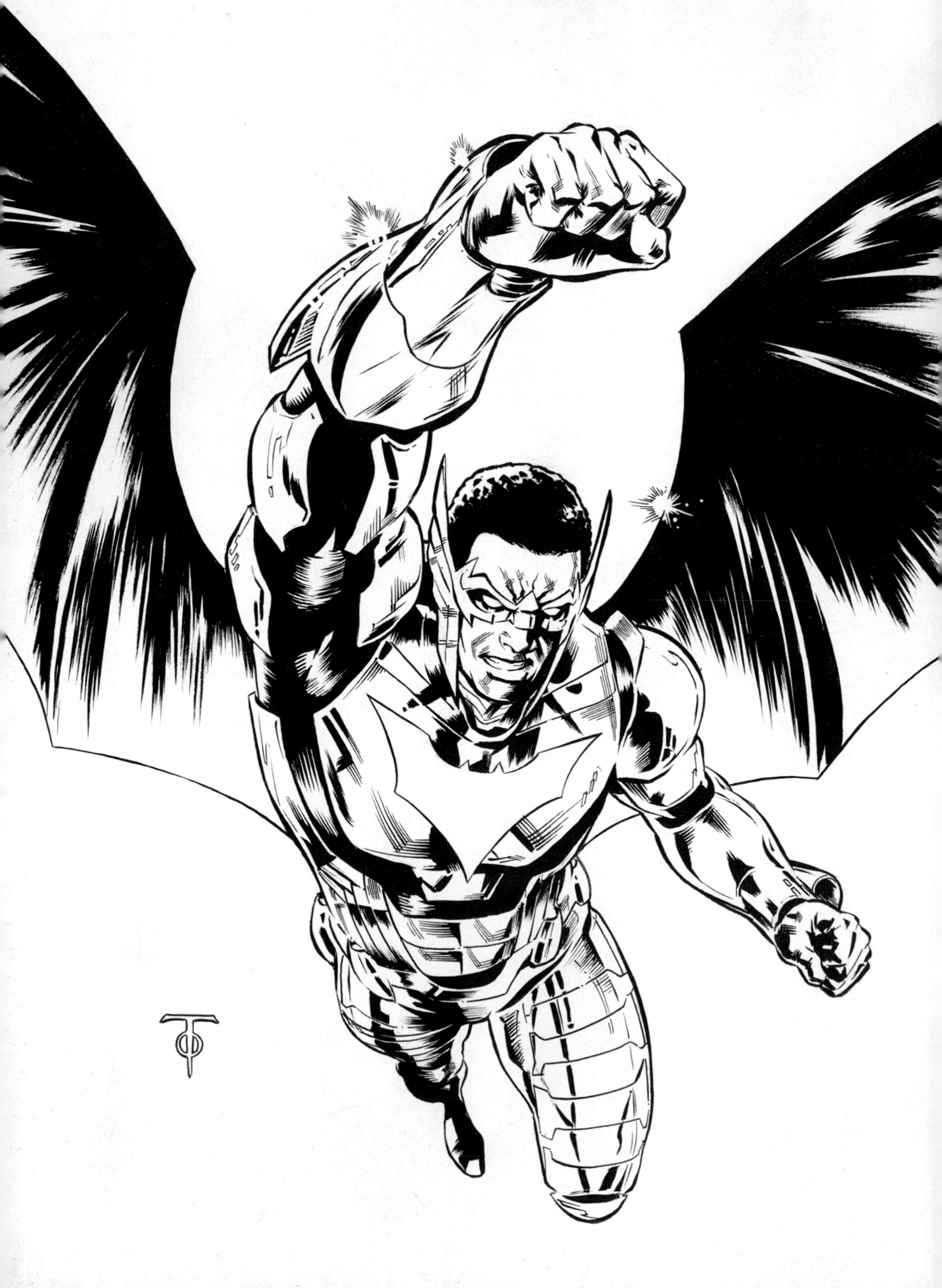

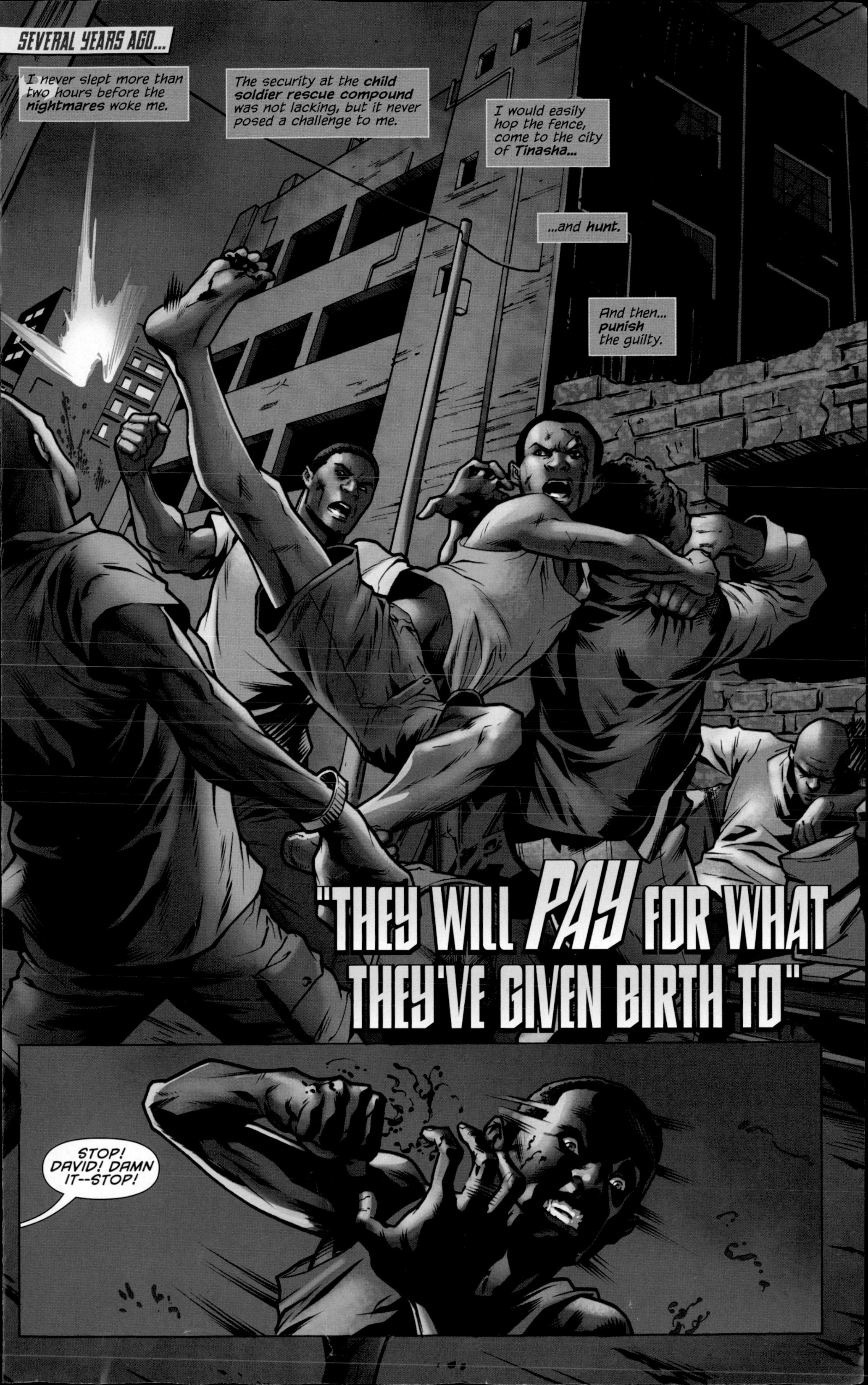
SEVERAL YEARS AGO...
I never slept more than two hours before the nightmares woke me.
The security at the child soldier rescue compound was not lacking, but it never posed a challenge to me.
I would easily hop the fence, come to the city of Tinasha...
...and hunt.
And then... punish the guilty.
"THEY WILL PAY FOR WHAT THEY'VE GIVEN BIRTH TO"
STOP! DAVID! DAMN IT--STOP!

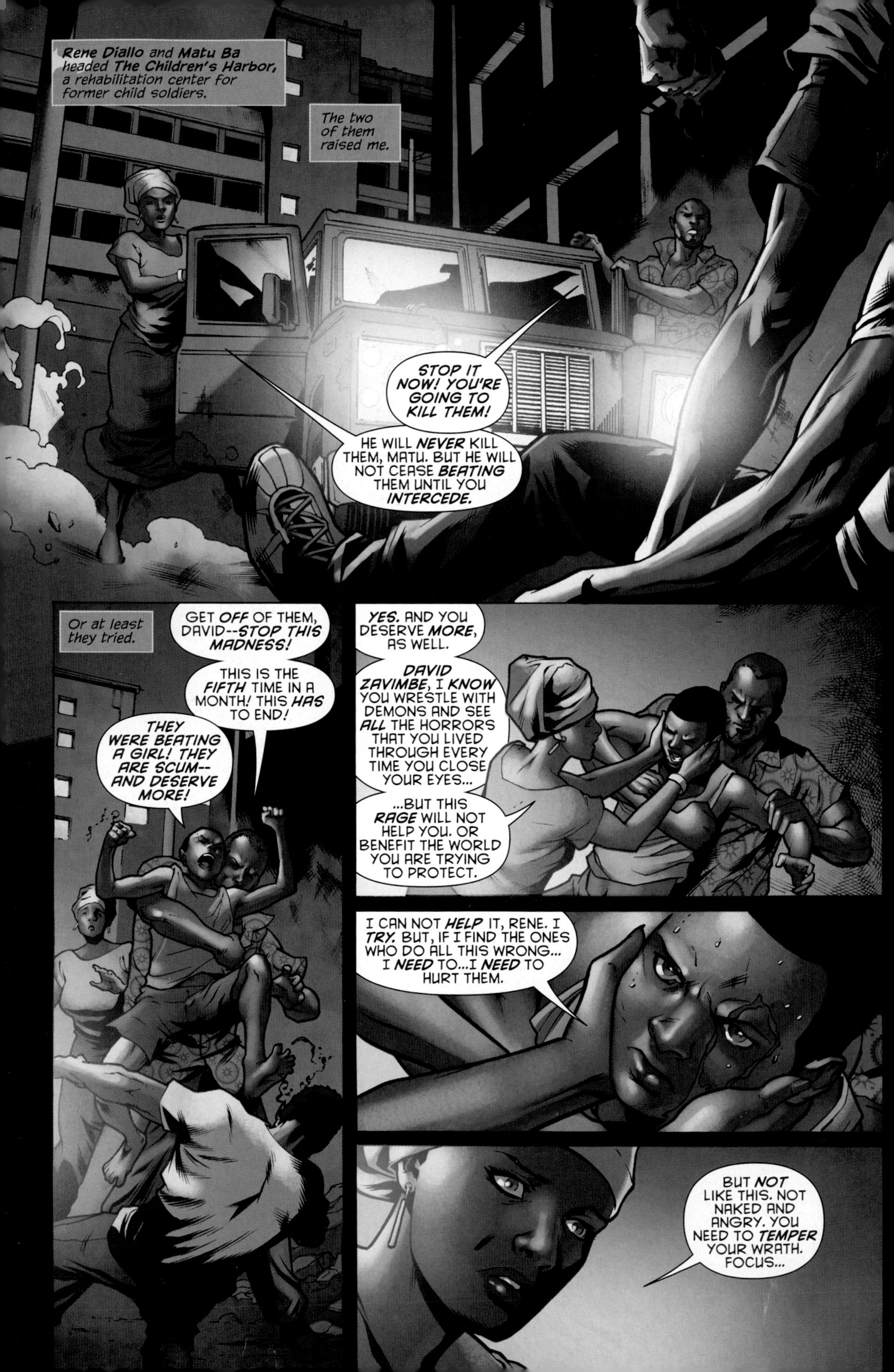
Rene Diallo and Matu Ba headed The Children's Harbor, a rehabilitation center for former child soldiers.
The two of them raised me.
STOP IT NOW! YOU'RE GOING TO KILL THEM!
HE WILL NEVER KILL THEM, MATU. BUT HE WILL NOT CEASE BEATING THEM UNTIL YOU INTERCEDE.
Or at least they tried.
GET OFF OF THEM, DAVID--STOP THIS MADNESS!
THIS IS THE FIFTH TIME IN A MONTH! THIS HAS TO END!
THEY WERE BEATING A GIRL! THEY ARE SCUM--AND DESERVE MORE!
YES. AND YOU DESERVE MORE, AS WELL.
DAVID ZAVIMBE, I KNOW YOU WRESTLE WITH DEMONS AND SEE ALL THE HORRORS THAT YOU LIVED THROUGH EVERY TIME YOU CLOSE YOUR EYES...
...BUT THIS RAGE WILL NOT HELP YOU. OR BENEFIT THE WORLD YOU ARE TRYING TO PROTECT.
I CAN NOT HELP IT, RENE. I TRY. BUT, IF I FIND THE ONES WHO DO ALL THIS WRONG... I NEED TO...I NEED TO HURT THEM.
BUT NOT LIKE THIS. NOT NAKED AND ANGRY. YOU NEED TO TEMPER YOUR WRATH. FOCUS...

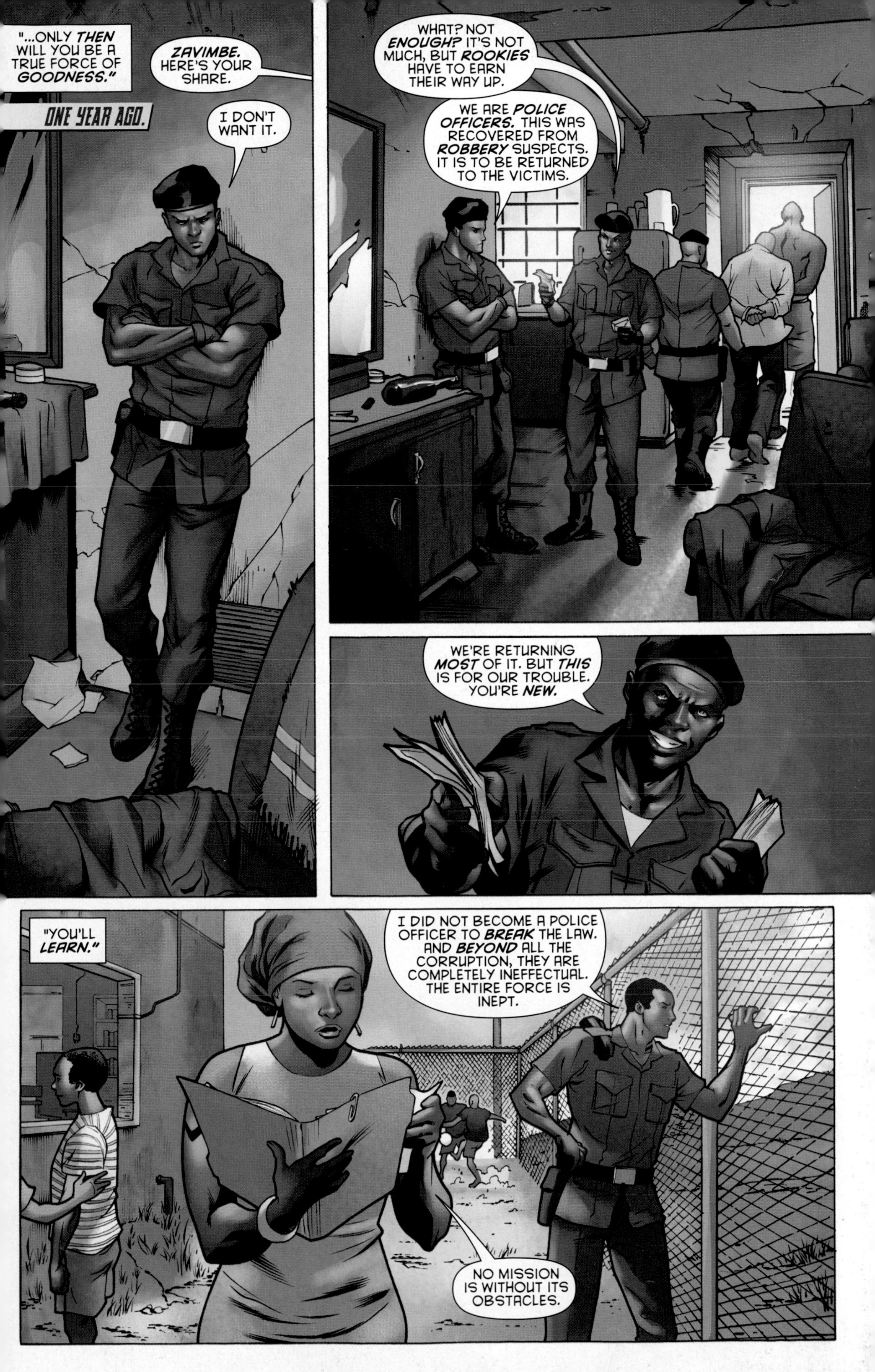
"...ONLY THEN WILL YOU BE A TRUE FORCE OF GOODNESS."
ZAVIMBE. HERE'S YOUR SHARE.
ONE YEAR AGO.
I DON'T WANT IT.
WHAT? NOT ENOUGH? IT'S NOT MUCH, BUT ROOKIES HAVE TO EARN THEIR WAY UP.
WE ARE POLICE OFFICERS. THIS WAS RECOVERED FROM ROBBERY SUSPECTS. IT IS TO BE RETURNED TO THE VICTIMS.
WE'RE RETURNING MOST OF IT. BUT THIS IS FOR OUR TROUBLE. YOU'RE NEW.
"YOU'LL LEARN."
I DID NOT BECOME A POLICE OFFICER TO BREAK THE LAW. AND BEYOND ALL THE CORRUPTION, THEY ARE COMPLETELY INEFFECTUAL. THE ENTIRE FORCE IS INEPT.
NO MISSION IS WITHOUT ITS OBSTACLES.

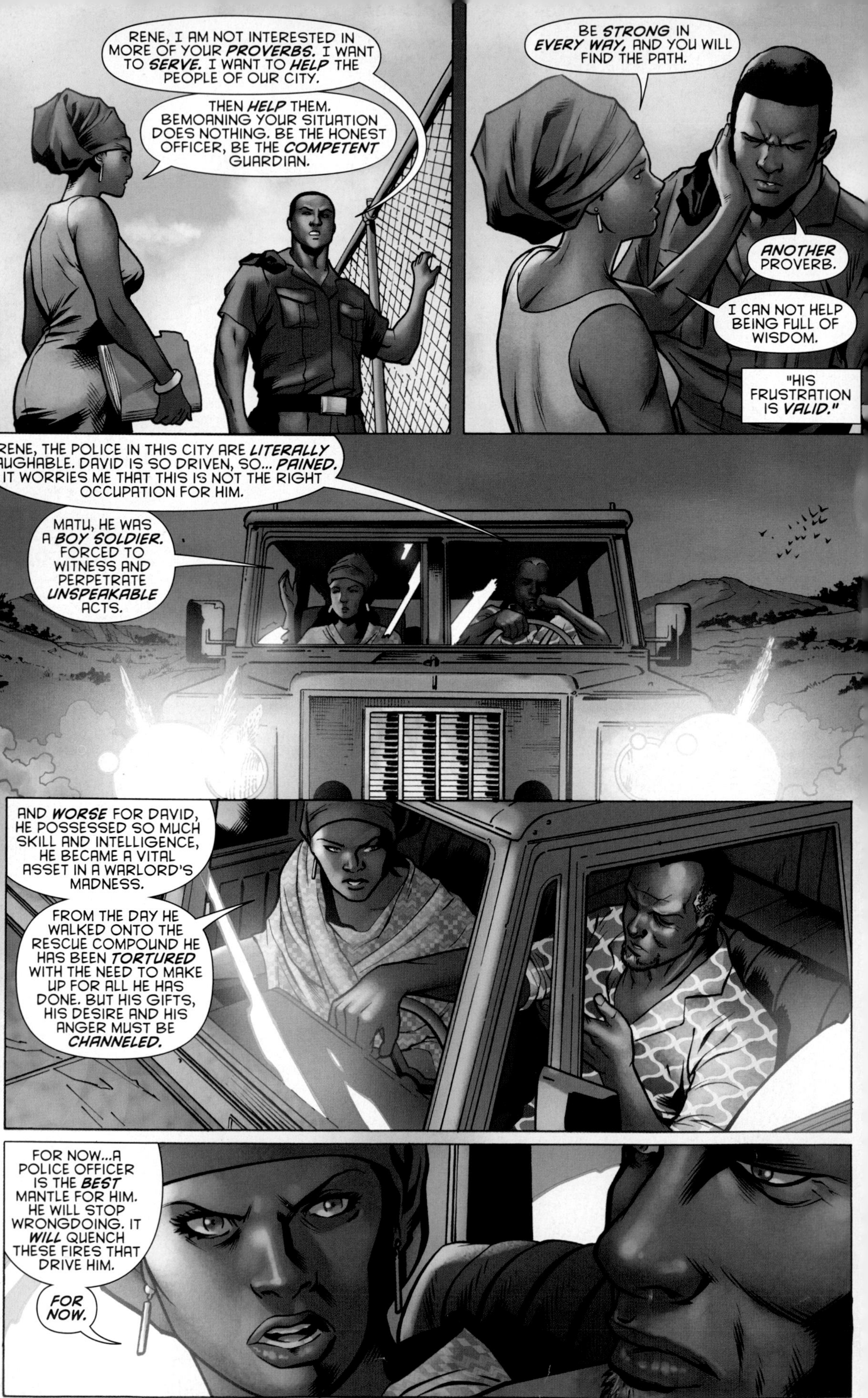
RENE, I AM NOT INTERESTED IN MORE OF YOUR PROVERBS. I WANT TO SERVE. I WANT TO HELP THE PEOPLE OF OUR CITY.
THEN HELP THEM. BEMOANING YOUR SITUATION DOES NOTHING. BE THE HONEST OFFICER, BE THE COMPETENT GUARDIAN.
BE STRONG IN EVERY WAY, AND YOU WILL FIND THE PATH.
ANOTHER PROVERB.
I CAN NOT HELP BEING FULL OF WISDOM.
"HIS FRUSTRATION IS VALID."
RENE, THE POLICE IN THIS CITY ARE LITERALLY LAUGHABLE. DAVID IS SO DRIVEN, SO... PAINED. IT WORRIES ME THAT THIS IS NOT THE RIGHT OCCUPATION FOR HIM.
MATU, HE WAS A BOY SOLDIER. FORCED TO WITNESS AND PERPETRATE UNSPEAKABLE ACTS.
AND WORSE FOR DAVID, HE POSSESSED SO MUCH SKILL AND INTELLIGENCE, HE BECAME A VITAL ASSET IN A WARLORD'S MADNESS.
FROM THE DAY HE WALKED ONTO THE RESCUE COMPOUND HE HAS BEEN TORTURED WITH THE NEED TO MAKE UP FOR ALL HE HAS DONE. BUT HIS GIFTS, HIS DESIRE AND HIS ANGER MUST BE CHANNELED.
FOR NOW...A POLICE OFFICER IS THE BEST MANTLE FOR HIM. HE WILL STOP WRONGDOING. IT WILL QUENCH THESE FIRES THAT DRIVE HIM.
FOR NOW.

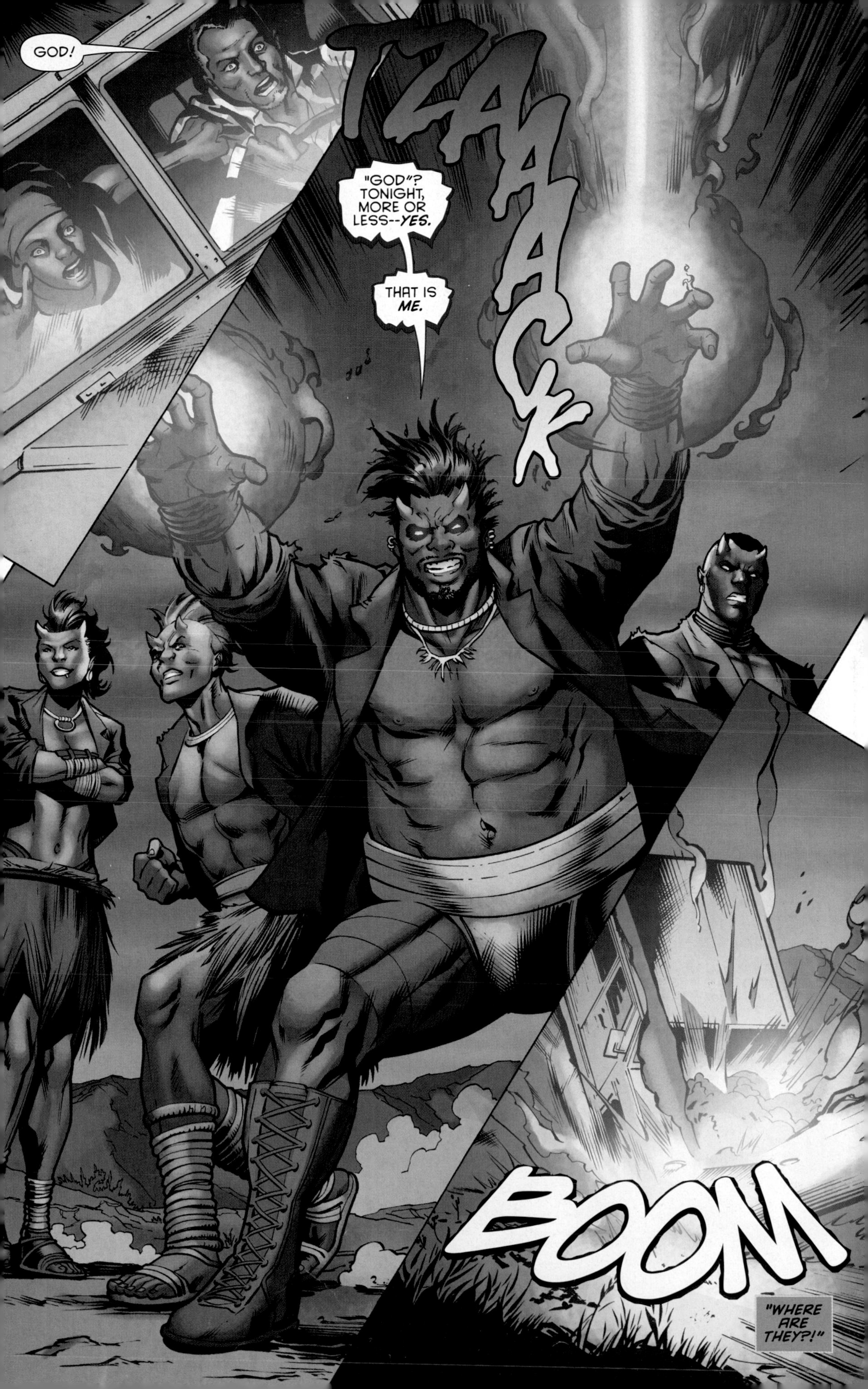
GOD!
TZAAACK
"GOD"? TONIGHT, MORE OR LESS--YES.
THAT IS ME.
BOOM
"WHERE ARE THEY?!"

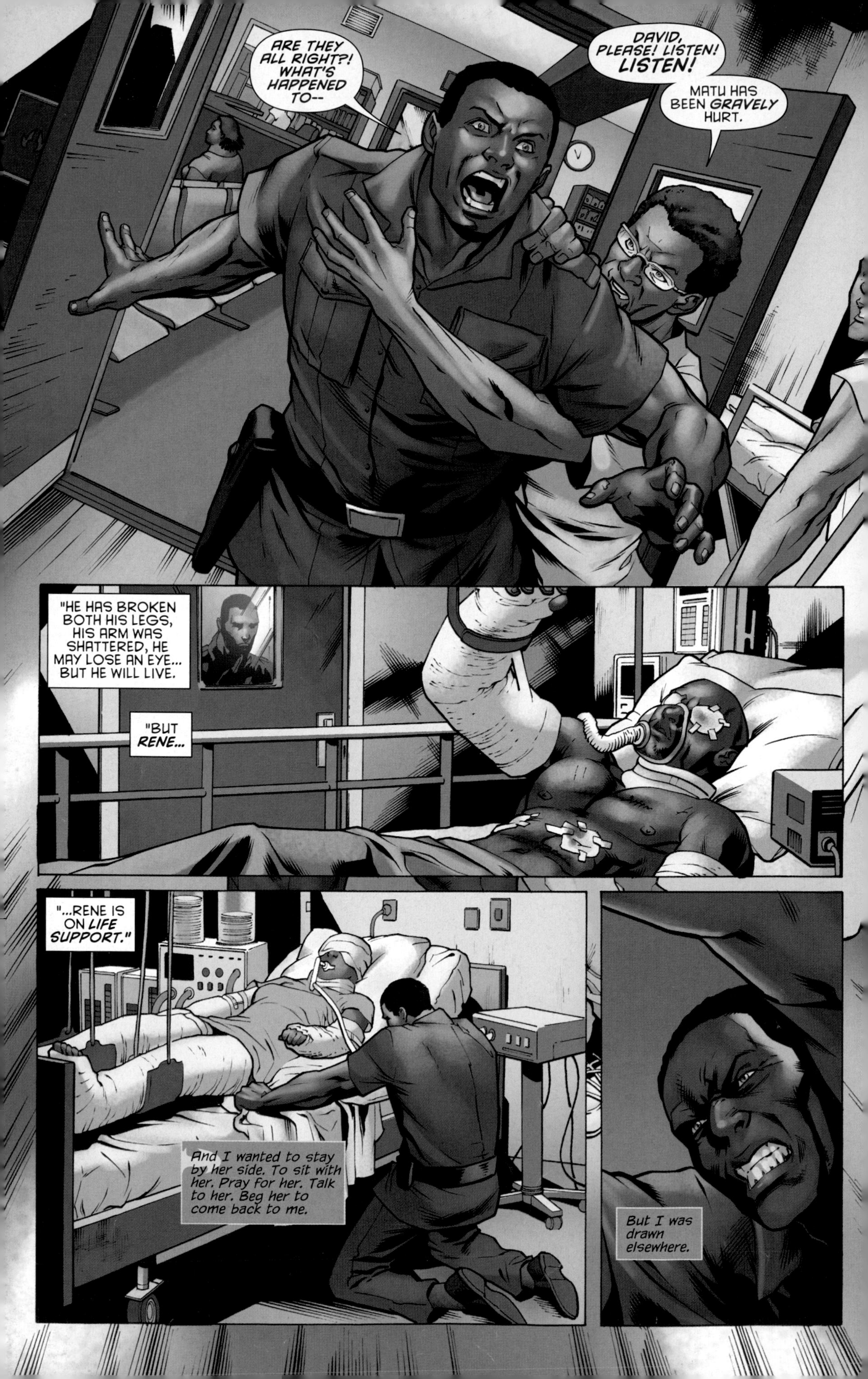
ARE THEY ALL RIGHT?! WHAT'S HAPPENED TO--
DAVID, PLEASE! LISTEN! LISTEN!
MATU HAS BEEN GRAVELY HURT.
"HE HAS BROKEN BOTH HIS LEGS, HIS ARM WAS SHATTERED, HE MAY LOSE AN EYE... BUT HE WILL LIVE.
"BUT RENE...
"...RENE IS ON LIFE SUPPORT."
And I wanted to stay by her side. To sit with her. Pray for her. Talk to her. Beg her to come back to me.
But I was drawn elsewhere.

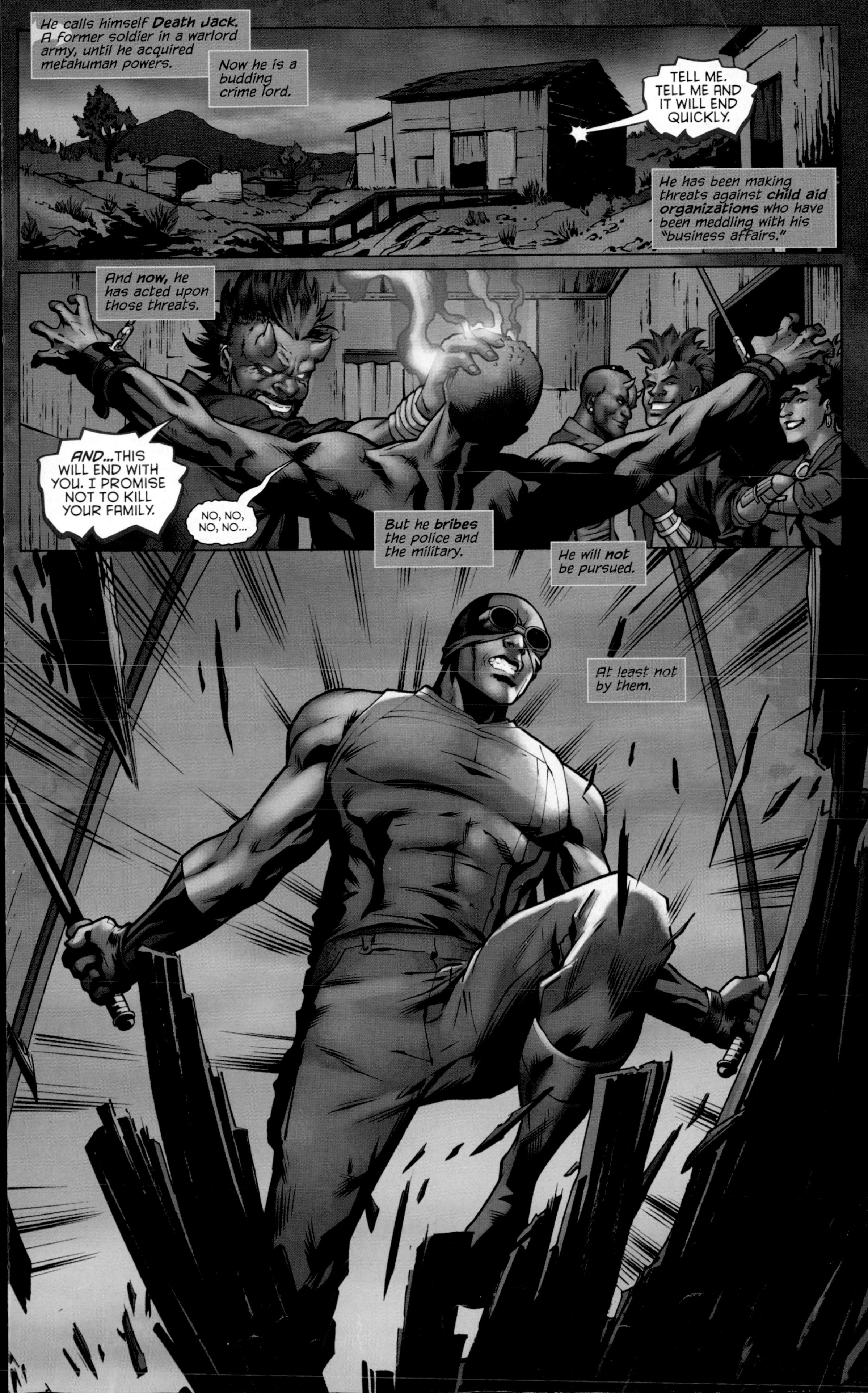
He calls himself Death Jack. A former soldier in a warlord army, until he acquired metahuman powers.
Now he is a budding crime lord.
TELL ME. TELL ME AND IT WILL END QUICKLY.
He has been making threats against child aid organizations who have been meddling with his "business affairs."
And now, he has acted upon those threats.
AND...THIS WILL END WITH YOU. I PROMISE NOT TO KILL YOUR FAMILY.
NO, NO, NO, NO...
But he bribes the police and the military.
He will not be pursued.
At least not by them.

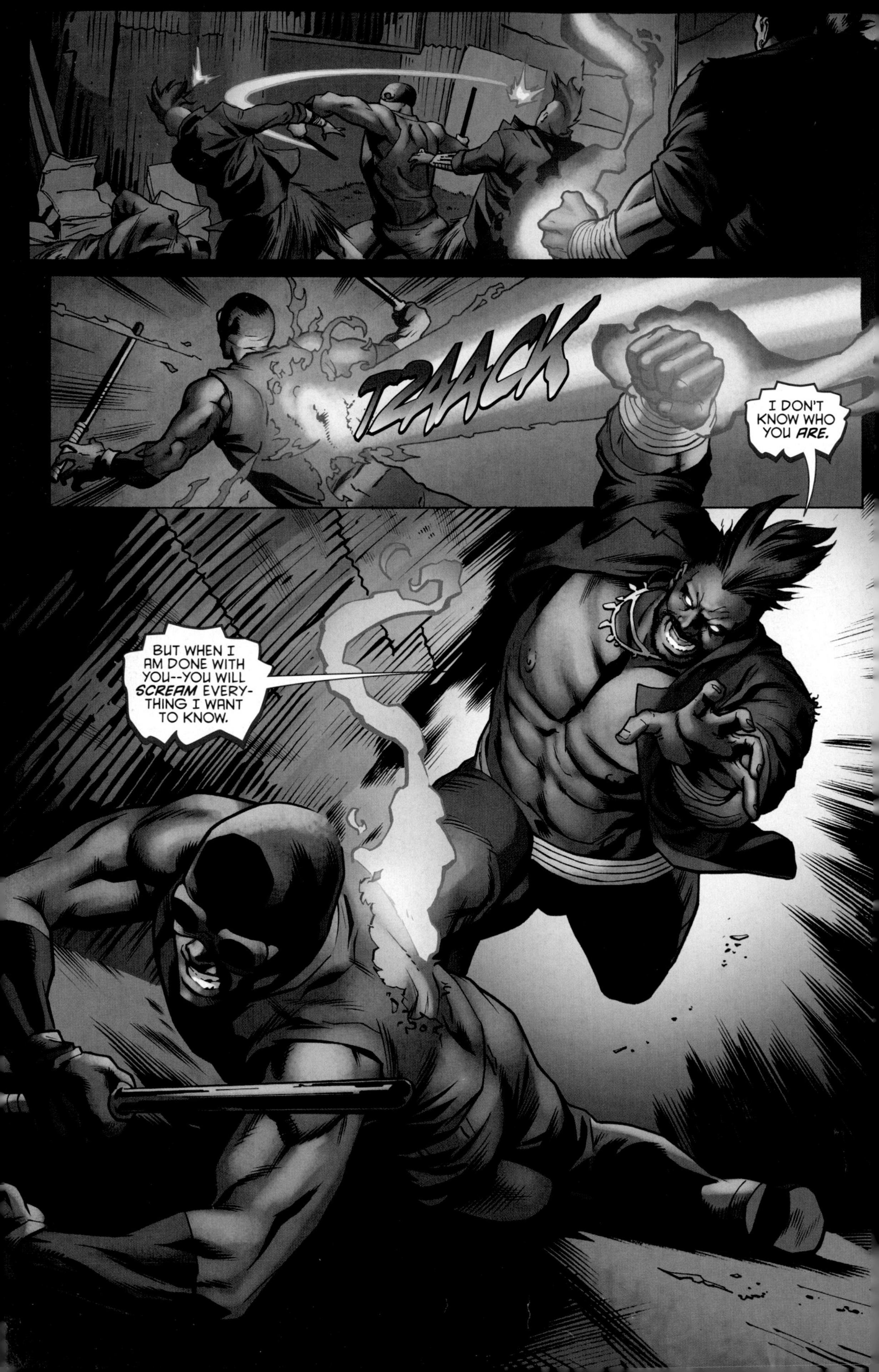
TRACK
I DON'T KNOW WHO YOU ARE.
BUT WHEN I AM DONE WITH YOU--YOU WILL SCREAM EVERY-THING I WANT TO KNOW.

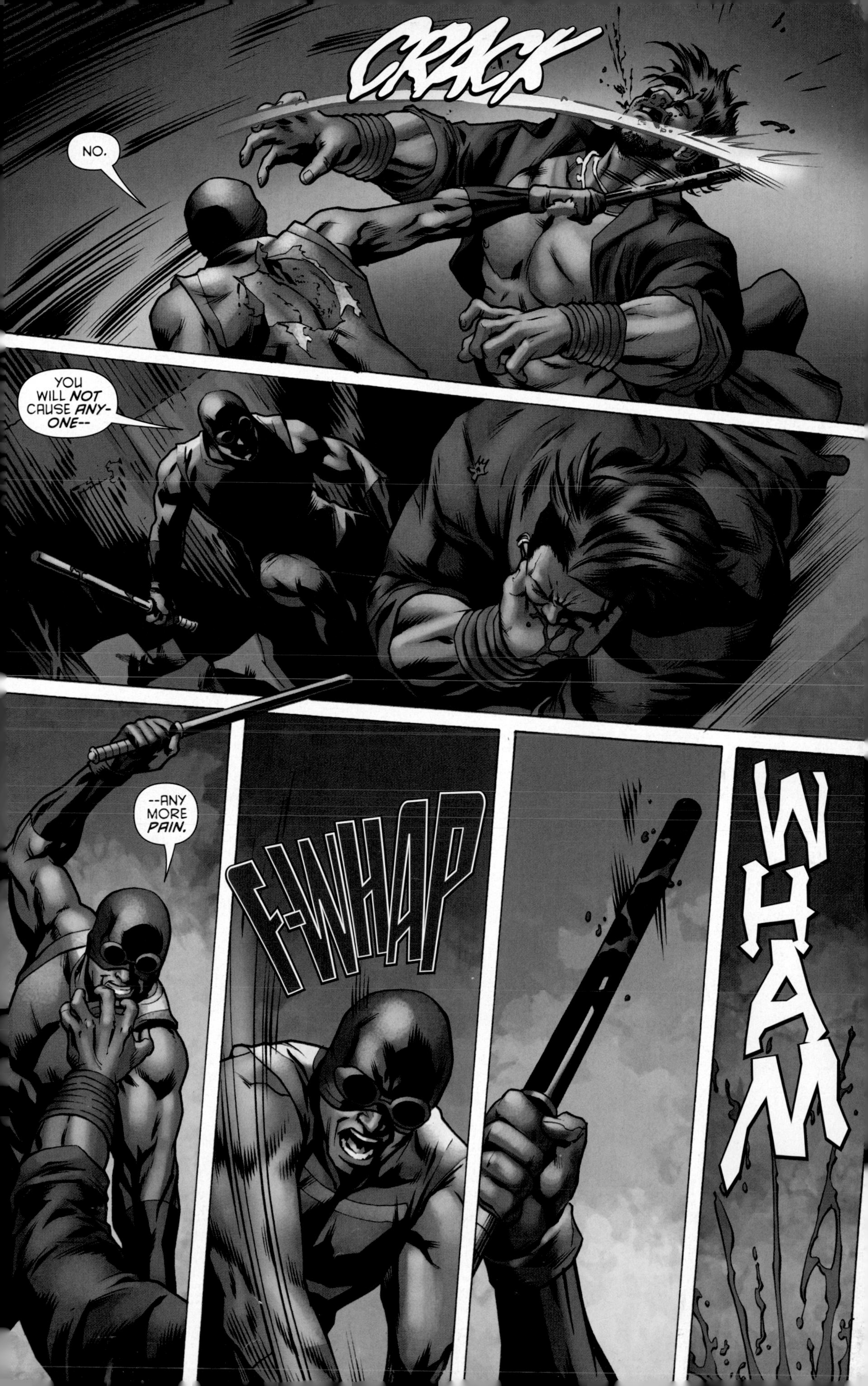
CRACK
NO.
YOU WILL NOT CAUSE ANY-ONE--
--ANY MORE PAIN.
F-WHAP
WHAM

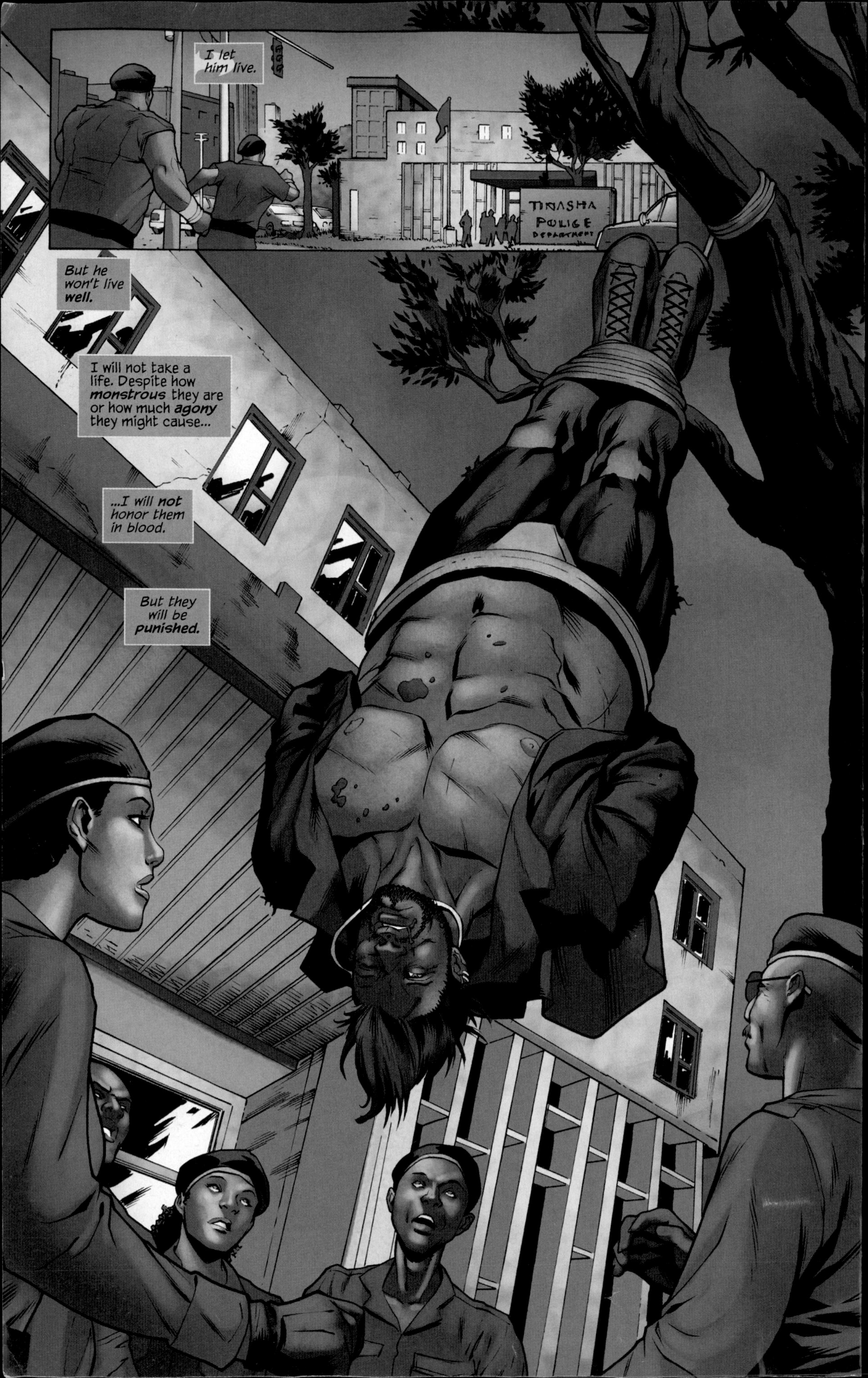

I let him live.
TINASHA POLICE DEPARTMENT
But he won't live **well.**
I will not take a life. Despite how ***monstrous*** they are or how much ***agony*** they might cause...
...I will ***not*** honor them in blood.
But they will be ***punished.***

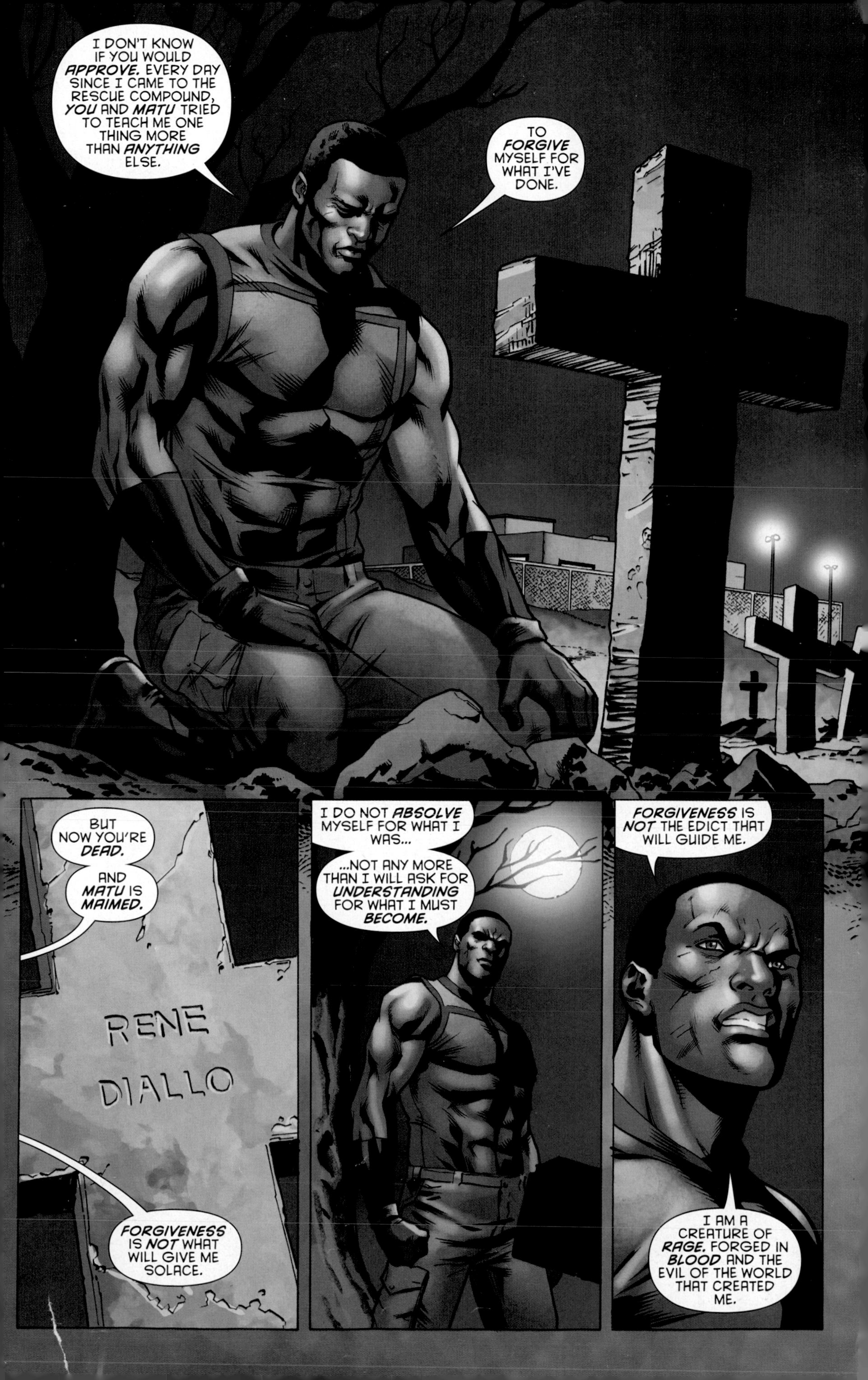
I DON'T KNOW IF YOU WOULD APPROVE. EVERY DAY SINCE I CAME TO THE RESCUE COMPOUND, YOU AND MATU TRIED TO TEACH ME ONE THING MORE THAN ANYTHING ELSE.
TO FORGIVE MYSELF FOR WHAT I'VE DONE.
BUT NOW YOU'RE DEAD.
AND MATU IS MAIMED.
RENE DIALLO
FORGIVENESS IS NOT WHAT WILL GIVE ME SOLACE.
I DO NOT ABSOLVE MYSELF FOR WHAT I WAS...
...NOT ANY MORE THAN I WILL ASK FOR UNDERSTANDING FOR WHAT I MUST BECOME.
FORGIVENESS IS NOT THE EDICT THAT WILL GUIDE ME.
I AM A CREATURE OF RAGE. FORGED IN BLOOD AND THE EVIL OF THE WORLD THAT CREATED ME.

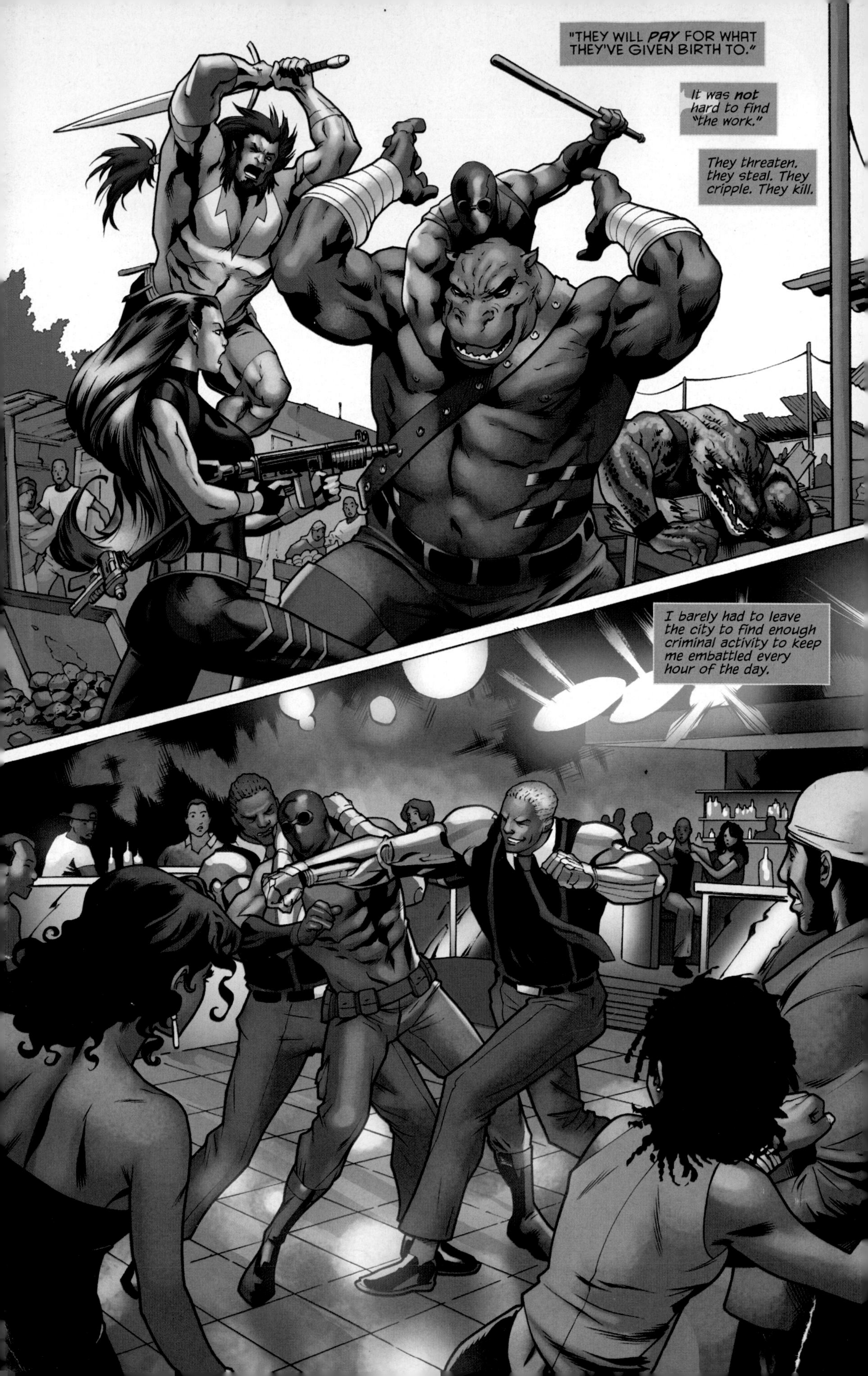
"THEY WILL PAY FOR WHAT THEY'VE GIVEN BIRTH TO."
It was not hard to find "the work."
They threaten. they steal. They cripple. They kill.
I barely had to leave the city to find enough criminal activity to keep me embattled every hour of the day.

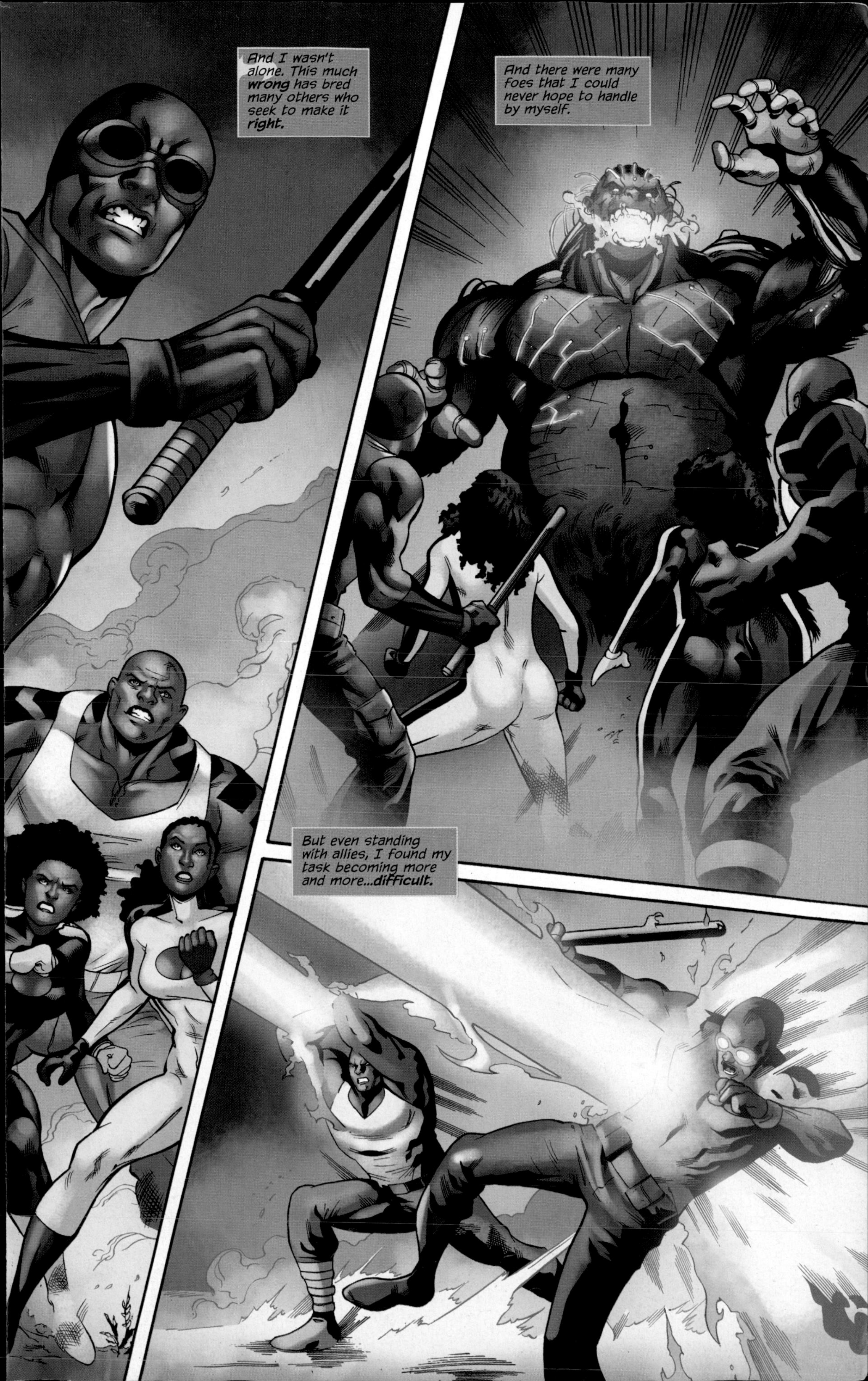
And I wasn't alone. This much wrong has bred many others who seek to make it right.
And there were many foes that I could never hope to handle by myself.
But even standing with allies, I found my task becoming more and more...difficult.

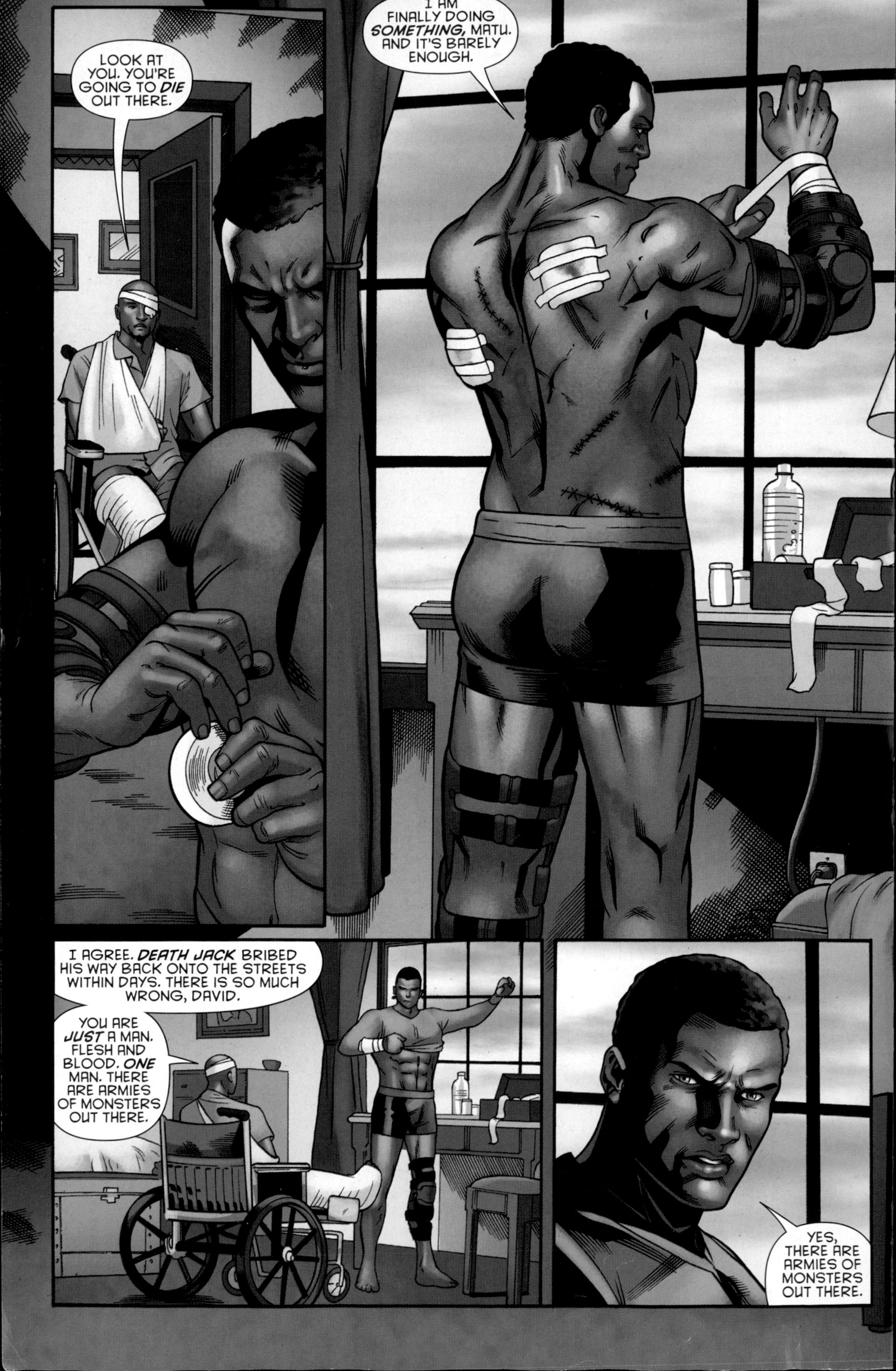
LOOK AT YOU. YOU'RE GOING TO *DIE* OUT THERE.
I AM FINALLY DOING *SOMETHING*, MATU. AND IT'S BARELY ENOUGH.
I AGREE. *DEATH JACK* BRIBED HIS WAY BACK ONTO THE STREETS WITHIN DAYS. THERE IS SO MUCH WRONG, DAVID.
YOU ARE *JUST* A MAN. FLESH AND BLOOD. *ONE* MAN. THERE ARE ARMIES OF MONSTERS OUT THERE.
YES, THERE ARE ARMIES OF MONSTERS OUT THERE.

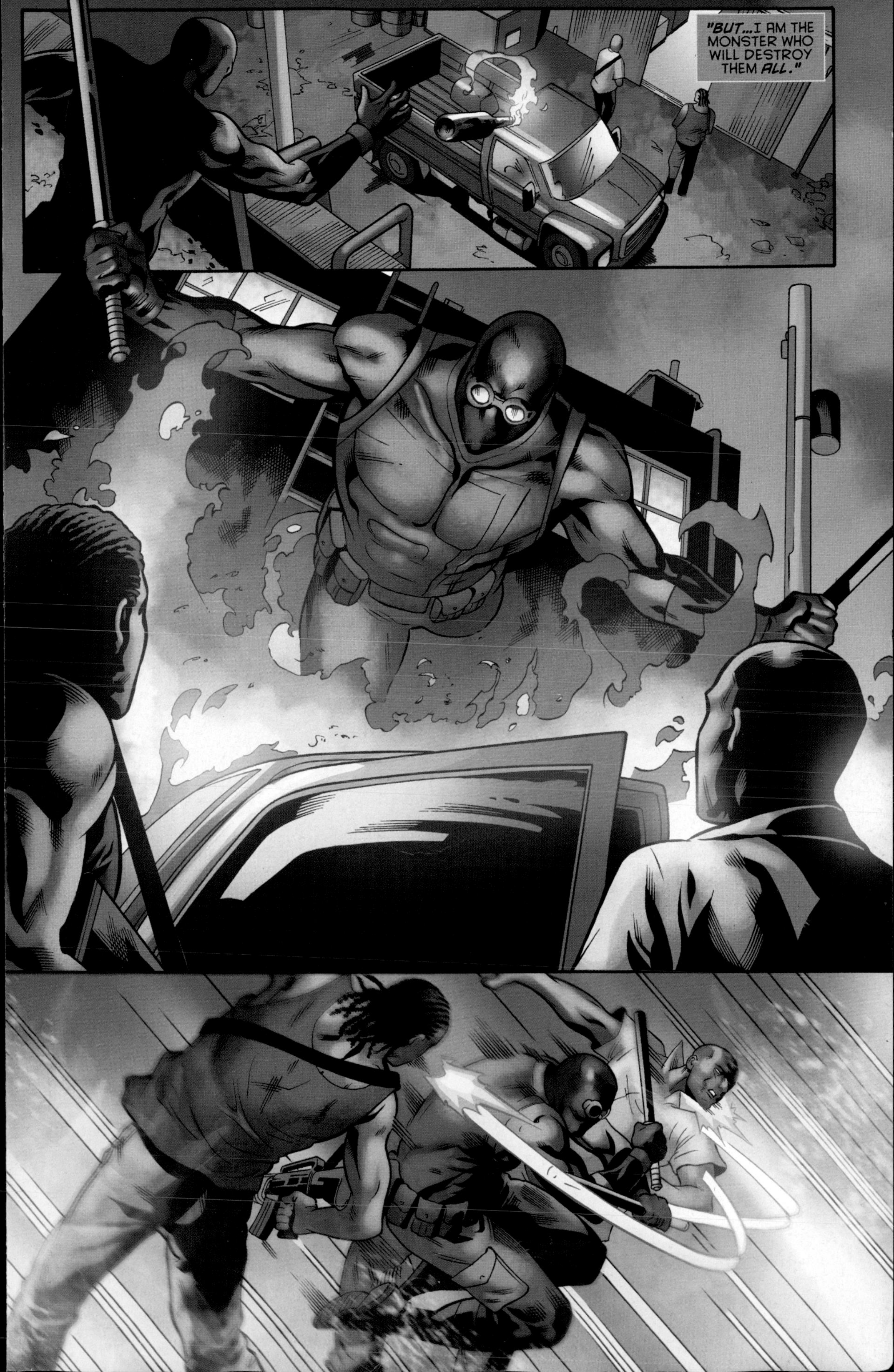
"BUT...I AM THE MONSTER WHO WILL DESTROY THEM ALL."

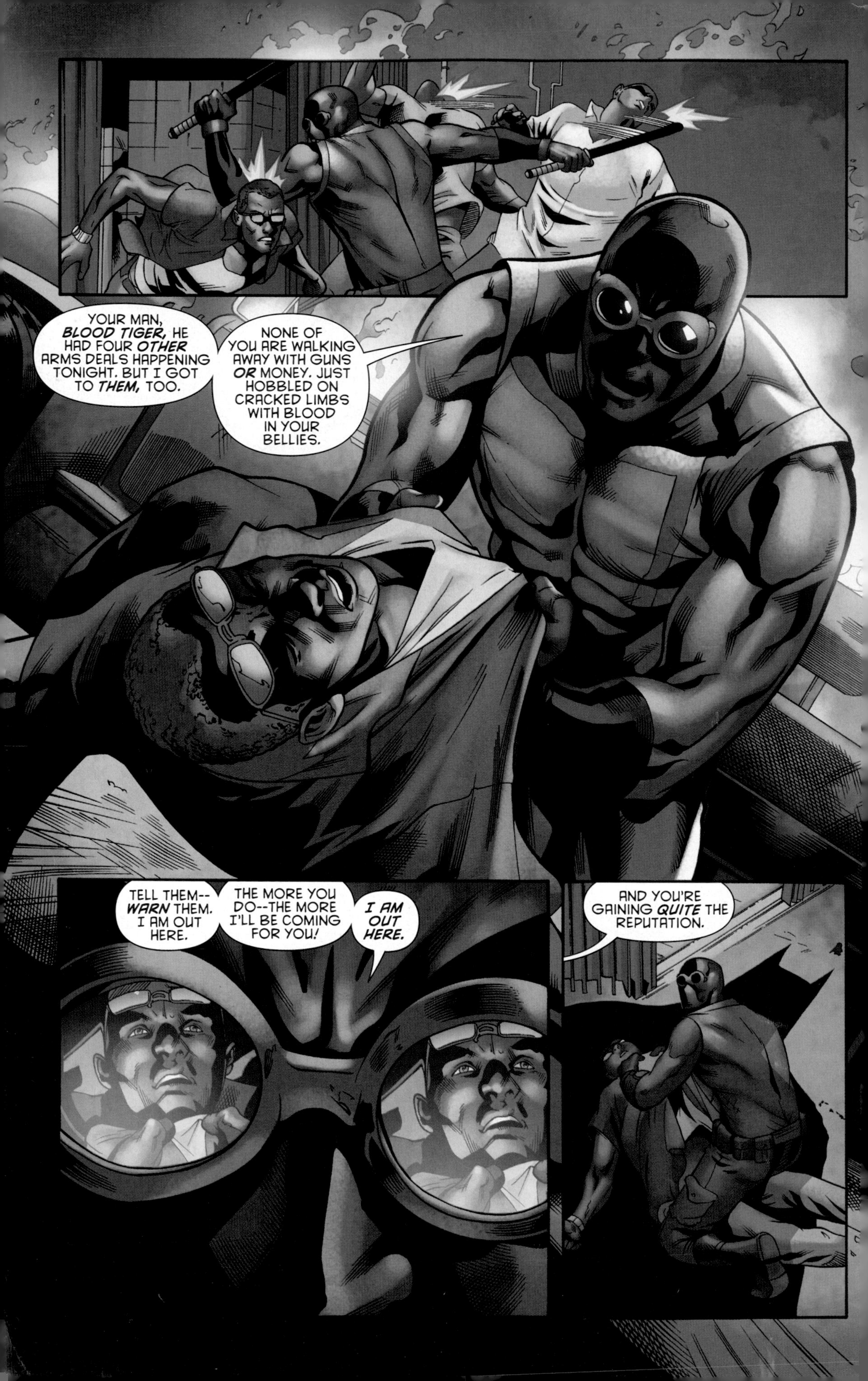
YOUR MAN, BLOOD TIGER, HE HAD FOUR OTHER ARMS DEALS HAPPENING TONIGHT. BUT I GOT TO THEM, TOO.
NONE OF YOU ARE WALKING AWAY WITH GUNS OR MONEY. JUST HOBBLED ON CRACKED LIMBS WITH BLOOD IN YOUR BELLIES.
TELL THEM-- WARN THEM. I AM OUT HERE.
THE MORE YOU DO--THE MORE I'LL BE COMING FOR YOU!
I AM OUT HERE.
AND YOU'RE GAINING QUITE THE REPUTATION.

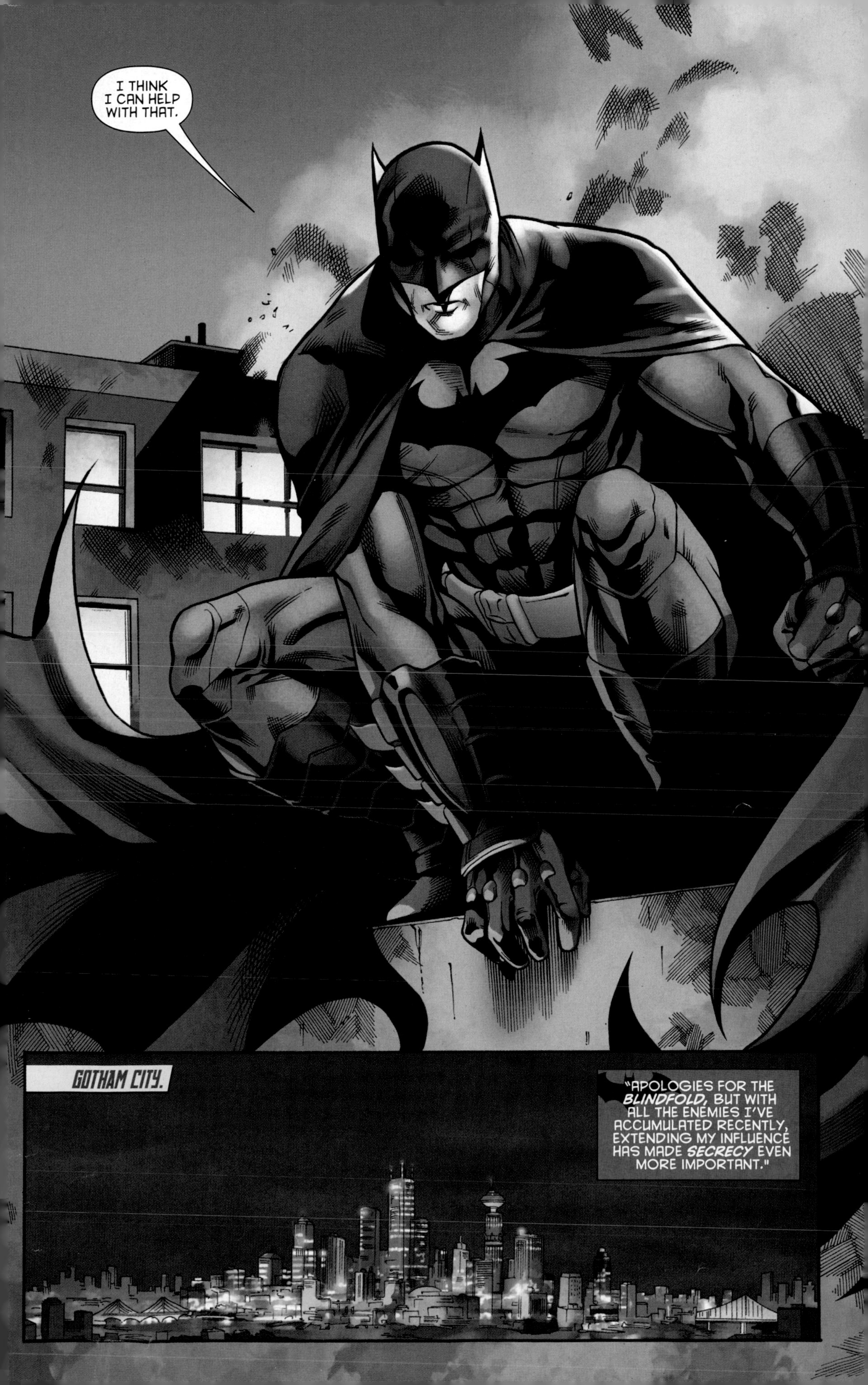
I THINK I CAN HELP WITH THAT.
GOTHAM CITY.
"APOLOGIES FOR THE BLINDFOLD, BUT WITH ALL THE ENEMIES I'VE ACCUMULATED RECENTLY, EXTENDING MY INFLUENCE HAS MADE SECRECY EVEN MORE IMPORTANT."

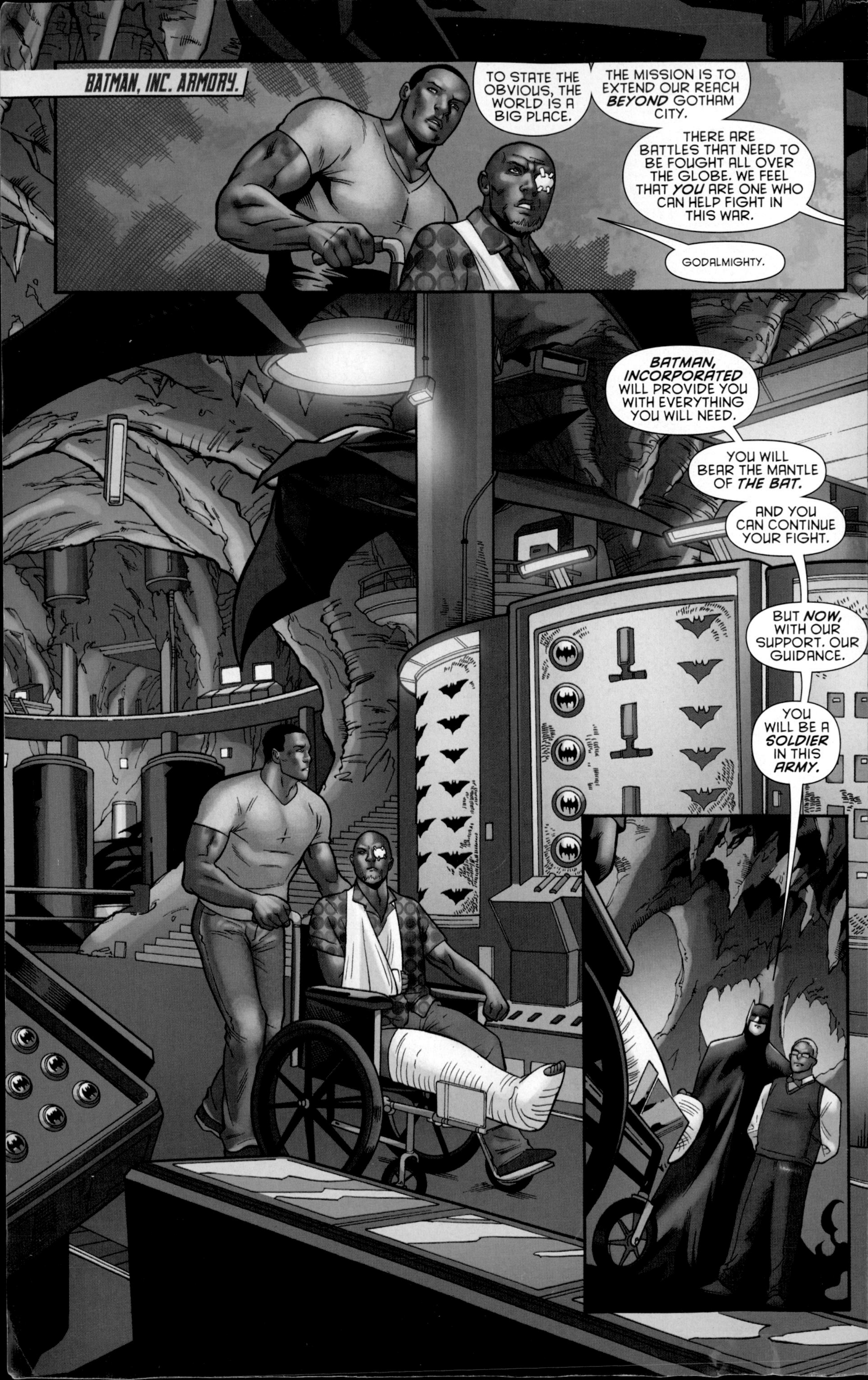
BATMAN, INC. ARMORY.
TO STATE THE OBVIOUS, THE WORLD IS A BIG PLACE.
THE MISSION IS TO EXTEND OUR REACH BEYOND GOTHAM CITY.
THERE ARE BATTLES THAT NEED TO BE FOUGHT ALL OVER THE GLOBE. WE FEEL THAT YOU ARE ONE WHO CAN HELP FIGHT IN THIS WAR.
GODALMIGHTY.
BATMAN, INCORPORATED WILL PROVIDE YOU WITH EVERYTHING YOU WILL NEED.
YOU WILL BEAR THE MANTLE OF THE BAT.
AND YOU CAN CONTINUE YOUR FIGHT.
BUT NOW, WITH OUR SUPPORT. OUR GUIDANCE.
YOU WILL BE A SOLDIER IN THIS ARMY.

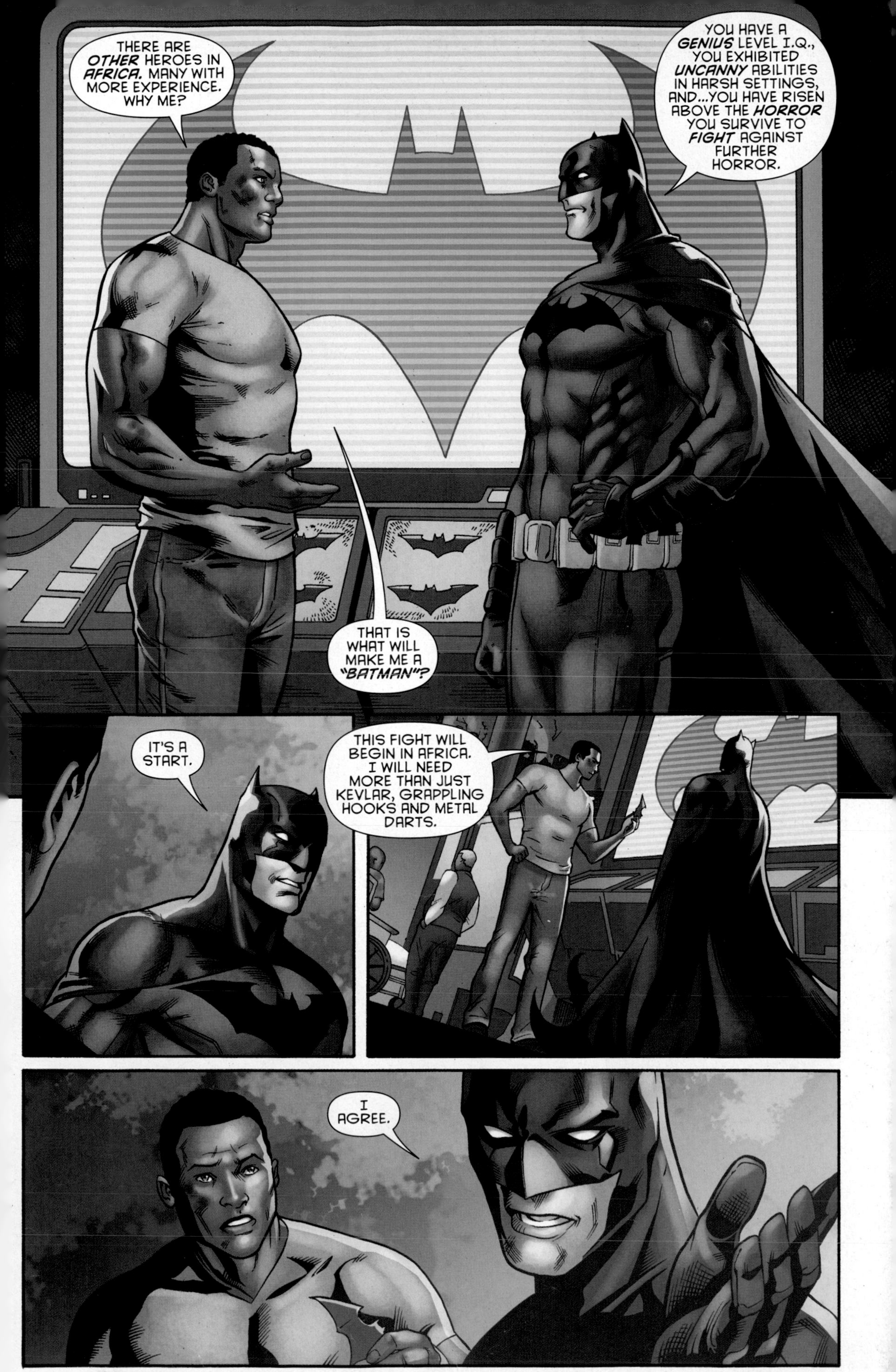
THERE ARE *OTHER* HEROES IN *AFRICA.* MANY WITH MORE EXPERIENCE. WHY ME?
YOU HAVE A *GENIUS* LEVEL I.Q., YOU EXHIBITED *UNCANNY* ABILITIES IN HARSH SETTINGS, AND...YOU HAVE RISEN ABOVE THE *HORROR* YOU SURVIVE TO *FIGHT* AGAINST FURTHER HORROR.
THAT IS WHAT WILL MAKE ME A *"BATMAN"?*
IT'S A START.
THIS FIGHT WILL BEGIN IN AFRICA. I WILL NEED MORE THAN JUST KEVLAR, GRAPPLING HOOKS AND METAL DARTS.
I AGREE.

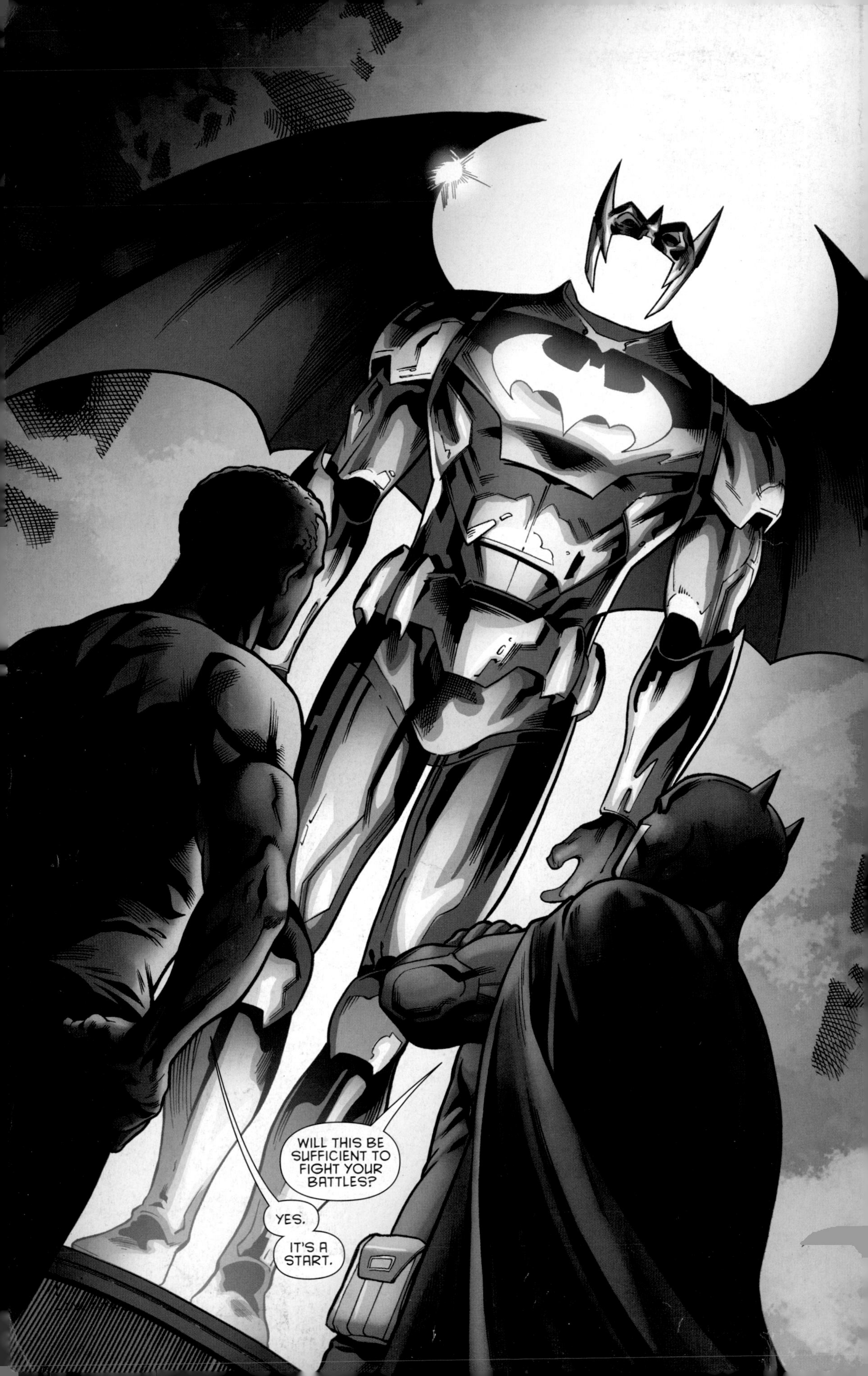
WILL THIS BE SUFFICIENT TO FIGHT YOUR BATTLES?
YES.
IT'S A START.

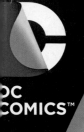

"Simone and artist Ardian Syaf not only do justice to Babs' legacy, but build in a new complexity that is the starting point for a future full of new storytelling possibilities. A hell of a ride."
—IGN

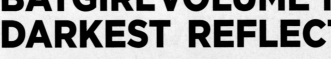

START AT THE BEGINNING!

BATGIRL VOLUME 1: THE DARKEST REFLECTION

BATWOMAN VOLUME 1: HYDROLOGY

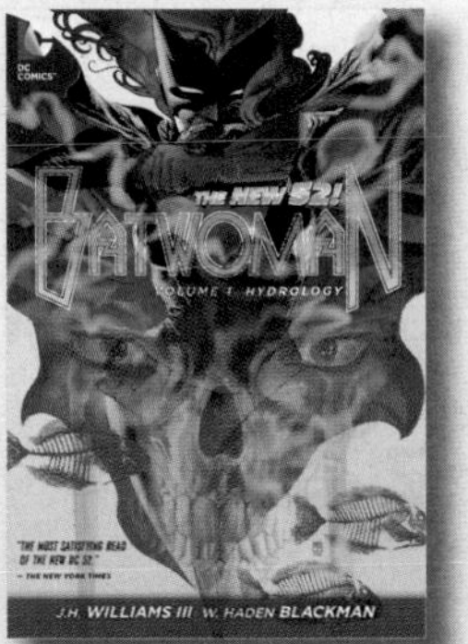
THE NEW 52!
BATWOMAN
VOLUME 1 HYDROLOGY
J.H. WILLIAMS III W. HADEN BLACKMAN

RED HOOD AND THE OUTLAWS VOLUME 1: REDEMPTION

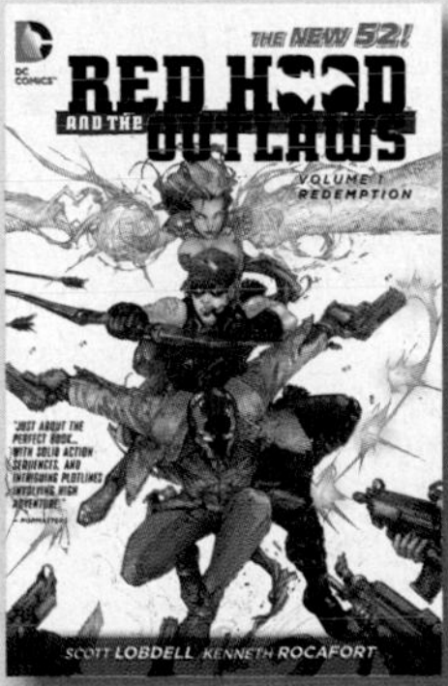
THE NEW 52!
RED HOOD AND THE OUTLAWS
VOLUME 1 REDEMPTION
SCOTT LOBDELL KENNETH ROCAFORT

BATWING VOLUME 1: THE LOST KINGDOM

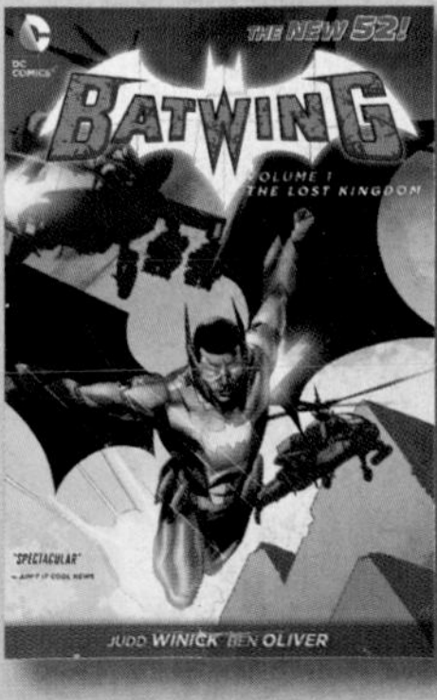
THE NEW 52!
BATWING
VOLUME 1 THE LOST KINGDOM
"SPECTACULAR"
JUDD WINICK BEN OLIVER

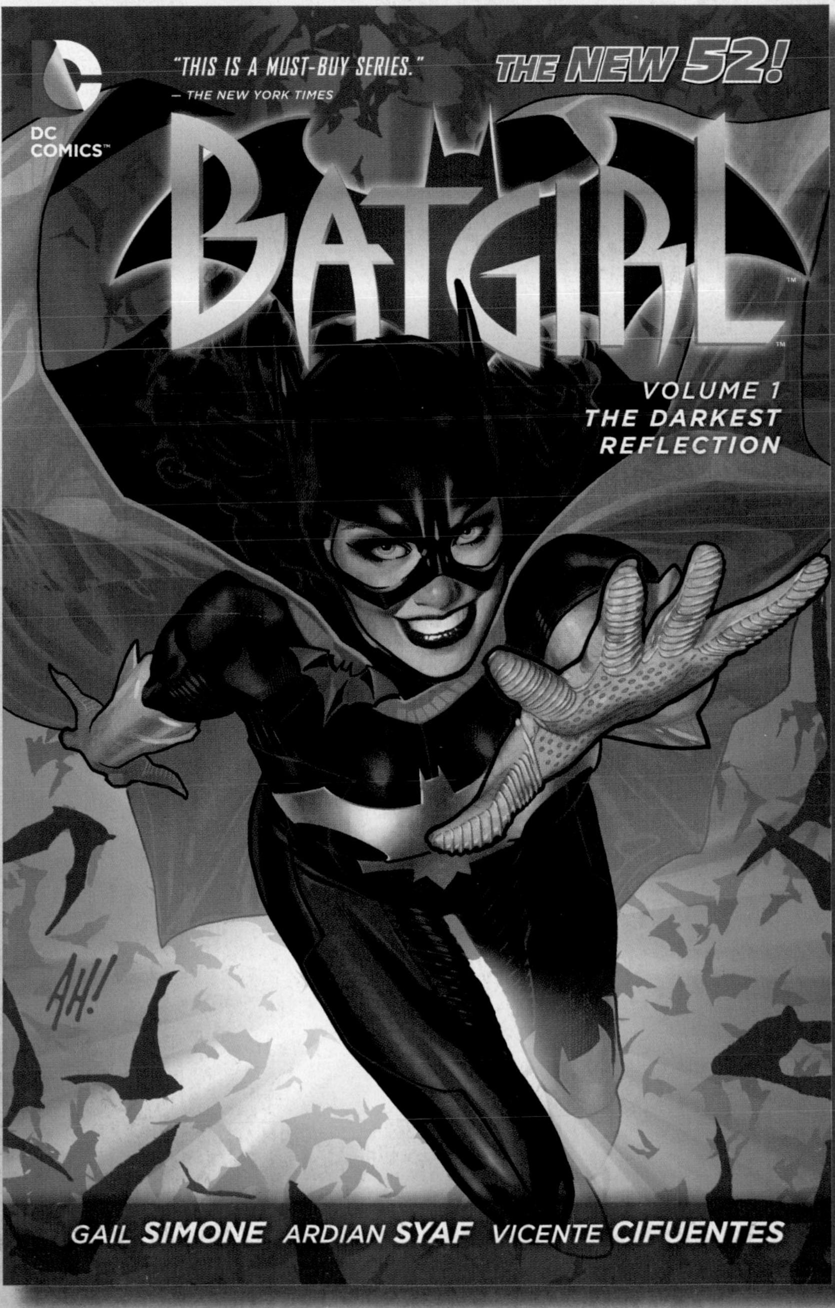
DC COMICS
"THIS IS A MUST-BUY SERIES."
— THE NEW YORK TIMES
THE NEW 52!
BATGIRL
VOLUME 1
THE DARKEST REFLECTION
GAIL SIMONE ARDIAN SYAF VICENTE CIFUENTES

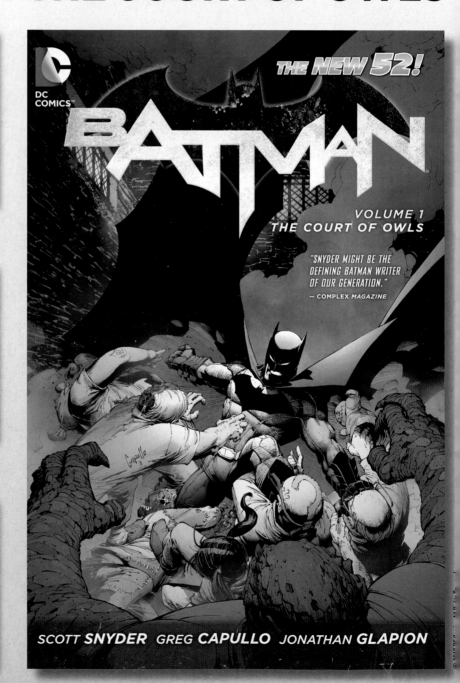